Public Finance in a Democratic Society

Collected Papers Volume I

Public Finance in a Democratic Society

Volume I:
Social Goods, Taxation and Fiscal Policy

Collected Papers of
RICHARD A. MUSGRAVE
H. H. Burbank Professor of Political Economy, Emeritus
Harvard University

Wheatsheaf
Books

DISTRIBUTED BY HARVESTER PRESS

First published in Great Britain in 1986 by
WHEATSHEAF BOOKS LTD
A DIVISION OF THE HARVESTER PRESS PUBLISHING GROUP
Publisher: John Spiers
Director of Publications: Edward Elgar
16 Ship Street, Brighton, Sussex

© Richard A. Musgrave, 1986

British Library Cataloguing in Publication Data
Musgrave, Richard A.
    Public finance in a democratic society : social
    goods, taxation and fiscal policy.
    Vol. 1
    1. Finance, Public
    I. Title
    336   HJ141

    ISBN 0–7450–0106–8

Typeset in Times Roman, 10 point by Photo·Graphics,
Honiton, Devon
Printed in Great Britain at the Alden Press, Oxford

THE HARVESTER PRESS GROUP
The Harvester Group comprises Harvester Press Limited (chiefly
publishing literature, fiction, philosophy, psychology, and science and
trade books); Harvester Press Microform Publications Ltd., (publishing
in microform previously unpublished archives, scarce printed sources,
and indexes to these collections); Wheatsheaf Books Limited (chiefly
publishing in economics, international politics, sociology, women's
studies and related social sciences); Certain Records Ltd., and John
Spiers Music Ltd. (music publishing).

Contents

In Retrospect*

My childhood was spent in Königstein, a small town near Frankfurt, Germany, a safe haven placed in a tumultuous world. Early memories recall departing troops in a flower-bedecked train in 1914; a defeated army returning four years later, with engines steaming; the arrival of French troops, quartered next door, presenting us children with a loaf of white bread. Then the revolution and the early years of the Weimar Republic; the murder of Walter Rathenau, hero of my youth; and the great inflation, yielding stacks of million-mark notes for us children to play with. Hindenburg's succession to the Presidency and shrinking hopes for the Weimar Republic. High school years in a school built in the image of Germany's youth movement, but lacking the moral fibre needed to stand up to what was to come. Concern with politics, pride in the Republic, and the hopes of the League of Nations. Love of literature, from Goethe and Schiller to Ibsen and Rilke. Hiking and canoeing the rivers, years to remember.

In 1930, I went to Munich to begin my study of economics, chosen as the field most likely to help me understand society and perhaps to help influence it. Requirements covered both law and economics, with von Zwiedineck-Südenhorst the outstanding professor. Academia, however, could not withstand the rising threat of the Nazi movement and its brutal intrusion into university life. A move to Heidelberg in 1931 brought closer attention to academic work. Jacob Marschak's seminar on Keynes' *Treatise* and the 'widow's cruse', as well as his work on social accounting, offered a challenge. Public finance emerged as my central interest. Alfred Weber's sociology seminar, based on the tradition of his brother Max, laid a foundation which was to reemerge later in my seminars of the 1970s. In 1933, I obtained the Diplom Volkswirt degree. Then came the Reichstag's fire, a last protest march that night, and days of book burnings in the University yard. The end of an era. The Weimar Republic, that ill-fated yet noble experiment in German democracy, had run its course.

In the fall of 1933, a fellowship from the International Institute of Education sent me to the United States. Good fortune, helped by my father's foresight and urging that I apply, thus permitted escape from the

---

* Bracketed references are to pertinent chapters in Volumes I and II.

disaster that was to follow. My first year in the United States was spent at the University of Rochester, with Professor Clausing my tutor and Marshall's *Principles* the text. I then proceeded to Harvard to undertake graduate work, in time to benefit from Taussig's last term of teaching Ec 11, the basic theory course. Thereafter, his sparse and socratic method yielded to Schumpeter's brilliant and sparkling style, replacing Ricardian puzzles with the elegance of Walrasian equations. Though uneasy in Schumpeter's overwhelming presence (Mephistopheles conversing with Wagner, the student), I admired his sweeping vision of economic theory and the social system, especially in his history of doctrine course.

Primary concern, however, was with the new modes of economic analysis which emerged in those years. Indeed, there could not have been a better time to be an economics graduate student than at the Harvard of the 1930s. All seemed to climax and fall into place: first, there was the rewriting of micro theory in the context of imperfect markets. Then there was the birth of macro theory in the Keynesian mode. Alvin Hansen's arrival from Minnesota in 1936 provided the drive [II, 17]. Tempered by the scepticism of John Williams, the fiscal policy seminar became the vehicle for exploring and expanding the new frontiers. The principles of fiscal policy [I, 24–6], of budgeting [I, 23, 27, 28], and of social security [II, 5–7] emerged, ideas which later were to become American institutions. There was a spirit of intellectual excitement and of finding the answers to the ills of the Great Depression. Many leading economists of later years were members of this group, including Paul Samuelson, Walter and Bill Salant, Lloyd Metzler, Sidney Alexander, Cary Brown, Benjamin Higgins, Emil Duprés, Henry Wallich, James Duesenberry, Robert Bishop, and many others.

While the seminar stressed the macro role of the public sector, my dissertation, encouraged by H. H. Burbank's generous support, stayed with its micro base. Here I could claim the comparative advantage (and what an advantage it was) of acquaintance with the continental literature— Austrian, Italian, and Swedish—which, in the 1880s and 1890s had attempted to apply marginal utility theory to the public sector.[1] One of my first publications opened this work to English-speaking colleagues [I, 1], and, so I like to think, offered the initial inducement which, twenty years later, led to Samuelson's famous solution. In contrast to the Lindahl model, the Pigovian framework offered an alternative approach, and the puzzle was how to merge the two strands. Completion of the thesis was followed by teaching and residency in Eliot House, the lively exchange at the tutors' table a suitable end to those fabulous Harvard years of the 1930s.

In the fall of 1939, having gained U.S. citizenship, I joined the Division of Research at the Board of Governors of the Federal Reserve System. The move to Washington brought a much-needed shift from academia to applied economics and policy-making. Emanuel Goldenweiser, the Board's Director of Research, soon banished the idea that technicians must not be policy makers: for whenever you chart the increase in money supply, he noted, your choice of scale determines its slope, and thereby guides the viewer's response. My initial assignment was in the banking section and my first job to forecast currency in circulation. I soon moved into fiscal analysis and then into security markets and debt management, a key concern of the Board during the War. In the later years, I served as assistant to Marriner Eccles, the Board's brilliant chairman, whose independent thinking and impatience with the waste of mass unemployment had made him a key contributor to the New Deal. This association afforded a fascinating insight into both the policy and politics of the monetary system, the battles for supremacy between the Board and the New York Fed, the struggle with the Treasury over rigid bond support, the ultimate emergence of the Accord, running battles with Congressman Chapman's House Banking and Currency Committee, and the International discussions leading to Bretton Woods.

Besides the business of the Board, there was lively academic activity as well. Evsey Domar had come to the Board in 1941, leading to our joint work on taxation and risk-taking [I, 10]. Ellis, Gerschenkron, Haberler, Hansen, and Machlup were on the Board's staff, and others were frequent visitors. There were weekly seminars, one memorable session with Keynes and Lerner where Keynes (as I recall it) mocked Abba's Keynesian outlook, suggesting instead that social security would allay over-saving in the postwar world.

But successful tenure in government, so I came to learn, leaves less and less space for research, and the time had come to return to teaching. In the fall of 1949, after a term at Swarthmore, I moved to the University of Michigan at Ann Arbor, eager to resume the problems of my thesis and to formulate my ideas on the nature of the public sector. Notwithstanding the shadow of the McCarthy years, the Michigan Department of the 1950s offered an idyllic setting in which to pursue research and teaching. The faculty—including Gardner Ackley, Kenneth Boulding, Larry Klein, Warren Smith, Wolf Stolper and Leonard Watkins—formed a cohesive working unit, receptive to each other's ideas and helpful in their exchange. Successive chapters of my manuscript were discussed as they emerged, with the hope of providing an integrated view of both the tax and expenditure sides of public finance. A brief quote from the preface may serve to suggest the spirit in which that work was undertaken:

Unlike some economic purists of today, I admit to more than only a scientific motivation; intelligent and civilized conduct of government and the delineation of its responsibilities are at the heart of democracy. Indeed, the conduct of government is the testing ground of social ethics and civilized living. Intelligent conduct of government requires an understanding of the economic relations involved; and the economists, by aiding in this understanding, may hope to contribute to a better society. This is why the field of public finance has seemed of particular interest to me; and this is why my interest in the field has been motivated by a search for the good society, no less than by scientific curiosity.[2]

The first task, however, was to build the *economics* of public finance and to do so in a systematic and comprehensive manner. The scheme was to distinguish between three major aspects of the problem, assigned to the allocation, distribution, and stabilisation 'branches' of the budget respectively [I, 2]. This three-branch model would permit a systematic arrangement of topics, falling under the respective headings; beyond that, it would show how mismanagement will result from confusion of issues, and how this may be avoided. I still find the three-branch model useful, not only as a pedagogical device, but also in analytical terms.

The distinction between allocation and distribution issues, inherent in this framework, also guided my view of social goods. Samuelson's application of Paretian efficiency to social goods had provided the fundamental solution. Based on the assumption that preferences are known, an omniscient referee could determine allocation and distribution in a general solution. My point of departure, following the Wicksellian tradition, did not allow for preferences to be given. A political process and voting was needed to secure preference revelation. To this the Lindahl model offered a normative solution, in line with my distinction between the allocation and distribution functions: for preferences to be revealed through voting, distribution of income must be taken as given; and a just solution to the financing of social goods, as Wicksell had put it, would presume a just distribution of income to begin with. This formulation has not been without critics, but I still find it a valid view of the problem, and one better designed to furnish a bridge between the theory and praxis of fiscal affairs [I, 4].

Taxes needed to finance public services were thus seen in benefit terms, with tax-transfer schemes used for distributional adjustments. In either case, however, an understanding of incidence would be needed to guide policy. The impact of taxes on households had to be traced from both the sources and the uses side of their accounts [I, 12], and the concept of differential incidence was developed to permit analysis of the tax as separate from the expenditure side of the budget. A controversial study of corporation tax incidence (jointly with Marian Krzyzaniak) followed,[3] and the burden distribution of the tax system was estimated [I, 13, 18]. This fed into my larger study on *The Theory of Public Finance*, which appeared at the close of my Michigan years.

Returning East, the years from 1958 to 1961 were spent on the faculty of Johns Hopkins University, with its unique departmental seminar, guided by Fritz Machlup's firm hand and enriched by the wisdom of Simon Kuznets' comments. Establishment of the Woodrow Wilson School then brought a move to Princeton. Involvement in tax reform, including the design of John Kennedy's investment credit, followed. Growth with equity emerged as a key concern of tax policy [I, 15], and seminar work supported by a Brookings grant addressed the economics of fiscal federalism [II, 1–4].[4]

My return to Harvard in 1965 was in response to a joint appointment in the Department of Economics and the Law School. The latter offered an opportunity to share the Federal Tax Seminar with Stanley Surrey, who was soon to return from his Treasury position [II, 21]. Langdell Hall's insistence on workable answers to complex problems (the Secretary needs to know!) and the students' delight in the technicalities of specifics, made a fascinating contrast to Littauer's pleasure in general and elegant, if hard to apply, models. These were also the years in which to share the excitement of the newly developing field of Economics and Law, including a seminar with Guido Calebresi, who visited Harvard in 1973. Application of economic reasoning to torts and contracts came as a natural extension of the economist's realm, even though I, the non-lawyer, at times felt that my legal colleagues were too willing to let Pareto efficiency replace a judicial sense of justice.

Oliver Goldman's International Tax Program met my long-standing interest in the application of fiscal policy to developing countries [II, 8, 9]. The first World Bank fiscal mission to Colombia, under Laughlin Currie's direction, had made the beginning (1948), continued in Burma (1954) and Korea (1967), both in association with Robert Nathan's missions. Direction of major tax missions in Colombia (1969) [II,10] and Bolivia (1976) soon followed.[5] These and other experiences found their residue in my study of Fiscal Systems.[6] The fiscal theorist in industrialised countries may be tempted to disregard the broader framework of society, but such would be fatal in developing countries where non-economic (cultural, social, political) constraints become decisive.

Teaching of public finance in the Economics Department was shared with Martin Feldstein, who had come to Harvard at the same time. Our joint offering of the Public Finance Seminar revived the lively tradition of earlier years, with emphasis shifted from the macro effects of the budget to micro issues of tax policy. New developments such as cost-benefit analysis [I, 5] and consumption as the base of personal taxation [I, 9, 21] had to be dealt with. But the major focus of tax reform, then as now, was with the personal income tax and the need for a broadened base [I, 17]. An undergraduate text, written jointly with Peggy Musgrave during the summer months in Vermont, appeared in 1971 and, now in its fourth edition, has made its friends around the country and abroad.[7]

Time also was claimed by the campus setting of the 1960s, involvement in the establishment of Harvard's Afro-American Studies Department, and response to the student concerns of those years. Unhappy with both the Marxist prescriptions of the radical left and my colleagues' view that such matters be left to sociology, I thought it necessary to address the broader issues of society and the place of economics therein. This provided the incentive for a new seminar under the Weberian heading of 'Economy and Society'. Following my Heidelberg tradition, the seminar was to transmit an awareness that social structure involves a complex, multi-dimensional web, including variables pertaining to values and traditions, as well as to the economists' world of resources and techniques. Conflicting theories of ideology were to be examined, including Weber's thesis (to which I hold) that though hypotheses may be value based, answers should be sought in an objective fashion. The seminar, spanning philosophical, sociological, and economics aspects of social structure, closed my teaching career with one of its most rewarding tasks. As good fortune had it, John Rawls' *Theory of Justice* had just appeared, and its brilliant vision, placed against Robert Nozick's Lockean counterpoint, greatly enriched those years [II, 15].

History, be it of ideas or events, does not stand still, and even the fiscal scene must share that fate. The growth of optimal taxation theory, following the Pigovian tradition of the 1920s, opened new vistas [I, 21]. Critical modelling of public sector behaviour, based on the new analytics of public choice, reflected a new mood and a fundamental change in perspective. Where my generation of fiscal economists had focused on normative policy rules to correct instances of market failure, emphasis was now on failure of the public sector and on hypotheses of bias in the democratic process. Such eventual swing in the Hegelian pendulum should have been expected, as policy failures do occur and need to be explored. The model, however, should not be designed, as has frequently been the case, to build failure into its very assumptions [II, 12]; nor should evidence of public sector failure be taken to prove perfection of the invisible hand. Both sectors, I continue to hold, play an essential role and their interaction enriches social life.

Retirement from Harvard in 1981 was followed by a move to the University of California at Santa Cruz, where my wife now teaches and I continue to lecture on an *ad hoc* basis. Blessed with a beautiful campus and a splendid library, we have found here a lovely setting for new endeavours.

This collection of papers, spanning a period of fifty years, is arranged by major themes and ordered chronologically within each. Essays addressing the nature of the public sector and the role of social goods are included in this first volume, as are essays in taxation and fiscal policy. Others, addressing problems of social security, fiscal federalism, budget growth and related issues follow in a second volume. This collection of essays reflects the development of my own perspective as well as that of fiscal analysis and, indeed, economics at large. Consequently, not all that was said in the earlier papers would stand today. New techniques have emerged, old problems have come to be seen in new perspectives, and new issues have come to the fore. Nevertheless, my basic theme has not changed. The public sector performs an essential and constructive role in democratic society and it is the task of fiscal economics to contribute to its equitable and efficient performance.

NOTES

1. See R. A. Musgrave and A. T. Peacock (eds.), 1958, *Classics in the Theory of Public Finance* (London: Macmillan).
2. R. A. Musgrave, 1959, *The Theory of Public Finance* (New York: McGraw-Hill).

3. R. A. Musgrave and M. Krzyzaniak, 1963, *The Incidence of the Corporation Income Tax* (Baltimore: The Johns Hopkins Press).
4. R. A. Musgrave, ed., 1965, *Essays in Fiscal Federalism* (Washington, D.C.: The Brookings Institution).
5. R. A. Musgrave and M. Gillis, 1971, *Fiscal Reform for Columbia* (International Tax Program, the Law School of Harvard University, Cambridge).
6. R. A. Musgrave, 1969, *Fiscal Systems* (New Haven: Yale University Press).
7. R. A. and P. B. Musgrave, 1973, *Public Finance in Theory and Practice* (New York: McGraw-Hill).

Part I
Fiscal Functions and Social Goods

1 The Voluntary Exchange Theory of Public Economy*
1939

The theoretical interpretation of public economy in terms of voluntary exchange dates back to the writings of the 1880s. Since then it has found acceptance among a considerable group of European authors and was brought to the attention of American readers by the English edition of De Marco's treatise [8]. The classical approach to the theory of public finance—with its neglect of the expenditure aspects of public economy and its overemphasis of the consideration of justice in its treatment of the revenue aspect of the problem—had left the revenue expenditure process outside the body of economic theory. Although the traditional benefit doctrine already contained the nucleus of an exchange interpretation of the revenue expenditure process, a thorough explanation of the process as a problem of value and price was not attempted until the reformulation of the value theory in terms of marginal subjective utility suggested an analogous interpretation of the theory of public economy. Notwithstanding their apparent similarity, the traditional benefit principle and the voluntary exchange theory of the revenue expenditure process differ distinctly. The benefit postulate was replaced by an analysis of the determination of absolute and relative tax shares on the basis of individual evaluation; previously postulated as an ethical standard, 'taxation according to benefit' was now arrived at as a condition of equilibrium resulting in the actual determination of the revenue expenditure process. This shift of approach is of significance for an appraisal of the voluntary exchange theory. While the premises of justice standards—as distinct from their translation into actual tax formulae—are, for purposes of economic analysis, to be considered as given factors, the construction of a theoretical model of public economy in terms of voluntary exchange is defective, if it constitutes a derivation from justice norms rather than a realistic interpretation of the actual revenue expenditure process.

* *Quarterly Journal of Economics* (1939) vol. LIII

I

In the following statement of the theory no history of the doctrine is given.[1] Instead, attention is concentrated upon what appears to be its central argument. The objective of the theory of public finance, it is argued, is to explain, in terms of rational economic action, the determination of the total volume of public expenditures and allocation of specific expenditure items, as well as the distribution of tax shares among different contributing taxpayers. Assuming that rational economic action must conform to the 'rationale' of a system of private enterprise, and encouraged by the advance of subjective value theory during the formative period of the doctrine, the proponents of the theory proceed to explain the revenue expenditure process as a phenomenon of economic value and price, determined by fundamentally the same 'laws' that govern market price in private economy. Taxes accordingly appear as voluntary payments rendered by the individual in exchange for services supplied by public economy, and in accordance with his evaluation of those services.

The reasoning in support of this general conclusion needs to be presented in more detail. At the outset it is postulated that those who govern 'act in the interest of those who are governed, and in accordance with economic considerations.'[2] Deviations from either of the two norms are considered incompatible with the theoretical model of a 'rational' revenue expenditure process. From the postulate of rational economic action, it follows that the public economy itself will undertake to supply only those goods and services in the production of which it is superior to private enterprise.[3] How the public economy is to procure the want satisfaction decided upon is, however, considered of secondary importance. The process through which such a decision is arrived at constitutes the primary problem. This decision, we note, is threefold. In determining the relative distribution of tax shares between various taxpayers a first choice must be made between the satisfaction of alternative wants by private households. If a given sum is to be raised from the taxpayers A and B jointly, A will have to reduce his private outlays to a lesser degree, if B will bear a larger share, and vice versa. In determining the application of the revenue sum derived, a second choice must be made between the satisfaction of alternative wants by public economy. If more is spent on armaments, less can be spent on education. In determining the total revenue to be collected or spent, a third choice must be made between the alternative satisfaction of wants decided upon by public economy and of wants decided upon by private households. If public expenditures are lower, smaller taxes will be needed and private spending need be curtailed less. This third decision, in turn, cannot be rendered without a knowledge of the relative distribution of tax shares and the expenditure allocation corresponding to varying revenue and expenditure totals. The three decisions, therefore, are mutually interdependent and must be rendered jointly.

In explanation of the formation of these decisions, the theory points to an analogous process in private economy, namely, the allocation of the total cost of production of two joint products *x* and *y* to the respective supply prices of the two products. This allocation, it is pointed out, is made, not according to cost imputation, but according to the demand prevailing for the two products respectively. If *A*, the purchaser of *x*, is willing to contribute only a small portion of the total cost of producing both *x* and *y*, then *B*, the purchaser of *y*, will be called upon to contribute a correspondingly larger share. The taxpayer *A*, it is argued, in desiring any given volume of public services is similarly confronted with the taxpayer *B*'s unwillingness to contribute more than a certain percentage of the total cost of these services. His dependence upon *B* results from the proposition that benefits derived from the supply of public services are not divisible into individual benefit shares, but are received jointly by all members of the community. The larger the volume of public services desired by *A*, the lower will be the percentage of total cost which *B* is prepared to contribute and hence the greater the percentage which *A* must contribute, if the given volume of public services is to be supplied. *B*'s offer to contribute varying percentages of total cost may, from *A*'s point of view, be interpreted as a supply schedule of public services, and similarly the offers of *A* from the point of view of *B*. Under the assumption of equal bargaining power—an examination of which will follow shortly—a final agreement between the two is reached at a volume of public services at which the sum of the percentage shares which both are willing to contribute equals 100 per cent of the cost of supplying these services.

Retaining the assumption of two taxpayers only, the solution may be illustrated diagrammatically.[4] Percentages of total cost contributed by *A* are measured along the vertical, and quantities of public services purchased, along the horizontal axis. aa indicates *A*'s offers to contribute varying percentages of total costs to the supply of varying amounts of public services. bb indicates *B*'s willingness to do likewise, his demand

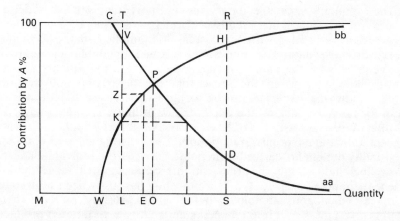

Figure 1.1

price being expressed as the percentage contribution which he expects A to make, i.e. as 100 minus the percentage contribution offered by himself. More than MO cannot be agreed upon, since for any quantity in excess of MO, MS for instance, B's demand price (requesting A to contribute SH per cent) falls below A's supply price (his willingness to contribute SD per cent). While the equilibrium may, according to the respective bargaining power of the two parties, be established anywhere to the left of O, MO will be the equilibrium supply, if 'equal' bargaining power is assumed. At MO marginal utility and price are equated for both parties, and the aggregate utility derived from the purchase of public services is maximised.

While the total volume of taxation and the distribution of relative tax shares is thus determined, the choice between alternative expenditure items still remains to be explained. This final difficulty is solved by postulating that the decisions concerning the allocation of public expenditure items and the distribution of cost shares are to be rendered simultaneously: the willingness of A or B to contribute any given percentage necessarily depends upon the prospective application of their contributions. Whether or not A is willing to accept a certain revenue expenditure project depends upon his comparative evaluation of the marginal benefit to be derived from the satisfaction of wants resulting from the prospective public expenditures and the marginal benefit to be derived from his private outlay of the potential tax contribution.

The preceding exposition of the theory agrees with Lindahl's version [4, p.85] which both in refinement and conciseness of argument is superior to those of other authors of the school. We cannot enter into a discussion here of divergent formulations of the doctrine, but proceed directly to a consideration of the theory as presented above.[5]

II

(1) The voluntary exchange theory has most frequently been criticised because of its underlying premises. Criticism of this type has been concerned in particular with the assumption, implicit in the exchange theory, that the nature of the wants satisfied by public economy is homogeneous with the nature of the wants satisfied by ordinary private outlays—homogeneous in the sense that the tax-paying and income-spending individual can evaluate comparatively the satisfaction derived in return for tax payments, on the one hand, or ordinary private outlays, on the other. With the exception of Sax, the assumption of want homogeneity is accepted by the adherents of the theory. Sax's dissent is based upon the indivisibility of benefits derived from public services into individual benefit shares. Such indivisibility, he argues, in turn renders individual evaluation of benefits impossible. [11, 308] This objection has justly been refuted by reference to analogous phenomena in the field of private economy, where different consumers join in the benefits derived from a common product, the indivisibility of which does not interfere with individual benefit

evaluation, e.g. a theatrical performance.[6] More frequently the assumption of want homogeneity has been objected to on a non-technical basis, generally from the point of view of an organic theory of the state. These objections, however, are metaphysical in nature and have to be discussed as such. Here the controversy seems largely due to failure to recognise the philosophical character of the issue. For the purposes of the present discussion, the assumption, particularly in the modified form in which it has been presented by Lindahl [6, p. 285] is accepted. Difficulties of individual evaluation, resulting from a deficient knowledge of the revenue expenditure process, relate to a different problem and can be overlooked at this point. It remains to be noted that the assumption of want homogeneity, though a necessary condition for the voluntary exchange theory of the revenue expenditure process,[7] is quite compatible with other interpretations of the latter. Opponents of the voluntary exchange theory are found on both sides of the issue, thus attesting to its limited significance. [10, p. 28].

The assumption of voluntary exchange, however, is more crucial in an appraisal of the theory. Considering the predominantly compulsory nature of the actual revenue expenditure process, this assumption must be rejected as highly unrealistic. Direct compulsion prevails in the legal enforcement of individual tax contributions, independently of the individual's willingness to share part of the burden.[8] The very fact that such enforcement appears universally necessary indicates the absence of a general willingness to comply with the obligation to contribute. The contention that fiscal policy in the modern community—democratic or authoritarian—is determined as a direct resultant of the mutual agreements of a multitude of contributors, acceptable to each and all of them, at best constitutes an unacceptable simplification of the highly intricate political process through which collective decisions are arrived at.[9] Indirectly the element of compulsion affects the behaviour of individuals in the formulation of collective decisions. In attempting to minimise their own contributions, political groups are concerned with the task of *forcing* a maximum contribution upon others, rather than with accepting the latter's voluntary offers—witness the example of poll taxpayers voting increased property tax rates.

In addition to analysing the effects of any given revenue expenditure project or the forces which determine the revenue expenditure process to take its given form, the student of public finance may attempt to establish a rationale of action which can serve as a standard of comparison in appraising the achievements of the actual revenue expenditure process. While a theory of public finance may be logically valid, notwithstanding the unrealistic nature of its assumptions, it fails to provide such a standard if the theoretical model constructed proves incompatible with the institutional and social framework in which modern public economy operates. In view of the unrealistic nature of the voluntary exchange assumption, the theory—quite apart from the internal logic of its argument—appears to be of little practical significance. While we may, at this stage, conclude that the theory fails to supply a realistic explanation of the revenue expenditure process as conducted in the actual world, it remains to be shown that it similarly fails to supply an acceptable standard of reference.

(2) Before approaching this latter problem, we turn to a consideration of the pricing process which the theory implies. Since this and the following paragraph are to deal with problems arising within the logic of the theory itself, the previously mentioned objections to the voluntary exchange assumption are waived for the time being. Following Lindahl's simplified statement of the problem [5, p. 85] we begin with the assumptions that only two parties participate in the bargaining process, that total services are voted upon at one single rate of cost distribution, and that all public services may be considered in the nature of a single product. The offer curves, as previously described, indicate the maximum contributions which the two parties are willing to make to the supply of varying amounts of public services. The curves accordingly are a function of both the tax-payers' monetary evaluation of public services and of the total cost of providing these services, the former being expressed as a percentage (or one hundred minus percentage) of the latter. Thus defined, the curves can be assumed to be independently determined and the theoretical case under consideration is, save for certain modifications, akin to that of simple barter. Instead of exchanging two different products, the two parties exchange the same product, or rather mutual offers to contribute varying percentages of the total costs of varying total supplies of services jointly consumed. As in Marshall's nut and apple exchange, there will be some equilibrium rate of exchange, 'at which both parties are willing to do business to the same extent.' If both parties are assumed to ignore the effects of their increased purchases upon price (i.e. changes in cost due to changes in ratio of cost distribution), the competitive solution suggested by Lindahl will result. Referring back to Figure 1.1, let the contributor *A* obtain the amount ML at the percentage contribution LK. *A* being willing to purchase the larger amount MU at the cost ratio LK, will proceed to vote larger supplies of services since, by assumption, he fails to consider that these cannot be obtained save at a less advantageous cost ratio. The supply accordingly will increase up to MO where, at the ratio of cost distribution indicated by P, equilibrium is established.

Once the problem of bargaining power is introduced, the case becomes much complicated. The competitive equilibrium P, as Lindahl points out, does not constitute, from the point of view of either party, the most advantageous of the possible equilibrium positions which may fall any-where on or to the left of the line CPW.[10] If *B*, for instance, can be induced to contribute KT per cent to the supply of ML, *A* may prefer not to ask for a larger quantity, realising that the latter can be obtained only at a changed ratio of cost distribution. Trying to maximise his advantage he will, technically speaking, proceed up to the point where marginal cost comes to exceed marginal benefit.[11] Considering that *A*'s advantage is *B*'s disadvan-tage, and vice versa, both parties will, once we discard the assumption that they fail to consider their influence upon price, attempt to establish equilibrium at the points most advantageous to themselves. Since their success in so doing depends upon their respective bargaining powers, this factor must be given closer consideration.

The problem of bargaining power, we note, is distinct from the previously considered problem of voluntary or compulsory action. While in the former instance it was argued that the premise of voluntary action as such is unrealistic, this assumption is granted for the purpose of the present discussion. Differences in bargaining power, therefore, refer to the effectiveness of the two parties in their respective attempts to conduct the bargaining process so as to arrive at the most advantageous equilibrium position without, however, impairing the voluntary nature of the other party's final decision. Lindahl's interpretation of bargaining power [4, p. 98] as implying either the ability of the party A to 'fool' the party B regarding the actual incidence of taxes imposed, or the ability of A to force B to pay taxes higher than he is willing to pay voluntarily is unsatisfactory. While insufficient information regarding incidence constitutes a bargaining disadvantage, it is of secondary importance; as a type of imperfection, it should be classed with fraudulent advertising and similarly deceptive practices. The imposition of force, on the other hand, is incompatible with the basic assumption of voluntary action and points to an altogether different interpretation of the revenue expenditure process. While we have argued previously that the element of compulsion is essential for a realistic theory of the revenue expenditure process, we now note that compulsion cannot be introduced into the voluntary exchange theory merely as an element of imperfection. If, and in so far as, compulsion prevails, the effect will not be that the equilibrium position is shifted along the offer curve of the weaker party to his disadvantage [4, p. 97], but rather that the entire analysis of voluntary exchange becomes invalid. The more common interpretations of bargaining power—such as ability to wait, which is dependent upon reserves or the nature of the product—are similarly inapplicable in this instance. The most significant interpretation of the term points, instead, to the degree to which a party is able to account for his own bidding upon price, directly and through the reaction of the other party.

After the consideration of effects upon price is introduced, the nature of the offer curves must be reconsidered. If the return offer which B may be expected to make depends upon A's initial bidding, then the latter—in announcing his offers for various supplies of public services—will account for this interdependence, and vice versa. In so far, therefore, as indirect effects are accounted for, the schedules as defined by Lindahl retain significance merely as stating a series of maximum offers that might be made, but the schedules can no longer be interpreted as defining offers that actually will be made. The assumption of two schedules, indicating the effective bidding of two parties as given independently, hence implies that both parties will refrain from considering the effects of their bidding, and thus in itself points to the competitive solution. In allowing for the consideration of effects, three cases may be distinguished. If A alone is assumed to consider the effects of his bidding, equilibrium will be established at the point most advantageous to him,[12] for instance L, where B is willing to contribute TK per cent of the total cost. If both parties are assumed to consider the effects of their bidding with different degrees of foresight (i.e. if unequal bargaining power is assumed), the solution will fall somewhere between the limits indicated by the maximum offers.[13] If both parties are assumed to be fully aware of the entire effects of their bidding, they will agree to choose that position where aggregate benefits are maximised and then share in the latter. Not considering differences in income utility, this position is, as pointed out by Lindahl [4, p. 92, n.1], reached at P and hence is identical with the previously discussed competitive solution where the contributors were assumed to refrain entirely from considering the effects of their bidding.

Assuming unequal bargaining power and hence an imperfectly competitive determination of the pricing process, the introduction of larger numbers raises a peculiar problem. While in the case of oligopoly the competitive solution results, once the number of parties has become sufficiently large to permit neglect of indirect effects [2, p. 48], no analogous argument holds in this instance. The individual contributor will not be in a position to argue that the more parties there are, the less risky will it become for him to agree to a larger volume of services, on the assumption that the other parties will not notice the increase in total supply and hence will refrain from reducing their percentage offer.[14] Since it is in the nature of the problem that all parties jointly benefit from the same total of public services,[15] one contributor X cannot, by assumption, vote an increase in the supply of services without calling the attention of the other contributors to his doing so. If the increase in benefits derived is too small to be noted by other contributors, then, by assumption, it is also too small to be noted by him. If, however, the other contributors are aware of the increase in the supply of services, they will necessarily react by reducing their percentage offer. This in turn means that X would have to contribute more. The solution, therefore, remains an imperfectly competitive one, even if the assumption of large numbers is introduced.[16]

If the remaining simplifying assumptions are corrected, further complications arise. The assumption that the entire supply of public services is purchased at one rate of cost distribution may, in view of actual budget procedure, be accepted. It must, however, be noted that this final ratio is but a composite of various offers to contribute different percentage shares to different parts of the product. The further assumption that there is only a single product is, therefore, more objectionable. If it is recognised that the product of public economy falls into different types of goods and services, it readily appears that the different parts of the product will not be equally desirable to the taxpayer. Such differences in evaluation may, as pointed out by Lindahl [5, p. 59], be expressed in the willingness to contribute varying percentage shares. While this solution is possible, it is not a realistic interpretation of the common 'log-rolling' activity of parliamentary pressure groups. The willingness of A to support B's special interest, in return for B's promise to support the interest of A, is based, in fact, upon the presupposition that both hope to exploit jointly a third party, *C*. This being against the interests of *C*, the success of the two other parties implies the element of compulsion. If *A* and *B* had to pay themselves for each other's benefit, no such agreement could be reached.[17]

The above discussion, although not claiming to give a thorough analysis of the problem as a question of pure theory, serves to put the nature of the pricing process into proper relief. Evidence from political reality—witness the pressure-group mechanism of modern parliamentary government—testifies overwhelmingly for the assumption of unequal bargaining power as defined above. Hence it follows that, if interpreted more realistically, the voluntary exchange theory points to an imperfectly competitive determination of the revenue expenditure process. The likelihood that a strong element of 'uncertainty' [6, p. 51] prevails in the political bargaining process adds the suspicion that the solution remains indeterminate. While in the foregoing paragraphs the voluntary exchange assumption in general was rejected as highly unrealistic, the present discussion is concluded with an analogous objection to the more specific assumptions from which a competitive solution of the pricing process will result.

(3) The conclusion that the nature of the pricing process is an imperfectly competitive one greatly affects the merits of the voluntary exchange theory as a solution of the problem of tax justice. Without intending to offer our own views concerning the merits of justice theories, we turn to consider the voluntary exchange theory in its relation to justice. According to Wicksell [16, p. 143] the term 'justice in taxation' may, as a matter of logic, be applied only on the assumption that a 'just' distribution of income prevails. Following this contention, Lindahl [5, p. 9] divides the requirements for 'justice in taxation' into, first, the socio-political problem of creating a just state of income distribution and, second, the fiscal problem of leaving the just distribution undisturbed by the revenue expenditure process. This requirement, in turn, is met by the competitive determination of public services and relative tax shares. The competitive solution arrived at provides a 'just' state of taxation: the correspondence between price and marginal utility prevailing for both parties indicates that they benefit 'equally' in accordance with the prevailing just state of distribution.[18] The solution, moreover, is equally compatible with 'ability' and 'benefit' principles; while the latter is considered the more basic theoretical principle, the former is a more practical rule of tax policy [5, p. 4].

The premise of the argument, i.e. the assumption that the prevailing income distribution is a just one, will be considered subsequently. The assumption is granted at this point. Then, by application of the conclusions obtained in the foregoing paragraph, it appears that, in so far as the exchange mechanism leads to an imperfectly competitive, rather than a competitive, equilibrium position, the marginal utility of public services to different taxpayers will differ more than in proportion to differences in the marginal utility of income (if the assumed 'just' state of distribution be one of unequal incomes) or will fail to be equal (if the 'just' state of distribution be equality of incomes). In either case, the relative welfare position of different individuals will have changed, thus indicating that the prevailing distribution of relative tax shares fails to conform to the standard of justice. If such is the case, the justice principles have to be applied extraneously, with the resulting reintroduction of the well-known difficulties implicit in the definition and application of justice standards.[19]

Neither can the premise of the argument, namely, the proposition that the concept of a 'just sector in an unjust whole' is logically fallacious, be accepted. If the competitively determined equilibrium position is assumed to be 'just', it naturally follows that the underlying income distribution must be 'just' and vice versa; but this is circular reasoning. Once the 'just' state of the revenue expenditure process is defined in terms other than that of competitive exchange equilibrium, there is no logical difficulty in assuming 'justice in taxation' to be coexistent with any state of distribution, just or unjust. Substituting a 'planned economy' interpretation of the revenue expenditure process for the voluntary exchange interpretation, we may well conceive of the public authority so arranging its revenues and outlays as to conform to some politically-determined standard of justice, without assuming the latter to be realised in the state of distribution in the economy at large. A logical difficulty arises only if the political authority is assumed to be omnipotent. If such were the case, we should be concerned with a planned economy proper and not with the problem under consideration, i.e. the operation of the revenue expenditure process within the framework of an economy predominantly organised as a system of private enterprise.

(4) Waiving the objections previously raised, we finally turn to consider the possible merits of the voluntary exchange theory in providing a standard of reference for the appraisal of actual revenue expenditure policies. The standard supplied is that of a 'neutral' revenue-expenditure system and readily follows from an interpretation of the revenue expenditure process in terms of voluntary exchange.[20] Interpreted as part of the exchange economy, public economy is by definition 'neutral' in the sense that it causes no disturbances extraneous to the exchange system. The neutrality condition, we note, merely refers to the assumption of voluntary exchange and is compatible with an imperfectly competitive determination of the pricing process. To provide a sufficient condition for an optimum arrangement of the revenue expenditure process, the condition of neutrality must, therefore, be supplemented by that of competitive determination of equilibrium output and cost shares. For purposes of the present argument attention is centred upon the former condition only.

The major problems confronting the student of contemporary public economy—e.g. the intricacies of shifting, the indirect effects of the revenue expenditure process, and the compensatory functions of public economy in the cycle—are concerned with the interaction of the two sectors of the economy, public and private. As such, these problems have, however, no place in the theory of the neutral revenue expenditure system. Shifting, to begin with, must be considered a result of 'extraneous' disturbances. This follows from the very nature of the shifting concept, which implies the pre-occurrence of an 'extraneous', that is, non-voluntary, intervention, in response to which the burden is transferred. If all taxes constituted voluntary payments, decided upon by the taxpayers, no shifting would occur; in so far as it does occur, it implies a deviation from neutrality and violation of the optimum condition. The existence of 'indirect effects' is equally incompatible with the condition of neutrality. While changes in the revenue expenditure process will necessarily cause changes from the prevailing position of general equilibrium, such secondary changes are akin to those resulting from primary changes in taste or choice between present and future satisfaction of wants. The revenue expenditure process, being a function of voluntary individual decision, cannot by itself affect the economic behaviour of the individual. If taxes are considered voluntary payments, the problem of possible effects upon saving, for instance, does not arise in the sense in which it appears if taxes are considered compulsory. The occurrence of 'indirect effects' of taxation—like that of shifting—must be preceded by an 'extraneous' intervention and similarly constitutes a deviation from neutrality [1, p. 451]. An analogous argument applies to the effects of public expenditures. In so far as taxes represent voluntary purchase payments for the supply of public services, the supply of these services cannot in turn act independently upon the taxpayers' primary decisions. Finally, the further incompatibility of the neutrality condition with any kind of fiscal policy aiming at the interference with, or supplementing of, the operation of private economy may be noted as self-evident.

This stated incompatibility of the neutrality condition with the most important aspects of the contemporary revenue expenditure process again points to the unrealistic nature of the voluntary exchange model. Notwithstanding the practical difficulties confronting the realisation of the neutrality condition in the actual conduct of the revenue expenditure process, the theoretical problem remains whether the best possible approximation to neutrality can be accepted as a criterion of a well-conducted revenue expenditure policy.[21] The question has to be viewed both in regard to shifting and indirect effects.

Shifting, if unpredictable and hence unaccounted for in the determination of policy, is disadvantageous both from a distributional and a general point of view: the burden impact is rendered arbitrary and the unforeseen chain of shifting movements may in turn result in a series of undesired indirect effects. A preference in favour of the tax not subject to shifting may be maintained, even if predictability of the shifting process is assumed. Then it may be shown that if a given revenue sum is to be collected from the same taxpayers by means of (a) a direct tax upon income or an equal *ad valorem* tax imposed upon all commodities, or (b) an unequal tax upon commodities, their loss in terms of total utility resulting from the second method of tax collection is likely to exceed, and cannot be smaller than, the one resulting from the first method. The argument upon which this preference rests is, however, subtle and unimportant in com-

parison with the disadvantages resulting from unforeseen shifting movements. The force of the theoretical case against the tax subject to shifting
accordingly depends upon the predictability of the shifting process as a
prerequisite for rational planning of taxation policy. As against the above
arguments in favour of the tax's 'staying put', considerations of political
and administrative expediency or advantages to be derived from the
resulting intended effects may speak in favour of the tax subject to shifting.
Results derived from balancing the various considerations will vary with
different cases; no dogmatic preference for either type of taxes in general
appears justified.

The requirement of minimising indirect effects is even less acceptable as
a criterion.[23] Assuming that a given revenue sum may be raised in either of
two ways, each alternative method will result in certain indirect effects.
The choice to be made, therefore, is between one set of effects and
another, not between more or less effects in general. In view of the major
importance which in modern public economy must be attributed to the
qualitative choice[24] between alternative effects, the neutrality condition of
minimising effects in general appears meaningless. This conclusion, we
note, is independent of the other problem, namely, whether or not fiscal
policy is, on general grounds, to be considered a desirable tool of economic
policy.[25] The contention that there is no good reason for dogmatically
assuming that the choice between different effects must be one between
lesser evils, and not an expression of positive preference, only raises
additional objections.

To summarise: as an interpretation of the actual revenue expenditure
process, the voluntary exchange theory was found unacceptable because of
the unrealistic nature of the voluntary exchange assumption in general and
of the competitive pricing assumption in particular. As a solution to the
theory of tax justice it was found strictly dependent upon the premise of
competitive pricing; the definition of the justice problem employed,
moreover, appeared excessively narrow. As standards of reference for
analysis and appraisal of actual revenue expenditure policies, the voluntary
exchange model and its corollary, the neutral revenue expenditure process,
were found unacceptable. Notwithstanding the ingenuity of the voluntary
exchange theory as presented by Lindahl, its claim[26] to provide a final
solution to the theoretical problem of the revenue expenditure process
appears, therefore, unjustified.

III

Rejection of the voluntary exchange theory of the revenue expenditure
process does not imply that a theoretical explanation of the process in
terms of rational economic action is impossible. We suggest, on the
contrary, that an analysis of public economy in terms of economic planning
supplies a more adequate model of the revenue expenditure process. In

this concluding part an attempt is made to sketch the lines along which such analysis may proceed.

The theoretical problem of public economy interpreted in terms of economic planning is not identical with that of central planning in the socialist economy. While in the case of the latter the planning function embraces most, or all, of the economic activity, the revenue expenditure process is assumed to operate within an economy which to a dominating extent is organised as a system of private enterprise. The problems of planning fall roughly into two groups. The first deals with the choice of wants to be satisfied, the second with the execution of such want satisfaction. Regarding the execution of want satisfaction, it suffices to say that the principle of least cost applies in the sphere of economic planning as well as in that of private enterprise. From this it follows that if public economy is to comply with the standards set by the theoretical model of rational planning, it will itself undertake, at minimum cost, the production of those goods and services only, in the supply of which it has an efficiency advantage over private enterprise. The planning problems which arise with the task of choosing between the satisfaction of alternative wants cannot be disposed of thus easily. The decision to be made is two-fold; it involves both the determination of the relative importance of alternative public outlays and the relative importance of alternative public and private outlays. If these decisions are to be translated into a rational revenue expenditure policy, so as to assure the satisfaction of wants in the order of their importance, two prerequisites must be met: the social value scales must be given, and changes in want satisfaction resulting from particular revenue or expenditure acts must be known. Both conditions will be considered in turn.

The formation of social value scales, in which relative positions of importance are assigned to the benefits derived from alternative public and private outlays, must be recognised as a highly complex process. Whether, for instance, a $1000 outlay on armaments is preferred to a similar outlay on playgrounds, or whether either of these objectives is preferred to the private outlay of potential taxpayers, depends upon a multitude of factors, political as well as cultural. The process by which social value scales are determined cannot, therefore, be disposed of by simplifying assumptions. Neither is such simplification necessary, since, for purposes of economic analysis, the scale of social wants may be considered as predetermined, just as the scale of individual tastes is considered a predetermined factor in traditional value theory.[27] Like the 'registration' of individual preference scales through the medium of market behaviour, social preference scales are registered through the medium of public policy. The fact that public policy constitutes the medium through which social value scales are expressed should not, however, lead to the conclusion that the actual conduct of the revenue expenditure process must, of necessity, provide the maximum satisfaction in accordance with the prevailing social preference scales. While such would be the case if the actual conduct of public economy fully complied with the standards set by the theoretical model of rational planning, the situation differs if deviations occur. These very deviations, in turn, constitute the subject-matter of practical analysis. The assumption of a predetermined scale of social wants must, therefore, be kept free from the fallacious reasoning that since public policy has decided to spend $N for the project X, the project X must be worth $N.[28]

The second prerequisite for rational planning is a knowledge of the changes in present and future want satisfaction resulting from any given conduct of the revenue expenditure process. Unless such information is available, planning errors are evidently unavoidable. If the cost of an expenditure project has been underestimated—whether the monetary outlay necessary for the completion of the project proves higher than expected or whether the indirect effects of the revenue collection deter production in other parts of the economy—a planning error has been made. Similarly, planning errors may result from failure to estimate correctly the benefits resulting from a scheduled outlay. The occurrence of planning errors in either case implies that the marginal benefit derived fails to equal the marginal cost, and thus indicates a deviation from the standards set by the theoretical model.[29] Both appraisal of the actual conduct of the revenue expenditure process in terms of its deviations from the standards set by the theoretical model and the minimisation of such deviations hence require close determination of the costs and benefits resulting from any revenue expenditure project.

The effects of the revenue expenditure process upon the state of want satisfaction include the directly accruing cost and benefit items as well as the more indirect effects. Regarding the former, an analysis in terms of personal gains or losses proves useful within certain limits. If full employment of resources is assumed, the intervention of public economy results in the shift of resources between alternative applications. Without considering, for the moment, the resulting indirect effects, such transfer will not lead to a change in monetary national income or in the volume of the 'heap' of goods [13, p. 142] which it represents. There will, however, be a change in the component elements of the 'heap', and with it a change in distribution. Determination of the costs and benefits resulting from the revenue expenditure process in this instance deals with the losses arising from the non-satisfaction of previously satisfied wants and the benefits derived from the satisfaction of previously unsatisfied wants. In so far as the problem falls within these limits, the question of personal loss and benefit incidence is the paramount one.[30]

Still neglecting the consideration of indirect effects, the problem loses its purely 'distributional' character once the assumption of full employment is discarded. If public economy puts to work otherwise unemployed resources, the cost problem assumes a different character: opportunity cost in this instance refers merely to alternative applications of resources by public economy and not to alternative applications by private and public economy as well, as was the case under the assumption of full employment. If the revenue expenditure process thus results in increased employment, the analysis in terms of individual loss and benefit incidence ceases to supply the most useful approach to the problem: an examination of the relationship between the revenue expenditure process and the national income becomes the more useful line of attack. Similarly, the analysis of indirect effects of the process proves more profitable if related to fluctuations in the national income, rather than to individual losses and benefits. Indirect effects, if related to changes in national income, assume a much more tangible form than if posited in terms of personal losses and benefits. For while these constitute the final determinants for changes in economic welfare, the assumption that an increase in real national income will, *ceteris paribus*, be accompanied by an increase in welfare does offer an acceptable working hypothesis.

As a result of the unprecedented expansion in the scope of public economy witnessed during the post-war period, those effects concerned with variations in the level and efficiency of employment of resources have become of primary importance. The traditional problem of shifts in the allocation of resources has been relegated to a secondary position. The standard of reference consequently will profitably be shifted from the incidence of individual losses and benefits to fluctuations in employment or national income. Notwithstanding its importance, such a shift must, however, be recognised as a change in emphasis only: the question of individual losses and benefits still remains an integral part of the planning problem.

The approach suggested is certainly far from final. It is neither as comprehensive nor as unambiguous as the previously discussed voluntary exchange theory. The encompassing charm of the latter is, however, attained at the cost of an unpermissible simplification of the socio-political process by which public value scales are formulated. As against such an alternative, it appears preferable to segregate the two problems; namely, first, the determination of social value scales and, second, the rational conduct of public economy on the basis of a given social value scale. The planning approach chooses the latter alternative. The criterion of fluctuations in national income again is more ambiguous than the neutrality condition which results from the voluntary exchange theory. While it appears relatively simple to determine whether any given conduct of the revenue expenditure process will result in a deviation from the prevailing state of equilibrium or non-equilibrium, the effects of the revenue expenditure process upon changes in the national income offer a highly complex problem.[31] The freedom from ambiguity of the neutrality condition is, however, of doubtful value, if the neutrality condition itself is useless in the analysis of contemporary problems of public economy. The theoretical construction of a 'rational model of public economy' is, we repeat, of significance only in so far as it supplies a scale of reference for analysing the deviations of the actual conduct of the revenue expenditure process from the standards set by the theoretical model. There is little merit in sacrificing the practical significance of our theoretical framework for the apparent benefit of unrealistic simplification.

NOTES

1. For the earliest presentation of the doctrine, cf. Sax [12] and De Marco [7]. In the further development, Wicksell's treatise [16] represents the most important contribution. For more recent formulations, cf. Sax [13]; Lindahl [4] (where a detailed survey of the literature may be found) and [5]; finally, De Marco's text [8], previously mentioned. (Further references will be to De Marco's later work only.)

2. Sax, ([13], p. 200). De Marco's definition of the coöperative state, where 'personal identity of producers and consumers can be assumed' involves the same assumptions. De Marco, ([8], p. 43). Wicksell's principle of voluntary and unanimous acceptance of tax measures similarly postulates the identity between subjects and objects of government. Wicksell, ([16], pp. 110 ff.) and Lindahl, ([5], pp. 14 ff., 85 ff.)

3. If taxes are voluntary payments in purchase of goods and services, then private supply, if cheaper, would of course be preferable to the public supply. This principle is, therefore, implicit in the voluntary exchange theory. For an explicit statement, cf. De Marco [8, p. 46].

4. The diagram represents an adaptation of the one employed by Lindahl [5, p. 89], to the more customary way of measuring quantity along the horizontal and price along the vertical axis.

5. Wicksell's exposition [16, p. 76] already contains the essentials of the above solution as elaborated by Lindahl.

   Sax's formulation of the theory is somewhat different. Sax [1] distinguishes between (1) the determination of relative tax shares based upon the mutual agreement of all taxpayers to contribute according to their *individual* 'value standards' (p. 21) and (2) the subsequent determination of total revenue sum and expenditure projects based upon *group* decision. Because of the indivisibility of total benefits into individual benefit shares, the group alone is considered capable of evaluating the benefits derived. The mutual agreement of taxpayers to contribute according to individual value standards refers to income utility only and does not account for differences in taste as to the desirability of public services. Sax's theory, therefore, is a voluntary exchange theory only in that taxpayers are considered as voluntarily purchasing public services to an amount and of a nature decided upon by group decision. Lindahl, on the contrary, assumes all three decisions to be determined by *individual* offers to contribute.

   De Marco's theory [8, p. 43] of the coöperative state, like that of Lindahl, interprets taxes as voluntary purchase payments. This contention rests on the assumed identity between producers and consumers and the political equilibrium resulting from the prevailing fluidity between governed and governing groups. Without considering other aspects of De Marco's study, it suffices to note the essential similarity between the theoretical model of rational public economy suggested by De Marco (the coöperative state) and the model suggested by Wicksell and Lindahl (the competitively determined revenue expenditure process).

6. De Marco, ([8], p. 118). For a discussion of Sax's further objection ([1], p. 230) that the taxpayers' choice implies the more difficult evaluation of total, rather than marginal, benefits derived from public services, cf. Lindahl [6, p. 284].

7. Sax's failure to accept this assumption places him, as previously noted, somewhat outside the group of 'voluntary exchange' theorists.

8. We note the theoretical difficulty which arises for the voluntary exchange theory in the event that some of the members of the community should attempt to benefit from public services without in turn being eager to contribute their share. While recognised as constituting a 'pathological group' [8, p. 114] and a 'problem' [1, p. 454], they are ruled out by the assumption of purely voluntary action. Assuming, however, for the sake of argument that all people act in the prescribed 'pathological' manner, the following problem arises: if the total cost of public services is covered by a large number of contributors, a reduction in the contribution of any one contributor will fail to affect notably the total supply of public services—either from the point of view of this contributor or in the eyes of other contributors who join in the consumption of the same indivisible services. Hence the reduction will result in a gain for the contributor in question without leading to reprisals. If all contributors should accordingly decide to reduce their contributions, the volume of public services will tend to shrink, and an unstable situation will result.

9. This does not imply that the formulation of policies cannot be traced back to individual want evaluations. We merely suggest that the extent to which individuals take part in the formation of collective decisions varies; and so do the motives underlying their participation and the channels through which their opinions are rendered effective.

10. We do not follow Lindahl's contention that only the line CPW should be considered as locus of possible equilibrium positions [5, p. 89]. The total cost of supplying ML, for instance, may be covered by the ratios of the cost distribution as indicated by Z as well as by those indicated by V or K. There is no reason to assume that one party only will pay less than its maximum offer. As long as total offers are in excess of one hundred per cent of cost, both may contribute less.

11. The problems of monopsony analysis considered from the point of view of utility theory—'treacherous ground' indeed [11, p. 215]—cannot be entered into here.

12. Let the amount ML be purchased, A contributing KL per cent. Then A, by offering a better rate to B—say, his willingness to contribute LZ per cent—may induce B to vote for a larger amount, since B, at the new ratio of cost distribution, is prepared to purchase as much as ME. Subsequently, by lowering his rate, A may induce B to pay his (B's) maximum offer for any new amount between L and E. In this way, A may, beginning from W, induce B to assume any point on WP which he wishes.

13. A more detailed discussion of the problem would have to distinguish between the consideration of, first, direct effects upon price or supply and, second, of indirect effects—i.e. the reaction of the other party. As in the case of duopoly, the solutions arrived at will, therefore, depend upon more specific assumptions regarding the nature of the bargaining process.

14. An attempt to purchase the same amount at a lower rate may, however, prove more successful. Cf. note 13.

15. The product of public economy is 'divisible', in the sense that its supply may be increased by small units, but 'indivisible', in the sense that no separate 'benefit shares' may be attributed to individual purchasers. Cf. the previously cited illustration of a theatrical performance.

16. Lindahl's solution for the case where there are more than two parties to the barter ([5], p. 93) suggests that the larger number may be reduced to two and that thus no new element is introduced into the problem. The reduction of

large numbers is to be achieved by means of successively determining joint offer curves expressing the combined offers of two parties for varying amounts of public services. This argument disregards the fact that the equilibrium arrived at between different parties may be an imperfectly competitive one. If this be the case, the final equilibrium will be dependent upon the successive grouping of the various parties. Thus a further element of indeterminateness appears.

17. If the offer curves are taken to refer to a combination of different types of public products, rather than one general product, the curves will furthermore become bulky and discontinuous. This follows from the different evaluation which different contributors will place upon different parts of the product.

18. We do not follow Myrdal's argument [18, p. 278] that the conduct of the revenue expenditure process so as to equalise marginal utilities of the tax outlays of different contributors is invalid as a standard for 'just' taxation. The standard of justice, Myrdal argues, should account for total rather than marginal utility which the contributor derives from public services. Cf. Myrdal [18]. As long as the revenue expenditure process is determined competitively on the basis of voluntary exchange, the question whether individual gains in terms of consumer's surplus are equal or not does not arise. Under the given assumptions such inequalities can arise only from initial inequalities in income or differences in taste. Both these factors, however, have been accounted for by assuming that a just income distribution prevails before the introduction of the revenue expenditure process.

19. These difficulties are theoretical (e.g. the definition of justice formulae and the determination of income utility for various taxpayers) as well as practical (e.g. the determination of incidence). Perhaps the most important objection is the inadequacy of the justice approach for the analysis of future or indirect effects of the revenue expenditure process, which, at present, may well be considered as of major importance.

20. While this development of the theory is not found in the writings of the previously quoted authors, its closeness to the central argument of the voluntary exchange theory calls for consideration in this connection. Cf. Benham [1, pp. 449 ff.] where the neutrality condition is deduced from the general argument of the theory.

21. It is but fair to note that Lindahl himself does not suggest that this is the case. His strict distinction between the 'purely fiscal' problem of tax justice, on the one hand, and the broader questions of social and economic policies, on the other, makes it clear that the competitive exchange model is designed to offer a solution to the former problem only, without at all relating to the latter. The above criticism accordingly applies to Lindahl only in the sense that a theoretical model of the revenue expenditure process which consciously excludes the most important aspects of the problem is of little practical significance.

22. The case may be conveniently demonstrated by means of the technique developed by Leontief [4].

Young [1, pp. 81 ff.] shows that, if certain simplifying assumptions are made, the form of tax collection may be considered irrelevant; once the assumptions are removed, the problem does, however, reappear. (A minor error in Young's argument may be pointed out in this connection. If an equal amount of revenue is to be obtained by imposing a tax upon commodity b, it would have to be taxed at *more* than half the rate imposed upon commodity a; the line from C through G does not bisect BD.)

23. As suggested by Benham [1, p. 445]. The fact that neutrality seems the only criterion which can be defined unambiguously does not render it acceptable, if, by definition, it is inapplicable to the solution of the major problems confronting modern public economy. The state of the revenue expenditure process which the neutrality condition defines is of no particular significance, unless the prevailing state of production and distribution is assumed to be the optimum one.

24. 'Qualitative' in the sense that alternative policies will operate upon production and distribution through different channels, affecting different parts of the economic mechanism. As pointed out below, resulting effects upon national income, rather than resulting deviations from prevailing equilibrium, are the decisive issue.

25. As in the case of shifting, a distinction between intended and unintended effects is, however, quite compatible with that of maximising intended effects, and accordingly is unrelated to the condition of general neutrality.

26. Cf. Lindahl's statement [5, p. 282], 'that by now the fundamentals of the theory which deals with the principles according to which the public household operates ... are laid down fairly definitely ... ; only in regard to details and refinement opinions still diverge....' A comparison with Mill's statement [9, p. 436] announcing the finality of his value theory is suggested.

27. This argument is compatible with the contention that the scale of social wants is dependent upon, and formed by, the opinions of individual members of the community. The process by which the scale results from individual opinions is, however, so complex that De Marco's demand that 'Theoretical inquiry must ... break down the state's calculations into the economic calculations of the individuals ...,' [8, p. 4] either results in undue simplification (witness the voluntary exchange assumption) or renders the problem too unwieldy for successful analysis. If it is the task of the theory to supply a model by reference to which the actual conduct of the revenue expenditure process may be appraised and analysed, the particular aspect of the problem concerned with the formulation of social value scales must, for reasons of expediency, be excluded. Since the conduct of the revenue expenditure process on the basis of a given social value scale is of primary interest, the tools of analysis should be formed accordingly.

28. The cost item $N can never be an indicator of value, unless 'sanctioned' by a corresponding demand. In the case of public economy, the conclusion that equality of cost and value prevails can be drawn only if it is assumed that no planning error has been made. Colm's argument, therefore, that we must assume a correspondence between service and cost in public economy [3, p. 74], analogous to the assumed correspondence between service and return in market economy, is misleading. If the value of the public service can be assumed to equal $N, $N is to be interpreted in its nature as a public demand price rather than as a cost item. Identity between the two can be assumed only if planning errors are ruled out.

29. Waste in the execution of any given expenditure project (assuming the supply of goods or services to be undertaken by the public economy itself) similarly represents a deviation from the standards set by the theoretical model.

30. It is recognised that the distributional problem is not eliminated by the planning interpretation of the revenue expenditure process. In the planning process individual losses must be 'weighed' in terms of the social value scale; they enter into the balance of benefits and losses *qua* 'social' rather than *qua* individual losses. If the scale is assumed to impose zero weights, the problem of

how tax formulae can be deduced from the principle of least sacrifice reappears. Although offering no solution for the distributional problem, the planning interpretation permits an analysis of the more important problems of indirect effects, without the confusing interference of distributional or justice considerations.

31. The relationship of the revenue expenditure process to fluctuations in national income meets—quite apart from the broad problems of causation—with specific statistical difficulties. Public services or goods supplied can be entered at their 'cost' value only after necessary corrections for planning errors have been made. The difficulties of double counting are considerable.

REFERENCES

[1] Benham, F. (1934) 'Notes on the Pure Theory of Public Finance', *Economica*, N.S.1.

[2] Chamberlin, E. (1935) *The Theory of Monopolistic Competition* (Cambridge, Mass.: Harvard University Press).

[3] Colm, G. (1927) *Volkswirtschaftliche Theorie der Staatsausgaben* (Tübingen: Mohr).

[4] Leontief, W. (1933) 'The Use of Indifference Curves in the Analysis of Foreign Trade', *Quarterly Journal of Economics*, 47.

[5] Lindahl, E. (1919) *Die Gerechtigkeit in der Besteuerung* (Lund: Gleerupska).

[6] —— (1928) 'Einige Strittige Frayen der Steuertheorie', in Mayer, H. (ed.), *Wirtschaftstheorie der Gegenwart*, vol. IV (Vienna).

[7] De Viti De Marco, A. (1888) *Il Carattere teoretico dell' economia finanziara*, Rome.

[8] —— (1936) *First Principles of Public Finance* (New York: Harcourt Brace).

[9] Mill, J. S. (1921) *Principles of Economics*, Ashley (ed.) (London: Longmans).

[10] Pfleiderer, O. (1930) *Die Staatswirtschaft und das Sozialprodukt* (Jena: Fischer).

[11] Robinson, J. (1933) *Economics of Imperfect Competition* (London: Macmillan).

[12] Sax, E. (1887) *Grundlegung der Theoretischen Staatswissenschaft* (Vienna).

[13] —— (1924) 'Die Wertungstheorie der Steuer,' *Zeitschrift für Volkswirtschaft und Sozialpolitik*, N.F. 4. Reprinted in part in Musgrave, R. A. and Peacock, A. (eds.), (1958) *Classics in the Theory of Public Finance* (London: Macmillan).

[14] Simons, H. (1937) Review of Robinson, *Economics of Imperfect Competition*, *Journal of Political Economy*.

[15] Stamp, J. (1930) *Wealth and Taxable Capacity* (Westminster: P.S. King).

[16] Wicksell, K. (1896) *Finanztheoretische Untersuchungen und das Steuerwesen Schweden's* (Jena: Fischer).

[17] Young, A. (1929) Book Review, *Economic Journal*, 39.

[18] Myrdal, G. (1933) *Das Politische Element in der Nationaloekonomischen Doktrinenbildung* (Berlin: Junker).

2   A Multiple Theory of Budget Determination*
1957

This paper is concerned with certain basic problems which arise in formulating a normative theory of the public household. Such a theory must include the revenue as well as the expenditure side of the household plan, and both must be determined as integral parts of the same system. The requirement is obvious, but it is not easily met. For one thing, the nature of budget policy is too heterogeneous to permit a unitary explanation. Various functions must be distinguished and dealt with separately, even though they are part of an interdependent system. For another, certain aspects of the problem lead us into the thin air of welfare economics, where as yet the oxygen has been prone to give out before the peak was scaled.

In approaching the design of a multiple budget theory I propose to distinguish between three major budget functions. These include (1) the function of providing for the *satisfaction of public wants*; (2) the function of providing for *adjustments in the distribution of income*; and (3) the function of *contributing to stabilisation*. While further functions could be added, these will do for present purposes. I shall assume that the fiscal department of our imaginary government is divided into three branches, dealing with these functions respectively, and begin with a look at the nature of each branch. Next I show how the sub-budgets of the various branches are determined as parts of an interdependent system and how a consolidated budget is derived by a clearing process. Finally, I consider some of the advantages and difficulties of the model.

THE FUNCTIONS OF THE THREE BRANCHES

I begin with the major problems encountered by the three branches.

* Finanzarchiv (1957) N. F. Heft 3. The 'three branches approach' to the budget model which has patterned much of my subsequent work was presented first in this paper and then formalised in my *Theory of Public Finance* (Ch. 3). See also Chapter 8 below.

1. Service Branch

The service branch poses the classical and most intriguing problem of public finance. Its function is to decide just what public wants should be satisfied, how much of such want satisfaction should be provided for, and who should bear the cost. In approaching his problem, the manager of the service branch will assume that a 'proper' state of distribution and full employment prevail, or, more precisely, that these objectives will be met by the operation of the other two branches. The problem, then, is to provide for the satisfaction of public wants free of direct charge, and paid for out of general tax revenue.[1]

What then do we mean by *public as distinct from private wants?* Before noting the difference between the two, let me emphasise an *essential similarity*. As I see it, both are *part of one and the same subjective preference systems of individuals;* in other words, *both are individual wants.* Recognition of this similarity is basic to our entire approach.[2] Beyond this, there is a *fundamental difference.* Goods and services supplied in the satisfaction of *private* wants *can be purchased by individuals* in *varying amounts.* Goods and services supplied in the satisfaction of *public* wants *must be consumed in equal amounts by all.* This has two implications.

First, there is a difference in the competitive solution of market price, assuming that such a solution could be obtained in both cases. In deriving a market demand schedule for goods and services supplied in the satisfaction of private wants, individual demand schedules are added horizontally to obtain market demand. Competitive equilibrium is determined at a uniform price where this market demand schedule intersects the supply schedule. Depending upon their particular preferences, individuals will consume varying amounts at the same price. In deriving a market demand schedule for goods and services supplied in the satisfaction of public wants, individual demand schedules (as first noted by Bowen [1, p. 177]) must be added vertically. The competitive solution now shows that while all individuals must consume the same amount, they will pay different prices. Or, putting the matter in the earlier terms of Lindahl [2, p. 89], A's demand schedule for such services (relating amount supplied to the per cent of total cost which he offers to assume) may be considered the supply schedule from B's point of view and vice versa; the equilibrium amount and cost allocation will then be determined at the intersection of these schedules where individual contributions total to 100 per cent.

Secondly, and more important, is the fact that this analogy between price determination in the two cases breaks down once it is viewed as an operational solution. Whereas demand schedules for the satisfaction of private wants are revealed in the auction process of the market, such is not the case for the satisfaction of public wants. Since the same amount will be consumed by all, individuals know that they cannot be excluded from the resulting benefits. This being the case, they are not forced to reveal their preferences through bidding in the market. The 'exclusion principle', which is essential to exchange, cannot be applied; and the market mechanism does not work.

Wicksell recognised this clearly in his early discussion of the problem and noted that a political process of decision-making must be substituted and enforced. Since decision by voting will hardly be unanimous, the result will not be optimal. However, the voting mechanism must be designed so as to approximate a true statement of preferences, and hence come as close as possible to that solution which would be obtained if the exclusion principle and the forces of the market could be applied. As Professor Samuelson [4] put it, there *is* a solution, but the question is how to find it.

The search for the best detecting technique, i.e. the best method of voting, offers interesting problems, related to Arrow's work in welfare economics. Without pursuing them here, let me note that I see little reason why majority vote should be given preference. The case for majority vote follows from Arrow's third condition that the result must not be influenced by the dropping out of 'irrelevant' alternatives. If this condition is adopted, the plurality vote is disqualified. On the contrary, it seems to me that all alternative budget arrangements should be considered as relevant, so that the results of plurality or even point voting may well be superior (at least in the absence of strategy) to those of majority rule.

Such, in briefest possible terms, is the problem of the service branch. Its budget, by the very nature of the service branch, must be balanced[3], and *the function of taxation* in this first context is *to place the cost of public want satisfaction with those whose wants are being satisfied.*

How does this approach relate to some of the earlier views on fiscal theory? There is a direct lineage to the benefit approach, or more specifically to its basic proposition that public services should be related to the people's wants for such services. Similarly, our view borrows from Lindahl's formulation provided that we interpret it as an optimal result and not as an operational solution. Viewed in operational terms, Lindahl's theory becomes a voluntary payment approach and overlooks the crucial fact that public wants, by their very nature, are not subject to the exclusion principle. Hence such wants are not revealed on a voluntary basis and the proper solution cannot be found through the market. It can be approximated only through a political process and compulsion in applying the decision reached by vote.

The *ability to pay principle* has the initial advantage of viewing the problem as outside the market, but beyond this it is seriously defective and bears little relation to our approach. Ability to pay theorists, including such outstanding thinkers as Mill, Edgeworth and Pigou, have concerned themselves with the tax side of the problem only. In other words, they have disregarded the problem of the service branch altogether. Least total sacrifice as the basic criterion of tax policy is a principle in distribution rather than in selecting public services and allocating their cost. If it is to be accepted as *the* principle by which the cost of public services should be allocated, then the same reasoning points to a general rearrangement of the distribution of income, beyond the arbitrary limit set by the size of the service budget. In other words, the ability to pay approach (quite apart from its intrinsic difficulties of utility measurement and comparison) deals with matters pertaining to the distribution rather than the service branch. Multiple pricing in the context of the service branch reflects differences in effective demands for the satisfaction of public wants, based on a given distribution of income. As such, it is not to be confused with distributional adjustments undertaken by the distribution branch. A case for progression at the level of the service branch follows if the income elasticity of demand for public wants typically exceeds unity. It has nothing to do with the slope of income utility schedules, traditionally considered the determinant of the proper degree of progression.

2. Distribution Branch

I now turn to the operation of this branch. The manager is instructed again to pursue his task on the assumption that the other branches will meet their objectives, i.e. that public wants are provided for and that full employment is maintained. To the extent that society wishes to undertake distributional adjustments, the tax-transfer mechanism of the public budget furnishes an efficient tool by which to accomplish them,[4] and one that provides least interference with the market. This, however, leaves open the difficult question of how to determine just what adjustments are to be made.

The least total sacrifice or maximum welfare approach of the 'old' welfare economics offered a simple solution to this problem, mitigated only by the need for considering the effects of equalisation upon the level of output at full employment. However, the assumptions of equal and comparable utility schedules, underlying the Edgeworth–Pigou type of analysis, are too dubious to permit objective conclusions, even if the goal of maximum total welfare is accepted; and similar, though perhaps less strenuous, objections still apply to Lerner's approach to the problem. The 'proper' state of distribution, therefore, cannot be derived as a simple exercise in maximisation from a given set of utility schedules. It must be thought of as *a problem in social choice*.

This, in the last resort, merely shifts the burden from determining the proper distribution of *income* to determining the proper distribution of *votes*; and presently we are returned to the fascinating (but not very conclusive) debate of the philosophers of natural law over the rules by which the social contract should be voted upon to begin with. Whatever is done, a value judgement of some sort lies at the bottom of any solution to the distribution problem.

Be this as it may, let us assume for present purposes that the 'proper' state of distribution is to be determined by social choice, based on an equal distribution of votes and with due allowance for its effects upon economic efficiency and social structure. Distributional readjustments thus decided upon will then be implemented through a tax-transfer plan. The distribution branch budget by its very nature is again balanced, ordinarily in the tax sense, and the function of taxes or transfers in this second context is to provide for the desired distributional corrections.

3. Stabilisation Branch

The problem of the stabilisation branch is familiar and may be dealt with very briefly. It is the function of this branch (in conjunction with other means of stabilisation, such as monetary and debt policy) to *maintain an appropriate level of aggregate demand*. Following the earlier pattern, the stabilisation branch is asked to solve its task in view of a given service branch budget and a given 'proper' state of distribution.

Reduced to its very simplest terms, the task of the stabilisation branch is to determine the inflationary or deflationary gap in the absence of stabilising action and to decide what level of taxes or transfers is required to close it. Beyond this, many complications enter into the conduct of stabilisation policy, but they need not be considered here. By its very nature, the budget of the stabilisation branch consists of either transfers or taxes. *The function of taxes and transfers* in this third case is *to check inflation or deflation*. The budget of this branch is always unbalanced except for the very special case (applicable in the classical system or at one particular point of the cycle) where a zero level of taxes and transfers is called for. Also, note that taxes or transfers will be distributed in line with the 'proper' distribution established by the distribution branch, i.e. they will be proportional to income after adjustment by the distribution branch but before taxes of the service branch.

4. Simultaneous Determination of Sub-budgets

Our brief description of the three sub-budgets shows how each branch pursues *its* objectives on the assumption that the others accomplish *theirs*. In other words, the three sub-budgets are determined as parts of a simultaneous system.

The underlying system may be defined in a set of equations, but its general structure will be evident from what has gone before. In the budget of the *service branch* we determine (or attempt to do so) the satisfaction of public wants and their cost allocation on the basis of individual preferences. In other words, we have demand functions for such wants based on preferences, relative prices of goods supplied in the satisfaction of various (public and private) wants, and a given state of distribution.[5] The service branch budget, as noted before, will usually be balanced. In the budget of the *distribution branch* we determine the distribution of earnings at full employment and decide what adjustments should be made to obtain the 'proper' state of distribution. The resulting tax-transfer system again leaves us with a balanced budget. In the budget of the *stabilisation branch* we determine total earnings at full employment and current prices. We then determine what total demand will be in the absence of stabilisation and find the inflationary or deflationary gap that need be closed.[6] Given the marginal propensity to consume with the 'proper' state of distribution, the necessary level of taxes or transfers is determined and distributed accordingly. As noted before, the stabilisation branch budget, if operative at all, will consist of taxes or transfers only and hence has either a deficit or a surplus.

5. Consolidation of Sub-budgets

After the three sub-budgets have been determined in this fashion, each might be put into effect by itself, but this would be a clumsy administrative procedure. While the goods and service expenditures of the service branch budget must be carried out as such, the taxes or transfers of the service, distribution and stabilisation branches might be cleared against each other, so that each individual will make one tax payment or will receive one transfer cheque only. The consolidated or administered budget will show a net deficit or surplus equal to that of the budget of the stabilisation branch.

The consolidation of the sub-budgets into a net plan facilitates administrative procedures, but we must not overlook the fact that the consolidated budget thus determined is merely a product of clearing, and that it hides the more important underlying policy objectives which are brought out only in the determination of the sub-budgets. For instance, taxes of the service branch might be allocated in a more or less proportional fashion, such as would be the case if the income elasticity of individual demands for public wants was typically unity; and the tax-transfer scheme of the distribution branch might transfer income from high to low brackets if it was held desirable to achieve a certain degree of equalisation. The tax structure of the consolidated budget would then still be progressive but less so than for the distribution branch alone; or it might express a quite different set of sub-plans.

THE DIVISION OF FUNCTIONS RECONSIDERED

I now turn to dealing with the advantages of, and objections to, the suggested division of functions.

1. Separation of Service and Stabilisation Branches

Let us begin with the separation of functions between the service and the stabilisation branches. The assumption of full employment for purposes of planning the budget of the service branch implies that the allocation of resources must be viewed within the context of a given total resource use. Since the optimum level of resource use can be established by the stabilisation branch without interference in the allocation of resources between private and public uses, it stands to reason that this allocation should be determined on the basis of a full employment income.

In more practical terms, our separation of functions has the advantage that it rules out ditch-digging to check a depression, as well as curtailing teachers' salaries or essential public works to check a boom. Also, it has the advantage of permitting Mr O, whose preferences for public wants are low, to support fiscal measures against depression; and of permitting Mr Y, whose preferences for public wants are high, to support fiscal measures to check a boom. In other words, the indicated separation helps to eliminate distortions in the politics of fiscal policy.

This, everyone will agree, is all to the good, but various objections have been raised to such a separation. A first group of objections is of a pragmatic sort and may be accepted readily without denying the essential principle. If the longer-run programme of public capital formation can be determined in advance, it may then be timed to compensate for cyclical variation. No serious inefficiency will arise since the adjustment will introduce difference in short-term timing only. If a serious depression is permitted to arise, public works rather than transfers will be needed for reasons of social morale. If the problem is one of meeting regional rather than general distress, public works rather than transfers may be called for. These and other exceptions must be granted and require qualification of our principle. But they do not invalidate the basic proposition that resource use for the satisfaction of public wants should be planned in a full employment context unless such special circumstances intervene.

Professor Samuelson [3, p. 180], however, has raised certain objections which, if correct, would invalidate this basic proposition. Put in somewhat exaggerated terms, the argument is that the very occurrence of a depression is evidence of the fact that there results a shift in individual preferences from private to public wants. Since the want pattern must be related to the allocation of resources at full employment, any decline in expenditures for the satisfaction of private wants must be taken to reflect an increase in the demand for the satisfaction of public wants. This being the case, a counter-cyclical movement in public goods and service expenditures (i.e. in the size of the service branch budget) is called for.

Let us apply the argument first to a classical system where Say's law holds sway. Also, let us suppose that the service branch problem is solved nicely so as to reflect rather fully the individual preferences for public wants. In such a system, changes in the structure of demand might occur, resulting in a vote for an increased service branch budget on the one side, and in a decrease in private expenditures on consumption or investment on the other. In such a system, a decline in the need for certain public wants (such as defence) will be reflected in increased outlays on other public as well as private wants. Allocation is clear-cut, but there would be no problem of stabilisation policy.

Now consider a system plagued by changing liquidity preference and rigidities, in short a system where depressions and inflations may occur. Here stabilisation policy will be called for, and here a decline or increase in expenditures on the satisfaction of private wants must be interpreted quite differently. A decline in this demand now does not signify a structural change in preferences from private to public wants within the context of a full employment income. Rather, it reflects a change in effective demand due to an unintended (in the micro sense) shrinkage of disposable income. There is no reason to expect in this case that a decline in expenditures on the satisfaction of private wants would (in the case of perfect public want determination) result in a vote for an increased service branch budget out of a full employment income; and hence there is no *a priori* reason for increasing the size of the service branch budget. As we have seen, the stabilisation function may be met by the operation of the stabilisation branch.

Professor Samuelson, in presenting his 'neo-classical synthesis', has emphasised that the problem of unemployment and inflation may be handled more or less readily, in principle at least if not in practice, so that we may again devote our attention to the more traditional problems of efficiency in resource use. This is correct, but I submit that the problem of efficiency is not as simple in the neo-classical system as it was in the classical case: the system, as it were, has lost its innocence, even though the problems of unemployment and inflation can be solved. The very need for stabilisation policy (and the choice among alternative approaches thereto) means that the division of the product between consumption and capital formation (the rate of growth) becomes a matter of public policy decision, whereas in the classical system it was determined by the market.[7]

2. Separation of Service and Distribution Branches

I now turn to the separation of functions between the service and the distribution branches. This procedure, shared by Wicksell and Lindahl, follows from our view of the service branch as providing for public wants in response to individual preferences. It is analogous to the assumption of given distribution made usually in discussing the efficiency of resource use in the private sector. Conclusions regarding the efficiency of allocation are necessarily based on the assumption of given effective demands and given states of distribution. Similarly, efficiency in the determination of public wants can be judged only on the basis of a given distribution of income and hence a given state of 'true' effective demand for the satisfaction of such wants.

Viewed on the more practical level of fiscal politics, this division of functions has the advantage of permitting Mr Y, who rates public wants high, to vote for a large service branch budget even though he does not favour income redistribution, and vice versa, for someone who favours distributional adjustments but opposes a large budget in the service branch. If the two functions are distinguished properly, the two tax plans are free to follow different patterns, and more efficient budget determination becomes possible.

Again, there are certain objections which may be raised against this separation of functions. A first objection points to the fact that goods and service expenditures of government frequently involve programmes which are not distributionally neutral, but whose very purpose it is to favour particular groups. To typify this situation, let us consider the case of free hospitals for the poor or public subsidies to low-cost housing. Such programmes may be interpreted as composed of (1) a transfer payment to low-income people, and (2) a requirement that the proceeds are used to purchase certain services, i.e. medical facilities or housing. As far as (1) is concerned, we have merely the redistribution function which ought to be taken care of in the budget of the distribution branch. But (2) introduces a new feature for which so far there is no place in our theoretical framework.

You will recall that we have defined public wants as wants which are not subject to the exclusion principle; but that the problem of the service branch nevertheless remained one of satisfying these wants in line with individual preferences and consumer sovereignty. The idea of a subsidy in kind—and this is what is involved in (2)—is a quite different matter. Here, as in the case of sumptuary taxes, public policy aims at interference with individual preferences; and frequently, such interference carries redistributional implications. I do not wish to say that interference of this sort is always bad, and that it may not at times result in an improved allocation of resources. The apparent willingness of the public to provide for a second car and a third fridge prior to assuring adequate education for their children is a case in point. However, this seems to me a special problem which should be distinguished from the more general theory of public wants. Where interference with individual preferences *is* desired, our schema must be expanded. Such wants—which for lack of a better name I refer to as merit wants—may be thought of as provided for in a separate branch. Here a strict separation from the distribution problem does, indeed, become untenable.

A second objection to the separation of service and distribution branches is more serious and comes closer to endangering the essential content of our scheme. We have noted that any concept of efficiency in resource allocation in response to given preference patterns must relate to a given state of distribution. If distribution is arbitrary, there is little point in adapting resource allocation to effective demands. In line with Wicksell and Lindahl we have therefore based our formulation of the service branch on the assumption that there exists a 'proper' state of distribution. Now, it might be argued that this is an artificial distinction. In dealing with the satisfaction of private wants, a political process is required to establish the 'proper' state of distribution, but from there on in the job will be done by the market. In dealing with the satisfaction of public wants a political process is needed not only in establishing the 'proper' state of distribution, but also in translating individual preferences into the service branch budget. Since a political process is needed at both stages, it might be concluded that there is no point in distinguishing between them.

There is considerable force to this argument, and I cannot brush it aside. Still, it is my judgement that a distinction between the two problems— between the two political processes, if you wish—remains useful. This I believe to be the case because the problem of the service branch, seen on the basis of a given distribution of income, may be handled by analogy to the market process. Individual preferences for alternative uses of one's resources include public as well as private wants. The difficulty is essentially one of getting people to *reveal* their preferences. Once these preferences are revealed, or an approximation thereto, a solution analogous to that of the market does exist. The problem of determining a 'proper' state of distribution, on the other hand, defies the tools of economic analysis altogether. Preferences with regard to the state of distribution are a more complex matter. The problem cannot be solved by analogy to the market, and little can be said about how the fiscal system should provide for it. Samuelson's conclusion that a solution exists but the problem is how to find it can be applied more readily to the case of the service branch than to that of the distribution branch.

3. Separation of Stabilisation and Distribution Branches

It remains to consider the separation of functions between the stabilisation and the distribution branches. Again, there is an obvious advantage if the appropriate use of fiscal policy as a stabilisation device is not interfered with by fears or hopes that such changes will carry the by-product of distributional adjustments. Similarly, there is an obvious advantage if distributional objectives can be formulated without having to allow for the possibility that one or another state of distribution may (in the absence of appropriate adjustments by the stabilisation branch) result in a higher or a lower level of demand. Thus, the case for or against a progressive tax structure may be decided on its own merits and independent of economic conditions. This is to be contrasted with a position which argues as a matter of stabilisation policy, that taxes ought to be progressive in the slump and regressive in the boom.

Again, some qualifications must be allowed for, but there appear to be no basic objections in this case. Possible effects of distributional changes upon the level of output at full employment are a different matter and must, of course, be taken into account.

In concluding, let me add that I do not recommend translation of this multiple budget plan into immediate legislative and administrative practice. While some practical applications may be possible, my primary concern here is with the components of a normative theory of the public household. The construction of such a theory, I believe, remains the heart of what is hopefully referred to as the science of public finance; and it needs to be straightened out before we can go very far in being helpful on the practical level.

NOTES

1. The question whether the government purchases such goods in the market or produces them itself is irrelevant in this context.
2. While we reject the notion that there are group wants as such, we do not deny in any way that individual preferences are affected significantly by social forces.
3. The budget must be balanced in the sense that private expenditures must be reduced so as to release resources for public use. Ordinarily this will mean tax finance. However, under special circumstances, loan finance may serve as a means of establishing inter-generation equity in the financing of public outlays on durable goods.
4. Other approaches are provision for maximum economic mobility and equal educational opportunity.

5. The state of distribution given for this purpose will include earnings plus distribution and stabilisation branch transfers, minus distribution and stabilisation branch taxes.
6. Total demand includes (1) outlays on consumption for private wants with the given 'proper' distribution of income, (2) outlays on private investment, and (3) outlays on the satisfaction of public wants or, if you wish, goods and service expenditures by the service branch. A complication which arises from the distinction between current and capital expenditures (the latter one accounted for on a use basis in the budget of the service branch, but on an expense basis in the budget of the stabilisation branch) may be overlooked here.
7. In response to this it might be argued that an equality between planned saving and investment might always be secured through monetary policy. This, however, is to carry the assumptions of the neo-classical synthesis too far. Moreover, it would limit fiscal policy to balanced budget changes in the level of expenditures in response to changes in the *structure* of demand rather than in *aggregate* demand, the latter being eliminated by monetary policy in the first place.

REFERENCES

[1] Bowen, H. (1948) *Towards Social Economy* (New York: Rinehart).
[2] Lindahl, E. (1919) *Gerechtigkeit in der Besteuerung* (Lund: Gleerupska).
[3] Samuelson, P. (1951) 'Principles and Rules in Fiscal Policy: A Neo-Classical Reformulation', in *Money, Trade and Economic Growth* (New York: Macmillan).
[4] —— (1954) 'The Pure Theory of Public Expenditures', *The Review of Economics and Statistics*, XXXV, 4.
[5] Wicksell, K. (1896) *Finanztheoretische Untersuchungen und das Steuerwesen Schweden's* (Jena: Fischer). For excerpts see R. A. Musgrave and A. Peacock (1958) *Classics in the Theory of Public Finance* (London: Macmillan).

3   On Merit Goods*
1959

The theory of the public sector, as developed in the 1950s and 1960s focused on the distinction between social (or public) and private goods. This was also the key issue of the Allocation Branch as treated in my *Theory of Public Finance*. Based on the framework of individual preference, consumer sovereignty and Pareto optimality, the issue was one which could be handled readily within the framework of conventional analysis. However, that study also posed the issue of merit wants (or merit goods) which added a further and less manageable dimension. Inclusion of the following excerpts from my 1959 volume seems appropriate, as the concept of merit goods has continued to haunt the discussion.

I

Exchange in the market depends on the existence of property titles to the things that are to be exchanged. If a consumer wishes to satisfy his desire for any particular commodity, he must meet the terms of exchange set by those who happen to possess this particular commodity, and vice versa. That is to say, he is excluded from the enjoyment of any particular commodity or service unless he is willing to pay the stipulated price to the owner. This may be referred to as the *exclusion principle*. Where it applies, the consumer must bid for the commodities he wants. His offer reveals the value he assigns to them and tells the entrepreneur what to produce under given cost conditions.

This mechanism breaks down with social wants, where the satisfaction derived by any individual consumer is independent of his own contribution.[1] Such, at least, is the case where the individual consumer is but one among many, and any contribution he may render covers only a small part of the total cost. Consider, for instance, such items as a flood-control project, the more general benefits of which accrue to an entire region; a sanitary campaign that raises the general level of health

---

* Richard Musgrave (1958) *The Theory of Public Finance* (New York: McGraw-Hill), pp. 9–14, 86–9, given here in a slightly edited version.

throughout an area; expenditures for the judiciary system that secure internal safety and enforce contractual obligations; or protection against foreign aggression. All these contribute to the welfare of the whole community. The benefits resulting from such services will accrue to all who live in the particular place or society where the services are rendered.[2] Some may benefit more than others, but everyone knows that his benefit will be independent of his particular contribution. Hence, as we have said, he cannot be relied upon to make a voluntary contribution. The government must step in, and compulsion is called for.

The difficulty thus created would be slight if the problem were merely one of collecting tax bills. Unfortunately, this is not the case. The tax collector, while important, does not solve the problem of the economist. The latter must determine what expenditures should be made and what taxes should be collected. To do this, a way must be found to determine people's true preferences in social wants, i.e. the preference pattern by which they rate the satisfaction of their total wants, private and social. The difficulty arises because the market mechanism fails as a device for registering consumer preferences. Since the services that satisfy social wants can be had without payment, the individual consumer need not reveal his evaluation thereof (and invite corresponding tax assessments!) through market bids. Because of this, signals are lacking and true preference scales for social wants are unknown. Such, at least, is the case with central finance. In the case of local finance, some registration of preferences may occur by moving from less to more congenial fiscal communities, a factor that will be disregarded for the time being.

Since the market mechanism fails to reveal consumer preferences in social wants, it may be asked what mechanism there is by which the government can determine the extent to which resources should be released for the satisfaction of such wants; the extent to which particular social wants should be satisfied; and the way in which the cost should be spread among the group. In a democratic society, the decision to satisfy one or another social want cannot be imposed in dictatorial form. It must be derived, somehow, from the effective preferences of the individual member of the group, as determined by his tastes and his 'proper' share in full-employment income.[3] A political process must be substituted for the market mechanism, and individuals must be made to adhere to the group decision. As shown later on, the problem is to determine the kind of voting process or group decision that offers the best approximation to the solution (or one of the solutions) that would be chosen if true preferences were known. The outcome of that decision will not please all who must contribute, so that some violation of private preferences occurs. But this is only the by-product of a process designed to meet private preferences for social goods.

Critics of this approach have noted that a sizeable part of budget activity does not deal with services consumed in equal amounts by all, but with services which are only partly of this sort [1, 4]. Typically, both social and private features are present. In response, we may grant that the case of the pure social good describes a polar situation, but this does not invalidate the usefulness of our approach. The general reasoning underlying our theory of social wants may be applied also to a mixed case, thereby translating the appropriate policy from one of complete subsidy (full tax finance) to one of partial subsidy (partial tax finance).[4]

II

The type of wants dealt with under social wants are wants whose satisfaction should be subject to the principle of consumer sovereignty. The basic rule is that resources should be allocated in response to the effective demand of consumers, determined by individual preferences and the prevailing state of distribution. Indeed, social wants are quite similar in this fundamental respect to private wants.

We now turn to our second category of public wants. Such wants may be met by services subject to the exclusion principle and may be satisfied by the market within the limits of effective demand. They become public wants if considered so meritorious that their satisfaction is provided for through the public budget, over and above what is provided for through the market and paid for by private buyers. This second type of public wants will be referred to as *merit wants*, and public services aimed at their satisfaction as merit goods.[5] Alternatively, certain wants may be stamped as undesirable, and their satisfaction may be discouraged through penalty taxation, as in the case of liquor.

The satisfaction of merit wants cannot be explained in the same terms as the satisfaction of social wants. While both are public wants in that they are provided for through the public budget, different principles apply. Social wants constitute a special problem because the same amount must be consumed by all, with all the difficulties to which this gives rise. Otherwise, the satisfaction of social wants falls within the realm of consumer sovereignty, as does the satisfaction of private wants. The satisfaction of merit wants, by its very nature, involves interference with the preferences of consumers.

To be sure, situations arise which seem to involve such interference, and a case of merit wants but on closer inspection involve social wants. Certain public wants may fall on the borderline between private and social wants, where the exclusion principle can be applied to part of the benefits gained but not to all. Budgetary provision for free educational services or for free health measures are cases in point. Such measures are of immediate benefit to the particular pupil or patient, but apart from this, everyone stands to gain from living in a more educated or healthier community. Wants that appear to be merit wants may involve substantial elements of social wants.

A further case for interference with consumer sovereignty, narrowly defined, may derive from the role of leadership in a democratic society. While consumer sovereignty is the general rule, situations may arise, within the context of a democratic community, where an informed group is justified in imposing its decision upon others. Few will deny that there is a case for regulating the sale of drugs or for providing certain health facilities. The advantages of education are more evident to the informed than the uninformed, thus justifying compulsion in the allocation of resources to education; interference in the preference patterns of families may be directed at protecting the interest of minors; the freedom to belong may override the freedom to exclude, and so forth. These are matters of learning and leadership which are an essential part of democracy reasonably defined and which justify the satisfaction of certain merit wants within a normative model.

The basic doctrine of consumer sovereignty, moreover, rests on the assumption of complete market knowledge and rational appraisal. In the modern economy, the consumer is subject to advertising, screaming at him through the media of mass communication and designed to sway his choice rather than to give complete information. Thus, there may arise a distortion in the preference structure that needs to be counteracted. The ideal of consumer sovereignty and the reality of consumer choice in high-pressure markets may be quite different things.

Situations such as these, however, only qualify the principle of consumer sovereignty in application, they do not displace the basic rule that the personal preferences of consumers are controlling. Yet the merit concept, as noted initially, seems to go further and to involve interference therewith. Can such a premise be incorporated into a normative model of the allocation branch?

One line of argument is advanced by writers who feel that public wants differ basically from private wants and thus do not appear in the private preference schedules of individuals. This view is taken by adherents of an organic theory of the state, who postulate the existence of group needs, or of needs that in some way or another are experienced by the 'group as a whole' [6, 8]. Since the group as such cannot speak, one wonders who is equipped to reveal group feelings. Unless they are given by intuition or experienced by proxy by the leader, we are left with an authoritarian system of preference determination. Whether such a system, or the organic view of society, is good or bad may be a matter of value judgement. All that need be said here is that the view is incompatible with a normative theory of public finances in a democratic setting.

More serious consideration should be given to critics who do not share the organic view yet want to reject a theory of the public household based upon individual preferences and anchored in the idea of consumer choice. This is said to overlook the essentially political character of the budget process and the essentially social nature of its objectives [2, 3]. To point up the difference between the budget process and the satisfaction of private wants, Colm suggests (1) that the contribution/benefit relationship for any one individual depends upon the decisions of the responsible organs of government and not upon a market process, and (2) that there are political tasks in a democracy that are only indirectly related to such individual needs as are expressed in the market place.

On closer consideration, Colm's first point is readily reconciled with our approach. We agree with Wicksell that budget determination is a political and not a market process. This is the case because political action is needed to translate individual preferences for social wants into a specific budget programme. Since the responsible organs of government in a democratic society are the electorate and their representatives, budget determination by these responsible organs is determination through the democratic process. This holds true even if allowance is made for the role of civil service and executive leadership.

Colm's second point introduces a difference in emphasis that may be more important. He holds that the individual voter dealing with political issues has a frame of reference quite distinct from that which underlies his allocation of income as a consumer. In the latter situation the voter acts as a private individual determined by self-interest and deals with his personal wants; in the former, he acts as a political being guided by his image of a good society. The two, Colm holds, are different things. Any theory of budget determination that is but an extension of the theory of consumer wants is said to overlook the essentially political nature of individual behaviour in relation to the budget problem.[6]

In evaluating this critique, let us consider first those social wants that do not involve great issues of state but deal with individual needs quite akin to those satisfied through the market. Instances of this sort are provided by fire protection, street cleaning, and many of the services rendered by local government. Here Colm's fundamental objection does not apply. The problem is strictly that of dealing with wants that are consumed in equal amounts by the group in question. In principle, at least, the individual voter should be called upon to contribute according to the benefits he receives from the services rendered.

At the other end of the scale, we deal with outlays such as those on defence, education and support of the arts. Here the voter's attitudes and preferences may be conditioned by his image of the good society and by influences extending far beyond matters of his immediate environment. His choices may be determined by what he considers a commitment to the cultural values of his community and to his image of a good society, rather than by the self-interest-based pattern of personal preferences which determine ordinary consumption choices in the market. However this may be, the structure of wants—including those for private, social and merit goods—must still be measured against the common constraint of scarce resources.

Taking an even broader view, decisions on budgetary matters may be combined with others that relate to the content of public policy (foreign policy X versus foreign policy Y) and have no immediate opportunity cost in terms of private wants. The difference, perhaps, is one of semantics more than substance: By replacing the term *contribution in accordance with benefits received* with *contribution in accordance with evaluation of services rendered*, the policy criterion is made neutral with regard to motivation. But the problem of merit goods cannot be exorcised from the discussion.

NOTES

1. In retrospect, it seems more appropriate to distinguish between social and private *goods* rather than social and private *wants*. The problem arises because the benefits derived from some goods are external, whereas those derived from others are internal. At the same time, the wants underlying provision for both types of goods are the personal wants of individual consumers and do not differ in nature.
2. It is evident that the case of social wants must involve joint consumption; but joint consumption, as usually defined, does not necessarily involve social wants. A circus performance involves joint consumption on the part of those who attend. Yet entrance fees can be charged, different amounts can be consumed by various people, and the service can be provided through the market. Demand schedules can be added horizontally. For a social want to arise, the condition of equal consumption must apply to all, whether they pay or not. In other words, we must combine the condition of joint consumption with that of inapplicability of the exclusion principle. Only then will demand schedules be added vertically.
3. As noted before, the budget of the allocation branch is planned on the assumption that the distribution branch has provided for the proper distribution of income and that the stabilisation branch has provided for a full-employment level of income.
4. Suppose that a given public service satisfies both social and private wants. We obtain a total demand schedule for social wants by vertical addition of individual schedules for the social want component, and a total schedule for private wants by horizontal addition of individual schedules for the private want component. Assume further (though this is not essential) that the social and private product components are matched on a 1:1 basis. We then deduct the total demand schedule for the social component from the supply schedule. The intersection of the supply schedule thus adjusted with the total demand schedule for private component shows the amount to be supplied (abscissa) and the part of the total unit cost to be paid for as price (ordinate). The vertical distance between the intersection and the unadjusted supply schedule shows the part of the unit cost to be provided for through the budget, i.e. by tax-financed subsidy. In the case of purely social wants, the subsidy is 100 per cent; while in the case of purely private wants it is zero per cent.
5. Whereas the issue of externalities arises in relation to various types of *goods*, the merit issue relates to the underlying nature of *wants*. Thus, the former distinction is better dealt with in terms of social vs. private *goods*, rather than social vs. private wants; but the latter is addressed more appropriately in terms of personal vs. merit *wants*. Such is the case, even though the problem has come to be referred to more generally as one of merit goods.
6. This discussion of Colm's position draws upon personal discussion as well as his writings, but the responsibility for appropriate interpretation remains mine.

REFERENCES

[1] Colm, G. (1956) 'Comments on Samuelson's *Theory of Public Finance*', *Review of Economics and Statistics*, vol. 32, no. 4.
[2] —— (1955) *Essays in Public Finance and Fiscal Policy* (New York: Oxford University Press).

[3] —— (1927) *Volkswirtschaftliche Theorie der Staatsausgaben: Ein Beitrag zur Finanztheorie* (Tübingen: Mohr).

[4] Margolis, J. (1955) 'A Comment on the *Pure Theory of Public Expenditures*', *Review of Economics and Statistics*, vol. 32, no. 4.

[5] Musgrave, R. and Peacock, A. (eds.) (1958) *Classics in the Theory of Public Finance* (London: Macmillan).

[6] Ritschl, H. (1925) *Theorie der Staatswirtschaft und Besteuerung* (Bonn: Schroeder), Ch. 1.

[7] —— (1931) *Gemeinwirtschaft und Kapitalistische Marktwirtschaft* (Tübingen: Mohr), pp. 32–43. For excerpts, see Musgrave and Peacock [5].

[8] Schäffle, A. (1873) *Das gesellschaftliche System der menschlichen Wirtschaft* (Tübingen), vol. I, p. 6.

4 Provision for Social Goods*
1969

THE THEORY OF SOCIAL GOODS

The theory of social goods deals with the features which distinguish social from private goods, and the problems encountered in making public provisions for the former. This theory has been developed rather fully with reference to the polar case of a pure social good, but its application to the important range of mixed goods remains to be explored. We begin with a review of the polar case and then proceed to the more complex situation of mixed goods. Emphasis will be on the nature of social goods and the characteristics of optimal provision. The equally important problem of how to implement this solution is dealt with only incidentally. The discussion will be in terms of current consumer goods, but essentially the same applies to that of durable consumer and intermediate goods.

Public Provision vs. Public Production
To begin with, we must distinguish between 'public provision' as we use the term, and public production. Public provision refers to a situation where certain goods are furnished to the consumer not in response to individual market purchases, but free of direct charge and through the budgetary process. Such public provision may take the form of public purchases from private firms or public production. Similarly, public production may involve goods which are sold to individual consumers in the market. The issue of resource allocation between social or private goods (whether produced publicly or privately) is the central theoretical issue of public finance or public economy as here understood. It is quite distinct from, and largely unrelated to, that of private vs. public management of production (whether of private or of social goods), i.e. to the traditional distinction between socialism and capitalism.

The problem of social goods, as here conceived, thus exists in both the socialist and the capitalist context. In the latter, certain characteristics of social goods require public provision through the budgetary process. In the

* From J. Margolis and H. Guitton (eds.) (1969) *Public Economics* (London: Macmillan/New York: St Martin's Press).

41

former, these very characteristics make it impossible to use the market (or queue) type of allocation applicable in a socialism with consumer choice [8]. Rather, such goods must again be allocated through a political system of preference determination quite analogous to that needed in the capitalist system.[1]

Subjective Preference Hypothesis

Next, one must choose between two approaches to the theory of social wants or social goods, involving two alternative premises regarding the underlying preference system. One approach is to argue that all allocation, whether to private or to social goods, is to be made in line with individual consumer preferences. The utility of defence along with that of door-locks and ice cream is included in the individual's preference function, and both goods should be provided in relation thereto. The social utility function relates to the ordering of welfare positions among individuals, but leaves the choice between particular goods to them. This excludes neither some degree of delegation of decision-making (be it to legislators or civil servants), nor implementation through a more or less imperfect mechanism of decision by voting. Nor does it presume extreme 'egotism' in individual behaviour. Some allowance may be made in the utility function A for utility derived by B. But it differs fundamentally from an alternative that postulates some élite or central authority (benevolent or not) which knows best, and imposes its preferences on the individual. A may be asked to consume Q_x even though he would prefer Q_y produced with the same resource input. The student of fiscal affairs who wishes to build a predictive model will investigate whether the existing set of institutions corresponds more closely to the one or the other system. But for purposes of a normative theory, which defines optimal fiscal behaviour, the choice between the two approaches is essentially ideological. It will not be discussed here and unless otherwise noted we shall proceed on the premise of individual choice.

This leaves us with an individualistic or subjective (as distinct from an imposed or collective) view of the preference system. At the same time, certain goods have characteristics which require group action to secure their provision, in line with individual preference. Such goods are here referred to as social goods. To emphasise that the distinguishing characteristic derives from the nature of the good, rather than the utility function, I now prefer the term 'social good' to my earlier terminology of 'social want' [10]. By the same token, the term 'imposed want' is preferable where the alternative system is considered.

THE POLAR CASE

Our first task is to determine the characteristics which must apply if a good is to be provided for publicly, i.e. to qualify as a social good. Much has been said about this in the literature, some helpful and some not. From this discussion there emerge two features which are most relevant and interesting. The first is the characteristic of non-rivalness in consumption, i.e. the existence of a beneficial consumption externality. The second is the characteristic of non-excludability from consumption. The two are distinct features and need not coincide. Each plays a different role.

Non-rivalness in Consumption

Social goods are defined as goods, the benefits from which are such that A's partaking therein does not interfere with the benefits derived by B. They differ from private goods, whose benefits are enjoyed by either A or B. The two goods enter the utility functions of A and B as $U_A = U_A(X_A, Y)$ and $U_B = U_B(X_B, Y)$ where X_A and X_B are the amounts of the private good X which are purchased by the two respectively, while Y is the total supply of the social good. The total output, subject to the transformation function, is given by $O = X_A + X_B + Y$.

The condition of non-rivalness in consumption (or, which is the same, the existence of beneficial consumption externalities) means that the same physical output (the fruits of the same factor input) is enjoyed by both A and B. This does not mean that the same subjective benefit must be derived, or even that precisely the same product quality is available to both. Consumer A who lives close to the police station has better protection than B who lives far away. Yet, the two consumption acts are non-rival, and we deal with a social good.

Due to the non-rivalness of consumption, individual demand curves are added vertically [2, p. 177], rather than horizontally as in the case of private goods. Or A's demand curve may be considered a supply curve from B's point of view and vice versa [9, p. 89]. The cost share payable by A will be the less, the more is paid by B, and the more additional consumers participate. Contrary to the case of private goods, a consumer will find it to his advantage to have tastes which are similar to those of others.

As Samuelson [13, 14] has shown, Pareto optimality for the supply of social goods requires that marginal cost equals the sum of the marginal rates of substitution of A and B, whereas for the private good it is equal to each of these two rates. Assuming preferences to be known, what does this imply for the pricing of social goods, and the possibility of separating allocational and distributional considerations in the public household?

Non-excludability from Consumption

Let us turn first to another characteristic difficulty of social goods, which relates to the process of preference determination. For the case of private goods, the market mechanism may be likened to an auction system, where the product goes to the highest bidder. Consumers must reveal their preferences, since otherwise they will be excluded from the enjoyment of the goods which they wish to purchase. But now consider the case of a social good, such as national defence, which is virtually such that no one can be excluded. As a result, consumers will be hesitant or unwilling to reveal true preferences. Being one among many, a consumer will argue that the total supply and hence the benefit which accrues to him will not be affected significantly by his contribution. If the government invites declaration of preferences and bills accordingly, he will respond by understating his preference. Since preference revelation is not secured automatically by the auction function of the market, another mechanism (e.g. voting procedures) must be substituted to determine preferences. This second difference stems from non-excludability and relates to the revelation of preferences.

While the case of defence combines non-rivalness in consumption with non-excludability, this is not a necessary situation. The existence of non-rivalness in consumption does not necessarily mean that exclusion is impossible; and the existence of rival consumption does not always mean that exclusion is possible. The first case is illustrated by an existing bridge which is not crowded, but which readily permits the charging of tolls. In this situation, charging of tolls is inefficient because it does not meet the Pareto condition for social goods. The second case is illustrated by A's apple orchard, the nectar of which is consumed by the bees of either B or C. In this case, market failure occurs because of non-excludability, even though we are dealing with rival consumption. Social (non-rival) goods need not be non-excludable goods, and vice versa. The occurrence of either feature calls for group action to secure proper provision, but for different reasons [1].

There are some situations where excludability is impossible (defence) and others where it is available at little or no cost (ice cream or use of bridge). In the former case, we have no choice in the matter. In the latter case, exclusion may be desirable but need not always be so. It should be applied only with regard to goods, the benefits of which are rival, but not with regard to goods whose benefits are non-rival. The non-crowded bridge should not be subject to tolls even if the gatekeeper is cheap or would be otherwise unemployable and hence involved no resource cost. The currently popular drive to 'internalise externalities' is thus subject to qualification. It should be added, however, that the situation with regard to external costs is asymmetrical. Such costs should be internalised even if non-rival. Whereas exclusion of additional consumers from the enjoyment of benefits is a loss, preventing the imposition of a burden on all is a gain.

The two preceding situations (excludability is impossible or available at zero cost) are not all-inclusive. In many cases excludability may be possible but at a significant cost. If the situation is such that exclusion should be applied if available at zero cost, the problem is then one of weighing the gains from exclusion (which forces revelation of preferences and obviates the need for a political mechanism of preference determination) against the costs. Thus, the cost of traffic congestion in New York City streets should be internalised, provided that the mechanism of so doing is not too costly. Exclusion technology is thus a factor in deciding what costs should be internalised. At the margin, the cost of internalising should be equated with the gain in consumer surplus which results therefrom.

Let us return to the double-polar case of a good which is both non-rival and non-excludable, such as defence. We have noted that the individual consumer, being one among many, will not reveal his true preference without the pressure of a voting system which imposes a mandatory decision. Such a voting system, though necessary to induce preference revelation, has its efficiency cost. For one thing, voting takes time and equipment; for another, the outcome will not please all participants. The economist's assignment for the political scientist is to solve the dilemma of devising a voting system which permits the best expression of preference (a system similar to point rather than majority voting) while giving least play to strategy (which might be most dominant under point voting).

This cost is avoidable in a situation where numbers are small. In this case, individual bargaining will be feasible, and non-excludability loses much of its significance. A market in externalities can be created [3], [5], [15], [17]. This, however, is not a pure gain, as the existence of small numbers creates a new set of imperfections. We have here another distinction between social and private goods. As I have noted earlier, the increase in numbers improves the market allocation of private goods, but only moves the social good from one trouble (small-number imperfection) to another (non-revelation) [10].

Optimal Allocation With Preferences Given, and the Distribution Issue

Let us now disregard the exclusion issue and its implications for revelation and assume that individual preferences are known to the planner. What then constitutes an optimal solution for the purely non-rival good?

The now classical formulation of the problem, as given by Samuelson [13], determines a set of feasible solutions, involving (1) different divisions of total output between the public good and the private good, and (2) different divisions of the total supply of private goods between A and B. All these solutions are Pareto optimal in that any departure from the set involves a loss to either A or B. The optimum optimorum is then chosen on the basis of a social utility function which weighs the relative welfare positions of A and B. The solution of the social goods problem is thus made part of the general problem of welfare maximisation including the *entire* issue of distribution and production choice of private goods.

This formulation meets the test of theoretical rigour and sweeping elegance and ranks among the great contributions to the theory of welfare economics as applied to public finance. Yet, it leaves the more parochially-inclined fiscal theorist somewhat dissatisfied. The extreme generality of the formulation renders it difficult to focus on the specifically fiscal problem and to relate the theoretical model to implementational schemes.

More attractive, from his point of view, is the spirit of the Lindahl formulation [9], especially as revised in a recent article by Johansen [7], and of my earlier attempt at restatement [10, p. 81]. In these models, the concern is directly with tax expenditure determination on the basis of a given initial state of distribution, following Wicksell's [16] proposition that

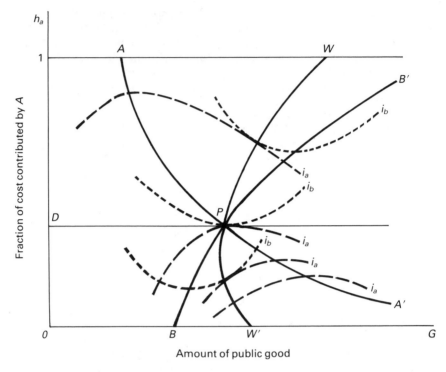

Figure 4.1: Johansen's exposition of Lindahl's diagram

the 'proper' distribution of the tax burden cannot be determined unless a 'proper' distribution of income is assumed to exist at the outset.

Johansen's analysis begins with a given state of distribution in terms of factor endowments. With the help of certain simplifying assumptions he derives an offer schedule for A, showing the preferred amount of social goods for various divisions of cost shares between A and B.[2] A similar curve is derived for B, and their intersection corresponds to the P point in the well-known Lindahl diagram [9, p. 89]. (See AA' and BB' in Fig. 4.1). As Johansen shows, this P point is one but not the only Pareto optimal solution, as it is only one among other points on the contract curve, WW' corresponding to different divisions of the welfare gain from the introduction of social goods between A and B. Since Johansen attaches no particular merit to the P point, he is still left with a distributional issue and need for a social utility function. However, the scope of the distributional problem is reduced, due to the initial assumption of a given distribution of resource endowment.

This formulation may be considered a special case of Samuelson's broader framework, but it is more attractive for purposes of fiscal theory as it permits us to focus explicitly on the crucial policy problem of tax shares. At the same time, it leaves open the question of why the initial state of resource endowment was considered proper. As long as the distribution of the gain from the introduction of social goods remains to be distributed, how is it possible to predetermine the 'proper' resource endowment? The social utility function, which determines the state of distribution, cannot relate merely to the distribution which would result in the absence of social goods, but must cover the entire resource use, including social goods. We are still left with an inconsistency which is successfully removed in Samuelson's general formulation.

But this is not the only possible solution. Instead of substituting this general formulation, the point *P* may be re-established (or established) as the optimal solution by hypothesising that the initial distribution of resource endowment has been derived from the social welfare function on the assumption that cost shares in the budget will be allocated according to a pricing rule which yields this result. Given my primary interest in developing a useful theory of public finance (the purpose of a theoretical tool being after all its applicability to relevant issues), I find this helpful for various reasons.

First, it suggests a method of pricing for social goods which is analogous to that of pricing for private goods in the sense that for each consumer there must be an equality of the marginal rates of substitution between social and private goods on the one side, and the ratio of *his* price for social goods and the *uniform* price for private goods on the other. The difference indicated by the italics denotes that the price of the social good to the individual (unlike that of the private good) is not equal to the marginal cost for the economy, but to the individual consumer's share therein.

Given this information, the provision of social goods may be considered an efficiency problem in resource use, analogous to the traditional practice with regard to private goods, where it is concluded that, in the absence of externalities and on the basis of a given distribution of resource endowment, the competitive solution is to be preferred. The allocation of both social and private goods follows a pricing rule and (contrary to the view which identifies economic issues with private goods [6]), one is as 'economic' as the other. There remains, to be sure, the difference that implementation of the pricing rule for private goods is achieved more readily than that for public goods, where non-excludability requires a political mechanism to secure preference revelation. But this is a problem of implementation, not different in kind from public controls to secure competition in private markets. Indeed, our pricing rule (choice of the *P* point) has the further advantage that it offers an operational reference point in evaluating the quality of alternative voting systems (e.g. qualified majority, plurality, etc.) as well as of parliamentary procedures (piecemeal vs. overall legislation in appropriating funds, ear-marking, combining tax and expenditure decisions, etc.) in approximating an optimal solution to the social goods problem. This is necessary if our theory is to be useful at a more applied level.

Above all, it is evident to the most casual observer that real-world decisions are frequently rendered inefficient because (as a matter of fiscal politics) allocation objectives are mixed with distributional objectives. Usually, these objectives can be implemented more economically through direct tax transfer measures, leaving the choice between social and private goods to be made on consumer-preference grounds.[3]

Addendum on Separation of Issues[4]

I remain convinced that the separation between allocation and distribution aspects offers a more useful approach to public finance theory, notwithstanding re-emphasis of their interdependence in Samuelson's paper. Unless a basis for separation is established, we are left with a theory of public expenditures or, better, resource use in which the tax problem has no conceptual place. But without this, the theory gives little aid to the analysis of fiscal problems as they actually arise. Hence the public finance theorist's need for a somewhat more parochial approach.

I grant that it is not possible to define the distribution goal merely in terms of resource endowment; and that it is not possible, by use of the Pareto rule, to determine *the* optimal allocation pattern. But suppose that the utility frontier has been determined and that a point thereon has been chosen as optimal. We may then work back to a distribution of resource endowments which corresponds to this point, provided that a specific pricing rule (e.g. marginal cost pricing) is followed. Having done so, allocation according to marginal cost pricing will be optimal.

I see no objection to this construction as an analytical device.[5] The question, rather, is whether it is a useful tool. The issue applies to both a world of private and of public goods. In the private good context, a move from a situation of average cost pricing to marginal cost pricing can be said unequivocally to involve a gain to society only if the relative welfare positions which result from marginal cost policy are considered desirable. Otherwise, the loss from worsened distribution may outweigh the gain in Pareto efficiency. Unless this condition is met (i.e. the distribution of resource endowment, given marginal cost pricing, is assumed to be correct), nothing can be said about the comparative merits of one or another market structure. There would be no basis (with regard to allocation objectives at least) for anti-trust policy, and the case against such measures as price maintenance legislation. I submit that this is not a reasonable judgement. One need not be a 'slave to Pareto optimality' to believe that more will be accomplished by retaining the fiction of 'proper' distribution when dealing with market structures, while applying distributional correctives directly with regard to income.

Much the same argument applies with regard to social goods. To be sure, the basic issue of distribution (how would one distribute income in a world of private goods which involve no externalities?) must be admitted as a problem of budget policy because, as just noted, it is accomplished better through direct redistribution (tax transfer measures) than through price adjustments. But there is much to be said for separating it from the additional problem of providing for social goods. By adopting our pricing rule, the latter may again be seen as an allocation issue, thereby expediting the provision of such goods in response to individual preferences and reducing the extent to which it is distorted by purely distributive considerations. While the implementation of the pricing rule is more difficult in the case of social goods, due to non-excludability and its consequences for revelation, this also renders the availability of a yardstick for efficient behaviour the more important. While Samuelson is correct in pointing out that too little has been done regarding the evaluation of alternative rules of decision-making, I do not take quite as nihilistic a view regarding the possibility of work in this area.

MIXED CASES

The preceding discussion has dealt with the case of a pure social good, i.e. a good the benefits of which are wholly non-rival. This approach has been subject to the criticism that this case does not exist, or, if at all, applies to defence only; and in fact most goods which give rise to private benefits also involve externalities in varying degrees and hence combine both social and private good characteristics. Granted that such is the case, it hardly renders the theoretical discussion of the polar case useless. Economic categories (not even the proverbial distinction between consumer and capital goods) rarely apply in pure form. We can do better, however, and show that the above analysis may be applied to at least some important types of mixed cases [11].

Case I. Social Goods with Limited Spillover

The utility function for the social good case was defined as $U_A = U_A(X_A, Y)$ and $U_B = U_B(X_B, Y)$, where Y is the social good. This may also be written as $U_A = U_A(X_A, Y_{PA} + Y_{PB})$ and $U_B = U_B(X_B, Y_{PA} + Y_{PB})$, where Y_{PA} are units of Y paid for by A, and Y_{PB} are units of Y paid for by B. Since the benefits derived by A from Y_{PB} are the same as those derived from Y_{PA}, and vice versa for B, the distinction between Y_{PA} and Y_{PB} is only a 'payment' matter. Both being fully beneficial to both A and B, the question of who pays and the 'location' of the direct consumption input may be disregarded. But suppose now that the situation is asymmetrical. The utility functions read $U_A = U_A(X_A, Y_A + Y_B)$ and $U_B = U_B(X_B, Y_B)$. X is again a purely private good. Consumption of X by A is useful to A but of no concern to B, and vice versa. Consumption of Y by B, however, is beneficial to A, and indeed a perfect substitute of own-consumption inputs by A. In other words, Y_B is a pure social good to A but a private good to B. The social good quality of Y is non-reciprocal. Anti-pollution measures undertaken by B who lives upstream are helpful to A who lives downstream, but not vice versa. The meaning of the subscript is now not merely one of finance but of 'initial consumption input'. The initial location of this consumption input, which was irrelevant in the case of the pure social good, is now of crucial importance. Since A does not care whether the consumption input is with A or with B, A will be prepared to subsidise B's consumption.

This type of limited spillover is of particular interest with regard to the interrelationship between fiscal units, be they localities or nations. If such unit is treated as a person, it being assumed that the respective community preferences are internally determined, the problem of benefit spillovers between fiscal units is indeed the same as that between individuals [18].

Before dealing with any particular situation, it is useful to develop a taxonomy of partial spillovers, which provides a bridge between purely private goods and purely social goods.

$U_A =$	$U_B =$			
	$U(Y_B)$	$U(Y_B+\beta Y_A)$	$U(Y_B+\gamma Y_A)$	$U(Y_B + Y_A)$
$U(Y_A)$	1	2	2	5
$U(Y_A + \beta Y_B)$	2	3	4	6
$U(Y_A + \gamma Y_B)$	2	4	3	6
$U(Y_A + Y_B)$	5	6	6	7

The subscripts A and B indicate in which community (or on behalf of which individual) the consumption input occurs. The β and γ coefficients indicate the benefit discounts or premiums attached to the foreign, relative to the own-input. If β in A's utility function is equal to 1, A is indifferent whether the consumption input occurs (one gallon of insect spray is released) in A or in B. If β equals 0·5, one input unit in B is worth one-half as much as to A as one input unit in A and so forth. The essential point is that insect spraying in B reduces pests not only in B but also in A, but that the input per gallon in B may well be less productive (in terms of reduction of pests in A) than would the input of the same gallon in A. The distribution of striking force between the members of an alliance is another illustration [12]. The values of γ and β are here assumed to be non-negative and not to exceed 1, but this is not a necessary assumption.

Case 1 will be recognised as the polar case of the private good, where there are no externalities at all, and case 7 as that of the pure social good, where there is full and reciprocal spillover. Situations 2 and 5 are situations of non-reciprocal spillover, with the spillover being partial in case 2 and full in 5. Cases 3, 4 and 6 involve reciprocal spillovers. In case 3 the reciprocal spillover is symmetrical, while in 4 and 6 it is not. In cases 5 and 6 at least one party benefits from spill-ins on a 1:1 basis, whereas in 2, 3 and 4 benefits from spill-ins are subject to a 'discount'.

To avoid confusion, let it be noted again that we are dealing here with consumption externalities. Own-consumption by (spraying in) A helps pest reduction in B. This is the case whether the spray is produced by A, B, or whether it is imported from C. The location of production remains a matter of trade theory in the traditional sense. A corresponding set of cases can be developed which deals with production externalities. Thus, the production of chemicals may generate unpleasant odours, which may or may not drift across the border. No one likes to live next to a smoke stack. This poses analogous problems, but they are not dealt with here.

Nor can we attempt to develop the consumption cases in detail, but a brief comment on case 2 may be useful to illustrate the nature of the problem. We compare an initial situation (1) where A and B each adjust their own purchases to that of the other party, but no side payments can be made, with a new situation (2) which comes about if side payments and negotiations are permitted. Adding a purely private good X to the picture (where both β and γ equal zero), it can be shown that the consumption of Y is increased when moving from (1) to (2). This is the case because income as well as substitution effects for both A and B favour increased consumption of Y.[6] At the same time, it does *not* follow that factor inputs into Y will be increased. In fact, it is quite possible that factor inputs will be decreased because consumption is shifted to the more efficient site, i.e. from A to B.[7] In case 3 where the spillover situation is symmetrical, such gain from relocation of factor input is not possible, and the introduction of side-payments may be expected to increase total inputs as well as consumption.

How does a situation of type 2 or 5 relate to the pure social good case of type 7? In case 5 for instance, Y is a fully private good for B but a fully social good for A. As a result, A will subsidise consumption by B, and resort to own-consumption only if the total supply which he desires at a price equal to cost or own-input, exceeds the amount for which B's marginal evaluation becomes zero. In the small number case, such a result might be approximated by bargaining. In the large number case, the A's will be called upon to pay taxes which are used to subsidise (though at less than 100 per cent) the purchases of own-inputs by the B's. We are left with a selective tax subsidy scheme, with a transfer from inefficient own-consumers or recipients of spill-ins to efficient own-consumers or originators of spill-outs.

Case II. Non-substitute Externalities

In case I we have dealt with situations where B's own-consumption of Y is a substitute for A's own-consumption of Y, even though the productivity per unit of input into B may be less, from A's point of view, than a similar input into A. Consider now a somewhat different situation. The utility functions are $U_A = U_A(X_A, Y_A, Y_B)$ and $U_B = U_B(X_B, Y_B, Y_A)$. This is a situation where A derives a benefit from B's consumption of Y, but this benefit is entirely different from (no direct substitute for) his own consumption of Y.[8] For instance, A may invest in his own education to raise his income, or to be better able to enjoy literature; and he may have an interest in B's education, either for altruistic reasons, or because this increases his safety or the pleasantness of his social environment. In this situation A will again be willing to subsidise B, and vice versa, but A's own demand for Y_A will not be related directly to the level of Y_B. Y_A and Y_B are rival rather than substitute commodities.

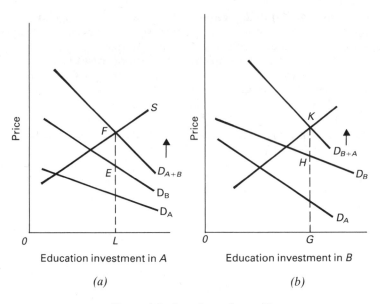

Figure 4.2: Interdependent utility

The situation regarding Y_A and Y_B is shown in Fig. 4.2, where (a) shows the demand for Y_A (education investment in *A*). D_A is *A*'s demand, D_B is *B*'s demand, and the two are added vertically into D_{A+B} or market demand. If *S* is the supply schedule (the cost of pencils which *A* needs for his studies), total input into *A* will equal *OL*. Adopting a solution analogous to Lindahl's *P* point, *A* will pay *EL* and *B* will pay *EF*. The subsidy rate received by *A* and paid by *B* equals *EF/FL*. Fig. 4.2(b) gives the same picture for education investment in *B*, with a subsidy rate equal to *HK/GK* and input equal to *OG*. Total education input (allowing compensation to be paid) equals *OL* + *OG*. Transferring the argument to the large number case, we arrive at a situation where everyone's own education becomes a social good for everyone else; but unlike the polar case, the solution is not provision through the budget with 100 per cent tax finance. Rather, we end up with a general tax subsidy scheme, where the rate of subsidy depends upon the relative weights of the private and social goods components of *Y*. The polar case of 100 per cent tax finance is but a limiting solution of the general theory of subsidy. It arises where the entire benefit is in social form, while private benefit is equal to zero.

Case III. Mixed Benefit Goods

Finally, consider a situation where the utility functions read $U_A = U_A(X_A, Y_A, Y_A + Y_B)$ and $U_B = U_B(X_B, Y_B, Y_B + Y_A)$. We are now dealing with a good which generates two types of benefits, one which is purely private and applies to own-consumption only; and another, which is wholly social and which is enjoyed equally independently of the locus of consumption input. This case bears similarities to and differs from both the preceding sets of situations. It is similar to the situations under case I in that Y_B and Y_A appear in additive form, but differs in that outside consumption is a substitute for only one, not all aspects of own-consumption. Discount coefficients may again be added as in case I. Also, this situation is similar to that of case II in that there are some aspects of own-consumption which cannot be substituted for by outside consumption; but it differs from it in that such benefits as are derived from outside consumption do serve as substitutes for some aspects of own-consumption.

The education case may again be drawn upon to illustrate this situation, it being as reasonable to interpret it in the case III as in the case II sense. *A* derives benefits from his own education such as higher earnings, but also values the environment of a close cultural society to which everyone's education (including his own) contributes. The attraction of the present formulation is that it neatly transforms the all-or-nothing case of the pure social good into a generalised theory of public subsidy. To simplify matters, we assume again that the proper solution of the pure social good case is given by the intersection of offer curves, i.e. the Lindahl–Johansen *P* point. Now let D_A^p and D_B^p in Fig. 4.3(a) be *A*'s and *B*'s demand curves for *Y* as a private good. Adding horizontally, we obtain the market demand schedule D_{A+B}^p. Similarly, let D_A^s and D_B^s in Fig. 4.3(b) be the respective marginal evaluation (offer) curves for *Y* as a social good. Adding vertically, we obtain the 'market' demand schedule D_{A+B}^s. Finally, in Fig. 4.3(c) we add the two market schedules vertically to obtain a total 'market' demand, including both features of *Y*.[9] We also enter D_{A+B}^p the market demand curve for *Y* as a private good. *S* is the industry supply schedule, showing the average cost per physical unit of *Y*. The horizontal axis in all three figures is drawn in the same scale.

Output is determined at *OE* with *A* purchasing *OH* and *B* purchasing *HE*. The market price, accounting for private benefit paid by each, is *OP* = *EF*; and *FB* is the unit subsidy, accounting for the social benefit. Of this, *FN* (see Fig. 4.3(b)) is contributed by *B* and *FR* = *NB* by *A*. Again, the traditional theory in terms of a 100 per cent tax and expenditure type of budgetary provision is converted into a general theory of subsidy. For a purely social good, D_{A+B}^p in Fig. 4.3(c) coincides with the horizontal axis, and the subsidy equals 100 per cent. For a purely private good, (D_{A+B}^p) coincides with $(D_{A+B}^p) + (D_{A+B}^s)$ and the subsidy is zero. We again have a general tax subsidy scheme, where all purchasers of the good receive the same subsidy rate. Even the smoke nuisance case can be incorporated into the argument by assuming D^s to be negative, in which case $(D_{A+B}^p) + (D_{A+B}^s)$ lies below (D_{A+B}^p) and a compensatory tax (the proceeds from which can be returned by lump-sum subsidy) is called for.

The analysis of cases *B* and *C*, as considered in the preceding sections, may be incorporated into the modern theory. Samuelson's derivation of the optimality condition may be adapted accordingly, the subsidy part of

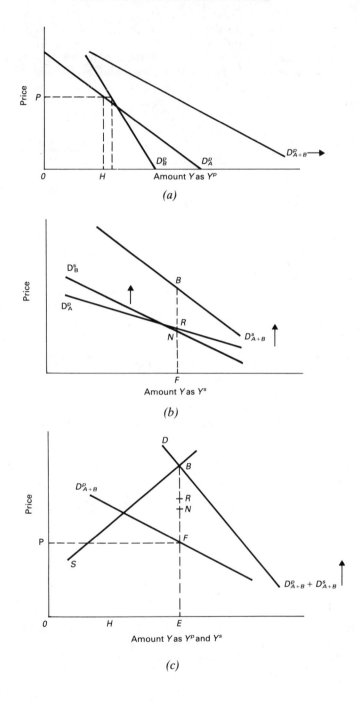

Figure 4.3: Mixed good

the cost being equated with the sum of the rates of substitution of A and B and the remainder with market price.

The fact that governments typically provide social goods where a 100 per cent subsidy is called for, but rarely where a lesser rate is indicated, shows a rigidity in social behaviour which leads to inefficient results. If many goods are indeed of the mixed type, an extensive set of subsidies at varying rates would be called for.

Determination of the proper subsidy rate is undertaken through the budget process and poses precisely the same difficulties (including non-revelation of preferences, choice of point on Johansen's WW' curve [7], etc.) already familiar from the polar case of social goods.

Addendum on Semantics[10]

Professor Samuelson rejects our taxonomy of p. 50, and proposes that one should draw only a single line between the knife-edge concept of the purely private good (my case 1) and all the rest. He has no use for my concept of a polar social good as defined by my case 7. The abandonment of monopoly as a counter-pole to competition in the theory of market structure is drawn upon as an analogy.

It seems to me that this analogy does not apply. Pure competition, presumably, is chosen as a point of departure because it is of particular interest (at least to the slaves of Pareto optimality) due to its welfare implications. Pure monopoly is but one among a wide range of 'imperfections' which may arise, reduction in numbers being but one of many ways in which reality may depart from the norm. Thus it does not provide an alternative pole. The situation differs with my cases 1 and 7. In the first case we deal with private benefit only, without externalities. In the second case, we deal with external benefits only, without private aspects. Thus, the first case involves a situation where (subject to the necessary distributional assumptions) the competitive market mechanism leads to an optimal result. The second case involves a situation where (given large numbers) nothing can be left to the guidance of voluntary market payments. In between these poles lies a situation where varying degrees of subsidy are called for. Case 7, therefore, constitutes a polar situation in a meaningful sense.

All this, of course, is quite compatible with Samuelson's claim that his general formulation covers all these cases in a formal fashion. Indeed, it was my very purpose to point out that similar analysis can be applied to mixed situations. But semantics, as the history of economic thought so well shows, is not a trivial matter; and I remain persuaded that systematic explanation of non-polar situations will be helpful, as they may point to different policy solution.

4 MERIT WANTS

In concluding, a word should be added regarding the role of merit wants. As noted, this entire discussion has been based on the assumption that social goods should be supplied in line with individual preferences. This may be objected to, because the critic feels that preferences should be imposed with certain limits by a chosen élite, be it because its members are better educated, possess greater innate wisdom, or belong to a particular party or sect. Or, it may be objected to simply as unrealistic since, in fact, a considerable part of budget expenditures go to provide goods (e.g. low-cost housing or milk for babies) which are rival in consumption and readily subject to exclusion. From this it may be concluded that society in fact wishes to impose a substantial degree of interference with consumer preference; and that therefore a theory of imposed choice should be incorporated into the fiscal model. Wants with regard to which consumer choice is abandoned and the satisfaction of which is imposed I have referred to as merit wants, and have argued that they remain outside the normative model [10, pp. 13 ff.].

A possible reconciliation may be obtained by granting that rational individual choice requires acquaintance with alternatives and that experimentation (even though it may involve imposed choice on a temporary basis) may be needed to obtain the necessary information. Temporary use of imposed choice may also be justified as an aid to the learning process. Thus, what appears to be imposed choice may be compatible, in the longer run, with the objective of intelligent free choice. This, however, is a somewhat uneasy position to one who may deplore the poor taste of the 'public', but would rather persuade than force them to choose otherwise. Yet, it is not without some validity in the realities of the social framework.

An alternative possibility of reconciliation emerges along these lines: Many of the phenomena which appear to be of the merit good type can actually be explained by interdependence of utilities. The situation is similar to that described in our case II, where A's utility function was given by $U_A = U_A(X_A, Y_A, Y_B)$. In other words, A derives a utility from his own consumption of Y, but he also derives a utility (though of a different kind) from B's consumption of Y. This, in fact, is a quite widespread attitude regarding the consumption of basic commodities, e.g. minimum requirements of food, shelter, health and so forth. The social philosophy of western society appears to be such that the freedom to tolerate inequality in the distribution of luxury consumption and saving is purchased at the cost of earmarked (specific) subsidies which assure equality in the consumption of necessities. Looked at in terms of this double standard, subsidies in kind, especially to low income groups, make sense; and what appeared to be the wholly different phenomena of merit wants may be incorporated into a subjective preference theory.

In *this* context, the position which views the problem in terms of social goods, rather than wants, also needs to be revised. However this may be, the case for reconciling merit wants with personal choice should not be carried too far: the possibility remains that choice is to be imposed *per se*, and here our basic analysis of social goods does not apply.

NOTES

1. At the same time, other aspects of the fiscal system (including the stabilisation and distribution functions, the specific function of taxes, and the extent to which merit wants are recognised) differ sharply under socialist and capitalist conditions [11, Part I].
2. The dashed indifference curves show combinations of public goods output (G) and cost shares (h_a) contributed by A among which taxpayer A is indifferent. They are derived from the taxpayers' basic preference patterns between a private good X and a public good G, and a given initial resource endowment in terms of X. The dotted indifference lines for B are concave to the abscissa, since $h_B = 1 - h_A$. The lines AA' and BB' show the most preferred values for various cost shares. The line WW', or contract curve, is the locus of the points on which the two sets of indifference curves are tangent. Only at point P do the most preferred positions coincide. Since the indifference curves in Fig. 4.1 refer to a given resource endowment, they will shift if the endowment is changed, and the WW' curve will shift accordingly.
3. This is not to deny that subsidies in kind may be appropriate in the merit good context.
4. This section has been added, to complement Samuelson's cross-references, in his paper.
5. Professor Samuelson is correct, however, in criticising certain aspects of my earlier version [10, pp. 80–5]. In particular (1) There is an inconsistency between the argument of p. 81 where the resource endowment is taken as given, and of p. 84, where the government is given the task of choosing among points on the utility frontier. If the given endowment distribution is accepted as 'correct', one must also stipulate a specific pricing rule as done on p. 85; and in this case one arrives at a specific point on the utility frontier. (2) Professor Samuelson is correct in pointing out that my utility frontier over range XY (p. 83) is a part of his frontier, each intermediate point reflecting a different pricing rule. (3) It was somewhat misleading to argue (p. 84) that indeterminacy arises in the case of public goods only. This is correct only if the prevailing distribution of endowments is assumed to stipulate marginal cost pricing for private goods, while making no such stipulation for social goods. The difference disappears if pricing rules are stipulated for both cases. (4) Professor Samuelson suggests that I am mistaken in requiring the budget for the 'allocation branch' to be balanced, since a subsidy is required for decreasing cost industries. I accept the principle that subsidy is needed in a truly decreasing cost case, but wonder how significant a factor this is for the broad range of social goods (pp. 136–40).
6. Williams [17] reaches the conclusion that consumption may rise or fall. This difference in result arises because Williams compares our initial situation (1) where A and B adjust themselves to the other's consumption of Y but *no* compensation is paid, with one (2) where compensation *must* be paid. With compensation mandatory, one party may come to be worse off. For him the income effect is negative and consumption may fall. Our comparison assumes moving from (1) to a situation (3) where compensation *may* be paid.
7. This very useful distinction between change in consumption and change in factor input has been advanced by Buchanan and Kafoglis [4].
8. The two demands are related only in the sense of general consumer equilibrium where, to some degree, the demand for *all* commodities is interdependent.

9. The reader may be puzzled why $D^P_A + D^P_B$, which has been added horizontally originally, is now included in a vertical addition. The reason is that the same physical output is available for both (joint) social use and (divided) private use.
10. This section has been added, subsequent to the Conference, to complement Professor Samuelson's cross-references.

REFERENCES

[1] Bator, F. (1958) 'The Anatomy of Market Failure', *Quarterly Journal of Economics*, LXXII.
[2] Bowen, H. (1948) *Towards Social Economy* (New York: Rinehart).
[3] Buchanan, J. (1962) 'Policy and the Pigouvian Margin', *Economica*, XXIX.
[4] —— and Kafoglis, M. (1963) 'A Note on Public Goods Supply', *American Economic Review*.
[5] Case, R. H. (1960) 'The Problem of Social Cost', *Journal of Law and Economics*, III.
[6] Ellis, H. (1950) 'The Economic Way of Thinking', *American Economic Review*, 40.
[7] Johansen, L. (1963) 'Some Notes on the Theory of Public Expenditures', *International Economic Review*, IV.
[8] Lange, O. and Taylor, F. (1938) *On the Economics of Socialism* (Minneapolis: University of Minnesota Press).
[9] Lindahl, E. (1910) *Die Gerechtigkeit in der Besteuerung* (Lund: Gleerupska).
[10] Musgrave, R. A. (1959) *The Theory of Public Finance* (New York: McGraw-Hill).
[11] Musgrave, R. A. (1967) *Fiscal Systems* (New Haven: Yale University Press).
[12] Olson, M. (1966) 'An Economic Theory of Alliances', *Review of Economics and Statistics*.
[13] Samuelson, P. (1955) 'Diagrammatic Exposition of a Theory of Public Expenditures', *Review of Economics and Statistics,* XXVI.
[14] —— (1969) 'Pure Theory of Public Expenditures and Taxation', in Margolis, J. and Guitton, H. (eds.), *Public Economics* (London: Macmillan).
[15] Turvey, R. (1963) 'On Divergencies between Social Cost and Private Cost', *Economica*, XXX.
[16] Wicksell, K. (1896) *Finanztheoretische Untersuchungen und das Steuerwesen Schweden's* (Vienna: Fischer).
[17] Wellisz, S. (1964) 'On External Diseconomies and the Government-Assisted Invisible Hand', *Economica,* N.S. 31.
[18] Williams, A. (1966) 'The Optimal Provision of Public Goods in a System of Local Government', *Journal of Political Economy*, LLXIV.

5 Cost-Benefit Analysis and the Theory of Public Finance* 1969

A theory of public finance remains unsatisfactory unless it comprises both the revenue and expenditure sides of the fiscal process. The classical (Ricardo–Mills–Edgeworth–Pigou) tradition of a 'taxation-only' view neglected this axiom. Holding expenditures unproductive, or disregarding them altogether, the task was to arrange taxes so as to impose equal (or least-total) sacrifice. As a theory of taxation, this approach collapsed with the old welfare economics, and as a theory of public finance, its exclusive concern with taxation by-passed the central problem of how to allocate resources for the provision of social goods. Subsequently, various attempts were made to combine the revenue and expenditure sides in a more satisfactory system. We shall note these briefly, and then consider how cost-benefit analysis fits into the picture.

I. PAST APPROACHES

The first attempt also came from A. C. Pigou. Although the early editions of his *Public Finance* stayed largely in the classical mould, subject only to added concern with announcement effects, it does contain an aside on public sector theory [20, Part I, ch. 7], drawn in the image of his prior *Economics of Welfare* [19]. The composition of public expenditures should be selected so as to equate their marginal social benefits; the composition of taxes should be chosen so as to minimise total social cost; and the size of the budget should be carried to the point where marginal benefits and costs are equal. There is nothing wrong with this view, but it says little beyond demanding in general terms that the public sector should be efficient. The real question is how costs and benefits are to be determined, and how they are related to each other.

Tax costs in terms of taxpayer sacrifice cannot be determined unless cardinal utility schedules are comparable and known. This was denied

---

* Richard Musgrave (1969) *The Journal of Economic Literature*, vol. VII.

(perhaps too vehemently so) by the new welfare economics. But, apart from this, the Pigovian model remains inadequate because it offers no mechanism by which benefits are to be measured. 'If a community were literally a unitary being, with the government as its brain,' as Pigou says, 'expenditures [paraphrasing] and taxes could be pushed up to the point where marginal benefits and costs are equal' [20, p. 50]. This formulation allows for both sides of the problem, but it still by-passes the main issue: the community is not a unitary being, and benefits must be valued (in the absence of specific reasons to the contrary) in terms of the preferences of consumers. While Pigou's welfare model is compatible with this requirement, it fails to show us how the requirement can be met.

Such was the state of affairs when I first studied the problem. Then came the Keynesian revolution, which elevated the fiscal mechanism to a strategic position in macroeconomic theory and policy. As distinct from the earlier emphasis on allocation and distribution, primary concern was now with fiscal effects on total demand. In the initial stages at least, exclusive emphasis was with the level of deficit and the expenditure side of the budget. When 'functional finance' reintroduced taxation as a policy tool [10, ch. 24], it was as an agent of deflation only, with the balanced budget theorem the symbol of the both sides approach. The traditional issues of efficient resource use and distribution were swamped by the newly discovered multiplier, or at best reduced to the 'ditch-digging' case against careless selection of public works.

A concerted return to the basic issues of allocation and distribution occurred in the 1950s, when English language literature first viewed the theory of public finance as one of social goods. The nature of social goods was defined in terms of goods the consumption of which is non-rival; and the conditions for efficient resource use in the provision of social goods were stated in terms of the 'new' welfare economics. In some respects, this was but a catching-up with Wicksell, who had written along these lines half a century before, and with Lindahl's development thereof.[1] But the job was now to be done more thoroughly. Samuelson's statement of Paretian efficiency for a world with both private and social goods was the basic step [22, 23]. While Samuelson referred to his formulation as a 'theory of public expenditures', this was too narrow a term. The formulation does not constitute an 'expenditure only' approach, analogous to the classical taxation only version. The opportunity cost of social goods use is made an integral part of the analysis, and the entire picture is included.

If taxation in the usual sense does not enter, neither do public expenditures. The generality of the formulation soars above such institutional trivia. An omniscient planner to whom available resources and techniques are given and all individual preferences are known, determines the choice of efficient outputs (including the division between public and private goods, and the assignment of the latter among consumers) for all possible states of welfare distribution, and then chooses the optimum optimorum by application of a social welfare function.

The special case of social goods was thus firmly incorporated into the general theory of welfare economics, but the new formulation left little or no footing from which to build a bridge towards an operational theory of public finance. Choosing this more parochial objective, I have preferred therefore to stay with the Wicksell–Lindahl tradition of separation between allocation and distribution issues. This separation can be reconciled with Samuelson's general formulation; and while I admit that nothing is gained thereby in the omniscient planner context, the separation of issues becomes essential if one is to link the normative model with the real-world problem of budget determination.

In that setting, an initial state of distribution exists, making it necessary to assign the opportunity cost of public resource use to individuals. Also preferences are unknown, so that a mechanism is needed to induce their revelation. These needs are met via a voting process which joins the tax and expenditure decisions, and the policy task is to design this process to implement an efficient pricing rule. Distribution objectives may then be met by redistributing money income, having in mind the pricing rule by which social goods are allocated and their cost charged. Allocation objectives may be met by approximating efficient project choice within the context of this pricing rule.

This much for past doctrine, as I see it. More recently, a new approach emerged and became of major interest to the younger generation of fiscal economists. This is the application of cost-benefit analysis to the determination of expenditure policy. While this approach has proved of great practical value in applying efficiency considerations to expenditure decisions, our concern here is not with its pragmatic use. Rather, I wish to examine how cost-benefit analysis relates to the central theory of social goods. Seen in this context, is it a step forward, or a throwback to a one-sided view of the budget, compensating, as it were, by lagged Hegelian logic for the taxation-only sins of the 1920s?

While this is a tempting interpretation of doctrinal development, it may also be too harsh a view. Whereas the classical theory of taxation-only dealt with minimising the costs of taxation without allowing for expenditure benefits, cost-benefit analysis by its very nature includes both the cost and benefit sides. An objective function is to be maximised, with both costs and benefits as arguments in that function. But this is not enough to make a theory of the public sector. The question is how costs enter the picture, and how they are related to the benefit side.

II. MEASURING BENEFITS

Consider first the question of what benefits should be included, and how such benefits should be measured. Unless distributional considerations are to be inserted into the objective function, cost-benefit analysts agree that purely pecuniary benefits should not be allowed for, but that all others (internal or external, direct or indirect, tangible or intangible) should ideally be included [21]. However, they cannot all be measured. Evaluation is easy where the goods provided are in the nature of private goods, and provision is through public sale so that benefits can be measured by market price. In this case, the planner merely performs functions usually assumed by the private firm, and the economics of that firm apply. The theory of public enterprise, selling private goods and producing without externalities, does not belong in the theory of public finance.

The more germane situations arise where there are inherent reasons for market failure. Among these, our concern is mainly with the provision of social goods, i.e. goods which are non-rival in consumption. Since their use by any one consumer does not interfere with that by another, it would be inefficient to make consumption contingent on a price payment, even where exclusion could be readily applied. Tolls are inappropriate for an uncrowded bridge.³ The fact that exclusion frequently cannot be applied, or at great cost only, further strengthens the conclusion that the auction system of the market is not available to evaluate the benefits.⁴ A political process is needed, and this involves tax and expenditure determination through the voting system.

Such at least is the case for social goods of the final or consumer good type. Uncrowded highways for pleasure driving, the delights of public parks, or the TV spectacle of a moon-landing, are cases in point. Here the benefit side of cost-benefit analysis collapses: while costs can be measured, benefits have to be stipulated if an optimisation procedure is to be applied. Such stipulation is not provided by cost-benefit analysis. In some cases, the cost of complementary private goods (travel costs to reach a park) may give some guidance to valuing the social good (enjoyment of the park itself) [11], but at best this sets only a lower limit to the benefit. Generally speaking, cost-benefit analysis provides no substitute for the basic problem of evaluation in the case of final social goods. All it can do is to expedite efficient decision-making after the basic problem of evaluation is solved. At the same time, cost-benefit analysis, even if based on arbitrary evaluations of final benefits, may be helpful: viewing the benefit as the dependent variable, the analysis may provide a test for how high evaluation must be to justify the outlay.

The situation is more manageable, however, where benefits are reflected in price change, or are made calculable with reference to price. Thus, the benefits from irrigation may be measured in terms of increased agricultural output; flood control results in cost-saving since measurable damage to capital assets or resources is avoided; better roads reduce automotive costs and save trucking time, which can be valued; public health measures reduce remedial care cost; investment in education raises earning power, and so forth.

The common characteristic of these cases is (1) that the social good is not a final but an intermediate good; i.e. a good which enters into the production of further output; and (2) that this further output is in the nature of a private good which may be valued efficiently at the market. While external effects on production cost have been dealt with in the general theory of externalities, the specific case of social goods *qua* intermediate goods has been neglected in the development of social good theory, nearly all of which has dealt with final goods.[5]

The intermediate social good has the same characteristic of non-rival use as has the final good; but this non-rival use is now by producers rather than consumers. Since it enters into a final private good, the benefit of such a social good can be measured in terms of the market price of this final (private) good. This measure of benefit can be inserted into the objective function, and the maximising procedure can be applied. It is thus in the case of the intermediate social good that cost-benefit analysis can perform most effectively. Notwithstanding past preoccupation of social goods theory with final goods, a large part of the social goods basket is clearly of this intermediate type, and this may explain why provision for social goods is in reality not as intractable as the theory suggests.

III. INVESTMENT DECISIONS

Until recently, at least, the primary application of cost-benefit analysis has been to public investment, rather than to the provision of short-lived goods. This may be due to concern with investment planning in developing countries, as well as the economist's fascination with the niceties of time discount analysis. Also, the very choice of the discount rate involves an externality problem, in that the social rate is usually held to fall short of the private rate. For our purposes, two aspects of the investment problem are of particular interest, i.e. (*1*) the relation between investment mix and total investment, and (*2*) the way in which the means of finance enter the profitability calculation.

Total Investment vs. Investment Mix
This problem may be seen most clearly if we suppose that the capital market is perfect, so that all rates of return, subject to risk differentials, are equalised. In this setting, we can speak of the internal rate of return on private investment, which in turn will equal the private rate of discount r_p. If we assume that the social rate of discount r_s equals r_p, a public investment will be undertaken if present value equals cost when using the discount rate r_p, or (which comes to the same) if its internal rate matches r_p. No conflict arises.

Now let $r_s < r_p$, which happens if investment involves social goods-type benefits which are not accounted for by the private market [1, 14, 15, 3]. In this case, the level of investment generated by the private sector will be too low from the social point of view. This may be compensated for either by raising private investment through monetary policy or other incentives, such as an investment subsidy; or it may be compensated for by adding public investment. If the former option is open, there is no *prima facie* case for public investment to be selected as a corrective for deficient total investment. The best solution, clearly, is to achieve both the proper level of total investment *and* the proper mix between public and private. This involves first a monetary or subsidy policy which equates the market rate of return with r_s, then a mix of public and private investment so as to equate returns at the margin, discounting by r_s in both cases.

But cost-benefit analysts tend to proceed without this two-step sequence. The prevailing discrepancy between r_s and r_p is taken as given and analysis then proceeds by the second best rule, that public investment should be made if it does not displace a 'better' private investment [13, p. 276]. To compare the value of alternative investments, the same social discount rate r_s is to be applied. A public investment is undertaken if the present value of the consumption stream which it generates exceeds its opportunity cost; and the latter is measured as the present value of the consumption stream forgone because the private investment is not made. But though no superior private investments are displaced, public investment as a policy instrument can neither raise the level of private investment to include projects which would be profitable if r_p were reduced to r_s, nor can it lengthen the structure of private investment to that which would hold at r_s.

These defects are avoided if the two policy objectives (adjustment in total investment, and its distribution between public and private) are distinguished and two instruments (equalisation of the private rate of return with r_s, and public investment) are used instead of public investment only. Cost-benefit analysts are aware of this but the trouble, they argue, is that the official who decides on public investment does not control fiscal or monetary policy. He must take the world with its given constraints, and if a pro-public investment bias results, this second best solution is still the best which the circumstances permit him. True enough, provided that the pragmatic nature of the approach is recognised and the need to loosen the constraints is not forgotten in the process.

Sources of Finance
Given the assumption of *perfect capital markets* and provided the government uses the private rate of discount r_p, the investment decision is independent of the source of finance. If resources are withdrawn from private investment, the least profitable investments (yielding r_p at the margin) will be surrendered. The present value of the consumption stream forgone, discounted at r_p, will be $1 per $ of investment that is withdrawn. If resources are withdrawn from consumption, the opportunity cost per $ of present consumption forgone is again valued at $1. Since the capital market is in equilibrium, the opportunity cost will be the same in both cases and the source of finance does not matter.

If the government uses a social discount rate r_s where $r_s < r_p$, the source of finance matters, even in the case of perfect capital markets [2]. If the resource withdrawal is from investment, the forgone consumption stream is discounted at r_s and the opportunity cost per $1 of private investment lost exceeds $1. But in the case of withdrawal from consumption, the opportunity cost will be $1. The opportunity cost will thus be greater where withdrawal is from investment. Accordingly, public investment is more likely to 'qualify' if tax-financed, where withdrawal is more largely from consumption, than if loan-financed, where withdrawal is more largely from investment. Matters are complicated further if reinvestment rates are to be considered. Since these differ among private investments, the result further depends on which particular investment is withdrawn. The outcome for loan finance thus depends upon the type of debt instrument which is issued.

Turning now to *imperfect capital markets*, we begin with a situation where a given rate r_s is applied. If the resource withdrawal is from private investment the opportunity cost now varies not only with the reinvestment rate, but also depends on the profitability of the particular investment which is displaced. The consumption stream forgone will differ, and so will its present value as discounted by r_s. If the resource withdrawal is from consumption, opportunity cost presumably is again valued on a 1:1 basis. Since tax finance, as previously noted, tends to fall on consumption while loan finance falls more largely on investment, the finance choice now matters even more in determining the opportunity cost.

Next, consider a situation where planners do not work with a given level of r_s, but wish to apply the private rate of discount r_p. If the resource withdrawal is from private investment, the consumption stream forgone again differs with the particular investment which is replaced. But there is now the additional difficulty of having to determine the level of r_p by which to discount both the private consumption stream which is forgone and the public stream which is to be gained. For lack of a single rate, some average of market rates has to be chosen. The government's borrowing rate, adjusted to include tax revenue forgone, may be a rough indicator [6].

A new twist enters if the resource withdrawal is from consumption. The particular rate (or combination of rates) available to the person whose consumption is reduced is now selected as the appropriate rate by which to discount the income stream generated by the public investment.[6] Since rates available to various consumers differ, the result depends on just what taxes are used and how they are shifted. Since low-income consumers borrow at higher rates, public investment will be less profitable and of shorter maturity with regressive than with progressive taxes. Since the bulk of public investment is financed by taxes, and since taxes fall largely on consumption, differentials in the interest rates confronting the consumer (rather than in the yields of displaced investments) are thus moved to the centre of the stage.

In summary, the sources of finance do not matter for the case of perfect capital markets with the use of r_n, but they are vitally important once r_s is used and especially if capital markets are imperfect. Since the choice of revenue policy determines whether displacement is in private investment or consumption, the revenue side affects the public investment decision. But revenue policy is taken as given, and is not linked (except via opportunity cost and the discount rate) to the basic task of evaluating the benefit stream. The linkage thus differs altogether from that demanded by a theory of social goods, where both sides of the budget are determined simultaneously, and neither side can be separated from the other.

IV. ALLOWING FOR DISTRIBUTIONAL OBJECTIVES

The addition of distributional considerations provides another instance where multiple targets are arrived at by use of a single instrument [1, 12, 24]. Distributional considerations may be included in the objective function by setting constraints regarding distributional effects, or by aiming at a 'grand efficiency' [24] which assigns value weights to particular distributional results.

It has been suggested that such weights may be derived from past policy, by assuming that past congressional action, be it in setting income tax rates[7] or in choosing investment projects,[8] did in fact reflect the true social welfare function. These techniques do not seem convincing to me, and I would prefer an explicit assignment of weights, based on deviation of income from the norm set by the poverty line, or some such concept. Let the administration, through the bureau of the budget, announce its scale of weights, and require all departments to use that scale. This, however, is not my main concern. Rather, it is with the very inclusion of such weights into the objective function for the particular investment, as against considering a policy package which combines various instruments to secure various targets.

Consider these two situations: in case 1 the choice is between building a park in location A or B, where A is a mountain top and B is a swamp, but the potential customers in A will be rich while those in B will be poor; and in case 2 the choice is between building a shipyard in D or E where D is Norfolk and E (to give an extreme illustration) is West Virginia. The cost will be lower in D but the income of potentially employed workers is lower in E. The objective function without redistributional weights calls for A and D; but with such weights B and E may win.

As I see it, the efficient choice is A and D, supplemented by the necessary distributional adjustment through a tax transfer mechanism from A or D to B or E. This is simply another aspect of what I consider to be the pragmatic case for the separation of allocation and distribution objectives. However, certain qualifications are in order.

(*1*) The political situation may be such that, for reasons of political strategy, the distributional objective can be 'put over' via investment in B and E, but not via a tax transfer mechanism. In this case, the *political* economist may favour B and E; though the solution is second-best in the absence of political constraints, he may consider it the best available measure to implement his views.[9]

(*2*) The community may prefer to redistribute by providing income in kind (the case for B) or by giving employment (the case for E) as against cash support. The employment choice in particular may make good sense;

but the social advantage of such decisions should then be specified and measured against its opportunity cost, be it the inferior park in B or the higher cost in E.

(3) In addition, and as a more technical objection, it has been suggested by Marglin that the excess burden involved in the redistribution process must be allowed for if equivalent policy packages (investment in B and E, or investment in A and D plus redistribution to B and E) are to be compared. This is a valid point, since by definition, distributional adjustments cannot be made through lump-sum taxes and lump-sum transfers. They must, by their very nature, be related to income, thus posing an excess burden problem. But it goes too far to conclude that, therefore, inclusion of distributional objectives becomes a 'matter of judgement' [14, p. 21]. The question is how heavy the excess burden will be.

If the investment is made in D, let the cost be C_D, and if it is made in E, let it be $C_E = (1 + \alpha)C_D$. If e is the excess burden as a percentage of the tax dollar, the total cost in D equals $(1 + e)C_D$ and the total cost in E equals $(1 + e)(1 + \alpha)C_D$. But investment in D requires additional transfer payments in E, equal to $(1 + \alpha)C_D$, and corresponding taxation in D. Both these involve an excess burden, so that the total cost $\dot{C}$ for investment in D becomes

$$\dot{C}_D = (1 + e)C_D + 2e(1 + \alpha)C_D$$

while that in E equals

$$\dot{C}_B = (1 + e)(1 + \alpha)C_D$$

There is thus a case for construction in E if $\dot{C}_B < \dot{C}_D$, that is if $\alpha < 2e/(1-e)$. If we set e equal to, say, 2 per cent,[10] we obtain $\alpha < 0.041$ as the condition for investment in E. It would seem that the excess burden factor can offset relatively minor cost differentials only. Even if extreme cases such as our shipyard example were discarded, α will typically be substantially larger, so that a strong case remains for a multiple-instrument approach.

Finally, if distributional effects of expenditures are included in the objective function, this would seem to call for a similar inclusion of the distributional effects of the financing mechanism [4]. This may be by-passed by ranking alternative public investments, while holding the source of finance constant, so that the distributional effects on the revenue side are the same. But they should be included in the function in the more general case where there is no budget constraint, and the scope of the public investment is to be determined.

In this case, revenue policy enters cost-benefit analysis not only via its bearing on opportunity cost and the rate of discount, but also through the distributional changes to which it gives rise. Moreover, revenue choice may be made a policy variable. Thereby, the approach becomes somewhat similar to the Pigouvian welfare model, except that policy weights are substituted for direct utility comparisons of disposable income. However, the basic weakness of the Pigouvian model is also retained. The tax and expenditure sides of the budget continue to be determined independently, and unrelated to the basic problem of benefit evaluation. The essential question of how to value final social goods—the essence of my 'allocation branch' problem—remains outside the system. Although the distribution function is included, it is permitted to enter into the allocation choice, rather than (as I think it should be) handled through a separate adjustment.

In concluding, let me note again that I do not wish to deprecate the practical value of cost-benefit analysis. Much is gained if a comprehensive assessment of project costs is made, accepting the existing policy constraints, and if benefits are measured for intermediate goods where this is possible. Having spent much of my time on tax analysis, which is equally partial, it would ill-behove me to deny the same treatment to the expenditure side. At the same time, it is well to note that cost-benefit analysis, even if combined with traditional tax analysis, does not provide a substitute theory of public finance. Though opportunity cost is allowed for and the revenue structure enters in peculiar ways, there is no basic linkage between the revenue and expenditure side, and hence no way to solve the valuation of final social goods. Moreover, by taking policy constraints for granted, and thus saddling the single instrument of public investment with multiple objectives (mix of public and private investment, correcting the level of total investment, correcting income distribution), the second-best nature of the approach is accepted perhaps too readily, thereby reducing its normative value where the use of multiple instruments (which can also be framed in cost-benefit terms) could give better results.

NOTES

1. See excerpts of Wicksell's and Lindahl's writing in Peacock and Musgrave [17].
2. To spell out this point, assume a world with private goods only, and no externalities or other causes for market failure. Competitive pricing then offers an efficient pricing rule. Given such a rule, there exists a desired state of welfare distribution which may be translated into a corresponding distribution of money income. We may then argue that public policy should be directed at (A) market-structure policies which will enable this pricing rule to function, and (B) distribution policies which are directed at obtaining the 'proper' (given this pricing rule) distribution of money income. This may be contrasted with an approach which argues that in the absence of proper distribution there is no presumption in favour of Pareto optimality; and that policy should always be ready to condone departures from Pareto-efficient pricing since such departures may be validated in a broader efficiency sense by resulting gains in distribution. The latter may be held as the best available solution if efficient decisions are precluded by political or other factors, but it does not seem suitable for a normative model.

   Precisely the same problem arises in the case of social goods, except that the choice of pricing rule (now through the political process) is less obvious. Nevertheless, some political mechanisms or voting systems are more efficient than others, and the task is to develop the system which offers the best approximation to an efficient solution. For further discussion see my article, 'Provision for Social Goods' [17].

3. Such is the case, at least, for an existing bridge. If a series of new investment is considered, the inefficiencies of charging tolls (while there is still traffic-slack) may have to be weighed against those of decision by political process.

4. Only where exclusion is inapplicable in the case of goods with rival consumption, does the inapplicability of exclusion become a primary and distinct cause for market failure. Improvement in exclusion technology then becomes the preferred solution.

5. I am indebted to John Head for pointing out to me that the intermediate goods case was dealt with in a brief note by Kaizuka [8]. Kaizuka shows that the efficiency condition (analogous to the consumer good case) now requires the sum of the marginal rates of substitution to be equal to the marginal rate of transformation. I also wish to thank Elisha Pazner for helpful discussion of this case.

6. See Krutilla and Eckstein [9, ch. 4]. While this procedure is ingenious, its meaning in a setting of imperfect capital markets is puzzling. If the rate of substitution of future for present consumption differs among consumers, and different rates of transformation apply in private investment, it is difficult to see why the rates applicable to the particular taxpayer should be controlling. To be sure, it is *his* consumption that is reduced, and this is relevant if distributional weights are to be attached. But I see little merit in applying the market rates available to him as a normative guide.

7. See Mera [16]. To begin with, I have no intuition as to the type of equal sacrifice (absolute, proportional, marginal) which Congress intended to implement. Nor do I know whether one should use actual liabilities (with loopholes) or statutory liabilities (without them). These difficulties arise, quite apart from the basic assumption that the legislative record could be taken to reflect a social welfare function.

8. See Weisbrod [24, p. 199]. If past investment decisions may be assumed to have been correct, why is cost-benefit analysis needed to validate future decisions?

9. The political case for including distributional objectives because policy constraints prohibit direct distributional adjustments, need be distinguished from the quite different analytical proposition that in Samuelson's model allocation and distribution issues are inherently inseparable.

10. Harberger's estimate for the excess burden of capital taxes is about 3 per cent of yield [5] while for the income tax the estimate is about 2 per cent [7].

REFERENCES

[1] Eckstein, O. (1959) 'A Survey of the Theory of Public Expenditure Criteria' in the National Bureau of Economic Research's *Conference on Public Finances: Needs, Sources and Utilization* (New York).

[2] Feldstein, M. S. (1964) 'Net Social Benefit Calculation and the Public Investment Decision', *Oxford Economic Papers* (N.S.), 16.

[3] —— (1964) 'The Social Time Preference Discount Rate in Cost-Benefit Analysis', *Economic Journal*, 74.

[4] Freeman, A. (1967) 'Income Distribution and Planning for Public Investment', *American Economic Review*, 57.

[5] Harberger, A. C. (1966) 'Efficiency Effects of Taxes on Income and Capital', in Krzyzaniak, M. (ed.), *Effects of Corporation Income Tax* (Detroit: Wayne State University Press).

[6] —— (1968) 'On the Opportunity Cost of Public Borrowing', in *Economic Analysis of Public Investment Decisions: Interest Rate Policy and Discounting Analysis*, Hearings Before the Joint Economic Committee, 90th Congress, 2nd Session (Washington: US Government Printing Office).

[7] —— (1964) 'Taxation, Resource Allocation and Welfare', in *The Role of Direct and Indirect Taxes in the Federal Revenue System*. A Conference Report of the National Bureau of Economic Research and the Brookings Institution (Princeton: Princeton University Press).

[8] Kaizuka, K. (1969) 'Public Goods and Decentralization of Production', *Review of Economic Statistics*, 47.

[9] Krutilla, J. V. and Eckstein, O. (1958) *Multiple Purpose River Development* (Baltimore: Johns Hopkins University Press).

[10] Lerner, A. P. (1944) *The Economics of Control* (New York: Macmillan).

[11] Mack, R. P. and Myers, S. (1965) 'Outdoor Recreation', in R. F. Dorfman (ed.), *Measuring Benefits of Government Investments* (Washington: The Brookings Institution).

[12] Marglin, S. A. (1962) 'Objectives of Water-Resource Development: A General Statement', in A. Maas *et al., Design of Water-Resource Systems* (Cambridge, Mass.: Harvard University Press).

[13] —— (1963) 'The Opportunity Costs of Public Investment', *Quarterly Journal of Economics*, 77.

[14] —— (1965) *Public Investment Criteria* (Cambridge, Mass.: MIT Press).

[15] —— (1963) 'The Social Rate of Discount and the Optimal Rate of Investment', *Quarterly Journal of Economics*, 77.

[16] Mera, K. (1969) 'Experimental Determination of Relative Marginal Utilities', *Quarterly Journal of Economics*.

[17] Musgrave, R. A. (1969) 'Provision for Social Goods', in J. Margolis and H. Guitton (eds.), *Public Economics* (New York: Macmillan).

[18] Peacock, A. and Musgrave, R. A. (eds.) (1958) *Classics in the Theory of Public Finance* (London: Macmillan).

[19] Pigou, A. C. (1924) *The Economics of Welfare* (London: Macmillan).

[20] —— (1928) *A Study in Public Finance* (London: Macmillan).

[21] Prest, A. R. and Turvey, R. (1965) 'Cost-Benefit Analysis: A Survey', *Economic Journal*, 75.

[22] Samuelson, P. A. (1954) 'The Pure Theory of Public Expenditures', *Review of Economic Statistics,* 36.

[23] —— (1969) 'Pure Theory of Public Expenditures and Taxation', in J. Margolis and H. Guitton (eds.), *Public Economics* (New York: Macmillan).

[24] Weisbrod, B. A. (1968) 'Income Redistribution Effects and Benefit-Cost Analysis', in S. B. Chase, Jr (ed.), *Problems in Public Expenditure Analysis* (Washington: The Brookings Institution).

6 Pareto-Optimal Redistribution: Comment* 1970

The analysis by Hochman and Rogers [2] of redistribution *qua* exercise in Pareto optimality offers a helpful and down-to-earth addition to other efforts in this direction [3]. Now that the case has been made, it is indeed difficult to see why this aspect had so long been neglected. However, the following comments seem in order.

I

The degree of 'redistribution' which occurs in the context of the Hochman–Rogers scheme is a function of (a) people's rate of substitution between the satisfaction derived from retaining income and that derived from giving it, and (b) the 'initial' distribution of earnings which exists before giving occurs. Whatever the values of (a), the outcome will differ depending on (b). Such, at least, will be the case unless everybody's rate of substitution is such that complete equality results. Pareto-optimal redistribution thus constitutes a *secondary redistribution* which depends on the initial distribution of earnings. This distribution is determined by such factors as inheritance, earning capacities, education and market structure. It may itself be changed through the political process. Such changes, referred to here as *primary redistribution*, are not a matter of voluntary giving, but of taking.

How is this primary redistribution decided upon? To the extent that it operates within the legal framework, it is performed through the voting mechanism. At a normative level, this explanation is not very helpful, however, since it merely raises the next issue, i.e. how the distribution of votes and the voting rules are to be decided on. Eventually, the problem becomes one of social contract determination. At a positive level, primary redistribution depends on the social structure and balance of power between income groups. As these change, corresponding changes occur in the voting decisions and/or voting rules.

_____

* *American Economic Review* (1976) vol. LX, 3.

II

Turning to an application of these concepts, how can the primary or non-consent component be distinguished from the secondary or Pareto component? Private redistribution or charity in the United States in 1976[1] accounted for about $12 billion. Assuming (somewhat unrealistically) that this giving is truly voluntary, it must be interpreted as being of the secondary type. But how should one interpret the much larger block of budgetary redistribution, which may well have exceeded $30 billion?

Hochman and Rogers assign this entire amount as well to the secondary category. This follows from their assumption of

an institutional setting in which freeriding, i.e. strategic behavior, is precluded so that the political mechanism through which interdependence is internalized accurately reflects the distributional preferences of individuals in this regard. (p. 548).

This permits them to treat the large number case as if it involved small numbers, but the assumption is not permissible.

Rather, the situation is similar to that of provision for social goods. Let us specify that Mutt's satisfaction from giving to Jeff derives from the fact that Jeff's consumption is increased. Mutt, therefore, derives the same satisfaction if the transfer originates with Sam. With small numbers, Mutt and Sam get together and negotiate their giving to Jeff.[3] But the situation differs if Mutt is confronted with 60 million Jeffs and Sams (households) instead of one. He will readily conclude that his giving will not contribute significantly to the welfare of the Jeffs, so that uncooperative behaviour on his part will not meet with retribution by the Sams. Some way must be found by which preferences are revealed and concerted action is agreed upon. Hence secondary (Pareto-optimal) redistribution must be implemented through the political process, just as such a process is needed for the provision of social goods. This is why secondary redistribution extends into the budgetary process.

But if so, how can it be distinguished from primary redistribution which also operates through the budget? The distinction is subtle but none the less important. In its secondary redistribution component, the budgetary process reflects an attempt to approximate what in the small number case would be accomplished voluntarily by individual bargains, and without compulsion. Since numbers are large, compulsion (the mandatory application of the voting decision) is needed to secure revelation of preferences, but it is a necessary evil only, not an objective in itself. Budgetary redistribution in its primary component, on the contrary, involves compulsion by its very nature: the Jeffs succeed in taking from the Mutts and Sams against their will.

The existing pattern of budgetary redistribution, therefore, includes both a secondary and a primary component. While I suspect that a substantial part is of the primary type, there is no simple test by which the two components may be distinguished in practice. Indeed, it would not be realistic to think of particular redistribution dollars as being assignable entirely to one or the other group. Both aspects are present and inter-twined in determining the redistributional pattern.

III

Finally, a word about the bearing of secondary redistribution on my distinction between allocation and distribution policy, a distinction which was formulated with primary redistribution in mind [4, ch. 1]. Allowing for the possibility of secondary redistribution moves part of the distribution issue into the framework of Pareto optimality, and in this sense aligns it with the 'allocation branch'. But this does not mean that policies to secure an efficient *product* mix must involve distributional considerations, and vice versa.

The Hochman–Rogers approach looks at Pareto-optimal redistribution, and I think correctly so, in terms of money income. Thus, two Pareto games are being played in two adjoining boxes. One involves the distribu-tion of money income, while the other involves the determination of the product mix with any given distribution. Mutt derives welfare from Jeff's increase in income, but accepts Jeff's preference pattern and decision on how to divide this income between oranges and apples.[4] As long as the interpersonal utility argument in Mutt's utility function is individualistic, my essential point of separation between allocation and distribution policies is retained. Redistribution should be handled in terms of income transfers, and not by pricing policy. I shall be pleased henceforth to divide my distribution branch into two compartments, D' being Pareto-optimal and D'' primary, but this is all that is needed.

The situation differs if Mutt values Jeff's consumption of oranges and apples in accordance with his own (Mutt's) rates of substitution. In this case, allocation and distribution are inseparable. The provision for merit goods may be interpreted in these terms, and is frequently linked with redistribution.[5] Equivalent in nature to a cash grant earmarked by the donor for specified uses, redistribution in kind may be of the secondary or primary type, but there is some presumption that it is secondary, since the claimant would hardly wish to restrict his choice in the primary case.

Redistribution, it appears, involves a complex set of transfers, primary or secondary, in cash or in kind, and operating both inside and outside of the budget. While the exploration of cash-giving in terms of Pareto optimality is instructive, it covers but a part of the problem and cannot claim to explain the entire phenomenon at hand.

NOTES

1. Charitable contributions claimed for itemised deductions in 1969 amounted to about $11.5 billion and the resulting tax revenue loss to over $3 billion, leaving about $8 billion of privately-financed contributions. To this let us add, say, $3.5 billion to account for contributions made by returns using the standard deduction, giving a total of about $12 billion of private contributions. This figure does not cover inter-family giving. Using the family as a unit, this is not considered a part of redistribution.

   The figure of $3.5 billion for non-itemised deductions is based on the following conjecture. Applying the ratio of contribution to *AGI* for returns with itemised deductions to returns with standard deductions, we obtain an upper limit of $6.5 billion. This, however, is surely an overestimate since non-itemisers may be expected to have a lower contribution ratio. The figure of $3.5 billion sets this ratio at roughly 50 per cent of that for itemisers.
2. This amount is the estimated total gain in net benefits (gain from public expenditures minus loss from taxation) on the part of those whose net benefits are positive. Obviously such estimates are difficult to obtain since they imply the entire scope of both tax and expenditure incidence, including the imputation of benefits from public services. For a discussion of the problems involved in estimating expenditure benefits, see Gillespie. The figure of $30 billion corresponds to Gillespie's estimate of $17.5 billion for a 1960 budget total of $133.6 billion, raised to allow for a budget total of $300 billion. The underlying figure of $17.5 billion assumes allocation of benefits from general expenditures (expenditures which do not permit specific allocation) in line with income. If such benefits are allocated on a *per capita* basis, the level of redistribution is nearly doubled.
3. The situation is similar if Mutt derives value from Jeff's giving because this maintains his net (after giving) income position relative to Jeff's. While Sam's position is improved, this does not carry adverse implications because he is too far down the line. If, on the other hand, Mutt's satisfaction derives from the fact that the gift originates with *himself*, he will be indifferent to gifts by others. In this case secondary giving will not call for budgetary action and be wholly private.
4. Dr Mutt, at his most sophisticated, realises that his welfare gain from giving depends on Jeff's welfare from receiving, and that the latter depends not only on changes in money income but also in relative prices. In this sense the allocation effects of giving are linked to the distribution effects. Dr Mutt will take into account prevailing price and market structures. In this connection, the problem is the same as that discussed in my defence of separation between allocation and primary redistribution issues.
5. I have suggested this approach as an explanation to the prevalence of merit goods [4].

REFERENCES

[1] Gillespie, I. (1965) 'Effect of Public Expenditures on the Distribution of Income', in R. A. Musgrave (ed.), *Essays in Fiscal Federalism* (Washington).

[2] Hochman, H. M. and Rogers, J. D. (1969) 'Pareto Optimal Redistribution', *American Economic Review*, 59.

[3] Kolm, S. C. (1966) 'The Optimal Production of Justice', in J. Margolis and H. Guitton (eds.), *Conference on the Analysis of the Public Sector, Biarritz, 1966* (New York).

[4] Musgrave, R. A. (1959) *The Theory of Public Finance* (New York: McGraw-Hill).

[5] —— (1969) 'Provision for Social Goods', in J. Margolis and H. Guitton (eds.), *Conference on the Analysis of the Public Sector, Biarritz, 1966* (New York).

7 Fiscal Functions: Order and Politics* 1981

It is not surprising and is indeed appropriate that fiscal policy, on both its tax and expenditure sides, should be among the most controversial of policy issues. The fiscal process, as much as any other democratic institution, occupies the middle ground between anarchy and absolute rule. It provides the forum on which interest groups and ideologies may clash without resort to the barricades, and on which compromise and cooperation may be sought. Located at the centre of dispute, the budget process can hardly be expected to function neatly and without error if only because it is created by the same conflicting interests which it must reconcile. Yet an orderly working of that process is essential to the conduct of public affairs and for this its multiple objectives must be understood.

Over the years, these objectives and their interaction have been central to my thinking on fiscal policy. My essential proposition, first made 25 years ago, was that budget policy involves multiple goals, including provision for social goods, adjustment in the distribution of income and stability with growth [2, chs. 1, 2]. I then argued that policy mixes may be developed which can meet these objectives together and without conflict, while failure to separate them involves conflict and poor policy design. At a time when there is a flood of proposals, frequently arbitrary, for constraining fiscal action, it may be well to review these propositions and to see what remedies emerge.

PROVISION FOR SOCIAL GOODS

The classical and still central function of budget policy is to provide for certain goods and services which, by their very nature, cannot be provided for efficiently through the market. The very logic of the market system requires that benefits and costs are internalised and accounted for by what buyers pay and suppliers charge. Where these conditions are not met and

* Acceptance paper, The Frank E. Seidman Distinguished Award in Political Economy, P. K. Seidman Foundation, 1981, Memphis, Tenn.

externalities occur, market failure results. The extreme case is that of
social goods, i.e. goods which, once provided, are available to all potential
consumers in equal amount and can be used by A and B without interfering
with their use by C and D. Because of this it is efficient to make benefits
available to all and free of direct charge. But given free availability, the
individual consumer has no occasion to purchase such services. Rather, the
individual will act as a freerider and rely on what is provided to all. This
becomes a zero-sum game since without buyers there will be no sellers
either. A political process is needed to provide for such goods.[1]

Let us look closely at what this process does or does not imply. The issue
to begin with is *not* one of public versus private production or ownership of
resources. National defence is provided for through the budget, but
military hardware may be purchased from private industry. Street-cleaning
is paid for by the town, but may be contracted out to a private firm. The
issue of public provision, therefore, is not one of private enterprise vs.
socialist organisation. Moreover, the provision of public goods is useful to
consumers in the same way as is their purchase of private goods. People's
preference maps include backyards as well as public parks and there is *no*
deep psychological difference in their wanting one or the other. Provision
for social goods, therefore, fits perfectly well into an individualistic view of
consumer demand. The efficient scope of their provision thus becomes a
function of factors such as consumer tastes, demography, technology and
the level of income. It should *not* be set by political ideology. Invention of
the automobile, to illustrate, called for road construction, thereby expanding the need for budgetary provision. This side-effect may have seemed
pleasing to liberals and unfortunate to conservatives, but their preferences
for driving should have nothing to do with this. The conservative may love
to travel while the liberal may like to stay at home.

What *is* involved in public provision is the need for a mechanism by
which individual preferences for social goods come to be revealed and
payments are made to defray the cost. For private goods, this dual
objective is met by forcing consumers to bid for what they want, thereby
revealing their preferences; and by paying in line with their bids, thereby
refunding the suppliers for their costs. The market serves as an auction
system and thus accomplishes both objectives. The problem is how to
create an analogue for social goods in the form of a political process.
Ideally, government would solicit taxpayers to enquire what social goods
they are willing to pay for, invite corresponding payments, and then
provide accordingly. This, however, would be self-defeating since, acting
as freeriders, taxpayers would tend to understate their true evaluation. The
essential problem, therefore, is to find a mechanism by which taxpayers are
induced to reveal their true preferences. This is accomplished—albeit in an
imperfect fashion—by using a voting system. Knowing that the outcome of
the vote will be mandatory, taxpayers will find it in their interest to vote so
as to have the outcome conform with their desires.

The question is how best to implement this process of choice. Two major
issues are involved, one being the voting rule and the other how issues are

defined. Regarding voting rules, I only note that any practicable system with mandatory acceptance of the outcome will fail to satisfy everyone concerned. Short of the extreme case of an unanimity rule, a dissatisfied minority will remain. As protection of minority interests is strengthened by requiring a larger majority, its extension also blocks the extent to which majority wishes can be served. The problem is one of balance, and I see little reason for deviating from the customary use of a simple majority rule. While some have argued that this rule is inherently biased towards over-expansion of social goods, I question this proposition [2]. Nor do the events of 1981 seem to support it. If there is to be reform of voting rules, the use of plurality as distinct from majority would seem the better direction.

However this may be, let me turn to the second and more fruitful issue of how the voting agenda should be arranged. Common sense tells us that for efficient decisions to be made, tax and expenditure issues should be decided jointly. How can a person decide whether to vote for or against a particular expenditure project without knowing what it will cost him or her? This linkage was recognised long ago by the great Swedish economist, Wicksell [6], who first addressed this problem almost 100 years ago. He suggested that tax and expenditure decisions be made jointly, so that voters can decide whether any particular project is worth the tax price which they are asked to pay. This is an eminently sensible proposition but not one that is followed. In practice actual procedure is at the other extreme. Expenditure decisions are made independent of tax votes, or are related only vaguely thereto. As a result, expenditure votes are not cost-conscious, nor are revenue votes benefit-conscious. The composition of the tax structure is determined without reference to the expenditure pattern and new expenditures are voted without specifying who pays. Such is still the case [in the USA] though the Budget Reform Act 1974 made some progress by requiring an overall budget limit to be set before dealing with specific appropriations.

The key question is how to establish a better nexus between tax and expenditure decisions. The answer clearly is not in earmarking of the traditional type, which assigns a particular tax to a particular expenditure function and lets expenditures vary with whatever that tax may yield. Rather, expenditure votes should be linked to their matching revenue votes when initially made. This may be done by tying various expenditure proposals to the same tax base, such as income, but different slabs of income tax would go to pay for different projects. Since various programmes are valued differently by different groups of the population, they would contribute different amounts of tax.

To permit such differentiation, suppose that appropriations were reorganised into a small number of committees, say five or so, with each responsible for public provision in a major programme area, including both the expenditure and tax sides of their programmes. Each committee might then determine its claim on the income base, or it might be given a base suitable as a proxy for the benefits generated by the particular service area.

Thus defence might be financed by a wealth tax, transportation by a gasoline tax, development by a value added tax, and so forth. In this way only those concerned with the potential benefit would enter into the vote, e.g. drivers would vote on an automotive tax to finance highways, while non-drivers would be indifferent. If instead the tax was assessed in line with income, non-drivers would vote nay, thereby blocking the wishes of the drivers.

I am aware that these thoughts involve a drastic departure from accepted standards of fiscal procedure. Breaking up the budget into components would seem to contradict the central principle of good budgeting, i.e. that there should be a simultaneous equating at the margin of the return obtained from *all* projects. True enough, but on closer consideration this principle—as indeed most accepted fiscal theory—applies to a setting in which preferences and the valuation of projects are known to the budgeteer. But it is of little use in a setting where preferences are unknown and must be determined before an allocation can occur. Similarly, my suggestions run counter to the widely accepted view (reflected also in my own writings on the good tax system) that there should be an equitable, ability to pay-based distribution of the *entire* tax bill, and not of its fragments. Once more, this equity rule is appropriate to the financing of public services in a setting in which expenditures are determined independent of the revenue pattern. Outlays are treated as if they were reparation payments to the moon and taxation is viewed simply as a necessary reduction in the income left for private use. At the same time, this equity rule does not meet a situation in which the need for preference revelation necessitates a linkage between both sides of the budget, i.e. where revenue needed to finance public services must be drawn from consumers in line with the benefits which they receive.

The principle that the cost of expenditures should be assigned when the project is voted upon, by its very nature, also suggests the requirement of a balanced budget. Deficit finance tends to understate the cost, while surplus finance tends to overstate it. There is however an important exception to this rule. Where the expenditures in question involve the provision of capital goods, loan finance is in order, as this permits future beneficiaries to share in the cost. This is an important consideration since a substantial part of public outlays on goods and services are in this group. A further qualification will be noted presently when the stabilisation aspect of budget policy is considered.

While these thoughts fall short of offering a workable solution, they at least point in the direction of constructive budget reform. This must be a reform designed to secure a better reflection of taxpayer preferences, with emphasis on the composition as well as the level of the budget, and *without* prejudice as to whether the budget is too large or too small. This view of reform differs sharply from current drives for constitutional limitation and other arbitrary barriers to free fiscal choice. These proposals are based on the contention that there is an inherent flaw in the democratic process, a flaw in which causes the budget to be over-expanded and calls for correction by wiser minds. I find this a questionable hypothesis and insufficiently proven to provide an unbiased basis for budgetary reform. Once more, recent events show that the democratic process may involve a budget policy which, though jerky, is by no means unidirectional.

ADJUSTING INCOME DISTRIBUTION

My preceding argument has been that taxation, used as an instrument for preference revelation, leads to a concept of taxation in line with benefits received. Such taxes may be expected to rise with income as higher-income consumers will value a common level of public services, say defence, more highly than low-income consumers. But this leaves open the question whether the benefit tax will rise less, as, or more rapidly than income. As a result, the burden distribution may prove regressive, proportional or progressive, depending on the price- and income-elasticity of demand for public services. But even if the tax turns out to be progressive, this should not be viewed as reflecting income redistribution. Rather, the benefit tax reflects the prevailing state of distribution and may thus be viewed as distributionally neutral.

At the same time, a benefit approach to the financing of public services is in no way incompatible with supplementation by a distinct set of tax-transfer measures designed to adjust the prevailing state of distribution. Indeed, it may well be argued—as Wicksell did from the outset—that benefit taxation can be considered just and equitable (in addition to being efficient) only if imposed on a just and equitable distribution of income. The argument here is precisely the same as for the pricing of private goods. While a competitive market results in efficient pricing, the outcome is equitable only if the pattern of effective demand which gives rise to such pricing is generated by an equitable distribution of income.

This takes me to the second concern of fiscal policy, which is the state of income distribution. While it is difficult to design an efficient mechanism for the provision of social goods, economic analysis at least offers some guidance in this undertaking. Such is not the case—or less so—when it comes to determining what constitutes the proper state of distribution. Philosophies regarding distributive justice differ, and so do views on the appropriate scope of redistributive policy. On one end of the scale there is John Locke's proposition, grounded in the philosophy of natural law, that one is entitled to the fruits of one's labour and that the state must not interfere therewith. Accordingly, no *taking* by taxation is permitted. Only those taxes are permitted which follow the benefit rule, providing a *quid pro quo* to the payee. Nozick, in his extension of the Lockean doctrine, even likens redistributive taxation to slavery since the payee is forced to work for the recipient [4]. On the other end of the scale, there is the proposition as recently argued by Rawls, that the accident of birth with its differential endowment of talent, wealth and position, does not establish a legitimate claim of desert [5]. The fruits of superior talent are subject to communal claim and not to personal entitlement, a view also expounded in Edward Bellamy's nineteenth century vision of an American Utopia [1]. Entitlement rather is to fair and equal treatment, a right held equally by all members of the community. In this setting, the distribution of earnings which results in the market must be adjusted to meet the standard of fairness, so that some degree of redistribution is required. Benefit taxes retain their place in the finance of social goods but the benefit principle ceases to reign as the universal rule of tax equity.

In matters of distributive justice, as elsewhere, polar positions are helpful to clarify issues but soon give way to qualification. Among those who start out with a Lockean view, few would prohibit all redistribution through the political process. While preferring reliance on charity or beneficence, as Adam Smith put it, most will accept governmental support in situations of severe poverty. At some point, appeal to charity yields to minimal rights. Those who begin with the opposite view of common entitlement must accept the fact that the size of the pie varies with the slicing. Short of compulsory labour, the transferer can substitute leisure for income; and since only income can be transferred but not leisure, redistribution in the last resort is conditioned by consent. Society, to paraphrase Karl Marx, may choose to give according to need; but it cannot assure contribution according to ability. Given this fact, even those who would divide a constant pie equally, will accept inequality if the pie is variable. The question is how much. John Rawls in his rule of maxi–min suggests that inequality be accepted to the extent that it permits a higher level of transfers to the bottom of the scale. Taxing the rich according to his rule is appropriate up to the point of maximum revenue but not beyond. A less stringent and more widely held view assigns some social weight to the transferer's loss, thus further limiting the appropriate scope of redistribution.

The degree of redistribution which a society chooses to undertake at a given time is conditioned by the prevailing distribution of income and the average income level. But distribution policy also reflects social attitudes and the balance of political power. Attitudes change and so does their legislative outcome. 'What they will call the spirit of the time', as Goethe put it, 'is but the people's own design in which the time reflects its image'.[2] Much of the growth of the public sector in recent decades has thus taken the form of distribution-oriented programmes, reflecting a liberal mood and the power of low to middle income coalitions. Whether this era of the welfare state has now come to an end remains to be seen, but one would not be surprised to find it a self-terminating process. After all, as the level of redistribution rises, so does the number of losers relative to that of gainers, so that the majority available for further action falls. This change in voting balance may be delayed as voting participation at the lower end of the scale rises, but once more this is a terminal process. Moreover, pro and con votes will not divide neatly in line with positions below and above the median income level. Low-income voters who aspire to move up will hesitate to lower their prospects, and demands for redistribution will be dampened by concern, real and induced, for adverse productivity effects.

For any given redistribution target there is the further question of what instruments should be used to implement it. In the longer run, the most attractive approach is not through redistribution at all, but through labour-market and training policies aimed at raising the earning power of the poor. But beyond this, some degree of redistribution is called for and here a tax transfer scheme offers the most direct approach. Discussed widely in the context of welfare reform a decade ago, this scheme has the advantage of securing the redistribution without interfering with how the funds are used by the recipient.[3]

The combination of a positive negative income tax has the further advantage that distributional adjustments are made without interfering with the provision of social goods. People who favour redistribution and prefer private goods would not have to vote for social goods, hoping that their financing will be more progressive than justified on benefit grounds. Others, who like public goods but not redistribution, would not have to oppose a larger budget fearing that it would involve such finance. In the historical perspective the first of these distortions reigned in the earlier stages of the welfare state. A levelling of income, which could not have been achieved politically via a tax-transfer scheme, could be achieved via progressive financing of an expanded provision for social goods. Under changed conditions, the second distortion now moves into action, with reduction of public services an excuse for cutting back on progressive taxation. Clearly, elimination of both biases would make for a more efficient conduct of fiscal affairs, and separation of the tax transfer scheme from benefit-financed provision of social goods would contribute thereto. There would, in short, be two sets of taxes, one to finance public services and the other (in the form of a positive-negative income tax) to adjust distribution. Their collection could be coordinated, especially if assessed on the same base, but they would differ in pattern.

With a tax-transfer scheme the most efficient instrument for fiscal redistribution, how can one explain that much of fiscal redistribution over recent decades has been through services in kind, such as health facilities, housing, food stamps or school lunches? Indeed, the only major cash transfers have been AFDC and the redistributive component of social security. In large degree, this prevalence of in-kind redistribution reflects the desire of payers to determine how the funds should be spent by payees. Payers agree to vote for redistributive programmes if they retain control, but not otherwise. Payees would rather have their funds without constraint but prefer conditional grants to no grants at all. There is nothing wrong with this outcome if seen from a Lockean entitlement position. The charitable donor can set the conditions of his gift and the donee remains free to accept or not. 'Einem geschenkten Gaul', so a German saying goes, 'sieht man nicht in's Maul.' The same holds for a modified Lockean view where entitlement to earnings is valid but subject to modification by majority rule. The transferer remains free to vote yea on conditional but nay on cash grants. Reliance on in-kind transfers, on the other hand, is inappropriate if seen from a common entitlement perspective, where the recipient has a right to support, independent of paternalistic imposition by high earners. But donor preference has not been the only factor in the growth of in-kind support. Such support enjoys the backing of supplying industries, e.g. agricultural support for food stamps or construction industry support for low-cost housing. Such support distorts the decision process since it is not available for cash transfers, the outlay of which is diffused more widely.

Given the important role of in-kind transfers, the fiscal process encounters another source of confusion, now between (1) the general provision for public services and their financing by benefit-type taxes, and (2) services provided as transfers in-kind and properly financed as part of a progressive tax transfer scheme. Indeed, it may not be easy to determine how particular provisions should be classified. Transfers in-kind, to be sure, may involve either social or private goods, while other provision involves social goods only. But social goods may not be equally important to all income groups. Suppose a particular social good is valued more highly by low-income earners so that its benefit finance may call for a regressive rate. Yet, finance by a progressive tax would turn such provision into redistribution in-kind. Once more, we have to recognise that such difficulties remain, even though I can offer no ready resolution thereof.

MACRO ASPECTS OF FISCAL POLICY

I now turn to the final concern of fiscal policy, its relation to employment, inflation and growth. The crucial policy variable in the Keynesian economics of the Great Depression was the magnitude of budget deficit. Full employment would require an adequate level of aggregate demand and, with monetary policy ineffective in the throes of the depression, this would have to be secured through budget policy. More specifically, the necessary increase in demand would have to be generated by a deficit-financed increase in public spending. Powerfully verified by the enormous expansion in economic activity during the second world war, the doctrine in the 1960s and 1970s had to be adjusted to the changed circumstances of inflation. Whereas increased spending had been seen as a means to employment creation, the same logic would now call for reduced spending as a means to cutting demand.

There is a fallacy in both positions. Given the exclusive emphasis of early Keynesian doctrine on government spending, expansionary policy had the by-product of increasing the size of the public sector. This side-effect made fiscal expansion attractive to the liberal position, as did the previously noted nexus between budget size and progressive taxation. This linkage between expansionary demand policy and budget expansion once more was a major factor not only in the depression context of the 1930s but well into the 1960s. Replayed in reverse, the later inflation setting came to call for reliance on expenditure cuts, a reverse bias now appealing to a conservative desire to reduce the size of the public sector.

Efficient conduct of public policy should and could avoid either bias. Measures to expand or restrain aggregate demand should be borne evenly by both the public and private sector and not place a disproportionate share on the former. For this purpose, primary reliance need be placed on tax rather than expenditure adjustments. To illustrate, suppose that federal expenditures account for $20 out of a GNP of $100, taxes take $20 and private outlays are $80. If there is to be a 10 per cent reduction in total outlays pro-rated over both sectors, public expenditures should be cut from $20 to $18 and private outlays from $80 to $72. Assuming for simplicity's sake that taxes reduce private expenditures on a 1:1 basis, taxes must be increased from $20 to $28. Thus a 40 per cent increase in tax rates is needed, as compared with an expenditure cut of 10 per cent. The differential is even larger if we allow for the fact that taxes are not reflected fully in reduced private outlay. A corresponding argument holds for expansionary action with the appropriate expenditure increase substantially below the rate of tax cut.

Returning to my theme of multiple-policy instruments, a third set of adjustments is thus called for. This takes the form of a tax or transfer which would lower or raise private income in proportional fashion, while being neutral with regard to both the provision for social goods and the distribution of income. A mechanism of this sort is in line with proposals made repeatedly over the years to grant executive authority for counter-cyclical tax changes to be made in a more or less neutral and across-the-board fashion. By separating stabilisation-oriented tax changes from the provision of public services and redistribution, fiscal policy may serve the objectives of stabilisation, and do so without interference with other aspects of budget. The previously noted rule that the public service budget should be balanced (except for loan finance of capital outlays) is thus rendered compatible with the rule that the budget as a whole may have to be in deficit or surplus, depending on the requirements of stabilisation policy. These in turn are set by the condition of the economy and the extent to which the necessary control of aggregate demand can be achieved through the means of monetary policy. Unnecessary to say, both have to work in conjunction, but reliance on monetary policy can hardly be so great as to relieve budget policy of this function. A requirement that the overall budget be in balance, therefore, is not compatible with sound economic management, and it would be most unfortunate to have it enshrined in the constitution.[4]

Apart from discretionary changes in tax and expenditure levels, allowance must be made for automatic responses of the fiscal system to changes in economic activity. Over the years, automatic revenue responses have come to be viewed as a desirable stabilising factor. As GNP falls, so will tax revenue, thereby creating a deficit which in turn cushions the decline. As GNP rises the reverse occurs, thus counteracting inflation. This mechanism fits well into the role of the budget as a stabilisation device provided that fluctuations are around a full-employment level and that automatic changes in revenue are not translated into corresponding changes in spending. If they result in such changes, as may well be the case, the stabilising effect is voided and the balance of public and private shares in GNP is disturbed.

These considerations are especially troublesome in the context of inflation, where the automatic revenue response of the income tax is accentuated by bracket creep. Revenue not only rises in proportion to the tax base but at a faster rate, since the nominal increase in incomes pushes given real incomes into higher-rate brackets. This has two effects. For one thing, the distribution of the tax burden undergoes hidden and arbitrary change since the degree of bracket creep differs over various parts of the income scale. For another, as revenue increases in real terms so that additional expenditures can be made, over and above what is needed to keep up with prices, without requiring explicit voter consent through raising tax rates. Or the built-in excess gain permits the legislature to please voters by reducing tax rates while maintaining services at their real level. Both consequences distort efficient policy decisions and may be avoided by indexing rate brackets. With indexing, now scheduled for 1985, revenue will increase in line with prices only, so that tax liabilities and services will remain constant in real terms. If inflation is to be checked, tax rates will then have to be raised in explicit fashion, or they will have to be reduced when expansion is needed.

All this relates to fiscal policy as an instrument for controlling aggregate demand. This role must be performed in conjunction with monetary policy. Both are important, and the bitter debate between Keynesians and monetarists as to which matters more is not very helpful. But as has become apparent in recent years, the control of aggregate demand, whether through fiscal or monetary tools, is hardly adequate to deal with the problem. In a setting of stagflation, raising aggregate demand may add to inflation rather than increase employment, while reducing demand may lower employment rather than check inflation. An environment must be created in which competing groups, unions and large firms, can be induced to stay within non-inflationary wage and price demands. Such schemes may involve the use of wage–price guidelines or of fiscal tools. These may take the form of income tax rebates to workers payable if wages are outrun by inflation, or penalty taxes on firms which grant inflationary wage increases. This opens new conflicts with traditional fiscal functions, but we shall not pursue them here.

Rather, I turn to the recently prominent concern with 'supply-side economics'. This new doctrine rejects the view, outlined above, that restriction of inflation should be through increased taxation. Raising taxes, so the argument goes, will reduce incentives thereby lowering output and increasing inflation. On the contrary, taxes should be cut to stimulate output, thereby checking inflation. There are two difficulties with that proposition. Seen in the context of short-run stabilisation, it is unrealistic to expect significant supply-side effects to occur. Such effects take time to develop. Moreover, as Say once taught us, additional production, whether for consumption or investment goods, also generates additional income. Thus additional output induced by tax reduction leaves excess demand unaffected. What is left is the additional demand due to the tax cut itself. However the administration's plan also provides for an offsetting budget cut, so that overall expenditures are largely unchanged as is the inflation picture. Responsibility for inflation control is left with monetary policy. As far as fiscal results are concerned, the major outcome is in the cutback of public programmes. Civil expenditures in particular are caught in the vice of tax reduction and rising defence outlays. Thus the bias of earlier fiscal policy is being replayed in reverse and with a vengeance.

While the supply-side doctrine has little merit for the short-run control of stabilisation, it does bear on the longer-run rate of economic growth. As economists have been well aware, growth policy not only calls for a rising level of demand, adequate to sustain a growing full employment output. This is an essential ingredient, but concern must also be with the rate of productivity growth. Such growth is desirable as it provides for a rising standard of living; and by permitting non-inflationary wage increases, it also helps to check inflation. Growth in turn requires capital formation and a mix of stabilisation policy which favours it. In line with this, the traditional 'neo-classical' recipe has called for a combination of tight budget to restrict consumption with easy money to provide cheap credit for investment. According to our earlier argument, the necessary degree of fiscal tightness could be secured by raising taxes without having to depress the provision of public services unduly. But if higher taxes required by the tight budget rule should depress economic incentives, the growth objective would be frustrated. Allowance for adverse productivity effects could thus shift the burden of fiscal tightness to the expenditure side of the budget, thereby curtailing provision for social goods and for distributional adjustments. With public capital formation, such as investment in human resources, an essential ingredient of growth, the pressure is on social goods of the consumption type. To recognise this problem one need not hold that consumption of social goods is less useful than consumption of private goods. Rather, the difference arises because social goods become available without direct charge and thus do not leave the consumer with an incentive to earn income in order to obtain them.

Resulting effects on economic incentives—work, saving and investment—will depend greatly on what taxes are used.[5] Taxes unrelated to economic activity such as a head tax may increase effort but they are hardly acceptable on other grounds. Discentives will be greater under a progressive income tax although it may be called for on other grounds. Even benefit-type taxes used to finance social goods will not by-pass the freerider problem. Potential conflict is sharpened as one turns to the redistribution function of fiscal policy, where the tax pattern is of the essence and progressive rates become unavoidable. Saving and investment decisions in the market economy depend largely on high-income recipients, so that the constraints on budgetary action are even greater.

While the existence of a potential incentive problem is evident, the magnitude of deterring effects are an empirical question and one about which much is to be learned. Recent studies suggest that effects on work effort are slight, especially for primary earners. Effects on saving are controversial and those on investment are even more difficult to measure. Much depends on how taxable income is defined and on how losses are treated. Moreover, the issue is not only one of fiscal economics but also of fiscal politics. Growth considerations not only impose a legitimate constraint on the tax structure but may also be used or abused to oppose equity goals of progressive taxation. Constructive tax reform, confronted with this controversy, should be directed at securing growth incentives in a way which will minimise interference with distributional objectives.

What can we conclude from this review of fiscal objectives, instruments and conflicts? Is it that bringing order out of chaos is a utopian undertaking, a forlorn task which had best be abandoned? I hope not. For one thing, even Utopias have their merit especially if accompanied by an awareness of the difficulties that bar their easy realisation. For another, much can be gained, even if not all resolved, by setting the framework for an orderly approach. The private sector has its problems and imperfections and so does the public. Both sectors have an essential role in our mixed economic system. Some may view this as an unfortunate necessity given by the exigencies of social affairs; but I would rather suggest that this dualism adds to the richness of social intercourse in a democratic society. A framework for budget policy, both democratic and efficient, is thus well worth reflection. It is so especially at a time when the call is for arbitrary restraint which may well weaken rather than improve the public sector.

NOTES

1. My concern is with the issues involved in the practical provision of social goods and not with the implications of their non-rivalness characteristics for the efficiency conditions of theoretical welfare economics. I also pass over another reason for public provision, i.e. a situation where exclusion, though desirable, is not feasible. For further discussion, see Musgrave and Musgrave [2, ch. 1].
2. Author's translation, *Faust*, Part I. 'Was ihr den Geist der Zeiten heisst, das ist im Grund der Herren eigner Geist in dem die Zeiten sich bespiegeln.'
3. Recent discussion in the optimal theory of taxation holds that dead-weight loss may be reduced by using an optimal mix of commodity taxes and subsidies, rather than a mechanism of income taxes and transfers. This, however, does not at this stage appear to be a practical scheme.
4. The major constitutional amendment now under consideration by Congress (Senate Joint Resolution 58) requires that planned outlays and receipts be in

balance unless a deficit is passed by a three-fifths vote of the whole number of both houses.

5. In line with the supply-side doctrine, the discussion is framed here in terms of deterring effects on factor supply. More precisely, economic theory views the problem in terms of resulting dead-weight loss, a loss which may result whether supply falls or rises. According to this more sophisticated view, the problem is not one of encouraging growth but of maintaiing neutrality in taxation effects.

REFERENCES

[1] Bellamy, E. (1960) *Looking Backward* (New York: New American Library), p. 76.
[2] Musgrave, R. A. and P. B. (1984) *Public Finance in Theory and Practice,* 4th edn. (New York: McGraw-Hill).
[3] —— (1984) 'Leviathan Cometh, or Does He?' in H. Ladd, and N. Tideman (eds.), *Tax and Expenditure Limitations* (Washington: Urban Institute).
[4] Nozick, R. (1974) *Anarchy, State and Utopia* (New York: Basic Books).
[5] Rawls, J. (1972) *A Theory of Justice* (Cambridge, Mass.: Harvard University Press).
[6] Wicksell, K., in Musgrave, R. A. and Peacock, A. (1958) *Classics in the Theory of Public Finance* (New York: Macmillan).

8 Public Finance, Now and Then*
1983

It is hardly necessary to express the pleasure and appreciation with which I participate in this event. To revisit with old friends, to return to the university which granted my first degree (as well, I might add, that of my father), to come back to the still lovely Neckar valley, all this is a matter of great delight, and I thank you for sharing it with me. It is difficult to believe that 50 years have passed (to avoid the even more frightening concept of a half century) since I received my Diplom-Volkswirt degree, and that we celebrated with a trip up to the Schloß to attend a performance of Beethoven's Ninth. There are many good memories of my two years here—of stimulating study and of good friends, as well as dubious ones such as the still present shadows of the George-Kreis with its substitution of capital letters for firm values. Also, there are the tragic events which marked that fateful year of 1933—a last torchlight parade in the wake of the Reichstag fire, the book burnings in the university's own yard and Alfred Weber courageously ordering the Swastika to be taken down, after it had been planted on the flagpole of the INSOSTA. All these are vivid memories, no less real for being long passed. Suffice it to add Germany's rebirth after the war as a democratic society and a staunch member of the European community has been a source of gratification to those of us who left Germany at that time, and an achievement which deserves our respect.

These are things which naturally come to my mind at this time, but they are not what I am to discuss here. Rather, I wish to reflect on how our science—the economics of public finance—has developed since then, and how I have fared in that process. The prime benefit of growing older (a course which is inevitable, though not to be confused with growing old) is that one becomes historian by osmosis, including that most exciting aspect of history which is the development of ideas. And for this public finance is an eminently suitable subject. Indeed, it would be hard to find another discipline so central to the interaction of economic analysis, social philoso-

---

* *Finanzarchiv* (1983), vol. 41, 1: paper presented at the award of a Dr *honoris causa* at Heidelberg University.

phy, political thought and changing institutions—a feature which, I suspect, was the reason why, from the beginning, I felt this to be my natural habitat in the broader landscape of economics.

TWO REGRESSIONS

And now to my topic. A look at public finance then (meaning the early 1930s) and now (meaning the early 1980s) covers a 50-year span of momentous change. Retracing it, I find myself moving between the development of the science and that of my own work. As a first tack, let me consider my work the dependent variable in the equation, and inquire what ideas and events should be assigned the largest and most significant coefficients on the other side. These would begin with my 'Heidelberg heritage', a term to be explained presently. Next would come my familiarity with the German writings of Wicksell and Lindahl. Then there would be the Great Depression and the rise of Keynesian economics, followed by the welfare economics of Pigou and my association with Paul Samuelson during the Harvard years and thereafter. Also there would be Schanz, reborn in Henry Simons' doctrine of broadbased income taxation as the ideal tax, with much time spent in the endeavour of tax reform. Finally, there comes the re-emergence of Pigouvian announcement effects in optimal taxation and its clash with the horizontal equity-based approach to tax analysis. Other variables might be added, but these, perhaps, would be deserving of the largest coefficients and the highest sigma ratings.

But this is only one perspective. Another might reverse the model, somewhat presumptuously to be sure, placing aspects of my own work on the right side of the equation and the development of fiscal analysis on the left. What part of approximately 10,000 pages encompassing, say 300,000 written words—a measure of output commensurate with the economist's prior that only that which can be measured is real—might be expected to yield coefficients which exhibit the right sign (hopefully have created insights rather than added to confusion) as well as a sigma sufficiently respectable to be noted? Without being aware of it at the time, my most important piece of intellectual baggage, when leaving Heidelberg for New York 50 years and three months ago, was my acquaintance with the writings of Wicksell and Lindahl. This acquaintance gave me a monopoly position *vis-à-vis* English-speaking (and only English-reading) students of our science, a comparative advantage which was to prove of great value in years to come. The subject of my first publication in the learned journals, my 1938 *Quarterly Journal of Economics* paper on the 'Voluntary Exchange Theory' not only gave me an early start, but later directed Samuelson's attention to the theory of social goods and his seminal contribution of the mid 1950s.

After having received my doctorate at Harvard in 1937, the decade of the 1940s was spent with the Federal Reserve Board in Washington, an invaluable experience of contact with the 'real world'. But getting ahead in an agency leads to rising operating responsibilities; and when I was about to be swamped by the technicalities of open-market operations, it seemed time to return to the sanctuary of the academic study. My intent then was to construct a modern system of fiscal economics which would encompass the macro and micro teachings of my Harvard years, as well as the subsequent policy experience. In this attempt—coming to fruition in my *Theory of Public Finance* in the late 1950s—I had the good fortune to write at a time which was ripe for just such an effort. The 1950s were pregnant with the theory of social goods and the Keynesian vision of public finances as employment creator as well as the central role of budget policy in the emerging welfare state. All this had to be integrated and provided the setting for my architectural design, a three-winged cathedral (with its branches of allocation, distribution and stabilisation) and a coordinating simultaneous process of budget determination in its nave. The idea thus was (and still is) that fiscal policies encompass a variety of objectives, but that these can be combined in a simultaneous and non-conflicting set of policy solutions. While much has been said over the years in criticism of this simple scheme, I still believe it to be useful, not only as a pedagogical device (a compliment made to damn with faint praise), but as a systematic approach to the structure of our science.

Without burdening you with undue detail, let me mention one other variable on the right side of the equation—a variable which, though ill-defined and precarious, has made its way and like the poet's *Besen*, will not go away. This is my category of merit goods and their role in the fiscal system. While all its siblings which populate my pages—such as social and mixed goods, differential incidence, built-in flexibility, benefit principle in local finance, and so forth—fit into the mainstream (Paretian, Walrasian, Keynesian) of modern economics, the merit good stands apart and does not. And though most of my work has bypassed its disturbing presence, the skeleton has remained in my closet and I am pleased to remain responsible for it.

Other arguments might be added but I shall now leave this parable of the two regressions, sparing you its extension into simultaneous estimating procedures which the complete model must in the end face up to. Instead, I shall consider a few selected issues—way stations in my wanderings through fiscal theory which I find of special concern. You must forgive me if these are handled in a somewhat introspective fashion, but perhaps this is not entirely inappropriate for today's occasion.

PUBLIC PROVISION AND THE NATURE OF THE PUBLIC SECTOR

In recent discussions I was asked repeatedly how my work was affected by my moving across the Atlantic and how it would have differed if the times had been conducive to remaining here? Like all counter-factual questions, this is difficult to answer. In either case my ideas would have changed over the decades and it is hard to separate out those changes which should be imputed to the change in location. But let me try.

To begin with, what are the important things that I took with me? Not, I should say, such early training in standard economics as I had acquired at that time. Adolf Weber's Allgemeine Volkswirtschaftslehre, which I had heard in Munich during my first term I now recall as a somewhat watered-down version of Cassel's *Sozialökonomie*, a good introduction but without great impact. Zwiedineck von Südenhorst, in the second term, was impressive, but as yet beyond my grasp. Perhaps it may also have been that the Zugspitze was more important than the Ludwigstrasse. Having transferred to Heidelberg in the autumn of 1931, Jacob Marschak's perusal of the equations in Keynes' *Treatise on Money*, with its parable of the widow's cruse was intriguing, as was Otto Pfleiderer's concern with the early development of social accounting as related to the public sector. My recollection of Arnold Bergsträsser's *Finanzwissenschaft* features Thomas Aquinas more than the tax system, but this might not have been so bad a choice. Beyond this, let me admit that most of the time spent in preparing for the final examination was given over to the legal rather than the economic fields. The reason evidently was that economics was more tolerant to improvisation than the legal subjects which were also required. Let me add here that my Heidelberg memories of economics are those of a tremendously complex and heterogeneous field, while the subject of law (organised neatly in a little red volume, the BGB) seemed structured and systematic. This impression was reversed when, coming to the United States, I found economic analysis a closely-knit and rigorous system, with common law an unmanageably broad and heterogeneous subject-matter.

Learning the trade of economics really began with my first year in the United States when, as an exchange student at the University of Rochester, I was exposed, under the guidance of Professor Clausing, to a sound foundation of Marshallian economics. Then came the years of graduate studies at Harvard, during that fabulous period of the 1930s (fabulous, that was, for graduate students in economics, not for those whose economic existence had been crushed by the Depression) when the world economy had collapsed and economists made their bid to save mankind. The new models of imperfect competition *à la* Robinson, Kaldor, and Chamberlain had restated micro theory in modern terms, replacing the old-fashioned model from Mill to Marshall, and at last permitting a real understanding of markets. In addition, the Keynesian revolution had arrived, showing how the economist could go about curing the world of its macro ills. With Alvin Hansen in the lead, all this created an atmosphere of optimism about economics, a unique aura of scientific bliss from which, I gather, my generation has never quite recovered—and for the absence of which I pity contemporary graduate students in our science.

These events thus swamped my previous training in economics, and the things which remained—to which I referred earlier as my Heidelberg heritage—were of a different kind. They were different, but no less important. This heritage was rooted in the intellectual tradition of Max

Weber, including (1) his broad-based view of economics as a social science, not just resource engineering, and (2) his concept of scientific analysis, with its distinction between but coexistence of value and objectivity, *Zweck-* and *Wertrationalität*. Among the most treasured items on my shelf, his *Wissenschaft als Beruf* has retained a unique position. From this I derived a lasting concern with normative matters, especially as applied to the role of the public sector in a democratic society.

The normative perspective was well rooted in the tradition of German Finanzwissenschaft. As I encountered it in my Heidelberg studies, there existed an essential difference between the nature of the public (*Staatswirtschaft*) as a mandatory and collective form of organisation (*Zwangs-* and *Kollektivwirtschaft*) and that of the market as an exchange economy (Tausch- und Individualwirtschaft). Among nineteenth-century writers, this distinction, if in various forms, runs from Adam Müller over Carl Dietzel and Schäffle to Adolph Wagner; and the debate over the nature of the Staatswirtschaft was resumed with new vigour in the 1920s and early 1930s, that is, the period preceeding and during my Heidelberg years. Beginning with Gerloff's central piece in the first edition of the *Handbuch der Finanzwissenschaft*, I must have been instructed that the public sector was a Zwangswirtschaft, scornfully rejecting Sax' effort to base public provision on individual utility calculus. Gerhard Colm, who later became a good friend and colleague in Washington affairs, was sceptical of the concept of communal as distinct from individual wants; yet, he saw a key difference between the two sectors. This was in the way in which wants are provided for. Whereas the market operates in response to the effective demand of individuals, provision in the public sector is decided upon by the '*massgebliche Instanzen*'. Rather than try to meet the demands of individuals, the Instanz may base its decision on cultural and political criteria, or it may simply respond to the wishes of powerful interest groups, Otto Pfleiderer who, as Alfred Weber's leading assistant, figures vividly in my memory of the Heidelberg years, also shared the rejection of an individual-utility based model and came close to Colm's view; but by accepting the *Instanz* as a legitimate decision-maker, he was able nevertheless to aggregate public services (evaluated at cost) and private goods in arriving at the *Sozialprodukt*.

Viewed as normative models, these theories fail to explain by what criteria the decision of the *Instanz* was to be legitimated; yet they seemed to claim more than furnishing a positive description of how government works. Ritschl, precariously but also more consistently, not only rejected subjective evaluation but went further. In line with Hegelian tradition, the *Staatswirtschaft* was viewed as *Gemeinwirtschaft*, with *Gemeinschaft* as its subject and the satisfaction of *Gemeinschaftsbedürfnisse* as its object. Sultan, also a member of the Heidelberg faculty of my time, found fault with all these approaches. Urging a sociological theory in the Marxist tradition, he called for a realistic analysis of public sector behaviour with allowance for social and political as well as economic factors.

These approaches differed in identifying what distinguishes the *Staats-*

wirtschaft from *Privatwirtschaft*, but they all felt that an important difference exists, a position which has remained a firm part of my thinking. But they also agreed in rejecting the relevance of individual preference analysis for the public sector, a proposition which I soon abandoned. My encounter with Pigou's *Economics of Welfare*, one of my favourite texts as graduate student, pointed to the strategic importance of externalities and the need for public provision to deal with them. The Hegelian distinction between communal and private wants and the sociological distinction between decision making processes was thus replaced by a more or less technological distinction between public and private goods.

The simple point is that provision for certain goods (e.g. goods which are non-excludable or non-rival in consumption) cannot be undertaken efficiently through the market, so that public provision is needed; and provision for such goods comprises the bulk of what I have called the allocation function of the budget. There is no reason why such goods should not enter into the utility function of consumers on a par with private goods. In short, there is no reason why marginal rates of substitution in consumption should not enter into the determination of efficient resource use in the provision for both types of goods. This holds even if it is granted, as I do, that society in some respects is more than an aggregation of individuals, and that in some instances traditions and common concerns override the independent preferences of the individual consumer. But these situations, i.e. the case of merit goods, are exceptions and not the rule. The bulk of public provision, and the goods which are to be included, does not rest on society's desire to override individual preferences, but to implement them. And where it is held desirable to override, this may apply to goods which are rival as well as to goods which are non-rival in consumption. Rigorous incorporation of social goods into the framework of Paretian efficiency is in order, and the blanket rejection of subjective utility (e.g. of the early contributions of Mazzola, Sax and Wicksell) which prevailed in my Heidelberg years had been a mistake.

But there remained another and less resolved aspect of the problem, i.e. how to actually secure an efficient provision of social goods. Here the roots of solution date back not to Pigou, who merely postulated, in Schäffle-like fashion, that public and private provision should be balanced so as to equate benefits at the margin. Rather, the key contribution here goes back to Wicksell. Wicksell, in his *Finanztheoretische Untersuchungen* (the most creative book in public finance ever written) bypassed the formal apparatus of welfare conditions (perhaps thinking it too academic) and directed his concern at just this more troublesome aspect of the individual subjective utility approach. He scornfully rejected as unrealistic the assumption, first advanced by Mazzola, that the political process of public provision and its finance through taxation functions in analogy to voluntary exchange in the market. Instead, he stressed the absence of voluntary preference revelation and the need for a political voting process to secure a solution. Aware that any solution by majority rule could offer only an approximation, he considered procedures (such as successive voting on alternative tax-expenditure bundles) which would do best in approximating an efficient outcome. He thus pioneered a normative approach to voting procedures, a model which links the efficiency problems of social goods provision to the applied issues of how an efficient solution can be achieved in practice. Samuelson, on the contrary, chose to set aside this aspect of the problem as leading into an unmanageable game-theoretical morass; but by sticking with the more tractable issue of efficiency conditions, this rendered social good theory somewhat of a scholastic exercise, of little help to improving the fiscal performance of the real world setting. I have tried to reestablish such a linkage, but this is not an easy task.

The Wicksell normative tradition of fiscal decision then was extended later into models of representative democracy as developed by Schumpeter and Downs. As distinct from this normative perspective, much of the recent work in fiscal choice takes a quite different tack. Optimising tools drawn from business behaviour in standard macro theory are applied to the behaviour of government officials, now somewhat derisively called 'bureaucrats' as distinct from their past role as 'civil servants'. These individuals are then assumed to pursue their self-interest by maximising the size of their budgets, with the typical result that the budget is shown to be larger than consumers would wish it to be. While I agree that social and private goods are joined in the same individual utility function, I do not believe that decision making in the public sphere must be of the same kind (i.e. profit or own-interest-maximising) as in the market-place. This takes too simplified a view of the political process and of the role of leadership in what is conceived to be the public interest. Moreover, I would prefer to view the positive theory of public finance more in terms of group interaction, with less stress on the behaviour of supposedly autonomous officials. Nevertheless, I welcome this new concern with the nature of the fiscal process. The pages which I have written on normative aspects should not be interpreted as denying the importance of positive models. Rather, they reflect my belief, quite in the Weberian tradition, that clarification of normative issues are not without bearing on what happens in the real world.

THE ROLE OF DISTRIBUTION

The remaining topics which I would like to raise, i.e. redistribution, stabilisation and tax structure design, will have to be dealt with in only summary fashion. As to redistribution: does it belong in public finance, how should it be implemented, and how much of it should there be?

The traditional literature of public finance had given mixed answers: with the exception of Edgeworth, distribution issues had entered the British literature only via the discussion of tax progression. But it had been more important in the German tradition. Wagner's *Sozialpolitische Zielsetzungen* of fiscal policy had introduced distribution as a major concern. But there was little if any mention of it in the literature of my Heidelberg years.

I found the same to be the case on the other side of the Atlantic, only more so. Pigou's discussion of sacrifice theories in the mid 1920s had still moved in the innocent framework of the old welfare economics with its cardinal and interpersonal utility comparisons, an approach which had fallen into disrepute by the time of my coming to Harvard. Respectable economists would accept Robbins' dictum that economics can deal with Pareto efficiency only, overlooking the fact that Pareto himself would not have shared this view. Since then two things happened. First, issues of distribution became so paramount a factor in budget policy, with transfer payments the dominant instrument of the welfare state, that to rule out distribution issues from public finance would indeed mean to rule out two-thirds of the problem. Moreover, and perhaps for just this reason, concern with optimal distribution was readmitted into the sanctuary of economics. The concept of the social welfare function appeared as another innovation of the Harvard years of the late 1930s and replaced cardinal utility comparison. Everyone felt virtuous with the new model, even though I have at times suspected that the difference may not be all that great. However this may be, allowance for distributional weights in terms of an assumed social welfare function became admissible and is now widely practised. I thus need not apologise for having included the distribution branch as a major fiscal function. What is more, I could not possibly have left it out of the picture. It is the distribution issue, more than anything else that makes economics a social science, and it is public finance as a social science that has been my concern.

There are just two points in the distribution issue which I would like to note here, as they are linked closely to my work. First, there is my separation of the distribution and allocation functions, following Wicksell's premise that there must be a just state of distribution before a system of just taxation (in the sense of benefit pricing) can be determined. Samuelson has criticised this separation as circular reasoning and he is correct in doing so in the context of his system, where an all-knowing referee determines the division of resources between public and private goods and the distribution of the latter among consumers. I have insisted, however, and still do so, that this separation is not redundant in a system which, moving closer to reality, realises that preferences are not known, but must be revealed through a voting system, a procedure which cannot be implemented without a given distribution of income. The voting system then enters into determining the distribution of income in line with an optimal distribution of welfare, and the system remains logically intact.

Secondly, there is the proposition contained in my initial model of the three branches, that redistribution should take the form of a tax-transfer process and thus be separable from a benefit tax financed allocation branch. Since then, two considerations arose which may render this doubtful. First, there is the fact that the willingness of donors to redistribute may be paternalistic in form, i.e. they may be willing to redistribute in the form of milk to poor babies but not in the form of cash (used to purchase beer) to poor parents. I grant this as an exception, although its application is to redistribution rather than to the initial problem of determining a just state of basic distribution.

More important is the objection raised by optimal taxation theory. Redistribution via income tax-financed cash transfers (i.e. a negative income tax) is superior in efficiency terms only under the very restrictive assumption of fixed leisure/income and fixed present/future consumption choices. Once these restrictions are relaxed, as they must be, an optimal set of redistributive measures may well involve a mix of excise taxes and subsidies, and may thus seem to interfere with the allocation function. However, such tax subsidy adjustments are not applicable to publicly provided goods only but also to private goods, so that they do not interfere with a basic differentiation between resource allocation to public goods and the issue of distribution.

In all, it still seems to me that as a rule of practical policy, the allocation–distribution separation, as well as primary reliance on an income tax-transfer mechanism, has much merit. Surely it would help to avoid distortions which arise if allocation objectives are restrained or enhanced by redistributional goals, and vice versa. The same, incidentally, holds for the introduction of redistributional weights into cost-benefit analysis.

STABILISATION

The fashion cycle in economic theory, in general, and in the theory of public finance, in particular, is nowhere illustrated better than in the changing role of macro issues. Macro theory preceding my Heidelberg years had focused on structural maladjustments leading to cyclical fluctuation, and Keynes' *Treatise on Money* had drawn attention to the role of liquidity and speculation. Public finances did not play a major role, without any inkling of what was to come. But there are always exceptions. Thus, macro issues were dealt with in one of the early writings of *Privatdozent* Neumark. In his study on 'Konjunktur und Steuern' (1930) he argued, as you may well know, that the built-in flexibility (he did not use that term) of various taxes differed, and concluded (contrary to later doctrine) that those taxes should be chosen which are stable over the cycle. Professor Rose also told me last year that the archives of this university still contain a seminar paper of mine dealing with the budget and the business cycle. He has now presented me this paper and I must confess that I shared the conventional conclusion that budget policy has little to offer in smoothing the cycle.

All this changed dramatically with the Keynesian revolution. Unemployment, so I learned at Harvard, arises when private investment falls short of full employment saving, and public dissaving (i.e. deficit-financed public spending) must be used to restore full employment balance. Very simple and, for that matter, still quite correct in the context of deep depression in which it was first presented. Alvin Hansen's fiscal policy seminar of the later 1930s, in which these problems were explored (remember that these were days in which the difference between ex-post and ex-ante equality of saving and investment was not all that obvious) became one of the most stimulating experiences of my early Harvard years, precisely because all this seemed so new and so promising a road to Utopia.

Presented in its most extreme form, Abba Lerner's theory of functional finance saw the role of taxation merely as a device to prevent an excessive rate of inflation, such as would result from outright reliance on printing-press finance. In my own view, the stabilisation function was important but not exclusively so, and once more the three-branch model served to show how stabilisation needs could be met without interfering with allocation and distribution goals. Unnecessary to say, this tends to be overlooked in practice. In the depression of the 1930s, the need for expansionary policies was taken as an excuse to increase the size of the budget; just as in the inflationary setting of today, the need for demand restriction is taken as an excuse to reduce it.

The fiscal role of stabilisation then came to be integrated with monetary policy into the neoclassical model of the 1950s, with both tools of stabilisation policy effective in their own way, and the selection of the policy mix serving to reconcile considerations of high employment, growth, and foreign balance. Thus integrated into the macro model, the stabilisation role of budget policy came to be separated from the more traditional aspects of public finance and was no longer included in many public finance courses. But this changed in recent years when inflation became an obvious fact and budget policy as a cause of, rather than a remedy to, inflation became the discussion topic of the day.

The current debate in the United States with its striking divergence of academic (apart from political) views is a case in point. What has changed to disrupt the neat world of the neoclassical model of two decades ago? Partly it was a changed perspective on governmental behaviour. Crucial for the Keynesian model as a policy instrument was the assumption that expenditure and tax parameters can be changed independent of each other. Thus, raising taxes in inflation would be stabilising, as would reduction in spending. But raising taxes becomes destabilising if increased revenue leads to increased spending, and expenditure cuts do not restrain demand if matched by tax reduction. Given such perverse behaviour, built-in stability becomes counter-productive and *Privatdozent* Neumark may still be proved correct.

Beyond this, the phenomena of stagflation, escalation and exogenous shocks, which have characterised the 1980s had debilitating effects on monetary and fiscal measures alike, and brought an end to the hope for fine-tuning which had peaked in the mid 1960s. New problems had to be dealt with and new problems, as is always the case, spawned new theories as well. As to the latter, little need be said about the emergence of 'supply side' economics. While effects of fiscal policy on potential growth may well be important in the longer-run perspective, the supply-side solution as a short-run remedy to recession and inflation has no merit. Halting inflation in the United States, after all, was accomplished via the time-honoured remedy of tight money and depression, with its great resource cost and social burdens. The more interesting new theoretical item, rather, is the neoclassical model of the rational expectation school. If correct, this model would suggest (1) that there is no difference between fiscal and monetary measures, since deficits lead consumers to anticipate the future burden of debt service which, in capitalised form, reduces their net worth as would a tax; and (2) that no systematic policy can have continuing effects on the level of real output since policy raises expectations which become a variable in private sector responses. Policy effects on expectations deserves more attention than they have been given and the construction of a macro model based on super-rational expectations with perfect foresight is a worthwhile undertaking. However, I find the assumptions underlying both propositions (1) and (2) so unrealistic as to make the model of little policy use. Indeed, after the storm is over, the neoclassical model (with due allowance for policy expectations) may well be vindicated as a reasonable policy tool. It will be supplemented, however, by selective policies which address structural maladjustments. These undoubtedly will include selective fiscal tools, but in a context different from that of demand management in the traditional sense.

THE GOOD TAX STRUCTURE

This brings me to my final topic, which is the quest for a good tax structure. While this has absorbed a good deal of my time, as it has for most of you, I must confess that it falls outside my theoretical design. As traditionally conceived, the nature of the good tax structure is viewed as dealing with taxation only, independent of the expenditure side of the budget. To be sure, it may be taken to encompass transfers, as these may be viewed as negative taxes, but linkage to the allocation branch is left out. The idea of the 'good' tax structure is thus dealt with as a distribution branch concept, and the crucial role of taxation in preference revelation, needed to determine composition and level of the allocation branch, is passed by. This holds for the equity strand of the 'good' tax theory, from Schanz over Haig to Simons and its role in the work of Neumark, Pechman, Shoup, myself and many of you. And it also holds for the efficiency strand from Pigou and Mirlees to Rose and its Heidelberg branch. Having laid bare my feelings of guilt at partaking in this basically flawed separation of issues, I shall now relapse and, in line with tax theory tradition, pretend that expenditures are an unrelated issue.

I begin with the search for the equitable tax base, defined as that most suited to measure ability to pay. Choice of the proper index is important to assure that people in equal position are treated equally, as well as to obtain a meaningful basis for differentiation among people with unequal capacity.

The concepts of both horizontal and vertical equity are only as good as the underlying index of capacity to pay. It is here that my German background fitted most readily into the American pattern. The thinking of Henry Simons, the intellectual father of the American income tax tradition, was influenced greatly by the extensive German literature on income concepts and in particular the writings of Georg Schanz. As a result, the norm of a comprehensive income base as accretion has been shared by American and German tax scholars. This has been the guiding star in our labours for tax reform, such as the integration of corporate and personal tax, inclusion of capital gains in the base, an economic concept of depreciation, and so on and so forth. We have not been very successful, but miracles may still happen. Perhaps things can turn better only after they have become bad enough, and the current call for a broad-based tax in the United States raises a hope.

While the thinking of my generation, in Germany as well as in the United States, has been mainly in terms of the income tax, the younger colleagues have advanced the case for a personal expenditure tax as a viable and preferable alternative. Though steeped in the income tax tradition, I have come to conclude (reluctantly, to be sure, as no one likes to lose capital in vested ideas!) that a consumption tax may indeed be preferable, at least so under very idealised conditions, calling among other things for inclusion of bequests in the consumption base.

There has also in recent years been a marked shift from an equity to an efficiency oriented view of the 'good' tax structure. Optimal taxation theory, though new in name, traces its lineage back to Pigou's announcement effects and is squarely rooted in the normative tradition of public finance. Efficiency in taxation obviously is important, and we must admit that the Schanz–Simons tradition has given it short shrift. Moreover, the presence of dead-weight loss enters in two ways. To say the least, dead-weight loss should be allowed for in the very formulation of equity. Equal treatment of equals involves equal welfare losses, and these comprise not only tax dollars paid, but also dead-weight losses. Beyond this, the occurrence of dead-weight loss poses efficiency as a further criterion of good tax performance, along with that of equity, and that may require a trade-off between the two.

There is thus no fundamental conflict between the two approaches. They supplement each other and need be linked. The difficulty, however, is that much of optimal taxation theory has been developed in a model where utility functions are assumed to be the same for all people, i.e. essentially in a one-person world, and hence in a setting in which the issue of horizontal equity does not even arise. This has bothered me greatly, but more recent work is becoming aware of the problem, and the conflict between these two approaches is being narrowed.

There are many other issues which I might have noted here, such as the advances in general equilibrium formulations of incidence theory, the great move forward in the empirical pursuit of research on taxation effects, the development of work in local finance built around the Tiebout effect (a concept born in my Michigan seminar of the 1950s) and the addition of cost-benefit analysis as a new chapel in the cathedral. But I must leave these aside here.

In closing, let me return to my Heidelberg heritage and admit that I have been increasingly tempted to go beyond the realm of fiscal economics. Concerned with economics as a social science, I have agreed with critics from the left that the neoclassical model in its modern form is indeed too narrow a view of the world. But in the Weberian tradition I have felt that a much needed broadening out can not be accomplished by letting this model compete with an equally closed and predetermined Marxian system. I have thus become much interested in the philosophical debate over forms of social justice and the role of the state, initiated by the writings of my (then) Harvard colleagues Rawls and Nozick. It is my hope that in years to come, I shall have the strength of character to forget about taxes and to focus on these broader issues. While the imperialism of economics (as distinct from economic imperialism) has made great advances over the last decade or two (witness the inroads of optimisation under uncertainty into social philosophy or the Paretian takeover of jurisprudence) I must confess some scepticism about these conquests. The economist's contribution, I think, should come not so much with reducing other disciplines to dealing with economic substance, but with trying to apply economic tools of analysis to substances which are not economic. This, I like to think, may establish a methodological linkage between the various social sciences—shadows of Max Weber once more and a return to my Heidelberg tradition.

Part II
Taxation

9   A Further Note on the Double
Taxation of Savings*
1939

Similar to previous formulations of the argument by J. S. Mill, Pigou and others, Fisher's [1] case for the exemption of saving outlays from the income tax base rests on the charge of double taxation.[1] Before defending the income tax against this charge we note that the case for or against the inclusion of savings cannot be decided on the ground of equity considerations only. If a heavier tax incidence on savings should be desired on grounds of policy considerations, double taxation, though perhaps disadvantageous from the equity point of view, would become advantageous and establish a case for rather than against the retention of a broader income tax base.

'Double taxation', an ambiguous and easily abused term, may, for present purposes be defined as taxation whose incidence results in an unintentionally discriminatory burden. The point of issue is whether the general income tax involves a hidden discrimination against income from saving or whether, on the contrary, Fisher's spending tax results in an analogous discrimination in favour of saved incomes.

We first consider the problem under the assumption of equal incomes and equal saving/spending habits of the various income receivers. A given percentage tax on all income will yield more revenue and hence impose a heavier tax burden upon the community than a similar percentage tax on incomes after the deduction of savings. A double taxation problem, in the sense of inter-individual discrimination, does not arise in this instance, due to the assumptions of equal incomes and saving/spending habits. As applied to different types of income the double taxation issue still exists but may be dealt with under the next set of assumptions.

We secondly assume equal incomes but varying saving/consumption ratios for various income receivers.[2] Now compare case A where we have a general income tax, with case B, where we have a spending tax yielding the same total revenue. Under B the 'savers' (people who save and invest a

---

* *American Economic Review* (1939) XXIX. For a later reconsideration, placed in a different framework, see p. 301 below.

large part of their income) are better-off relative to the 'spenders' (people who consume a large part of their income) than they would be under A. While this is true, it fails to prove that under A the savers are the victims of undue double taxation. The existence or non-existence of double taxation is, we believe, a theoretical problem, not a matter of arithmetical proof or disproof. The following points are made in support of the contention that no double taxation prevails:

(a) The original income received and taxed in period 1 is, after its investment, crystallised in the invested capital sum. At any later date it may be withdrawn and transformed into consumption income *without suffering a second tax deduction*. The original income is thus taxed but once, whether or not consumption has been delayed. This holds, no matter whether the income is taxed before investment or, as Fisher suggests, the tax is imposed after disinvestment has occurred.

(b) As distinct from the original income which at any time may be recovered tax-free by way of disinvestment, the income from investment accrued during period 2 constitutes a new and additional income. Notwithstanding the merits of Fisher's income concept for purposes of general theory, we find no necessity to use the same income concept for all purposes. The investment of the original income is made and found profitable from the point of view of time preference, in anticipation of the *net* interest return. From the individual's point of view—and this is the relevant factor if we consider his capacity to pay taxes—there is no difference between such interest income and, say, a wage income. The tax on interest is not a duplication of the taxation of the original income in period 1. Whether in the light of capital theory the capital value is derived from its income, or vice versa, is an interesting but altogether different problem [2, n. 490; 3, p. 89].

(c) Lastly, a comparison of the results of taxes on income and taxes on spending is relevant. We begin with the assumption that the originally invested income is disinvested at a later point, and shall subsequently consider the case of continued investment. Under Fisher's scheme, taxation of the original income takes place at the time of its later disinvestment. If the original income is hoarded rather than invested, it is irrelevant which method of taxation is applied. In either case the same percentage tax will be imposed upon the same capital sum; since no interest has accrued, the difference will be one of timing only. If the original income is invested, a given percentage tax on income will over the period from income receipt to disinvestment bear harder on the 'saver' than a tax payable at the time of disinvestment yielding the same amount. The cause of the excess burden on the saver lies in his loss of interest, resulting from the tax reduction of the original income before the investment was made.

From a logical point of view Fisher's statement that the income tax discriminates against savings is no more valid than the opposite contention that the spending tax discriminates against spending. If, however, the problem is considered one of individual capacity to pay taxes rather than one of logic, the general income tax is superior. The additional burden upon the saver is justified: the saver, when investing his original income *did* experience an addition to his economic capacity, independent from later interest receipts. The case for the income tax is further strengthened if the investment of the original income is assumed to continue. Under Fisher's scheme no tax would be collected under such a condition. The range of income tax brackets would be narrowed enormously; a miserly millionaire may well fall into a lower spending bracket than an extravagant middle-class income earner. Such procedure would fail to produce a fair appraisal of the individual's tax-paying ability which is dependent upon additions to capital reserves as well as upon additions to income.

As pointed out initially, equity considerations form but part of the problem. Fisher's spending tax stands in direct contrast to the opinion, expressed by a growing group of economists, that a shift of the tax burden from consumption to saving appears desirable in so far as this is feasible without producing deterrent effects upon investment. The spending tax, while certain to encourage saving, is much less certain to encourage investment and is hence apt to widen the gap between the propensity to consume and the inducement to invest.

NOTES

1. The argument presented in this note has in part been stated previously by Guillebaud [2] and later by Simons [3, p. 89]. In view of Professor Fisher's [1] article a restatement and further clarification of the issue appears desirable.
2. A third set of assumptions of unequal incomes and varying income/saving ratios may be distinguished. The discussion of this case is omitted since it is analogous to the above treatment under the second set of assumptions.

REFERENCES

[1] Fisher, I. (1939) 'Double Taxation of Savings', *American Economic Review*, 29.
[2] Guillebaud, C. (1935) 'Income Tax and Double Taxation', *Economic Journal*, 45.
[3] Simons, H. (1938) *Personal Income Taxation*, (Chicago: Chicago University Press).

10 Proportional Income Taxation and Risk-Taking*
1944

The effects of income taxation on investment have been discussed in economic literature with varying emphases. Prior to the débâcle of the late 1920s the detrimental effects of taxation upon the volume of savings were stressed. During the 1930s economic thinking and experience indicated that the decision to invest constitutes a crucial link between the setting-aside of savings and the flow of funds into actual investment. Accordingly, the emphasis of the discussion was shifted to the effects of taxation on the investment of available funds, particularly on investment in risky ventures. In this paper we examine the basic aspects of this problem, which will be of vital importance after the war.

SUMMARY AND CONCLUSIONS

An investment involves the possibility of a loss. It will not be undertaken unless the expected return appears sufficiently promising. In every investment decision the investor must weigh the advantage of a greater return, or *yield*, against the disadvantage of a possible loss, or *risk*. These two variables serve as tools for the analysis of the problem.

The effects of taxation upon risk-taking are analysed in two steps: first, we consider how the imposition of a tax under varying conditions affects the yield and the risk of an investment (or, more correctly, of a whole combination of various assets); second, we enquire how the investor will react to these changes. That the tax reduces the yield is entirely evident and has been much emphasised; but the equally important fact that the tax may also reduce the degree of risk has received little attention. Its significance was noted by Simons [15] and has been pointed out by Lerner [9] to whom this paper owes a considerable debt.

By imposing an income tax on the investor, the Treasury appoints itself as his partner, who will always share in his gains but whose share in his

* With E. D. Domar (1944) *Quarterly Journal of Economics*, 58, 3.

losses will depend upon the investor's ability to offset losses against other income. Three cases may be distinguished:

1. If losses cannot be offset, the investor carries the entire burden of the loss. The tax reduces the yield (and even by a higher percentage than the tax rate), but leaves the degree of risk unchanged, so that the compensation per unit of risk-taking is reduced. This is the case most frequently discussed in the literature.
2. If a complete offset of losses is possible, the result is very different. Suppose the investor receives an income of $1000, which is independent of the investment in question, so that after a 25 per cent tax he retains $750. If he now makes an investment and suffers a loss of $200, this loss can be fully deducted from his other income, so that only $800 remains subject to tax. Accordingly, the tax is reduced to $200 and his total income remaining after the loss, net of the tax, is now $600, as compared with $750 before the investment was made and the loss suffered. The net loss is thus only $150, the remaining $50, or 25 per cent, having been absorbed by the Treasury in the form of a reduced tax bill on the investor's other income. The yield *and* the risk of the investment have been reduced by the rate of the tax, so that the return per unit of risk-taking remains unchanged.
3. If only a partial offset of losses is possible, the yield is reduced by a greater percentage than the degree of risk, and the results fall between those of cases (1) and (2).

How will the investor react to these changes in yield and risk which the tax has produced? Prior to the tax, he was in an equilibrium position, which gave him the most advantageous combination of yield and risk available. After one or both of these variables are changed he may wish to change his position, that is, take more or less risk. We again consider the same three cases:

1. Since without loss offset the yield is cut, while risk is unchanged, the compensation for risk-taking is reduced. Risk-taking has become less attractive, so that the investor will want to take less risk. But the reduction in yield also means a lower income from his investments. To restore his income, the investor will try to take more risk, since risky investments can be expected to have a higher yield. These two forces are operating in opposite directions. Theoretically the result is uncertain; practical evidence would indicate that the investor is likely to shift in the direction of less risk.
2. If losses can be offset, and the Treasury assumes part of the risk as well as of the yield, a distinction must be drawn between *private risk* (and yield), which is carried by the investor, and the *total risk* (and yield), which includes also the share borne by the Treasury. It is the private risk (and yield) of an investment that is reduced by the tax; the total risk (and yield) remains, of course, unchanged. Since the private risk and yield are reduced by the same percentage, risk-taking has not become less attractive. The inducement to take less risk, which was present in the first case, has disappeared. The investor's income, however, has been reduced and, to

restore it, he will take more risk, although the private risk taken after adjustment to the tax need not equal the pre-tax level. If the investor had retained the original asset combination, its total risk would have remained the same. But since the investor was shown to adjust his asset combination so as to increase his private risk above the unadjusted level to which it was lowered by the tax, total risk must have increased above the pre-tax level. 3. Under conditions of partial loss deduction, the yield is reduced by a greater percentage than risk. Both forces will be operating as in case (1), and the outcome will be uncertain. But there appears little doubt that the higher is the rate of loss offset, the higher will be the degree of risk taken after the tax.

The assumptions under which these conclusions have been reached are developed later on and are summarised in the final section.

A shift towards a more risky investment (or rather, asset combination) may be accomplished by reducing the proportion of the investor's total assets held in cash, that is, by larger total investment, or through a change from less to more risky investments. There is no question that increased risk-taking in either or both forms is highly desirable (except during acute boom conditions) and that therefore a higher degree of loss deduction is of vital importance. The extent to which loss offset is possible in actual practice depends on the offset provisions in the tax laws and upon the availability of other income in each instance.

There are limited provisions for loss offset in the tax law. Since a tax is imposed on net income, the law necessarily permits the offset of investment losses realised in a given period against income received in that period, subject, however, to the important limitation that, with minor exceptions, capital losses can be offset against capital gains only. The likelihood that sufficient other income will be available to the taxpayer is increased greatly if losses made in one period can be carried forward or backward against income made in other periods. The personal and corporation income tax law [at the time of writing] provide[d] for a limited carry-back and carry-forward (two years each) of business net operating losses and for a five year carry-forward of long-term capital losses. Possible changes in the rate schedule introduce additional uncertainties into the investor's calculations.

The extent to which investors may utilise these provisions depends upon the availability of other income. Here the position of various taxpayers differs greatly. A large corporation or a large-scale financial investor may undertake a risky investment as a side-line, and know that possible losses are covered by other income which is reasonably certain to be derived from the main line of business. It is not necessary, of course, that the losses should be realised in the form of capital losses; they may also take the form of a lower taxable income resulting from depreciation costs being charged against other income. Further, a large corporation is assured of the possibility of loss offset as long as the investment in question does not exceed the minimum net income (low as it may be relative to total invested capital) which the management is reasonably certain to derive during the period of carry-over. Thus, if a public utility or a life insurance company were to make a small investment (small relative to other income from operations or interest on gilt-edged bonds) in a very risky venture, it could be quite certain of a loss offset, and would thus have a great advantage over a small competitor who might consider the same venture. The discrimination is even more flagrant in the case of loss carry-back, which gives an 'old' corporation (that is, a corporation with past net income) the certainty of possible loss offset, thus placing it in a very advantageous position as compared with a new company. Inequities of this type will tend to increase economic concentration, and may lower the volume of new investment.

It is evident that the tax law should be adjusted to create the most favourable possible condition for loss offset for all types of investors. This raises numerous technical problems which are not considered in this paper. A careful analysis should be made of the length of the carry-over period required for this purpose, and, if necessary and feasible, unlimited carry-forward of losses should be permitted, supplemented by a limited carry-back. The possibilities of averaging income over a period of years should also be explored, and the present differential treatment of capital gains and losses, as well as the possibility of providing more flexible depreciation schedules, should be examined. These considerations by no means apply to the corporation tax only, but are equally if not more important with respect to the personal income tax.

A less orthodox alternative to an extended carry-over of losses might be considered, under which the Treasury would reimburse the taxpayer during the very period in which the net loss was made. Besides encouraging risk-taking, an arrangement of this kind might also contribute to cyclical stability by raising effective tax rates during prosperity and lowering them during depression. Even if some loss in revenue results, the condition for investment will be more favourable under a somewhat higher tax rate, together with more complete loss offset than under a lower tax rate accompanied by more imperfect offset conditions.

In the following five sections, the analysis is carried out in greater detail. In Section II the general rationale of investment behaviour is described. In Sections III, IV and V* the effects of taxation on risk-taking are examined under the assumptions of no loss offset, full loss offset, and partial loss offset, respectively. Some limitations of the analysis are reviewed in Section VI.

II. THE RATIONALE OF INVESTMENT BEHAVIOUR

The essence of our problem is the change in the investor's behaviour under the impact of the tax. Just as the usual theory of tax-shifting is but an

---

* This section is omitted in this volume, and Section VI of the original paper renumbered V.

application of the principles of price theory to a particular change in data caused by the imposition of a tax, so the solution of the present problem consists in applying a theory of investment behaviour to a similar change. Although the discussion of various investment problems is common in economic literature, no integrated theory of investment behaviour applicable to the analysis of effects of taxation has come to our attention. While this is not the place to develop such a theory, it will be necessary to agree at the outset on those aspects of investment behaviour which are directly related to our problem. For purposes of simplicity, our analysis is mainly concerned with the case of financial investment, some special characteristics of real investment being mentioned in the closing section. In addition, the following assumptions are made: (*a*) a *given* amount of investment funds is available to the investor; (*b*) investments are divisible into small units, that is, 'lumpiness' is excluded; (*c*) the investment market is perfectly atomistic, so that the investor can neglect the effect of his decisions on yields; (*d*) the investor's expectations gross of the tax are unaffected by the imposition of the tax and by resulting government expenditures.

To handle our problem, quantitative values for the yield and the degree of risk of an investment are needed; and in the absence of a better approach they are obtained by means of a probability distribution which the investor will construct for each available investment opportunity [2, 11].[1] Each possible yield, positive or negative, will include the recurrent income from the investment (such as interest or dividends), as well as the change in capital value which the investor expects to realise. Thus, no distinction is made here between capital gains and other income or capital losses and other losses. Each expected yield will be net of all monetary costs of investment. The dollar amounts are transformed into percentage yields on the amount invested by a process similar to that used by Keynes in defining the marginal efficiency of capital.[2] In constructing the probability distribution, the investor will consider all those circumstances which appear significant to him, such as the period of holding, possible developments during this period, and the conditions accompanying the sale. Thus, not only expectations regarding the specific investment and general market developments will be included, but also personal circumstances, such as a sudden need for cash because of a broken arm. Since income for tax purposes is always expressed in dollar amounts, our analysis is carried out in cash terms, cash being used as the numéraire.

From the probability distribution thus constructed, the investor will compute the mathematical expectation of the percentage yields, to be indicated by y.[3] It will prove helpful in the following discussion to separate y into its negative component r and its positive component g. Thus, if $q_1, q_2 \ldots q_k, q_{k+1} \ldots q_n$ are the expected rates of return, such that $q_i < q_{i+1}$ and $q_k = 0$, and if the probability of the occurrence of q_i is p_i, so that

$\sum\limits_{i=1}^{n} p_i = 1$, we arrive at the following definitions:

$$r = - \sum_{i=1}^{k} q_i p_i^4 \qquad (10\text{-}1)$$

$$g = \sum_{i=k+1}^{n} q_i p_i \qquad (10\text{-}2)$$

$$y = \sum_{i=1}^{n} q_i p_i = g - r \qquad (10\text{-}3)$$

The magnitude of the actuarial value is not the only factor determining the investor's choice. Other characteristics must also be considered, though for purposes of this analysis their number must be limited.

Investment decisions are made in spite of uncertainty with respect to the relevant data and their implications. No investor is sure that his estimated probability distribution is entirely correct, but the degree of uncertainty will vary with different investors and different investments. It will be a factor in the investment decision. Yet it is extremely difficult to express the degree of uncertainty involved in workable terms.[5] For our purpose it is sufficient to say that the prevalence of uncertainty may induce the investor to require a somewhat higher return than would be required otherwise.

The very fact that the actuarial value is based on a probability distribution indicates that the investment involves some degree of doubt as to whether or not the actual return will fall within specified limits. The investor will undoubtedly be interested in a number of limits, and in comparing two investments with different actuarial values may or may not wish to apply the same limits to each. Of all possible questions which the investor may ask, the most important one, it appears to us, is concerned with the probability of the actual yield being less than zero, that is, with the probability of a loss. This is the essence of *risk*.[6] Since the investor is not only interested in the probability of a negative return, but also in the chances of suffering losses of various magnitudes, the coefficient of risk should be defined more precisely as a function of losses and their probabilities. This can be done most simply by defining risk as the already familiar expression r, i.e. the summation of all possible losses multiplied by their respective probabilities as defined in (10–1).[7]

By considering r, the most relevant aspect of the dispersion of the probability distribution is accounted for in our analysis. If an investor is to undertake an investment involving a possible loss of his wealth, a compensation will definitely be demanded. The case is less clear in regard to other aspects of the dispersion. If a choice is to be made between investments with different probability distributions, but which have the same yield and risk, it may well be that one investor would prefer the possibility of a large gain, although the probability of obtaining an even moderate return may be low, while another investor would prefer a greater probability of obtaining a moderate return, even though the possibility of a substantial gain may be small. It is thus not clear that a greater dispersion, other things being equal, represents a disutility and commands a market return. This is not to say that the dispersion of the distribution will not be a factor in investment decisions. A more elaborate analysis would allow for additional variables defining the shape of the probability distribution, for example, in terms of the standard deviation, the probability of obtaining less or more than a given 'minimum yield', or the probability of suffering more or less than a given 'maximum loss'. For purposes of this analysis, however, it is assumed that the investor will consider changes in y and r only.[8]

From the preceding discussion we thus emerge with two tools of analysis: r, the degree of risk, and y, the yield of the investment, which is regarded as a compensation for risk-taking. Aside from the already considered question whether a compensation is needed for the uncertainty and dispersion of the probability distribution, the definition of y as the compensation for risk-taking may meet with two objections. First, it may be argued that y should also contain a compensation for the necessary effort of making an investment. Second, the reader will wonder what has happened to the compensation for parting with liquidity.

As stated previously, y is defined as net of all monetary costs of investment, so that the only element that is disregarded is the personal 'effort' of making the investment. But this effort is subject to enormous economies of large scale, which are also available to smaller investors through the services of investment trusts. It appears to be of no great importance. In those few cases, however, where the element of personal effort may affect the results, it will be taken into consideration.[9]

The problem of liquidity remains to be considered. As expounded by Keynes [8, chs. 13, 15] cash is held because of the speculative, precautionary and income (and business) motives. The speculative motive refers to possible losses due to changes in interest rate, and thus represents a component of our concept of risk. The same holds true for the precautionary motive, which is concerned with the possibility of a loss due to the unavailability of cash at some future date. The analysis of the income motive results in a similar conclusion: the reason why an investor does not invest all his funds up to his last dollar is the knowledge that he will need some cash for current expenditures at an early date, so that the investment of the last portion of his funds would almost certainly result in a net loss, since investment expenses would be large relative to gross yield and a rush sale would probably be necessary. Thus, the three elements of the liquidity preference represent nothing but the fear of loss, and are therefore accounted for in our probability distribution and in the values of y and r.[10]

So far, the discussion has referred to single investments. Actually the investor is concerned with obtaining the most desirable use of all his assets, consisting of various investments and cash. It should be noted that a distinction is made here between an *investment combination*, which refers to that part of the investor's wealth which is not held in cash form, and an *asset combination*, which includes both investments and cash. It will be convenient to assume, at first, that the investor intends to invest all his funds, and then to introduce varying holdings of cash. To the extent that the probability distributions of various possible investments are independent of one another, their combination will reduce the degree of risk in accordance with the usual probability theory. But actually the probability distributions of most investments are somewhat interdependent, primarily due to their common dependence on general business conditions. A careful selection of investments may thus be more important than the choice of a large number of different investments.

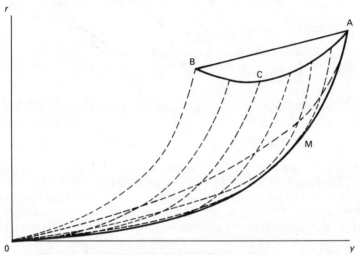

Figure 10.1: The optimum asset curve

Let the ordinate and abscissa of the points *A* and *B* in Fig. 10.1 indicate the degree of risk and the yield of two different asset combinations consisting *entirely* of the investments *A* and *B* respectively. Thus no cash is held at all. If the two investments are combined, the magnitudes of the *r* and *y* of each combination will depend upon the *r* and *y* of the components, the ratio at which they are combined, and their degree of independence. If they are completely interdependent, the magnitudes of *y* and *r* of the combinations will equal the weighted averages of the components and will hence be located on a straight line *AB*. If, as is more likely to be the case, they are more or less independent, the *r* of each combination will be more or less below the weighted average of the *r* of the components. This reflects the principle that diversification reduces the dispersion of a probability distribution. Therefore the *r*'s and *y*'s will fall on a curve such as *ACB*.

Besides investments, the investor's asset combination will also include a proportion of cash. Cash differs from investments by having a zero risk and zero yield. Cash holdings are riskless, since they can not give rise to losses. This is the case because opportunity costs—that is, income not received because investment opportunities were missed—do not enter our analysis. Losses or gains in the real value of cash, due to price changes, are excluded

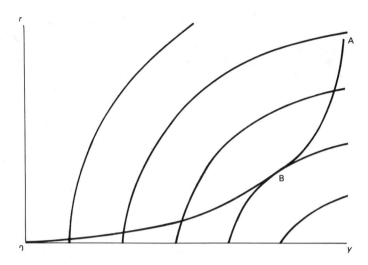

Figure 10.2: The equilibrium position

likewise, because the entire analysis is in terms of cash. An expected appreciation or depreciation of investments due to general price changes is already accounted for in the estimating of probable gains and losses. Therefore in Fig. 10.1 an asset combination consisting of cash only is located at the origin.

Beginning with an asset combination consisting of investments only, such as represented by a point C, the investor can move his combination towards the origin by increasing the proportion of his assets held in cash. The dotted curve CO described by this movement will be called the *cash investment curve*. As the proportion of cash increases, the risk and the yield of the whole asset combination decline, since cash has zero risk and yield. The point C will move towards O, not along a straight line, but rather along a curve of the type CO, since r falls faster than y. The reason is that as the proportion of cash in the asset combination increases, it becomes less likely that a forced sale under unfavourable conditions will be necessary. Therefore the risk of the *investment* combination will decline, while its yield may even rise.[11]

The cash-investment curve as drawn in Figure 10.1, does not indicate the proportion of cash in the asset combination corresponding to any given point on the curve. To measure the cash ratio, a third dimension would be needed. This is an important limitation of our analysis, since it makes it impossible to allocate changes in risk to changes in cash holdings and changes in the riskiness of investments held.

In order to find the best available asset combination, the investor will draw all possible cash-investment curves between each point indicating an investment combination and the origin, as shown by the dotted curves in

Figure 10.1. It is evident that for each level of risk there will be a large (infinite) number of asset combinations with varying proportions of the investments *A, B* and cash. Of these, however, only the one with the highest yield is relevant.[12] The locus of these points of maximum yield, *AMO*, is the curve which describes the investor's evaluation of the market situation and which is the principal tool for our analysis. We shall call it the *optimum asset curve*.[13]

In order to determine the investor's choice of the best position on the optimum asset curve, a preference map between *y* and *r* can be constructed. Again *y* is measured along the abscissa and *r* along the ordinate. The essence of the map is a comparison between the investor's advantage of obtaining income and the disadvantage of jeopardising his wealth. In our analysis both income and losses, measured in terms of *y* and *r*, are expressed as percentage rates on a given dollar amount of wealth. Therefore, any changes in wealth will result in a change in the indifference map.[14] But since the amount of wealth is assumed to be constant, changes in percentage returns are equivalent to corresponding changes in income.

The indifference map presented in Fig. 10.2 and in the other figures is constructed on the basis of the following conditions: it is assumed, first, that for any individual the marginal utility of income declines with increasing income, and second, that the marginal disutility of risk-taking rises with increasing risk. We also assume the marginal utility of income to be independent of risk, and vice versa. Our analysis being limited to the immediate effects of a tax on investment, without regard for secondary effects such as changes in wealth, this assumption appears reasonable.

Since the slope of each indifference curve, or *the marginal rate of risk-taking*, equals the ratio of the marginal utility of income to the marginal disutility of risk, the slopes of the indifference curves must be positive: an increase in *y* along any indifference curve must be accompanied by an increase in *r*, and vice versa. The application of the two assumptions, stated above, to the preference map gives the indifference curves the following three properties:

1. The slope of any one indifference curve must be decreasing upward and to the right. This is the result of either one or both assumptions.
2. The slopes of the indifference curves must decline with increasing values of *y* for any given value of *r*—the result of the first assumption.
3. The slopes of the indifference curves must decline with increasing values of *r* for any given value of *y*—the result of the second assumption.

Property (1), used throughout our argument, is more certain than properties (2) and (3), since it holds true even if either one of the assumptions is omitted. Property (3) is not needed for our purposes.[15] Finally, property (2), which rests on the first assumption only, is used throughout our discussion, but sceptics who do not believe in it will find comfort in the footnotes below.[16]

The equilibrium position of the investor can now be easily found by establishing the point of tangency of the optimum asset curve, *ABO*, with one of the indifference curves, as shown by point *B* on Figure 10.2.

III. TAXATION WITHOUT LOSS OFFSET

We turn now to the effects of a tax on investment. By imposing a tax without loss offset, the Treasury shares in the investor's gains, while leaving his losses unchanged. We consider first the effects of the tax on the magnitudes of y and r, and then the investor's reaction to this change.

Let the rate of the tax be indicated by t, $(0<t<1)$, and let y_t, r_t, and g_t indicate the magnitudes of these variables after the tax. From (1) and (2) it is evident that

$$g_t = g\,(1-t) \text{ and} \tag{10-4}$$
$$r_t = r, \tag{10-5}$$

since by assumption, no losses can be deducted.[17]
Therefore,

$$y_t = g\,(1-t)-r = y\,(1-t)-rt \tag{10-6}$$

From (10-6) we find that

$$y_t < y\,(1-t). \tag{10-7}$$

Thus the rate of yield is reduced by a greater percentage than the rate of the tax. This, of course, should be expected, because all gains are reduced by the rate of the tax, while all losses are left unchanged. When $t \geq y/g$, we obtain $y_t \leq 0$. In other words, if the tax is sufficiently high, the rate of yield becomes zero or negative.

It is often stated that the yield of more risky investments is hit particularly hard by a tax. It is not clear whether this statement should be interpreted in the absolute or relative sense. To the extent that more risky investments have a higher yield, they will obviously suffer a greater absolute reduction. Similarly, out of any two investments with the same degree of risk, the one with a higher yield—that is, the more attractive one—will be hit harder in the absolute sense. It appears to us, however, that the relative reduction is the more significant of the two, and there the argument is far from evident.

Let a indicate the fraction by which y is reduced by the tax so that

$$a = \frac{y-y_t}{y} \tag{10-8}$$

Substituting the values of y and y_t from (10-3) and (10-6), we obtain[18]

$$a = \left(1 + \frac{r}{y}\right) t. \tag{10-9}$$

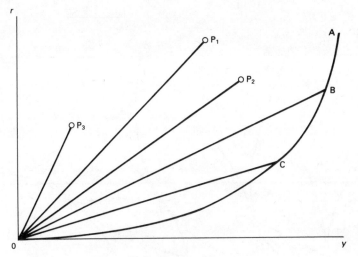

Figure 10.3: Tax sensitiveness

Thus, a is not a function of risk, but of r/y. This expression may be called the degree of tax sensitiveness, and will be indicated by s.

Figure 10.3 shows that s can be interpreted geometrically as being the slope of the line connecting any point representing a given asset combination with the origin. It also demonstrates that the degree of risk and the degree of tax sensitiveness are different concepts, and that there is no apparent reason in general why a higher degree of risk should be accompanied by a higher degree of tax sensitiveness. Thus, while the degrees of risk of the points p_1, p_2 and p_3 are $r_1 > r_2 > r_3$, their degrees of tax sensitiveness are $s_3 > s_1 > s_2$. It must be noted, however, that if a comparison is made among points located on the same optimum asset curve, $ABCO$, a point with a higher degree of risk (B) will also be more tax sensitive than a point with a lower degree of risk (C).[19]

As the yield is cut by the tax, the investor may wish to change the asset combination chosen by him prior to the imposition of the tax. The adjustment will depend upon both the reduction in yields and the investor's preferences. It will be the result of the income and substitution effects. On the one hand, the tax will reduce the compensation per unit of risk y/r, because y is reduced while r is left unchanged. The investor will therefore tend to take less risk. On the other hand, a reduction in y means that his total income is reduced, which will induce him to take more risk. The substitution and income effects will thus work in opposite directions, and the outcome will depend upon the circumstances of each case. The situation is somewhat similar to that in the labour market, where a fall in wage rates may or may not result in a decreased supply of labour. General opinion and empirical evidence would indicate, however, that a shift towards less risk appears more likely.

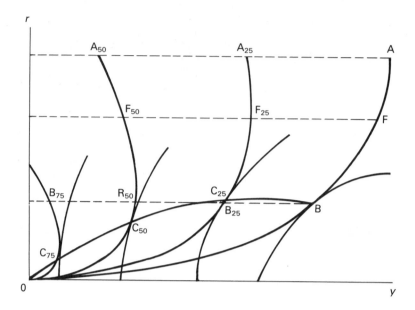

Figure 10.4: No loss offset

A geometrical analysis of the problem may permit some more definite conclusions. Let *ABO* in Fig. 10.4 indicate the position of the optimum asset curve prior to the imposition of the tax, and let *B* be the equilibrium point. When a tax is imposed, each point of the asset curve suffers a reduction in *y*, in accordance with its degree of tax sensitiveness. It will move to the left along a horizontal line, since the degree of risk remains unchanged by the tax. Thus, any point *F* moves to F_{25}, F_{50}, etc., and so does the whole asset curve, *ABO*, which now becomes $A_{25}B_{25}O$, $A_{50}B_{50}O$, and so on, the subscripts indicating the rate of the tax. Because the tax sensitiveness of any point on the asset curve rises with risk, the upper part of the curve bends leftward as the tax rate increases, so that, as shown in Fig. 10.4, its upper part becomes negative, if the tax is sufficiently heavy.

The investor who before the tax was located at the equilibrium point *B*, will, after a 25 per cent tax, find himself at B_{25}. This point is not an equilibrium position. He will therefore move up along the asset curve $A_{25}B_{25}O$ to the new equilibrium position C_{25}, located at the point of tangency of $A_{25}B_{25}O$ with an indifference curve, where his risk will exceed that taken before the tax. In the case of a 50 per cent tax, the corresponding adjustment would have been a downward move from B_{50} to C_{50}. It should be noted that the price of risk-taking *y/r* falls (increases) as the investor moves up (down) the optimum asset curve, which produces a secondary substitution effect and acts as a check to his movement.

Whenever an investor shifts to a more risky asset combination, he may do so by taking more risky investments or holding less cash or, most likely, by applying both methods at the same time.

As the optimum asset curve moves to the left, the new equilibrium positions describe the curve $BC_{25}C_{50}C_{75}O$, which will be called the *tax asset curve* (Fig. 10.4). It first rises and then gradually falls towards the origin. Its shape, proceeding this time from left to right, can be explained in the following manner. If the return on risk-taking is close to zero—that is, if market prospects are extremely poor—the investor will take little risk, if any. As the market improves, he will take more risk. Finally, as his income increases, due to improved market conditions, he may once more become less willing to take risk. The result is determined by the interaction between the substitution and income effects.[20]

It follows that if an investor (with a given amount of wealth) is optimistic about the market outlook, so that the optimum asset curve is further down and to the right, the effect of a tax on risk-taking is more favourable or less detrimental than in the case of a darker market outlook. If the tax is very heavy, the investor may prefer to hold his entire assets in cash.

The subjective nature of the problem should be emphasised. The indifference curves, by their very definition, are only expressions of the investor's preferences, and the optimum asset curve represents his personal evaluation of the market situation. Since the same market situation may appear more favourable to one investor than to another, it is quite possible that a given tax may induce the more optimistic investor to take more risk, while driving his more pessimistic colleague out of the market. But the general conclusion is likely to hold that a relatively low tax imposed under depressed economic conditions, when expectations are bad, may have more harmful effects on investments than a much higher tax imposed under more favourable conditions.[21]

The argument is frequently presented that income taxes discourage risk-taking, because (1) the yield from risky investments is particularly sensitive to taxation, and (2) because more tax-sensitive investments are avoided by the investor.[22] The first part of the argument has already been dealt with above (p. 118). In regard to the second part, it must be emphasised that tax sensitiveness is by no means the only factor which determines the investor's reaction to the tax. As has been shown, his choice depends both on the original position of the optimum asset curve and on its movement, as well as on the slopes of the indifference curves. Unless special assumptions are made in respect to these factors, the choice need not be in favour of the less tax-sensitive investment. As a matter of fact, the concept of tax sensitiveness is not a very essential part of the argument, and the whole problem could well be analysed without it.

Another version of the argument runs as follows. Prior to imposition of a tax, the investor is indifferent between a more risky investment, bearing, say, 10 per cent, and a less risky investment, bearing, say, 3 per cent, the difference of 7 per cent being just sufficient to compensate the investor for the additional risk of the second investment. If now a 50 per cent tax is imposed and both yields are cut by one-half (in fact, they are likely to be reduced by different percentages), the difference is reduced to 3.5 per cent, which is not sufficient to compensate for the difference in risk. Hence the conclusion that the investor will take the less risky investment. Evidently the argument implies that the investor will be indifferent between any two investments (or asset combinations) as long as the difference between their rates of yield remains constant, irrespective of the level of the yields themselves. This means that the indifference curves are assumed to be horizontally parallel or, in other words, that the marginal utility of income is constant. (For a discussion of this special case, the reader is referred to notes 16 and 21.)

IV. TAXATION WITH FULL LOSS OFFSET

We shall now assume a complete offset of losses. This implies that the investor is assured of a sufficient amount of income derived from other sources (than the asset combination), and that adequate provisions for loss offset are made in the law. If he suffers a loss from his asset combination, he can then reduce his other taxable income by the magnitude of the loss. Thus, his total tax liability is decreased by an amount equal to the loss multiplied by the tax rate, so that this part of the loss is recovered. In other words, full loss offset means that whenever the investor suffers a loss, the Treasury reimburses him for a fraction of the loss equal to the tax rate. The Treasury thus becomes a partner who shares equally in both losses and gains.

Under these conditions, not only are the expected gains in the probability distribution cut by a percentage equal to the tax rate, but all losses are reduced likewise. We therefore have from (10-1), (10-2) and (10-3)

$$r_t = r(1 - t) \tag{10-10}$$
$$g_t = g(1 - t) \tag{10-11}$$
$$y_t = g_t - r_t = y(1 - t) \tag{10-12}$$

Thus, both the degree of risk and the yield are reduced by a percentage exactly equal to the rate of the tax. The question of tax sensitiveness does not arise here at all, because all asset combinations (or investments) suffer the same percentage reduction.[23] These results are in sharp contrast with those of the preceding case, where no loss offset was possible, so that we may expect the investor's reaction to be markedly different.

Before proceeding further, we must make a distinction between *total yield* and *private yield* and between *total risk* and *private risk*. The imposition of the tax reduces the yield and the degree of risk which are left to the investor, or his *private* yield and *private* risk, in the manner already described; but the *total* yield and the *total* risk of the given asset combination are entirely unaffected by the tax. The fractions of yield and risk which the tax takes away from the investor are simply transferred to the Treasury.[24] The symbols y_t and r_t refer to private yield and degree of risk, respectively. Total yield and degree of risk, being unchanged by the tax, are still denoted by y and r. Since our main problem is the effect of the tax on *total risk-taking*, not much use will be made of the difference between y and y_t; but the distinction between r and r_t will be extremely important. This distinction was not needed in the preceding case, where it was assumed that no loss offset was possible. Since in that case the Treasury did not share in risk, private risk and total risk were necessarily equal. From the point of view of the economy as a whole, it is, of course, total risk that is important, not private risk.

Faced with a reduction in private yield and private risk, the investor will try to readjust his asset combination. His reaction can again be studied in terms of the income and substitution effect. This time, however, the tax produces no initial substitution effect, because the price of risk-taking (y/r) is unchanged, the yield and the degree of risk being reduced in the same proportion. The income effect will make the investor shift to an asset combination with higher risk. This increase in private risk taken (though not necessarily to or above the private risk taken before the tax) also implies an increase in total risk, since from (10-10)

$$r = r_t \cdot \frac{1}{(1 - t)} \ .$$

Thus we reach the important and somewhat unexpected conclusion that the imposition of the tax will increase the total risk taken.

A geometric demonstration will help to clarify this result. Let ABO in Fig. 10.5 be the position of the optimum asset curve before the tax, and let B be the optimum point. Since the imposition of the tax reduces y and r equally by the percentage of the tax rate, any point F on ABO moves towards the origin along a straight line FO, covering a fraction of the distance from F to O equal to the tax rate, so that if the new position of F is F_t we have $FF_t/FO = t$. Similarly, the entire curve ABO moves to a new position, $A_tB_tO_t$ and the investor, who prior to the tax was at the equilibrium point B, now finds himself at B_t.

Finding himself at B_t, the investor discovers that, while holding the identical asset combination, his net return (after tax) has fallen by a fraction equal to the rate of the tax, and so has his private risk. He will then find that he can improve his position by moving from B_t to C_t, the point of tangency of the optimum asset curve, in its new position, with an indifference curve. Since, as shown before, the imposition of the tax will produce an income effect only, the point C_t must be above B_t. This statement can be readily proven geometrically.[25]

From the fact that private risk taken after adjustment to the tax exceeds private risk taken prior to this adjustment (although not necessarily private risk taken prior to the tax), it follows that *total risk taken after the tax will exceed total risk taken before the tax*. To find the total risk point, E_t, corresponding to the private risk point C_t, we can either apply the formulae

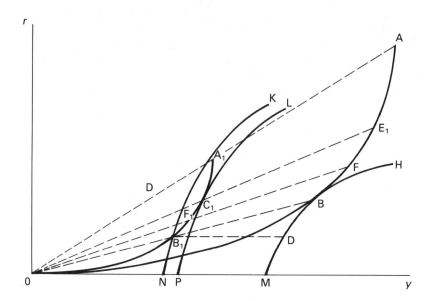

Figure 10.5: Full loss offset and constant tax

$r = r_t[1/(1-t)]$ and $y = y_t[1/(1-t)]$, or draw the line C_tO and extend it to its intersection with ABO, which gives the position of E_t. The total risk (and yield) of any optimum asset combination being unaffected by the tax, it is still represented by its original position on the optimum asset curve. Since C_t is above B_t, E_t must be above B.[26]

The relationship between the level of total risk and the rate of tax remains to be considered. As the tax rate increases, the optimum asset curve ABO moves towards the origin, taking the positions $A_{25}B_{25}O$, $A_{50}B_{50}O$, etc., as shown on Fig. 10.6, the subscripts indicating the corresponding tax rates. The new equilibrium positions located at its tangency points with the indifference curves describe the already familiar tax asset curve, $BC_{25}C_{50}C_{75}D$. This time, however, this curve indicates only the private degree of risk (and yield) taken by the investor under given tax rates, and will be referred to as the private tax asset curve.

In Fig. 10.6 the private tax asset curve first rises with an increasing tax rate from B to somewhat beyond C_{25}, and then falls towards the origin, this movement again depending upon the investor's evaluation of market conditions prior to the tax, and the shapes of the indifference curves.[27] Since the equal percentage reduction of y and r leaves the ratio y/r unchanged, it may appear surprising that the private tax asset curve should fall at all; that is, that under certain conditions the investor should fail to recover the degree of private risk taken before the tax. When a given (say, 50 per cent) tax is imposed, the investor will find his original equilibrium point B moved to B_{50}, and again readjust his position in the direction of increased private risk by moving up along the new optimum asset curve $A_{50}B_{50}O$. If the latter were a straight line passing through the origin, he would be able to return to the original point B, thus taking just as much risk as he did prior to the tax; but as the slope of $A_{50}B_{50}O$ increases with increasing risk, the investor finds that the ratio y/r diminishes as he goes up along $A_{50}B_{50}O$; this secondary substitution effect will finally stop his upward movement. In the general case, it cannot be said whether any given tax will cause the investor to stop short of or exceed the *private* risk taken prior to the imposition of the tax. But as in the preceding case, a comparatively favourable market and lower tax rate will be conducive to a higher level of private risk.

From the point of view of the economy, the question whether the pre-tax level of private risk is recovered is relatively unimportant. What matters is the degree of total risk taken jointly by the investor and the government. By extending the lines OC_{25}, OC_{50}, OC_{75}, etc. to their intersection with ABO, we find the corresponding points E_{25}, E_{50}, E_{75}, etc., indicating the degrees of total risk which will correspond to the investor's adjustment to various tax rates. We have already proved that all *these* points must fall above the pre-tax equilibrium B; it can be shown by a similar proof that the degree of *total* risk taken will be the higher the higher the tax rate. This, of course, is not an argument for a tax rate approaching 100 per cent. The

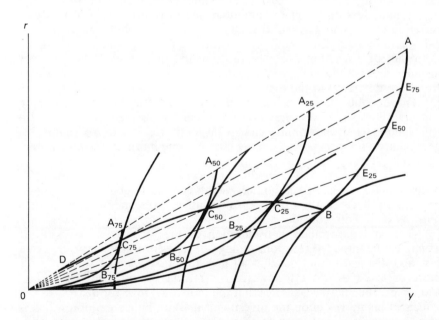

Figure 10.6: Full loss offset and variable tax

simplifying assumptions upon which the conclusion rests must be kept in mind. In addition, the results for the economy would obviously be chaotic, if the government were to invite everybody to invest his funds in whatever project he chooses with a 'no loss' (and 'no gain') guarantee.

V. QUALIFICATIONS

In the preceding analysis the problem has been considered in a simplified form. A review of the major limitations is now in order.

(1) Our analysis has been based upon the probability approach to risk theory. Lacking better alternatives, this approach was introduced in order to obtain numerical values for y and r. It appears that, under the impact of a tax, these values behave in a manner quite compatible with common-sense considerations. If definitions for risk and yield were obtained on the basis of some different approach, their behaviour under the impact of a tax would probably be very similar. If it is denied that numerical values can be obtained, no method for a precise analysis of the problem appears to be available.

(2) We have assumed that the investor's behaviour is concerned with changes in y and r, only because these variables appear to us the most important. Undoubtedly there are other characteristics of the probability distribution in which the investor may be interested, such as the probability of obtaining less than a given minimum rate of return, the probability of suffering more than a given loss, the probability of obtaining very large gains, and so forth. Like r and y, each of these variables will also change as the result of a tax, but not necessarily in the same way. If the investor includes these additional variables, the outcome may in some cases differ from that described in the text.

(3) Throughout our discussion the investor's wealth was assumed to be constant. Now, it is likely that as the result of the tax the investor's wealth will change, which in turn may change his indifference pattern. That is, his general attitude towards risk-taking may become more or less favourable. This secondary adjustment has not been taken into account, since the analysis is limited to the immediate effects of the tax on the investor's decisions. The effect of taxation on wealth is in itself a complex problem, particularly because the effects of alternative taxes and/or expenditures must be taken into consideration.

(4) Our analysis omits a consideration of the 'investment market'. It examines the intended reactions of any one investor to the imposition of a tax, and disregards the fact that all investors may want to shift towards more or less risk, thereby lowering or raising the price of risk-taking. Moreover, the analysis assumes that the individual investor disregards the effects of his moves upon the investment market, an assumption which is clearly unrealistic with respect to important groups of investment decisions, and which we hope to reconsider at a later date.

(5) The probability approach as used here is more nearly applicable to the case of the financial investor than to 'real' investment decisions. The manager of a corporation about to decide which of his plants he should expand, and what equipment he should purchase, is confronted with fewer and more unique investment alternatives than is the financial investor, and is thus unable to achieve an equal degree of diversification. Certain considerations which might be of little importance for the financial investor, such as those related to maintaining competitive advantages, might be very significant for him. On the whole, however, it is likely that the rationale of real investment decisions would move along similar lines, and that the general conclusions here arrived at would also apply to the case of real investment.

(6) The effects of a proportional tax only have been considered. If the case of a progressive tax is examined, additional complications arise. The entire shape of the probability distribution, and its right tail in particular, become of great importance, so that it is very doubtful whether it remains sufficient to describe the distribution in terms of y and r. Given a progressive rate schedule, tax savings due to loss offset are likely to be made at different (mostly lower, but possibly higher) rates than those which would have been imposed on the gains. These considerations would modify some of the conclusions reached here, but the case for loss deduction would become even stronger. In an analysis of progressive rates, the related problem of discrimination against fluctuating incomes, and its elimination through averaging, becomes of particular importance.

NOTES

1. The probability approach to risk theory implies that it is 'reasonable to set up the assumption of quantified probability estimates as an idealisation of actual business practice' [5]. Objections may be raised to this assumption, as in fact they may be raised against most any feature of the *homo economicus*. For purposes of this paper, which does not discuss risk theory as such, the probability method is adopted, because no satisfactory alternative approach to the subject of risk theory has been developed. The theory of investment behaviour, as developed by Shackle [13, 14], divides expectations into those which would and would not cause 'surprise', and thus avoids having to attach numerical probabilities to all expected yields. It appears to us that the resulting indeterminacy makes it impossible to derive satisfactory tools for the comparison of relative advantages of different investments and therefore for the analysis of taxation effects.

2. That is, the investor will compute the rate of discount which equates the present value of the prospective returns with the amount invested [8, n. 135; 2 chs. 13, 14].

3. The use of the mathematical expectation appears to us to be superior to that of the most probable value, employed by some other authors in similar problems. If, for reasons of simplicity, the probability distribution is to be represented by one variable, the latter should reflect as much as possible the changes in any

part of the probability distribution. The significance of this condition for an analysis of taxation effects will be seen presently.

4. Since the values of all qs from the beginning to qk are negative, r is positive.

5. The uncertainty factor has been emphasised in discussions of investment behaviour, according to which the investor is, in fact, confronted, not with a single probability distribution, but with a probability distribution of probability distributions. Hart [6] has pointed out that the problem of uncertainty cannot be solved by boiling down the set of probability distributions into a single 'super' distribution, since the latter would conceal certain characteristics of the component distributions which are relevant for economic planning. This paper being a first step in the analysis of our subject, these complications, which will hardly affect the major results, are avoided here.

6. The term 'risk' has been given different connotations by various authors, but it has been generally described as a property of a known probability distribution. It has been expressed, for instance, as the probability of obtaining a smaller return than γ [11, p. 776] or as the coefficient of variation. The expression in the text appears to be most useful for our purposes, because among the factors underlying investment behaviour and affected by a proportional tax we regard risk as defined in the text as by far the most important.

The term 'uncertainty' usually applies to anticipations where the probability distribution itself is not exactly known. This is in general agreement with Professor Knight's use of the term, although 'uncertainty' in his sense would appear to apply only where probability estimates are assumed not to be cardinal [6].

7. A further refinement of our definition of risk may be made. If the market pays a return on an entirely riskless investment, the investor when purchasing a given investment incurs not only the risk of losing a part of his present wealth, but also of losing the opportunity of obtaining a certain return from a riskless investment. If, therefore, the return on an entirely riskless investment is equal to l, expected losses should be measured, not from the zero point of the probability distribution, but from l. Thus, if in our original probability distribution of $q_1, q_2 \ldots q^k \ldots q_m \ldots q_n$ there is a $q_m = l$, the adjusted degree of risk may be redefined as

$$r' = - \sum_{i=1}^{m} (q_i - l) \, pi = - \sum_{i=1}^{k} q_i pi + \left(- \sum_{i=k+1}^{m} q_i pi + l \sum_{i=1}^{m} p_i \right) = r + \lambda.$$

In an economy like that of the United States, the difference between r and r' is likely to be of minor importance, since l may be expected to be quite small or zero. Therefore, this correction may be omitted for most of the argument and will be mentioned only where it may be particularly significant.

8. This limitation would probably not be acceptable for the analysis of a progressive tax, for which the entire shape of the probability distribution would be important.

9. Thus, if it can be assumed that the net investment effort requires a minimum compensation, to be indicated by e, which is a constant percentage rate on the amount invested, then the adjusted compensation for risk-taking may be redefined as $y' = y - e$.

10. This view of the supply price for investment funds has certain implications for the theory of interest. If the return for waiting is zero (which, of course, depends upon institutional and other factors) and if Keynes' liquidity prefer-

ence represents merely special types of risk, the question must be asked why the return for these elements of risk (namely, marketability and changes in the interest rate) should be separated from other risk factors and identified as *the* rate of interest. This does not mean that for certain purposes a distinction between various types of risk might not be useful, but the more inclusive is the definition of interest—that is, the more complete the different types of risk the return for which is included—the clearer becomes the need for discarding the idea of *the* rate of interest and for talking about the returns available on different investments. We hope to develop this idea at a future date.

11. It is quite possible that, as the investor moves down along the cash investment curve, the yield of the whole asset combination may increase at first, since he will escape the probable loss that would result from the investment of the last portion of his funds. In order to analyse what happens on the upper part of the curve, it would be necessary to allow for the possibility of borrowing, which may become profitable as the investor moves up along the curve. We prefer to disregard borrowing, so as not to complicate the general discussion.

12. It follows from the subsequent analysis that the imposition of a tax will not change the yield rating of various asset combinations with the same degree of risk.

13. The optimum asset curve can be expected to be smooth and continuous, because we have assumed an infinite divisibility of all assets. The investor can, therefore, combine the three assets, namely, the investment A, B and cash, in an infinite number of proportions which, most likely, will eliminate kinks. The case will be even stronger if more than two investments are considered.

14. The indifference map could also have been expressed in dollar amounts. Then the pattern would have been independent of changes in wealth, which would have been reflected in a shift of the optimum asset curve. For the purposes of the present analysis, the approach chosen seemed more convenient.

15. The second assumption and property (3) are included here for the sake of completeness only. They would enter into the analysis of related problems, such as the effects of insurance against loss on risk-taking.

16. If the marginal utility of income is assumed to be constant, the slopes of the indifference curves will be constant with increasing values of y for any given value of r. In other words, the curves will be horizontally parallel. If income utility is thus assumed constant, the second assumption (increasing disutility of risk-taking) must be applied, since the tax will produce no effects on risk-taking whatsoever, if both income utility and risk disutility are held constant.

    For a more thorough discussion of the properties of indifference curves, see Schultz [12, p. 183], and Hicks [7, ch. 1].

17. If instead of r we use r', as defined in footnote 7, the tax will reduce the adjusted degree of risk somewhat. Since the tax reduced the yield of a perfectly safe investment as of all other investments, λ becomes $\lambda(1-t)$ and $r'_t = r+\lambda(1-t)$, which is smaller than $r' = r+\lambda$. But since λ is likely to be small, the reduction in risk will not be substantial.

$$a = \frac{y-y'}{y} = \frac{y-y(1-t)+rt}{y} = \left(1 + \frac{r}{y}\right)t.$$

19. The problem becomes more complex in the case of progressive taxation. To the extent that probability distributions with a higher degree of risk are also characterised by a longer right tail, they will probably be more tax-sensitive than less risky distributions.

20. The faster the slopes of the indifference curves fall as the rate of yield increases along any given horizontal line, that is, the more the investor's marginal rate of risk-taking is (inversely) affected by the size of his income, the sooner will the tax asset curve begin to fall. Since an increasing tax rate makes the investor move from right to left, an investor who 'tires' quickly of taking risk as his income increases, is more apt to shift to more risky investments as a result of the tax than is another investor whose willingness to take risk is less affected by the size of his income. In the extreme case, the investor who insists on a given income, irrespective of the risk involved, will be taking higher and higher risk as the rate of the tax increases.

21. As promised above, the argument is reconsidered on the assumption that the marginal utility of income remains constant with an increasing y, so that the indifference curves are horizontally parallel. In that case, there is no income effect. The tax asset curve moves downward throughout, and the investor takes less risk.

22. See, for instance, Moulton [10, p. 296], and for the version of the argument presented in the following paragraph, Black [1, p. 2223].

23. This statement must be modified, if the minimum compensation for effort defined in note 9 is taken into consideration. Then we have $y'_t = y_t - e$ and the percentage reduction of the adjusted yield is

$$a' = \frac{y' - y'_t}{y'} = \frac{y - e - y(1-t) + e}{y'} = t\left(1 + \frac{e}{y'}\right).$$

It follows, therefore, that the yield is reduced by a greater percentage than the rate of the tax. If $t \geq y'/y$, we get $y'_t \leq 0$, so that the adjusted yield can become zero or negative, if the tax is sufficientiy high. But since e is small, y'/y is very close to 1, and therefore, to achieve this result, the tax rate must be very high.

The adjusted degree of tax sensitiveness now becomes

$$s' = \frac{e}{y'}$$

Since e is a constant, s' depends on y' only and varies inversely with it. To the extent that a higher y' is accompanied by a higher r (or r'), more risky asset combinations are less tax sensitive. Again, since e is small, this difference in tax sensitiveness is hardly important.

24. The statement that the total degree of risk is unaffected by the tax is perhaps misleading, because it implies that public and private risk are interchangeable. Quite possibly the concept of total risk is illegitimate, because it represents a combination of heterogeneous items. *Public* risk-taking presents a most interesting problem, which certainly deserves further investigation. It remains true, however, that changes in 'total risk'—which for any given investment equals private risk before the tax—reflect the changes in the magnitude and direction of capital flows.

25. The first proposition is that the slope of KB_tN at B_t must be greater than the slope of HBM at B. This follows from the fact that (a) at the point B the slopes of ABO and HBM are equal and therefore are both smaller than the slope of HBM at D, since by assumption, the slope along any given indifference curve falls with increasing y and r, and that (b) the slope of KB_tN at B_t must be equal or greater than the slope of HBM at D. A second proposition is that the slope of A_tB_tO at B_t will be equal to the slope of ABO at B: the slope of ABO at any point (y, r) is dr/dy. Similarly, the slope of A_tB_tO at a corresponding point $(y_t,$

r_t) is dr_t/dy_t. But since $y_t = y(1-t)$ and $r_t = r(1-t)$, we have $dy_t = dy(1-t)$, $dr_t = dr(1-t)$ and hence $dr_t/dy_t = dr/dy$. From these two propositions it follows that at B_t the slope of A_tB_tO must be smaller than the slope of KB_tN. Therefore, B_t cannot be the new point of equilibrium, at which the slopes of A_tB_tO and the indifference curve must be equal. Since the slope of A_tB_tO increases while moving upward and to the right, while that of any indifference curves decreases, the new equilibrium point C must be to the right and above B_t.

26. Continuing the story of note 21, we must review the argument on the assumption of a constant marginal utility of income. As explained above an increasing marginal disutility of risk-taking must then be assumed. The conclusion reached in the text that the imposition of the tax will increase the level of total risk taken still holds, because the price of risk-taking is unchanged, while the marginal disutility of risk is reduced by the reduction in private risk. It should be noted that the geometric proof given in the preceding note does not depend on the assumption that the slopes of the indifference curves fall along a given horizontal line.

27. In Fig. 10.6 the tax asset curve is not continued beyond D, because as the tax continues to increase, there are no points of tangency between the subsequent positions of the optimum asset curve and the indifference curves below the line ADO. In order to make use of the tangency points above ADO, borrowing must be introduced, which is excluded in this paper. In the absence of borrowing, the tax asset curve will proceed along the straight line DO.

REFERENCES

[1] Black, D. (1939) *The Incidence of Income Taxes* (London: Macmillan).
[2] Fisher, I. (1906) *The Nature of Capital and Income* (New York: 1906).
[3] Guillebaud, C. (1935) 'Income Tax and Double Taxation', *Economic Journal*, 45.
[4] Haig, R. (1921) 'The Concept of Income', in Haig, R. (ed.), *The Federal Income Tax* (New York: Haig).
[5] Hart, A. (1940) 'Uncertainty and Inducements to Invest', *The Review of Economics and Statistics*, 8.
[6] —— (1942) *Studies in Mathematical Economics and Econometrics* (Chicago: University of Chicago Press), pp. 110–18.
[7] Hicks, J. (1939) *Value and Capital* (Oxford: Oxford University Press), Ch. 1.
[8] Keynes, J. M. (1936) *The General Theory of Employment, Interest and Money* (New York: Harcourt Brace).
[9] Lerner, A. (1940) *Economics of Control* (New York: Macmillan).
[10] Moulton, H. (1940) *Capital Expansion, Employment and Economic Stability* (Washington, D.C.: The Brookings Institution).
[11] Pigou, A. (1920) *The Economics of Welfare* (London: Macmillan), Appendix 1.
[12] Schultz, H. (1938) *The Theory and Measurement of Demand* (Chicago: University of Chicago Press), pp. 18–22.
[13] Shackle, G. (1940) 'The Nature of Inducement to Invest', *The Review of Economics and Statistics*, 8.
[14] —— (1942) 'A Theory of Investment Decisions', *Oxford Economic Papers*, 6.
[15] Simons, H. (1938) *Personal Income Taxation* (Chicago: University of Chicago Press).

11   Income Tax Progression, 1929–48*
   1948

The expansion of federal taxation during the last two decades has featured increased reliance upon the personal income tax. From the rate low in 1929 to the rate peak in the second world war, income tax liabilities were raised on seven occasions. Notwithstanding subsequent reductions, present [1948] liabilities remain well above pre-war levels. While most people feel that income tax progression increased, the concept of 'increased' or 'decreased' progression is ambiguous. In fact, the results depend entirely on how the degree of progression is measured.

The usual failure to attach precise meaning to the concepts of increase or decrease in progression may be due to the ease with which the existence of progression, proportionality, or regression is distinguished [7, Part II, ch. 2; 10]. It is generally agreed that a rate structure is progressive where the average rate of tax (i.e. tax liability as a percentage of income) rises when moving up the income scale; proportional where the average rate remains constant; and regressive where the average rate falls with the rising income. In other words, the rate structure is progressive where the marginal rate (i.e. the increment in tax liability as a percentage of the increment in income) exceeds the average rate, proportional where it equals the average rate, and regressive where it lies below the average rate.[1] As may be seen from Fig. 11.1, the conditions of progression were met for the entire range of taxable incomes throughout our period.

Difficulties only arise because these basic definitions are compatible with numerous alternative measures of the *degree* of progression and regression, and here there is no general agreement on which measure to use. Yet various measures if applied to any one rate structure will show different degrees of change in progression when moving up the income scale; in certain cases, the movements may even be in opposite directions. Moreover, the degree of progression at specific points in the income scale may rise or fall when moving from one rate structure to another, depending upon the measure employed. Statements about changes in the pattern of progression are useful only if accompanied by a definition of the particular measure used.

---

* With Tun Thin (1948) *The Journal of Political Economy*, vol. LVI, no. 6.

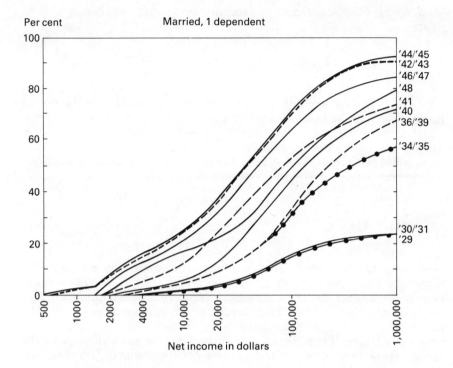

Figure 11.1: Average rates applicable in various income years

In this paper various measures will be distinguished and applied to changes in rates during the 1930s and 1940s. Subsequently, policy implications of the various measures will be considered.

AVERAGE RATE PROGRESSION

Since a tax structure is defined to be progressive when the average rate increases with rising income, the degree of progression may be measured by the rate of change in the average rate of tax

$$\frac{\dfrac{T_1}{Y_1} - \dfrac{T_0}{Y_0}}{Y_1 - Y_0},$$

where T_1 is the tax liability for income Y_1, and T_0 is the tax liability for income Y_0 with $Y_1 > Y_0$. This measure of progression, mentioned by Pigou

[7, p. 65], is here referred to as average rate progression; it may also be written as

$$\frac{1}{Y_1}\,(M_{1-0} - A_0),$$

where A_0 is the average rate of tax for income Y_0, and M_{1-0} is the rate of tax applicable to the marginal income $Y_1 - Y_0$. Average rate progression is equal to zero when the tax is proportional, positive when the tax is progressive, and negative when the tax is regressive.

Average tax progression, which measures the rate of change of the average rate of tax, may also be written as

$$\frac{d}{dY}\left(\frac{f(Y)}{Y}\right),$$

where infinitesimal changes in Y are considered, and T is expressed as a continuous function of Y. Thus, average rate progression measures the slope of a curve obtained by plotting on an arithmetic scale the average rate of tax against the taxpayer's net income (before exemptions). This relationship is shown in Fig. 11.2. Several observations may be drawn from it.

Since the slope of the average rate curve is not the same throughout the income range, it is evident that the degree of progression differs at various

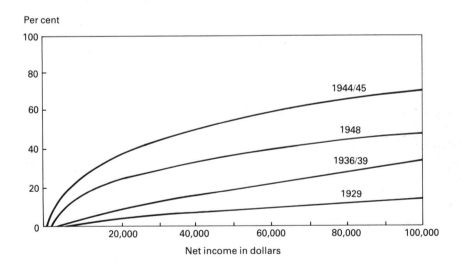

Figure 11.2: Average rates applicable in various income years

income points or over various income ranges. Therefore we cannot express the degree of progression for different points or ranges by the use of a constant coefficient, such as could be applied if the slope were the same throughout the income range.[2] Fig. 11.2 also shows that the slope of the average rate curve declines more or less continuously. That is, average rate progression at successive points in the income scale tends to fall when moving up the scale. This tendency for progression to decline is readily explained. The rate structure of a progressive income tax is subject to the condition that the marginal rate rises throughout the income range until a peak rate is reached which for ordinary-type income taxes cannot exceed 100 per cent and may fall far short of this level. It follows that the differential between the marginal and the average rate tends to fall when moving up the income scale; and hence average rate progression, obtained by dividing this more or less decreasing difference by increasing income, tends to decrease as income increases.

Consider now changes in the degree of progression at any one point in the income scale, which result when moving from one rate structure to another. From our definition of average rate progression, it follows that the degree of progression is unchanged for all points in the income scale if the average rate is raised or lowered throughout by the same *number* of percentage points, that is, if there is a parallel shift in the average rate curve.[3] In the case of increased yield requirements, for instance, a taxpayer who previously paid 20 per cent may now pay 23 per cent, and a taxpayer who previously paid 70 per cent may now pay 73 per cent, assuming the three-point increase to meet the requirement for increased yield. Similarly, average rate progression is increased if the increment in percentage points rises when moving up the income scale,[4] or decreased, if the increment in percentage points falls. In the case of yield decline, the situation is reversed: progression is increased if the decrement in percentage points falls with rising incomes, and it is decreased if the decrement rises.[5]

Changes in average rate progression, accordingly, may be analysed in terms of incremental average rates, obtained by deducting the rates applicable in earlier years from those applicable later on. Incremental rates imposed by successive Revenue Acts are shown in Fig. 11.3. The incremental rates obtained by deducting the rates applicable in 1930/31 from those applicable in 1934/35 rose with rising income. Hence the increase in rates tended to result in increased point progression throughout the income scale. Rates applicable in 1936/39 exceeded those for 1934/35 in the high income range only, but again incremental rates were increasing. The increase in rates applicable in 1940 over those applicable in 1936/39 for the first time involved an incremental rate which was declining over part of the income scale. The incremental rate rose for incomes up to about $85,000 but declined beyond this point. That is, average rate progression was increased for the larger part of the income range but was reduced for incomes above the $85,000 level. The picture was similar for the increase in rates applicable in 1941 over those applicable in 1940, although in this case the point beyond which incremental rates declined was moved down to

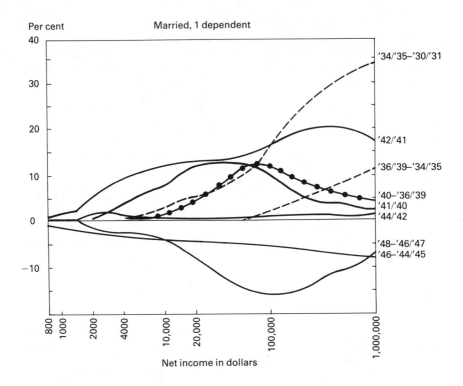

Figure 11.3: Incremental average rates of tax

about $40,000. The major wartime increase in rates applicable in 1942/43 again raised progression sharply for all but the very top incomes, while the new rates applicable in 1944/45 brought little further change except for increased progression at the bottom of the scale. The lowering of rates applicable in 1946/47 involved decremental rates which rose when moving up the scale and thus reduced progression throughout. The reduction applicable in 1948 again reduced progression for incomes up to $100,000 but increased progression beyond this point.

Considering successive rate changes during the 1930s, we thus find that average rate progression was increased at all points in the income scale but, beginning with 1940, we have noted a tendency for incremental rates to decline above a certain point in the scale. This tendency reflects hesitancy to permit marginal (and eventually average) rates to reach levels which are considered excessive for various points in the scale. After rates applicable in the higher income ranges have reached substantial levels, less leeway remains for further increases in these rates and relatively greater reliance comes to be placed upon the next lower income ranges. The larger the ratio of required yield to taxable income, the greater will tend to be the share contributed by the lower incomes, a process which is accentuated by the fact that the size of the tax base widens out toward the bottom. The relatively high level of top-bracket surtax rates which had already been reached by the end of the thirties, combined with the additional yield requirements for war financing, set the stage for further rate increases which involved falling incremental rates and hence declining progression for at least part of the income range.

Table 11.1: *Coefficients of average rate progression for selected income ranges*

Net income before exemp- tions (in $1000)	Revenue Acts applicable in			
	1929	1936/39	1944/45	1948
2–4	.005	.350	4.075	3.900
4–6	.060	.500	1.750	1.350
6–8	.035	.500	1.400	.950
8–10	.150	.550	1.250	.650
10–20	.190	.380	1.110	.540
20–40	.190	.355	.720	.460
40–60	.165	.280	.430	.350
60–100	.118	.298	.268	.220
100–200	.042	.153	.117	.125
200–400	.011	.053	.034	.054
400–600	.004	.030	.011	.012
600–1,000	.002	.012	.003	.013

Numerical values for average rate progression are shown in Table 11.1. The coefficients of progression have been computed for certain income ranges rather than points of income. This is preferable for technical reasons and also more significant in assessing rate developments.[6] The coefficients of progression on the whole tend to fall when moving up the income scale.[7] Considering the change from the 1929 to the 1936/39 schedules, we find that progression increased for all the ranges shown, and the same applies to all but the five top ranges in the 1936/39 to 1944/45 adjustment. In the post-war rate reduction, finally, progression is reduced for all but the four top ranges.

MARGINAL RATE PROGRESSION

Our first measure of progression referred to the rate of change in the average rate of tax. As an alternative, we might consider the *rate of change in the marginal rate* of tax, a second measure of progression suggested by

Pigou. This coefficient of progression, here referred to as marginal rate progression, is defined as

$$\frac{\dfrac{T_2 - T_1}{Y_2 - Y_1} - \dfrac{T_1 - T_0}{Y_1 - Y_0}}{Y_2 - Y_1}$$

where Y_2 is slightly in excess of Y_1, and Y_1 is slightly in excess of Y_0. The coefficient may be re-written as

$$\frac{M_{2-1} - M_{1-0}}{Y_2 - Y_1} \ .$$

A proportional tax structure is again indicated by a coefficient of zero, a progressive structure by a positive coefficient, and a regressive structure by a negative coefficient.[8] Assuming the marginal rate curve to be a smooth line and considering infinitesimal changes in income, marginal rate progression may be expressed as

$$\frac{d^2}{dY^2} \, [f(Y)] \ ,$$

which measures the slope of the marginal rate curves similar to those shown in Fig. 11.4 but smoothed out.

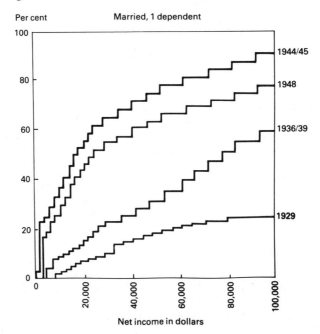

Figure 11.4: Marginal rates applicable in various income years

From previously-noted properties of rate structure it follows that marginal as well as average rate progression will tend to decline when moving up the income scale. From Fig. 11.4 we find that the slopes of the marginal rate schedules (assuming a trend to be drawn through the bracket steps) tend to flatten out with rising incomes. Next we return to a comparison between the patterns of progression under different rate schedules. We again have the principle that progression remains unchanged if the schedule is shifted parallel, that is, in this case, if the marginal rate of tax is raised or lowered by an equal number of percentage points all along the line. Examples of incremental marginal rates from which changes in marginal rate progression may be determined are given in Fig. 11.5. Again we note a tendency for incremental marginal rates to decrease beyond a certain point in the income scale. The explanation is similar to that offered in the preceding discussion of incremental average rates.

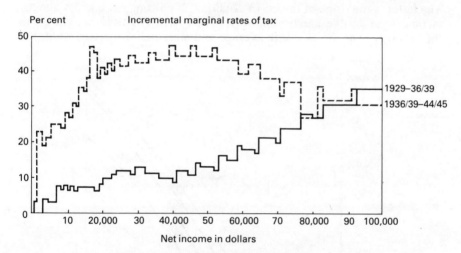

Figure 11.5: Incremental marginal rates of tax

LIABILITY PROGRESSION

We now consider a measure of progression, here referred to as liability progression, which is based on changes in the amount of tax liability. It is defined as the *ratio of the percentage change in tax liability to the concurrent percentage change in income*. Analogous to price elasticity, liability progression may be written as

$$\frac{T_1 - T_0}{T_0} \cdot \frac{Y_0}{Y_1 - Y_0} \, ,$$

which is equal to M_{1-0}/A_0.[9] The coefficient will equal 1 where the tax is proportional, exceed 1 where the tax is progressive, and fall short of 1 where the tax is regressive. The new coefficient is wholly compatible with our initial definition of progression and regression in terms of rising and falling average rate.[10]

Considering small changes in income, liability progression may also be expressed as

$$\frac{d\,f(Y)}{d(Y)} \cdot \frac{Y}{f(Y)}$$

or

$$\frac{d \log f(Y)}{d \log Y}.$$

The latter is the slope of the curve obtained by plotting tax liability against income on a double logarithmic scale. Such liability curves are shown in Fig. 11.6. As was the case with average and marginal rate progression, the

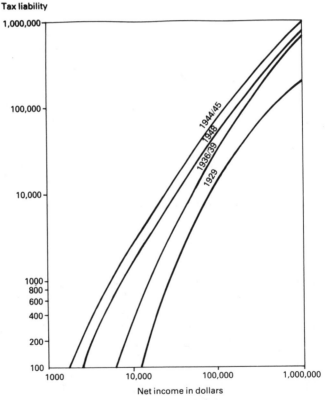

Figure 11.6: Relation of tax liability to income

degree of progression again tends to decline when moving up the income scale. That is to say, the slopes of the liability curves flatten out, and it follows from the formula why this should be the case.[11]

Turning to changes in the pattern of progression between different Revenue Acts, we now have the rule that liability progression will remain the same at all points in the income scale if there is an equal *proportionate* change in average rates all along the line. In other words, the liability curves plotted on a double logarithmic scale must be shifted in a parallel fashion. For instance, a taxpayer who formerly paid 20 per cent now pays 22 per cent, and a taxpayer who formerly paid 70 per cent now pays 77 per cent, assuming the required increase in yield to be met by this 10 per cent rise in rates. For an increase in yield, the rate structure becomes more (less) progressive if the proportionate increase in average rate rises (falls) with rising incomes, and the reverse relationship holds for a decline in rates.

We have seen previously that the upward changes in rate structure enacted during the 1930s and the war years were such, in most instances, as to raise the average rate by a greater *number* of percentage points for large than for small incomes. Hence, we found that average rate progression at given points in the income scale tended to rise with successive Revenue Acts during the 1930s and war years. These same rate adjustments, however, tended to result in *fractional* increases in average rates which were less for large than for small incomes, and liability progression, consequently, tended to decline over the same period. These contrary results are not surprising if one considers that slight advances in the number of percentage points at the bottom of the income scale, where initial rates are low, involve rather substantial fractional increases; at the same time, even substantial additions to the number of percentage points

Table 11.2: Coefficients of liability progression for selected income ranges

Net income before exemp-	Revenue Acts applicable in			
tions (in $1000)	1929	1936/39	1944/45	1948
2–4	3.000	3.000	2.092	2.522
4–6	4.518	2.813	1.485	1.579
6–8	2.467	2.219	1.463	1.497
8–10	4.285	2.465	1.559	1.374
10–20	2.475	1.808	1.451	1.381
20–40	2.029	1.748	1.427	1.452
40–60	1.952	1.772	1.373	1.506
60–100	1.598	1.807	1.309	1.391
100–200	1.345	1.485	1.200	1.305
200–400	1.147	1.255	1.109	1.218
400–600	1.083	1.199	1.054	1.065
600–1,000	1.050	1.139	1.037	1.146

at the top of the scale, where initial rates are high, will involve relatively small fractional increases. The same principle repeats itself with regard to post-war rate reductions. These reductions tended to increase liability progression, since percentage cuts in average rates were less for the high than for the low incomes. As noted before, they also resulted in reduced average rate progression, since top-bracket rates were reduced by a larger number of percentage points than bottom-bracket rates.

Numerical values for liability progression are shown in Table 11.2.[12] For reasons previously noted, the numerical values again are given for selected income ranges rather than for points of income. The table shows that liability progression tends to fall off when moving from lower to higher income ranges. It also reveals that the coefficient of progression for given income ranges tends to decline when comparing successive Revenue Acts during the 1930s and the war years and to rise when considering the post-war rate reduction.

RESIDUAL INCOME PROGRESSION

In the preceding section the degree of progression was measured as the ratio of percentage change in tax liability to the percentage change in income. Instead, the degree of progression may be measured as the *ratio of the percentage change in income after tax to the percentage change in income before tax*. This new measure of progression, here referred to as residual income progression, is defined as

$$\frac{(Y_1 - T_1) - (Y_0 - T_0)}{Y_0 - T_0} \cdot \frac{Y_0}{Y_1 - Y_0},$$

which may also be written as $(1 - M_{1-0})/(1 - A_0)$.[13] A proportional rate of tax will again give a coefficient of 1; but, as is easily seen from the formula, progression in this case is indicated by a coefficient of less than 1, while regression is expressed by a coefficient of over 1. Again, this measure of progression is fully compatible with our initial definitions of progression and regression.[14]

For small changes in income, residual income progression may also be written as

$$\frac{d[Y - f(Y)]}{dY} \cdot \frac{Y}{Y - f(Y)}$$

or

$$\frac{d \log [Y - f(Y)]}{d \log Y}.$$

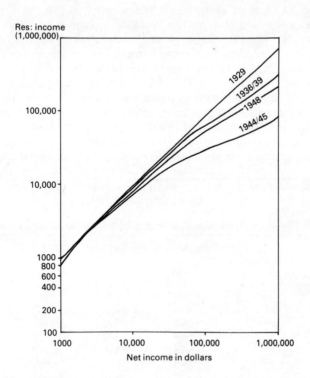

Figure 11.7: Relation of residual income to income

The latter is the slope of the curve obtained by plotting income after tax against income on a double logarithmic scale. Such residual income curves are shown in Fig. 11.7.

Moving up the income scale under any one rate structure, the results in the case of residual income progression are opposite to those obtained with the three preceding measures. Whereas these all registered declining progression with rising income, residual income progression increases when moving up the income scale. Increased progression is now reflected by a falling slope of the residual income curve in Fig. 11.7. The tendency for residual income progression to rise extends up to a very high point in the income scale; beyond this point, when the marginal rate approaches constancy, residual income progression begins to fall.[15]

Again we turn to changes in progression at given points in the income scale which result when moving from one rate schedule to another. For residual income progression to remain constant at all points in the income scale there must be an equal proportionate change in residual income all along the line. The residual income curves plotted on a double logarithmic scale (Fig. 11.7) must again be shifted parallel. An increase in yield will require a downward shift in the residual income curve and vice versa. Inspection of Fig. 11.7 shows that the downward shift in the residual income curve tended to be greater throughout for larger than for smaller incomes. That is, residual income progression tended to rise throughout the 1930s and the war years. The picture is thus similar to that provided by average and marginal rate progression except that in this case the continuous increase in progression extends into very high income ranges. The changes in residual income progression brought about by the post-war rate reductions are also similar to those in average rate progression. The percentage increase in residual incomes as well as the decrease in the number of average rate points was greater on the whole for larger than for smaller incomes, and both types of progression declined accordingly.

Table 11.3: *Coefficients of residual income progression for selected income ranges*

Net income before exemptions (in $1000)	Revenue Acts applicable in			
	1929	1936/39	1944/45	1948
2–4	.999	.999	.842	.845
4–6	.999	.976	.897	.927
6–8	.998	.999	.888	.924
8–10	.998	.999	.831	.935
10–20	.973	.945	.791	.911
20–40	.946	.896	.649	.833
40–60	.920	.831	.545	.736
60–100	.900	.690	.427	.708
100–200	.929	.646	.343	.636
200–400	.963	.694	.371	.583
400–600	.978	.689	.575	.846
600–1,000	.986	.729	.640	.567

Numerical values for residual income progression are shown in Table 11.3.[16] With the exception of the very top of the scale, the coefficients tend to rise (i.e. progression tends to fall) when moving from lower to higher income ranges under any one rate structure. Comparing successive Revenue Acts during the 1930s and the war years, the coefficients tend to fall (progression to increase) for all ranges shown. In the post-war rate reduction the coefficients increase (progression declines) except for the very top of our ranges.

EFFECTIVE PROGRESSION

All the above measures of progression belong to the same family. They are merely different mathematical expressions of the relationship between income and tax. We now turn to a quite different approach where the degree of progression depends not only upon the rate structure but also upon the distribution of income.

The new measure of progression, here referred to as effective progression, measures the extent to which a given tax structure results in a *shift in the distribution of income toward equality*.[17] As suggested by Gini, the coefficient of equality may be expressed with reference to a Lorenz distribution as the ratio of (1) the area limited by the x axis, the income distribution line and a vertical line at the point indicating 100 per cent of income recipients, to (2) the area limited by the x axis, the diagonal and the same vertical line. Effective progression is then expressed as E_a/E_b, where E_a is the coefficient of equality of the distribution of income after tax and E_b is the coefficient applicable before tax. Effective progression will be equal to 1 where the tax structure is proportional, exceed 1 in the case of progression, and fall short of 1 in the case of regression. The measure is again compatible with our initial definition of progression and regression.

The degree of effective progression of a given rate structure depends upon the distribution of income to which it is applied. If the distribution of income before tax is perfectly equal, both a proportional and a highly progressive rate structure will have coefficients of effective progression equal to 1. If the income distribution before tax is assumed to be unequal, the coefficient of progression for the progressive rate structure will rise above 1. The less equal is the distribution of income before tax, the more potent will be a progressive tax structure in equalising income. Moreover, effective progression depends upon the general level of rates as well as upon the steepness of the rate structure as such. If we move from a lower to a higher yield structure, both of which have the same average rate progression at all points in the income scale, the degree of effective progression will increase. Also, the shift to a higher rate structure may involve increased effective progression even though there is some decline in average rate progression. Conversely, effective progression will fall off when moving toward a lower yield level while maintaining average rate progression, and it may decline even though average rate progression rises somewhat. The matter is different, however, for residual income progression. If residual income progression remains unchanged, effective progression remains constant as well; and, if residual income progression changes, effective progression will necessarily move in the same direction though the rate of change may differ.

Effective progression also differs from our preceding measures of structural progression in that it is useful primarily for measuring the degree of progression of the rate structure as a whole, whereas structural progression is applicable to specific points of income or income ranges only. Effective progression may also be applied to smaller income ranges; but, since it refers to changes in income distribution, it is not applicable to a mere income point.

No attempts are made in this connection to furnish quantitative measures of effective progression. In order to calculate such coefficients, the

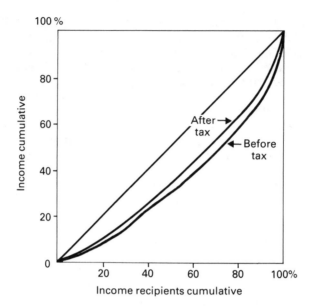

Figure 11.8: Distribution of income before and after 1948 tax

various Revenue Acts must be applied to the same basic income distribution. This procedure is subject to considerable error and may yield misleading results, since the coefficient of equality is rather insensitive to changes in distribution. This may be seen readily from experimentation with Lorenz distributions and can be illustrated with reference to the present situation. Using a recent set of estimates of income distribution, it appears that the coefficient of equality for the distribution of income before tax is .853. The coefficient of equality after tax is .872; and the coefficient of progression, accordingly, is 1.022. The coefficient of progression which, with the given distribution of income before tax, would make for a completely equal distribution of income after tax is 1.17. The two distributions before and after the 1948 tax are shown in Fig. 11.8. Distributions obtained by applying the 1929 and 1936/39 rate structures would fall between the two distribution lines there shown, whereas the line for income after 1945 tax rates would probably fall slightly to the left of the 1948 line.

POLICY IMPLICATIONS

So far we have been concerned with the mathematical properties of various measures of progression. It remains to consider their significance for policy purposes.

Some definite observations may be made regarding the merits of our various measures from the point of view of special interest groups. Let us assume that there is to be a change in the level of yield, and, to simplify matters, let the taxpayers be divided into two groups representing the 'rich' and the 'poor', respectively. Each group will want the change in yield to involve a shift in the burden distribution which is in its own interest. Yet, as a matter of political strategy, each group will wish to place its proposal in as moderate a light as possible. That is, each group will wish to minimise the apparent deviation of its proposal from the prevailing degree of progression.

This in turn determines each group's preference between the various measures of structural progression. If the change is one of yield increase, it follows from our preceding discussion that the interest of the high-income group will be served best by adopting the concept of average rate progression. Its further order of preference will be for marginal rate progression and liability progression, with residual income progression giving the least favourable results. The preference of the low-income group, of course, will be in the reverse order. It follows also that what is the rich man's order of preference for rate increase is the poor man's order of preference for rate reduction, and vice versa.

The political implications of various definitions of progression are brought out quite neatly in the [1947] debate on income tax reduction. Treasury representatives and their supporters objected to an across-the-board percentage cut in tax rates because this would decrease the progressivity of the income tax. They insisted that, in order to hold progression constant, rates would have to be cut by an equal number of percentage points [12]. Representatives of the Congressional majority and their proponents insisted that to maintain progression it was necessary to reduce rates by an equal fraction of percentage points [12], [13]. Each party then preferred the reduction pattern compatible with its definition of progression.

If we are to say which interpretation of progression is the 'correct' one, a broader context is needed. Public policy, evidently, cannot rest on preferences between mathematical formulae. One frame of reference is supplied by the traditional equity theory which lays down certain rules for the distribution of the tax burden. To implement the rules, two steps are involved. First, it is necessary to choose between various formulations of the equity condition, such as equal, equal proportional, or equal marginal sacrifice. Second, it is necessary to find the shape of each taxpayer's income utility curve and to assume that the utility curves of various individuals are comparable. Given these conditions, it is then possible to determine the rate structure which, for any given distribution of income and level of yield, will result in a 'proper' burden allocation. If there is to be a change in yield, it is similarly possible to derive the 'proper' changes in rate structure.

The above dispute thus reduces itself to the question whether the 'proper' burden distribution is maintained if rates are cut so as to hold average rate progression constant or so as to hold liability progression constant. When it is assumed that the burden distribution prior to the rate cut is not the 'proper' one, it is obviously impossible to give a general answer. Similarly, there is clearly no general answer if different taxpayers are assumed to have different income utility curves. However, let us suppose that the initial burden distribution is the 'proper' one, 'proper', that is, in terms of equal or equal proportional sacrifice. Suppose also that the same utility curve may be applied to all taxpayers. Even then it appears, subject to some very special cases, that *changes in rate structure required to change the level of yield in conformity with the equity conditions will involve changes in the pattern of progression, whichever of our definitions of progression is used.* The Treasury position that average rate progression is the only logical measure and the Congressional majority view that equity considerations require maintenance of liability progression are both mistaken. To be sure, if the 'correct' rate structure applicable prior to the rate reduction was progressive, it is most likely that a 'correct' downward adjustment will also require a drop in average rate progression, i.e. a greater reduction in the number of percentage points for higher incomes. Yet it does not follow that the cut in the number of percentage points for higher incomes should exceed that for lower incomes in the very pattern which would maintain liability progression unchanged. Depending upon the conditions involved (such as the amount of change in yield, the distribution of income, and the shape of the income utility curve), the number of points differential in the rate reduction for high and low incomes may well deviate from this pattern.[18]

The assumptions involved in this type of argument, moreover, are hardly realistic. The burden distribution prior to the adjustment may well not be the 'correct' one. And if the relative burden imposed upon one part of the income range is too high or too low initially, there is no reason why an adjustment to a more proper burden distribution might not be secured in the context of a reduction as well as an increase in yield. Quite apart from this, it is most doubtful whether the traditional theory of equity can be applied in this fashion. The assumption of identical income utility curves is most precarious, and it is only on the basis of this assumption that a general answer can be obtained. Indeed, the much narrower framework of modern welfare economics rejects the very notion of inter-personal utility comparisons, and, if this view is adopted, the very basis of equity theory is lost.[19]

The concept of effective progression, perhaps, provides a more useful if less subtle approach. While the various measures of structural progression are merely technical devices which have no economic significance as such, effective progression furnishes a direct measure of the equalising effects of a tax; and this, after all, is the essence of any progression policy. Effective progression as here defined, however, is an approximation only. One and the same coefficient of progression may reflect quite different patterns of change between the distributions of income before and after tax. Yet, it is certainly significant to know whether the equalising effect has occurred among, say, the upper two quarters of income recipients or among the upper and lower half. Given adequate data, it will be desirable to supplement the coefficient of effective progression by measures which permit a more detailed comparison between the various income distributions, such as the percentage of income received by various quartiles of recipients.

NOTES

1. If tax liability T is expressed as a function of income Y as $T = f(Y)$, the average rate of tax is equal to $[f(Y)]/Y$, and increases, remains constant, or decreases as

$$\frac{d}{dY}\left(\frac{f(Y)}{Y}\right) \text{ is } \gtreqless 0.$$

$$\frac{d}{dY}\left(\frac{f(Y)}{Y}\right) = \frac{1}{Y^2}\left[Yf'(Y) - f(Y)\right]$$

$$= \frac{1}{Y}\left[f'(Y) - \frac{f(Y)}{Y}\right]$$

$$= \frac{1}{Y}(M - A),$$

where $M = f'(Y)$, and $A = [f(Y)]/Y$. Therefore, $[f(Y)]/Y$ increases, remains constant, or decreases as $(M - A) \gtreqless 0$.

2. Provided that a curve may be fitted to the rate structure, one may develop a more complex expression from which progression can be measured at various points in the income scale by substituting the corresponding values of income.

3. If the average rate function prior to change is $(f(Y))/Y$, the new function equals

$$\frac{f(Y)}{Y} + k.$$

The new degree of progression is equal to

$$\frac{d}{dY}\left(\frac{f(Y)}{Y} + k\right) = \frac{d}{dY}\left(\frac{f(Y)}{Y}\right),$$

which is the old degree of progression. The text discussion disregards certain difficulties encountered at the bottom of the income scale if it is assumed that there is an equal change in the number of percentage points throughout. In the case of rate reduction, this assumption implies an increase in exemptions, and (short of making the very unrealistic assumption of negative rates) this means reduced progression for incomes now released from tax. Similarly, for rate increases we have a reduction in exemption which will result in increased progression for the newly included incomes. This difficulty does not arise in connection with liability progression and residual income progression. Slitor [11, p. 310, n. 4] overlooks the fact that exemptions must rise if the average rate is reduced by an equal number of points throughout. Therefore, progression will remain constant (except for the incomes now released) and will not decline as suggested by Slitor.

4. The new average rate function in this case, for instance, may become

$$\frac{f(Y)}{Y} + k\,Y,$$

where $k > 0$. The new degree of progression then equals

$$\frac{d}{d\,Y}\left(\frac{f(Y)}{Y} + k\,Y\right) = \frac{d}{d\,Y}\left(\frac{f\,(Y)}{Y}\right) + k,$$

and is, therefore, greater than the old degree of progression.

5. The latter is the case when, in note 7 $k < 0$.

6. From the formula $1/Y\,(M - A)$ it is seen that progression depends upon the marginal as well as the average rate. Since the marginal rate rises by bracket steps, the movement of point progression, while generally downward, is in a zigzag line. This introduces an arbitrary element into comparison between progressions at different income points. For comparison between different Revenue Acts the results in terms of point progression suffer from the fact that the marginal rate corresponding to an average rate at any given point in the scale depends upon the entire preceding rate structure. Hence the relationship between $(M - A)$ at one single point in the scale cannot be compared for successive Revenue Acts.

7. Because the results are affected by the ranges chosen, this does not hold throughout, especially at the beginning of the scale. If point progression is used, the coefficient will fall throughout, though, as noted, the decline will be in a zigzag fashion.

8. The basic definition of progression as an increasing average rate is compatible with the definition of progression as an increasing marginal rate only under the condition that the marginal rate is continuously rising (at a decreasing rate) when moving up the income scale. Since the marginal rate does not rise continuously but steps up by income brackets, we have certain income ranges for which the rate structure is proportional according to the marginal rate progression, while it is progressive according to the average rate progression. The fact that this holds even for the first bracket is due to the existence of exemptions. If we disregard the brackets and think of 'marginal rate trend', this difficulty disappears.

Shun-Hsin Chou [1] attempts to prove mathematically that average rate progression and marginal rate progression are necessarily compatible without posing the condition of a continuously rising marginal rate. This is not the case, because the marginal rate curve may obviously decline while average rate rises. Shun-Hsin Chou's conclusion rests on the erroneous assumption that, if a variable is greater than another variable, the derivatives of the respective variables must necessarily stand in the same relationship.

9. Liability progression equals

$$\frac{d\,f(Y)}{d\,Y}\frac{Y}{f\,(Y)} = \frac{\dfrac{d\,f(Y)}{d\,Y}}{\dfrac{f\,(Y)}{Y}} = \frac{M}{A}.$$

10. It can be proved that if

$$\frac{d}{dY}\left(\frac{f(Y)}{Y}\right) \gtreqless 0,$$

then

$$f'(Y)\frac{Y}{f(Y)} \gtreqless 1,$$

for

$$\frac{d}{dY}\left(\frac{f(Y)}{Y}\right)$$

$$= \frac{1}{Y^2}\{Yf'(Y) - f(Y)\} \gtreqless 0,$$

that is,

$$\frac{Yf'(Y)}{f(Y)} - 1 \gtreqless 0$$

or

$$\frac{Yf'(Y)}{f(Y)} \gtreqless 1.$$

11. M/A will fall as long as $(\Delta M)/(\Delta A) < M/A$, where ΔM and ΔA are increments to M and A, when moving up the income scale. This is clearly the case for the entire income scale as a whole, because $M > A$ at the beginning and $M = A$ at the end. However, it is possible that $(\Delta M)/(\Delta A) > M/A$ for some point of the income range, especially if the marginal rate curve is not a smooth curve but rises in abrupt brackets.

12. Using a measure of arc elasticity, the formula for residual income progression becomes

$$\frac{(Y_1 - T_1) - (Y_0 - T_0)}{Y_1 - Y_0}$$

$$\times \frac{Y_1 + Y_0}{(Y_1 - T_1) + (Y_0 - T_0)}.$$

13. Residual income progression equals

$$\frac{Y}{Y - f(Y)}\frac{d}{dY}[Y - f(Y)]$$

$$= \frac{Y}{Y - f(Y)}[1 - f'(Y)]$$

$$= \frac{1 - f'(Y)}{1 - \dfrac{f(Y)}{Y}}$$

$$= \frac{1 - M}{1 - A}.$$

Another possible measure of degree of progression is the rate of change in residual rate, which equals

$$\frac{d}{dY}\left(1 - \frac{f(Y)}{Y}\right)$$

$$= -\frac{d}{dY}\left(\frac{d(Y)}{Y}\right),$$

which is numerically equal but opposite in sign to average rate progression.

14. It can be shown that if

$$\frac{d}{dY}\left(\frac{f(Y)}{Y}\right) \gtreqless 0,$$

then

$$\frac{1 - f'(Y)}{1 - \dfrac{f(Y)}{Y}} \lesseqgtr 1.$$

$$\frac{d}{dY}\left(\frac{f(Y)}{Y}\right)$$

$$= \frac{1}{Y^2}[Yf'(Y) - f(Y)] \gtreqless 0,$$

$$-f(Y) \lesseqgtr -Yf'(Y)$$

$$Y - f(Y) \lesseqgtr Y - Yf'(Y)$$

$$1 - \frac{f(Y)}{Y} \lesseqgtr 1 - f'(Y)$$

$$\frac{1 - f'(Y)}{1 - \dfrac{f(Y)}{Y}} \lesseqgtr 1.$$

15. $(1 - M)/(1 - A)$ will fall if $(\Delta M)/(\Delta A) > (1 - M)/(1 - A)$, where ΔM and ΔA are as defined in note 14. Now for a progressive tax $(1 - M)/(1 - A)$ is always less than

1, because M/A is always greater than 1. However, at the beginning of the income scale $(\Delta M)/(\Delta A)$ is likely to be greater than 1 (the marginal rate being stepped up quickly), whereas later on it falls below 1 (the marginal rate leading the average rate in approaching the maximum). Thus $(1 - M)/(1 - A)$ falls first and then rises. If we consider the entire income scale, the net result will be a rise in $(1 - M)/(1 - A)$, since A is zero at the beginning but approaches M at the end of the scale. The marginal rate flattens out at an earlier point so that $(\Delta M)/(\Delta A)$ rapidly approaches zero. Note, however, that the point at which $(\Delta M)/(\Delta A)$ falls below 1 is *not* the point at which $(1 - M)/(1 - A)$ starts to increase, the actual turning-point being at a somewhat lower income, where $(\Delta M)/(\Delta A)$ begins to fall below $(1 - M)/(1 - A)$.

16. Using a measure of arc elasticity, the formula for liability progression becomes

$$\frac{T_1 - T_0}{Y_1 - Y_0} \cdot \frac{Y_1 + Y_0}{T_1 + T_0}.$$

17. For a somewhat similar definition of progression see Dalton [2, p. 153].
18. Pigou [7, pp. 97 ff.] discusses certain general relationships between equity rules and progression formulas. To meet the condition of equal marginal sacrifice, we need only know that the income utility curve is downward-sloping. In the other cases the slope must be known. Thus, Pigou shows that the condition of equal proportional sacrifice leads to a progressive rate structure as long as the income utility curve is downward-sloping, while the condition of equal sacrifice requires a progressive rate structure only if the income utility curve is inclined more steeply than a rectangular hyperbola. In both cases the required *degree* of progression (following any one definition) will depend upon the slope. And Pigou notes that, given the equal sacrifice rule, a change in yield will require the same fractional change in rates for all incomes only if the 'proper' rate is proportional to begin with, i.e. if the income utility curve is of unit elasticity. In all other cases the required change in the rate structure will involve different fractional changes for different incomes.

    Changes in rate structure required to adjust for changes in yields, in conformance with equal proportional sacrifice and on the assumption that the initial rate structure was 'proper', are discussed by Preinreich [9].
19. Lerner's solution [6, p. 30] rejects the assumption of identical or known income utility curves but retains the assumption of downward-sloping and comparable curves. By adding the assumption that there is an equal probability, as between any two taxpayers, that one or the other has the 'higher' curve, Lerner concludes that there is a case on probability grounds in favour of an equal distribution. If this approach is accepted, a solution for the 'proper' burden distribution is readily obtained where the equity criterion is stated in terms of equal marginal sacrifice, but the information assumed in the Lerner model is not sufficient to give a solution for the equal or equal proportional sacrifice formulations.

REFERENCES

[1] Chou, S. (1945) *The Capital Levy* (New York: King's Crown Press).
[2] Dalton, H. (1936) *Principles of Public Finance* (London: Routledge), p. 153.
[3] Fisher, I. (1906) *The Nature of Capital and Income* (New York: Macmillan).

[4] Keynes, J. (1936) *The General Theory of Employment, Interest and Money* (New York: Harcourt Brace).

[5] Lerner, A. (1943) 'Functional Finance and the Federal Debt', *Social Research*, 10.

[6] —— (1944) *Economics of Control* (New York: Macmillan), p. 30.

[7] Pigou, A. C. (1928) *A Study in Public Finance* (London: Macmillan).

[8] —— (1932) *The Economics of Welfare* (London: Macmillan).

[9] Preinreich, G. (1948) 'Progressive Taxation and Sacrifice', *American Economic Review,* 38.

[10] Simons, H. (1938) *Personal Income Taxation* (Chicago: University of Chicago Press).

[11] Slitor, R. (1948) 'The Measurement of Progressivity and Built-In Flexibility', *Quarterly Journal of Economics*, 62.

[12] US Senate Committee on Finance (1947) *Individual Income Tax Reduction*, pp. 18, 99–103, 167, 523.

[13] US House of Representatives, Committee on Ways and Means (1947) Report no. 180, p. 8.

12 On Incidence*
1953

The purpose of this paper is to compare the incidence of excise and of income taxes in a general equilibrium setting. This is not an easy proposition. Lest we get lost at the outset, it will be useful to begin our analysis with the simple case of an all-consumption economy. Thereafter, we proceed to a somewhat more realistic setting of a neoclassical model where capital formation is allowed for. The final and more complex case of a liquidity preference model is considered but briefly at this time.

INCIDENCE IN THE ALL-CONSUMPTION MODEL

First, it will be well to define some terms used in the following discussion. In studying the 'incidence' and 'effects' of taxation, we begin with a state of equilibrium containing a given structure of taxes and of public expenditures as an integral part. Now some changes in budget policy are made, adjustments occur, and a new equilibrium is reached; and we compare the old with the new situation.

In appraising the total change that has occurred, various aspects of change may be distinguished. Thus, we shall want to know whether resources have been transferred between public and private use. This is a function of changes in public goods and service expenditures and may be referred to as 'resource transfer'. Also, we shall want to know what changes, if any, have occurred in the distribution of real income available for private use. This I refer to as 'incidence'. Finally, we shall want to know whether a change in total output has resulted. This one may refer to as 'output effects'. All three are interdependent but separately measurable aspects of the overall change. Whatever the merits of these particular definitions, at least they are free of the ambiguity which so frequently attaches to the term 'incidence' and 'effects' of taxation.

We may consider now various kinds of budget adjustment and measure the resulting changes in distribution or incidence. For instance, we may raise or lower tax yield, while holding public expenditures constant.[1] This I

* *The Journal of Political Economy* (1953), vol. LXI, No. 4.

refer to as 'absolute incidence'.[2] Or we may substitute one tax for another tax of equal yield. This I refer to as 'differential incidence'. Or we may trace the distributional change that results when taxes and expenditures are increased by equal amounts. This I refer to as 'balanced budget incidence'. Other combinations might be considered as well.[3] Any of these approaches is permissible and may have its use, provided it is followed through consistently.

Incidence a function of relative price change

Changes in the state of distribution which result from changes in tax policy depend on changes in *relative* factor and product prices. In an exchange economy each individual is linked to the market (1) by the price he obtains from the sale of his services, and (2) by the price he must pay for the products he purchases. When a change in tax policy is made, he may find his relative position changed on both the sources and the uses side of his budget.

On the sources side, he may find that his disposable income has changed, be it due to a change in his earnings or in his personal tax liabilities. On the uses side, he may find that the prices of the products which he purchases have changed, be it because of changes in cost due to changes in demand or because of changes in the taxation of products. When assessing the resulting change in any individual's position, we must account for changes in his position on both the sources and the uses side.

To illustrate, consider a situation in which there are two individuals, A and B, selling two factors n and m and buying two products x and y, respectively. Now A's position improves relative to that of B if the price of n rises relative to that of m and/or if the price of x falls relative to that of y; and the reverse relationships hold for B. If we wish to measure the change in A's income position, we may express the same as $\Delta R = \Delta E - \Delta T_p - Q_r \Delta P_r + Q_f \Delta P_f$. where ΔR is the change in real income, ΔE the change in earnings, ΔT_p the change in personal taxes, Q_r and Q_f the new amounts bought of products the prices of which have risen and fallen respectively, and ΔP_r and ΔP_f the respective decreases or increases in product prices.[4] Incidence measures changes in the distribution of income as defined in ΔR.

Relative price changes a function of tax discrimination

Next we note that changes in relative prices (and hence incidence) which follow particular changes in tax policy depend on the degree of generality or lack of generality (discrimination) which is inherent in particular taxes. This is the important factor, not whether we are concerned with income or with product taxes.

In the circular-flow system of our all-consumption model, all transactions may be divided into factor transactions and product transactions.[5] Any one tax will be assessed on one or the other type of transaction, but it may be general or it may be discriminatory in various respects.[6] The classification in Table 12.1 provides a useful point of departure.

Table 12.1 *Types of tax discrimination*

	Tax is applicable to			
	All sellers, all buyers	Some sellers, all buyers	Some buyers, all sellers	Some buyers, some sellers
Tax on products:				
all	1	5	9	13
some	2	6	10	14
Tax on factors:				
all	3	7	11	15
some	4	8	12	16

General Taxes. Consider first the incidence of general taxes. As shown in Table 12.1, there are two types of truly general taxes: item 1, which applies to all product transactions, and item 3, which applies to all factor transactions.

A first rule to be noted is that it is a matter of indifference whether such a tax is imposed on the seller's or on the buyer's side of the market. In the case of a tax on product transactions, it is a matter of indifference whether it takes the form of a general sales tax or a general spendings tax. In the case of a tax on all factor transactions, it is a matter of indifference whether it takes the form of an income tax or of a tax on factor purchases. Substitution of the spendings for the sales tax leaves the situation unchanged, as does substitution of the factor purchase for the income tax. This similarity, which was noted first by Edgeworth, holds for discriminatory as well as for general taxes but is of particular importance in the latter case.[7]

Second, and more interesting, we find that there is no difference between a tax on all *factor* transactions and a tax on all *product* transactions. Substitution of the one for the other will leave relative product and factor prices unchanged. While absolute prices may change as a result, relative values, and hence incidence, remain unchanged. Thus we arrive at the important conclusion that a truly general income and sales tax are identical in the all-consumption model.

Granted that truly general taxes on product and on factor transactions are identical, so that differential incidence is neutral, what can we say about the absolute incidence of such taxes? Once we pose the problem in these terms, assumptions must be made about public expenditures. Suppose that a general tax of this sort is introduced, while public expenditures are raised by the same amount. If we assume (*a*) that factor supplies are inelastic, (*b*) that the pattern of private demand does not change with the decline in income available for private use, and (*c*) that public demand is directed at precisely the resources released by private demand, we may conclude that the balanced budget incidence of such a tax-expenditure plan will leave relative positions unchanged. Absolute budget incidence in this case will be proportional.

How realistic are these assumptions? The assumption of inelastic factor supplies is not tenable for the case of a partial tax, but it may be fairly realistic in the present setting of a truly general tax. If the supplies of various factors are more or less elastic, relative rates of return—for example, wage rates paid for various skills—before tax will change in favour of the more elastic factor. Relative income positions, in this case, will change.[8] The assumption of a constant pattern of demand is not realistic. Individual preferences will change with a change in income available for private use, and the government's preference pattern is likely to differ from that of private purchasers. Thus changes in the pattern of demand will result and affect individual positions with regard to both uses and sources of income. However, under most circumstances we may expect such changes in individual positions to occur equally among individuals in all size brackets of income. To the extent that this is the case, such changes will affect individual positions but will not alter the size distribution of income by income brackets. In this sense of the term the incidence of the entire budget operation will remain proportional.[9]

Discriminatory Taxes. We now turn to the differential incidence of various discriminatory taxes. Let us begin with item 2, a tax on product transactions applicable to all transactors but to certain products only.

Substitution of such a tax for a general tax (be it item 1 or item 3 of Table 12.1) results in an increase in the price of taxed products relative to that of tax-free products. Also, it results in a reduction in the earnings of factors with a comparative advantage in the production of taxed products relative to factors with a comparative advantage in the production of tax-free products. In all, this will improve the income position of those whose preference patterns favour tax-free products and whose earnings are from factors directed primarily at the production of tax-free products. Also, it will worsen the income positions of those who are primarily consumers or suppliers of taxed products. There is reason to expect that incidence, in this case, will depend primarily on changes in income use (relative product prices) rather than in earnings (relative factor prices).[10]

Similar reasoning may be applied to item 4, which is a discriminatory tax on factor transactions. Here we find an improvement in the income position of those who supply tax-free factors and whose consumption patterns feature products primarily produced with tax-free factors. In this case adjustments on the earnings side are likely to be of major importance.[11]

The analysis may be expanded to allow for various types of discrimination against particular transactors. A tax on all product transactions (item 5) may be confined to corporations or chain stores. A tax on all factor transactions (item 7) may be confined to transactors with large incomes, as is the case with surtax rates under the income tax. Or we may combine various types of discriminations, as under a progressive income tax (discriminating against large incomes) which permits lower rates for capital gains (discriminating against earned income). At various stages of the analysis, pairs or families of equal-yield taxes may be established which, though different in their assessment base, give the same or rather similar result in terms of incidence. This is possible in particular if we define incidence not in terms of changes in individual positions but in the distribution of income (net of tax) by income brackets.[12] Thus a discriminatory product tax applicable to all transactors (for example, a sales tax on cigarettes) may be matched with a tax on income applicable to all income sources but subject to a scale of regression which will match the weight of cigarette outlays in budget patterns. On the other hand, it would be difficult or impossible to match a discriminatory product tax applicable to all transactors with a discriminatory factor tax applicable to all transactors. Depending upon prevailing interrelationships between earnings patterns and patterns of income use, matching may or may not be possible in various cases.

Absolute price adjustments

The entire discussion so far has been in terms of *relative* prices and earnings. This is indeed the important part of the problem. However, tax adjustments in the real world involve changes in absolute as well as relative prices, a calamity which has led to much confusion in the theory of incidence and, for that matter, in the treatment of taxes in the social accounts.

In our all-consumption model the quantity theory can be put to work. It is appropriate here to assume that the total money supply is in the form of transaction money and that the payments velocity of transaction money is fixed. Thus, the given money supply fixes the total volume of payments which can be performed. Assume now that government transactions (in taxes or expenditures) involve the same payment velocity as do private payments or stand in some fixed ratio to them. This permits us to determine what will happen to absolute prices or to the money supply as changes in budget policy are made. If such changes expand or contract the structure of payments while the money supply stays constant, a larger or a smaller total of transactions must be accommodated by the same volume of payments in money terms. To permit this, the unit of payment or the price level must adjust itself accordingly. This simple principle is illustrated in Table 12.2 for general taxes and in Table 12.3 for discriminatory taxes, it being assumed in both cases that transaction velocity for all transactions is equal to 20.

For the case of a *general tax*, we may assume a one-product economy and treat the private sector as a whole. We begin with the pre-budget situation shown in column 1 and introduce a budget. This budget is to permit the government to purchase four-tenths of total output and is to be financed by

Table 12.2 Price adjustments to general taxes

	Before tax	Income tax		Sales tax				
				Gov. purchases taxable		Gov. purchases tax-free		
		Constant money supply	Constant price level	Constant money supply	Tax added to price	Constant money supply	Public price constant	Private price constant
	(1)	(2)	(3)	(4)	(5)	(6)	(7)	(8)
Consumer sector, A's and B's transactions:								
1. Wages, in dollars	100.00	83.33	100.00	60.00	100.00	71.40	100.00	60.00
2. Income tax, in dollars		33.33	40.00					
3. Purchase payments in dollars	100.00	50.00	60.00	60.00	100.00	71.40	100.00	60.00
4. Price per unit, in dollars	1.00	0.83	1.00	1.00	1.66	1.19	1.66	1.00
5. Units bought	100	60	60	60	60	60	60	60
Business sector:								
6. Receipts from private sector, in dollars	100.00	50.00	60.00	60.00	100.00	71.40	100.00	60.00
7. Receipts from public sector, in dollars		33.33	40.00	40.00	66.66	28.56	40.00	24.00
8. Wage payments, in dollars	100.00	83.33	100.00	60.00	100.00	71.40	100.00	60.00
9. Gross receipts tax, in dollars				40.00	66.66	28.56	40.00	24.00
Government sector:								
10. Income tax receipts, in dollars		33.33	40.00					
11. Excise tax receipts, in dollars				30.00	66.66	28.56	40.00	24.00
12. Expenditures, in dollars		33.33	40.00	30.00	66.66	28.56	40.00	24.00
13. Price per unit, in dollars		0.83	1.00	1.00	1.66	0.71	1.00	0.60
14. Units bought		40	40	40	40	40	40	40

All sectors:

15. GNP (6+7), in dollars	100.00	83.33	100.00	166.66	100.00	140.00	84.00
16. Total payments (2+6+7+8+9), in dollars	200.00	200.00	240.00	333.33	200.00	280.00	168.00
17. Price level, average	1.00	0.83	1.00	1.66	1.00	1.40	0.84
18. Money supply, in dollars	10.00	10.00	12.00	16.66	10.00	14.00	8.40
19. Transaction velocity	20	20	20	20	20	20	20

Notes:

*Figures are rounded. Computation of the various columns was as follows:

Column 1 is self-explanatory, the transaction velocity being assumed at 20.

Column 2 is determined by the following conditions: (1) $E = VM$; (2) $E = W + Ti + P + G$; (3) $Ti = Gi$; (4) $P = W - Ti$; (5) $G = 40p$; and (6) $G + P = 100p$, where E = total payments, M = money supply, W = wage payments, Ti = income tax payments, P = private purchase payments, G = government purchase payments, and p = unit price. Given $M = \$10$ and $V = 20$, we determine E, W, Ti, P, G, and p.

Column 3 is determined by the same conditions as column 2. However, we now take $V = 20$ and $p = \$1$ as given and solve for E, W, Ti, P, G, and M.

Column 4 is determined by the conditions (1) $E = VM$; (2) $E = W + P + T_s + G$; (3) $P = W$; (4) $T_s = G$; (5) $G = 40p$; and (6) $G + P = 100p$, where T_s is sales tax payments. Given M and V, we solve for E, W, T_s, P, G, and p.

Column 5 is determined by the conditions (1) $E = VM$; (2) $E = W + P + T_s + G$; (3) $W = P$; (4) $T_s = G$; (5) $G = 40p$; (6) $G + P = 100p$; and (7) $p = 1 + T_s/100$. Given $V = 20$, we solve for E, W, T_s, P, G, p, and M.

Column 6 is determined by the conditions (1) $E = VM$; (2) $E = W + P + T_s + G$; (3) $W = P$; (4) $T_s = G$; (5) $G = 40pg$; (6) $P = 60pp$; and (7) $pg = pp - T_s/60$, where pg = price payable by government and pp = price payable by private buyers. Given $V = 20$ and $M = 100$, we can determine E, W, P, T_s, G, pg and pp.

Column 7 is determined by the same conditions as column 6 except that M is not given and (8) $pg = 1$ is added.

Column 8 is determined in a way similar to column 7 except that we now have (8) $pp = 1$.

various types of taxes. Government purchases are assumed to be made at competitive prices.

The case of balanced budget incidence for a general income tax-financed budget is shown in columns 2 and 3. In column 2 we assume that the money supply (line 18) is held constant, so that the level of money payments (line 16) must be unchanged as well. But the payment structure has been lengthened. As before, business disburses its entire proceeds in wage payments; and, as before, wage income is paid out, income tax payments taking the place of former purchase payments. But the purchase payments of the government are added. As total money payments are unchanged, the unit of payment—the level of factor and product prices (lines 1 and 4)—must fall.[13] In column 3 we assume that the price level is to remain constant. This means that the level of money payments (line 16) must rise and that the money supply (line 18) is expanded to permit this.

Now let us assume that the same expenditures are to be financed by a sales tax, applicable to government and private purchases alike. In column 4 we show a situation in which such a tax is absorbed in reduced factor payments, product prices remaining unchanged. In this case introduction of the budget does not lengthen the structure of transactions.[14] Therefore, the price level is unchanged with a constant money supply. In column 5 we show a situation in which imposition of the tax leaves factor payments unchanged, while product prices rise by the amount of tax. In this case total payments expand and the money supply must be increased.

The situation is somewhat different if the sales tax leaves government purchases tax-free. Three situations may be distinguished in this case. First, we may assume a constant money supply. As shown in column 6, this means that factor prices fall, prices to private buyers rise, prices to public buyers fall, and the average price level remains unchanged. Second, we may assume that prices paid by private buyers rise by the amount of tax, while prices paid by the government remain constant. As shown in column 7, this leaves wages unchanged, but the money supply must expand. Finally, we may assume that prices paid by private buyers remain constant. As shown in column 8, this implies a reduction in prices paid by government, a fall in wages, and a contraction in money supply.

Comparison of the various cases gives a picture of differential incidence. It shows that resulting changes in absolute prices are a function of changes (or lack of changes) in money supply. This, of course, must be the case by virtue of our quantity-theory assumptions. More important, we find that the resulting incidence—the division of the real product between the private and the public sectors, as shown in lines 5 and 14—is the same throughout. Differential incidence is neutral. This result is entirely unaffected by differences in the respective patterns of absolute price change.

In Table 12.3 similar adjustments are shown for a set of *discriminatory taxes*. For this purpose, the private sector is divided between Mr A and Mr B, where A consumes product *x*, while B consumes product *y*. To simplify matters, we assume that A and B are similar with regard to their sources of earnings and that the costs of producing a unit of *x* and *y* are equal. In

Table 12.3 *Price adjustments to partial taxes*

| | Before tax | Partial income tax | | Partial sales tax (Government purchases tax-free) | | |
| | | Constant money supply | Constant prices | Constant money supply | Price of tax-free product constant | Price of taxed product constant |
	(1)	(2)	(3)	(4)	(5)	(6)
Consumer sector, Mr A:						
1. Wages	50.00	41.66	50.00	35.70	50.00	10.00
2. Income tax		33.33	40.00			
3. Purchase payments	50.00	8.34	10.00	35.70	50.00	10.00
4. Price of x	1.00	0.83	1.00	3.57	5.00	1.00
5. Units of x bought	50	10	10	10	10	10
Consumer sector, Mr B:						
6. Wages	50.00	41.66	50.00	35.70	50.00	10.00
7. Purchase payments	50.00	41.66	50.00	35.70	50.00	10.00
8. Price of y	1.00	0.83	1.00	0.71	1.00	0.20
9. Units of y bought	50	50	50	50	50	50
Business sector:						
10. Receipts from private sector	100.00	50.00	60.00	71.40	100.00	20.00
11. Receipts from public sector		33.	40.00	28.56	40.00	8.00
12. Wage payments	100.00	83.33	100.00	71.40	100.00	20.00
13. Gross receipts tax				28.56	40.00	8.00
Government sector:						
14. Income tax receipts		33.33	40.00			
15. Excise tax receipts				28.56	40.00	8.00
16. Expenditures		33.33	40.00	28.56	40.00	8.00
17. Units bought		40	40	40	40	40
All sectors:						
18. GNP (10+11), in dollars	100.00	83.33	100.00	200.00	140.00	28.00
19. Total payments, in dollars	200.00	200.00	240.00	200.00	280.00	56.00
20. Price level, average	1.00	0.83	1.00	1.00	1.40	0.28
21. Money supply, in dollars	10.00	10.00	12.00	10.00	14.00	2.80
22. Transaction velocity	20	20	20	20	20	20

* Figures are rounded. Computations are similar to those of Table 2 but somewhat more complicated.

column 1 we repeat the pre-budget situation of Table 12.2 but now divide
the consumer sector between A and B. As before, a budget is introduced
and the government is to buy four-tenths of the total product. However,
the entire burden is now to fall on A. To simplify matters, let us assume
that the government wishes to purchase x, thus taking over the units which
are released by A.

Placing of the entire burden on A might be accomplished through a
partial income tax on A. The balanced budget incidence for a partial
income tax-financed budget is shown in columns 2 and 3. As before,
column 2 is based on a constant money supply and column 3 on a constant
price level. The resulting changes in prices and money supply are the same
as for the general tax. The only difference is that the entire income tax is
now obtained from A, so that B's real income position remains what it was
prior to introduction of the budget.

Alternatively, placing the burden on A might be accomplished through a
sales tax on x, the product bought by A, government purchases being
assumed tax-free. As a result, the price of x may rise relative to that of y.
As before, we begin with the assumption of a constant money supply. This
is shown in column 4. As a result of introducing the sales tax-financed
budget we find that wages and the price of y fall, while the price of x rises.
On the average, prices and the total volume of payments are unchanged.[15]
Next, we hold the price of y constant. As shown in column 5, wages stay
unchanged, the price of x rises, total payments and the money supply
expand. Finally, we hold the price of x constant. As shown in column 6,
wages decline, the price of y falls, total payments and the money supply
contract.

The principle is the same as for the general tax. Resulting changes in
absolute prices are a function of changes in the money supply. This must be
so because it is the money supply which determines total payment in
money terms. More important, incidence is again unaffected by alternative
monetary assumptions. The division of the real product between A, B, and
the government—as shown in lines 5, 9, and 17—is precisely the same in all
cases. *Whether we assume that the tax is shifted 'forward' as in column 5 or
'backward' as in column 6 does not make the slightest difference.* This being
the case, we must be careful not to refer to these manipulations as a
'monetary theory' of incidence. There is no such thing in the present model
where liquidity preference is excluded. The theory of incidence is inherently a theory of relative prices, while monetary manipulations in this setting
bear on the price level only.

Imperfect competition

The preceding argument has been based on the assumption of competitive
pricing in both factor and product markets. If imperfections are allowed
for, the equivalence between pairs of taxes, prevailing under perfect
competition, might be broken. A tax on the gross receipts of a monopolist
is still equivalent to a spendings tax on a competitive group of buyers who

purchase from him. But the tax on the monopolist's gross receipts is not equivalent to a tax on his cost payments which are net of monopoly profits. A tax on wage income may (but need not) be equivalent to a tax on cost payments to labour, depending on what view of the matter is taken in bargaining policy, and so forth.

Also, it may well be under conditions of imperfect competition that the outcome will not be indifferent to the direction of the initial adjustment.[16] If the price of the taxed product remains unchanged and factor costs are reduced, the prices of tax-free products may not be reduced correspondingly, as part of the savings in cost may be absorbed in increased monopoly profits. Collective bargaining may react differently to changes in real wages depending on whether prices or money wages are involved, and so on. Such complications will arise especially where market positions do not express perfect profit maximisation but where restraint is used or where a shock is required to induce a revision of price output positions.

Also, it may be noted that the adjustment process takes time, so that the initial movement of relative prices is of major importance. All these considerations introduce important qualifications, but they are disregarded for purposes of the present discussion.

INCIDENCE IN THE CAPITAL-FORMATION ECONOMY

We now turn to our second model, which allows for saving and capital formation. Liquidity preference, however, is ruled out for the time being. Savings out of full-employment income are always invested in the purchase of capital goods, and no balances other than transaction money are held. As before, changes in budget policy are introduced into this system, and we want to see how the resulting adjustment differs from that of the all-consumption model. In particular, let us (1) compare the adjustments to a general and a discriminatory income tax, and (2) examine what can be said in this setting about the relationship between a general income and a general product tax.

Cost/price relationships
To begin with, let us consider briefly the cost/price relationships involved in the present model. As before, we assume a competitive factor and product market.

To simplify matters, let us suppose that capital goods are produced instantaneously by the input of labour only. They are then permitted to ripen into consumer goods. At the end of the ripening process, further labour may be added 'directly' to the capital good, the cost of 'direct' labour input being the smaller relative to total cost, the more capital intensive production has become. In this system the cost of the unripened capital goods equals the labour cost of producing capital goods. The cost of the consumer good equals the labour cost of the capital plus interest thereon plus the cost of labour added directly. Also, the price of the capital good equals the discounted value of the consumer good net of the direct labour cost.[17] Factor shares in turn are divided between wages paid for the supply of labour and interest paid for the supply of savings required to permit the ripening process.

Budget financed by general income tax

We begin with the balanced budget incidence of a budget financed by a proportional income tax. As this is a general income tax, it will apply to earnings from both factors (labour and the supply of funds or waiting) alike. If we assume that the supply of both factors is inelastic to the rate of return, introduction of the budget will leave factor inputs unchanged in the first instance.[18] Marginal products remain unchanged, as does the division of earnings before tax between wages and interest.[19] Wage-earners and interest recipients find their disposable incomes reduced at the same rate. Relative prices of consumer and capital goods are unchanged as well. This being the case, the relative positions of wage-earners and interest recipients remain unchanged. The incidence of the budget turns out to be proportional, the result being the same so far as for the all-consumption model.

But in the capital-formation model this is only part of the picture. Relative factor inputs will not remain unchanged over time. Introduction of the budget reduces incomes available for private use and hence the private supply of savings. This will be the case even if we assume that the supply of savings is inelastic to interest; all that need be assumed (if we may use a Keynesian term in a classical context) is that the marginal propensity to consume out of disposable income be positive. Assuming public expenditures to be for consumer goods, introduction of the budget will lead to a reduction in the rate of capital formation.[20]

If capital formation declines, the capital stock, and hence total output, will be less at any future date. Capital will be scarcer, relative to labour, than it would have been otherwise. As a result, the rate of interest will be higher, and the distribution of factor shares between interest and wages will differ from what it would have been in the absence of the budget. As the interest rate is higher, the price of capital goods will be lower relative to that of consumer goods. These longer-run adjustments, resulting from the change in capital stock, will modify our short-run conclusion that the incidence of the budget is proportional. However, there is no simple way of telling just whose position will be favoured [2].

Substitution of discriminatory income tax

We now turn to the differential incidence which results when the general tax is replaced by a discriminatory income tax.

1. Let the general income tax be replaced by an equal-yield income tax which applies to earnings from all factors but to employment in certain uses (industries) only.

We here encounter the important and familiar distinction between incidence in the short and in the long run. In the short run, the supply of capital to particular uses is highly inelastic. In the long run, it is highly elastic. The elasticity of labour supply similarly is greater with regard to partial than to general markets, but the time factor is less marked. From this some familiar conclusions follow which need not be developed here.

2. Next, let the general income tax be replaced by a discriminatory income tax covering all industries but applicable to interest income only. This case is of particular importance for our later discussion of a product tax on capital goods.

Suppose again that the supply of savings is inelastic to the rate of return. In this case, factor inputs remain unchanged.[21] The relative prices of consumer and capital goods remain unchanged, as do wage and interest earnings before tax. But wage-earnings after tax increase relative to interest earnings after tax. Since interest income as a percentage of total family income rises and wage income falls when moving up the income scale, we must conclude that the differential incidence of our tax substitution is regressive.

This comparison relates to changes in the income position of typical individuals at various points in the income scale. But consider now a comparison between various individuals at the same level of income. The problem is relatively simple if we can divide all people between type A (people who receive wage income only and spend all of it on consumption) and type B (people who receive interest income only and save all of it). In this case, substitution of the partial tax is obviously to the advantage of group A and places the entire burden on group B.

The case is less obvious if we compare the positions of type C (people whose income is mostly from wages but who are heavy savers) and type D (people whose income is largely from interest but who are heavy consumers). While our measure of change in relative income position shows that C is favoured and D is harmed by the substitution of taxes, this result is obvious for the immediate period only. In a longer view, it is not at all evident that, put to a vote, C would favour and D would oppose substitution of a tax on interest for a general income tax. C, after all, is moving toward the position of B. He will, in future years, suffer increasingly from the high tax on interest. D, on the other hand, may dissave and thus move toward the position of A. If so, he will be burdened decreasingly by the tax on interest. Looked at this way, it appears that the concept of incidence had best be related to a particular timespan: C might gain in the short but lose in the long run, and vice versa for D.[22]

General tax on consumer goods

We now proceed to a general tax on transactions in consumer goods, a general sales tax, so called, to be substituted for a general income tax. In dealing with this matter, we meet confusion unless we distinguish clearly between two problems.[23] Problem 1 is to inquire into the absolute budget incidence of a budget financed by a proportional income tax. This having been done, problem 2 is to determine how incidence is changed when a sales tax is substituted for the proportional income tax. Problem 1 has been discussed already. Let us assume now that factor supplies are inelastic to the rate of return, so that, in the short run at least, the incidence of the income tax-financed budget will be proportional, that is, leave relative income positions unchanged. Our present concern is with problem 2 only.

Suppose now that a general sales tax on consumer goods is substituted for a general income tax. The conventional conclusion is that this substitution relieves those who save and places the entire burden on the consumer. The usual argument is that as the tax on consumer goods is imposed, the prices of such goods will rise by the amount of tax and that therefore the burden is on the consumer. While the conclusion is substantially correct, the reasoning involves two fallacies. First, we cannot be sure that the prices of consumer goods will rise. It may also be that consumer goods prices are unchanged, while cost payments to factors are reduced. As shown above, what happens depends on our monetary assumptions.[24] Second, and assuming that prices did rise, no conclusions as to incidence can be drawn therefrom. As shown above, incidence depends on changes in relative price, and these are independent of change in absolute prices or price levels.

The first fallacy was noted several years ago by Brown [1] and was extended recently in an important contribution .by Rolph [5]. Both recognise that it is not necessary for the prices of taxed products to rise. In fact, they rather overshoot the mark and hold that the adjustment *must* be in terms of constant prices and reduced factor payments.[25] But this is a minor matter. The important point, if I see the problem correctly, is that the Brown–Rolph position still contains the second fallacy: it implies that the tax does not fall on the consumer and that it is equivalent in incidence to a proportional income tax *because* the initial adjustment takes the form of reduction in factor payments. This conclusion does not follow. The assumption that factor payments are reduced does not prove that the tax falls on all individuals alike, just as the conventional assumption of increase in prices does not prove that the tax falls on the consumer only. The direction of adjustment does not determine incidence, and it must not be confused with incidence.

Let us restate the problem with this in mind. The price of consumer goods equals cost payments to the factors of production employed in the making of consumer goods. The tax, therefore, may be thought of as a tax on cost payments. By our earlier argument, a tax on all cost payments is similar to a tax on all factor earnings. As one is substituted for the other, we merely remove the wedge between factor earnings and disposable income and replace the same by an equivalent wedge between firm receipts and factor payments. Both wedges are non-discriminatory and chargeable equally against all factor payments. Substitution of the products tax leaves unchanged the distribution of factor earnings and disposable incomes.

But to conclude that the two taxes are similar on the income sources side does not prove that they are similar on balance. We must consider also what happens with regard to income uses. Here we find that relative prices do not remain unchanged. The market price of consumer goods will rise relative to the price of (unripened) capital goods. This follows from our basic relationship between consumer and capital good prices. In the absence of a product tax, the price of capital goods equals the discounted price of consumer goods. After the product tax is imposed, the price of capital goods equals the discounted price of consumer goods net of tax.[26] In the short run at least, factor inputs will be unchanged by our tax substitution. Therefore the efficiency of investment or the rate of discount will be unchanged. Capital good prices accordingly remain unchanged relative to the net prices of consumer goods but fall relative to their market price.

The argument has been stated in relative terms but might be formulated readily in terms of absolute price changes. If we assume that the absolute price of consumer goods rises by the amount of tax, we find that the price of capital goods remains unchanged, as do disposable money incomes of wage and interest recipients.[27] If we assume that the absolute price of consumer goods remains unchanged, we find that the price of capital goods falls, as do disposable money incomes of interest and wage recipients.[28] The results in terms of change in relative positions are the same in both cases.

For purposes of interpretation, consider the second adjustment, leaving disposable money incomes unchanged while the price of capital goods falls. In all, we find (a) that relative positions are unchanged in terms of disposable money income, (b) that relative positions are unchanged in terms of disposable real income if the incomes of consumers and savers alike are deflated by the same price index, and (c) that consumers have suffered relative to savers if we deflate their respective incomes by the prices of consumer or of capital goods, depending on which are being bought respectively. If we choose interpretation (b) we conclude that a proportional income tax and a general tax on consumer goods are similar in incidence. If we choose interpretation (c) we conclude that the latter tax falls on the consumer.[29] Since consumption as a fraction of income falls when moving up the income scale, this means that differential incidence is regressive.

In the all-consumption model it was evident that (c) was the proper approach. As all income was consumed, income and relative income positions could be defined only in terms of current consumption. Now we may choose between two possible concepts of income, one being accretion to wealth in terms of potential consumption power and the other being accretion to wealth in terms of goods purchased, be it consumer or capital goods. If we choose the first concept, incomes of consumers and savers alike must be deflated by consumer good prices, and there is no difference in incidence between our two taxes.[30] If we choose the second concept, we conclude that the tax on consumer goods falls on the consumer.

The choice between two concepts, as most matters of equity, is essentially a point in social philosophy rather than in science. But as I see it, much is to be said in favour of the second view. If we accept the potential consumption concept, we imply that it is a matter of indifference to Jones, who saves a large part of his income, whether a tax on consumer goods is substituted for a general income tax.[31] Yet, this permits Jones to maintain his preceding consumption standards while accumulating more capital goods. To be sure, the potential consumption value of this accumulation is not increased at the outset. But accumulation of wealth gives satisfaction as such; moreover, dissaving, and hence tax payment, may never occur. Be this as it may, payment of the tax is postponed, and interest on it may be earned. This latter aspect, it appears, is a real advantage which goes beyond the debate of income concepts. Moreover, the potential consumption concept implies that it is a matter of indifference to Smith, who consumes his entire income, whether the tax on consumer goods is substituted for the income tax. Yet Smith obtains less consumer goods after the tax than before and cannot help but feel that his position has worsened.[32] In all, I find it reasonable to conclude that the tax falls on the consumer.[33]

Whatever our interpretation of the short-run result, it is evident that substitution of the tax on consumer goods *will* lead in time to a transfer of resources from consumer to capital good production. This need be the case because savers now obtain more capital goods for their saving, while consumers obtain less consumer goods. However, the increased return on savings in terms of capital goods may increase the supply of savings. As the capital stock is increased, this will lead to further changes in relative positions with regard to both sources and uses of income. Whatever the precise outcome, it is evident that the state of affairs does not remain the same as the one tax is substituted for the other.

General tax on capital goods

Finally, let us consider what happens if the general income tax is replaced by a tax on transactions in capital goods.[34]

We assume for the time being that our substitution leaves the supply of labour and of saving unchanged. The proceeds from the sale of consumer goods are divided in the same ratios as before between payments for direct labour input and for capital goods. But part of the latter share goes to pay for the tax on capital goods. Less is left to pay for the labour input into capital goods and to the suppliers of saving. The rate of return to labour used in the making of capital goods cannot be reduced, since it must equal that paid for the direct labour input into consumer goods. The tax must be absorbed, therefore, in reduced payments to the supplier of funds.[35] Earnings from interest fall relative to earnings from wages. Both wage-earners and interest recipients benefit equally from the removal of the income tax, so that, on balance, the disposable income of interest recipients declines relative to that of wage-earners. This result, we note, is similar to that obtained previously for the discriminatory tax on interest income.

The net price of (unripened) capital goods remains unchanged relative to that of consumer goods, as it did for the discriminatory tax on interest income. The net price of (unripened) capital goods is determined by the wage rate and remains unchanged relative to the cost of the direct labour input into consumer goods. But the cost of this direct labour input remains unchanged as a fraction of the total cost (or price) of consumer goods. Therefore, the net price of (unripened) capital goods remains unchanged relative to consumer goods.[36]

As before, we may translate the argument from relative to absolute terms. If, for instance, the price of consumer goods stays put, so will the net price of capital goods. Interest recipients find their disposable income reduced, while wage recipients find their disposable income increased.

There is no difficulty in interpreting the immediate result. The burden of the new tax is on interest recipients, and wage-earners are relieved of tax. Since interest rises as a fraction of income when moving up the income scale, the differential incidence of our tax substitution is regressive. While the immediate result is independent of income use, a longer-run view must allow for the fact that current uses of income determine future sources of earnings. Complications arise, similar to those considered in our preceding discussion of the tax on interest income.

Also, longer-run analysis must allow again for changes in capital stock. As the tax on capital goods (or interest income) is substituted for the general income tax, it is likely that resources will be transferred from the production of capital goods to that of consumer goods. This will be the case because interest recipients as a group tend to have a higher propensity to save than do wage recipients,[37] or it may be the case because the resulting reduction in the net rate of return may lead individuals to substitute consumption for savings. Resulting changes in the rate of growth, as noticed throughout this discussion, will qualify our short-run results.

General tax on all product transactions

Our conclusions may now be combined into the case of a general tax on all product transactions, covering consumer and capital goods alike.

Since the tax on capital goods is equivalent to a tax on interest income, a tax on capital goods and consumer goods will be equivalent to a general income tax if the tax on consumer goods is equivalent to a tax on wage income.

This is the case if (1) we take the view that the tax on consumer goods falls on the consumer and if (2) we consider a universe in which all wage income is consumed and all interest income is saved. The conclusion does not hold once we allow for wage-earners who save and interest recipients who consume. The simple equivalence between a general income and a general product tax, which we found to prevail in the all-consumption model, does not hold for the present case.[38]

INCIDENCE IN THE LIQUIDITY PREFERENCE MODEL

Space does not permit reconsideration of the problem in the more realistic setting of a liquidity preference model. We note only some of the major respects in which the argument need be qualified.

1. If liquidity preference is allowed for, the direction of adjustment cannot be predicted as a simple function of monetary policy. The balances need to expedite 'forward' adjustments may be provided for from holdings of asset money, or funds released by 'backward' adjustments may be absorbed into asset money. The direction of adjustment, therefore, becomes a matter of market behaviour. Under conditions of imperfect competition, substitution of an excise for an income tax, in my judgement, is likely to be reflected in increased prices rather than in reduced factor payments, the upward rigidity of prices being considerably less than the downward rigidity of wages.

Resulting changes in the supply of asset money may affect the rate of interest and investment, so that different directions of adjustment may, in fact, lead to different end results. This possibility must be allowed for, but I doubt whether it is of very great importance.

2. In interpreting the results of a tax on consumer goods, we have distinguished between income as accretion of potential consumption power and income as accretion of consumer and/or capital goods. Allowing for liquidity preference, the latter concept is expanded to include accretion in terms of money balances. This raises the awkward problem of just what price index should be applied to such balances.

3. In the preceding discussion, continuous reference was made to taxes which do or do not affect the supply of savings. This was important, as the supply of savings was the determinant of the level of capital formation and the rate of growth. With liquidity preference allowed for, the obvious link between saving and capital formation is broken. The impact of taxation on saving is now of importance primarily in terms of its non-impact on consumption and hence on the level of consumption expenditure. Taxation effects on investment may still operate through qualitative changes in the supply of savings, but effects on the willingness to invest available funds become of primary importance.

4. Owing to these factors, adjustments in budget policy may result in changes in the aggregate level of prices or employment. These in turn may give rise to further changes in the state of distribution. Now it may well be argued that incidence analysis should be neutralised from such effects by assuming that offsetting stabilising policies are applied. Much can be said for this formulation because incidence, as a consideration of tax policy, should be concerned with the distribution of a given income total.

But if we assume that such stabilising moves are made, just what devices of stabilisation are to be used? If it is to be monetary policy, we do in effect come to discuss the joint incidence of monetary and tax policy. Since aggregate demand is determined by both monetary and fiscal policy, we cannot readily isolate fiscal policy by holding monetary policy constant. Rather, we may be driven to consider the differential incidence of various packages of stabilisation measures, including the incidence of monetary no less than the incidence of tax policy.

NOTES

1. The implicit assumption is that the gain in yield will be withdrawn from the system or that yield lost will be replaced by printing-press finance.
2. Absolute tax incidence, as stated in the text, is defined as the change in income positions which results when the level of taxation is changed while public expenditures are held constant. It is to be contrasted with differential tax incidence, which measures the change in distribution when one equal-yield tax is substituted for another. With regard to expenditure changes, we may speak similarly of absolute and differential expenditure incidence.

    The reader is warned that the term 'absolute' is used merely as the opposite of 'differential'. In particular, the term 'absolute tax incidence' does not imply in any way that introduction of a tax imposes an absolute burden on the group as a whole, as results from resource transfer to public use. Resource transfer is the result of expenditure and not of tax changes. For a more detailed discussion of these concepts see Musgrave [4].
3. Cases of absolute tax and absolute expenditure incidence may be combined to give the incidence of tax expenditure adjustments which do not balance.
4. Alternatively, we may write $\Delta R = (E_1 - T_{p1})/P_1 - (E_0 - T_{p0})/P_0$, where P_0 is the price index weighted according to expenditures for the first period and P_1 the corresponding index weighted according to expenditures after adjustment to the tax change.

    This abbreviated statement of a difficult problem is given to indicate at least in broad outline what is meant by a measure of incidence. The suggested measure is far from perfect. Gains and losses among various individuals will not necessarily cancel when one tax is replaced by another, or net losses will not necessarily equal yield as the budget is increased. These difficulties may arise even though factor inputs remain unchanged, but they can hardly be avoided. For the present purposes it will suffice to note that the measurement of incidence would remain a difficult matter even if all the changes in economic data resulting from a change in tax policy were known.
5. To simplify matters, we assume that all products involve only a single state of production.
6. We disregard here the special case of lump-sum taxes which are not assessed on economic acts.
7. In the case of discriminatory taxes, characteristics of either buyers or sellers may be made the basis of discrimination, thus requiring that the tax be assessed on the buyer's or on the seller's side.
8. Note that our operational measure is in terms of change in deflated disposable money income. It does not allow for the burden or gain which results from a reallocation of time between effort and leisure. Nor does it allow for the complex of problems associated with the 'excess burden' of indirect taxes.
9. It is implied here that incidence is to be measured in terms of change in the

distribution of income by size brackets, that is, in the Lorenz curve. See my paper referred to in n. 2 above.

10. Reference is again to incidence in terms of change in the distribution of income by size brackets. A tax applicable to certain products only will raise their price relative to others. As there exists a systematic relationship between income size and budget patterns, this change in relative price is likely to alter the size distribution of real income. Resulting changes in earnings, on the contrary, will tend to be distributionally neutral. Except for unusual cases, there is no reason to expect that resulting changes in relative factor returns should accrue primarily to high or to low income brackets.

11. In this case there is likely to exist a systematic relationship between earnings change and income size, as various factors may be chosen for discriminatory or favourable treatment because the income accrues primarily to high or to low income groups. But there is no particular reason, in this case, to expect the prices of products bought by high income groups to rise or fall relative to those of products bought by low-income groups.

12. As shown at the outset, our definition of change in distribution allows not only for changes in the distribution of disposable money income but also for changes in the prices of products bought.

13. A different conclusion is reached if source-withholding is assumed. In this case income tax payments take the place of wage payments, and public purchase payments take the place of private purchase payments. The payment structure is not lengthened, and a constant money supply leaves prices unchanged. The result is similar to that of column 4, Table 12.2.

14. Sales tax payments by the firm take the place of wage payments, and public purchase payments take the place of private purchase payments. See note 13.

15. For the purposes of the text, discussion is in terms of budget incidence, comparing each result with the no-budget situation. Alternatively, comparisons may be made between the various tax situations, thus giving the results in terms of differential incidence.

16. An additional difference may arise from the presence of a money illusion in the consumption function.

17. Disregarding considerations of risk, the rate of discount is the internal rate of discount which equates the present value of the future income stream with cost.

18. If factor supplies are elastic, the relative position of the suppliers of various factors will change, even without considering the longer-run aspects noted in the next paragraph of the text. As indicated in our discussion of the all-consumption model, the relative position of those who supply the more elastic factor will tend to improve. See n. 23 below.

19. We make the simplifying assumption that there occurs no change in the pattern of demand as between more and less capital-intensive products.

20. If the government spends on capital goods, the direction of the argument is reversed, but the principle is the same.

21. From a longer-run point of view, this may again require qualification, as the community's propensity to save, and hence the rate of accumulation, may be affected by the tax substitution. This may be the case either because savings are elastic to the net (after-tax) return or because the propensity to save (at any given level of income) is related to the fraction of income derived from interest.

22. In other words, we might compare the present values of future tax burdens imposed on C and D by the respective taxes. These values will depend on C's and D's future budget plans.

23. In Part II of my earlier paper [4] I was not aware of the importance of this distinction. Indeed, failure to distinguish between problems 1 and 2 led to an error in interpretation which should be corrected here.

   My earlier conclusion was that the results of substituting a sales tax on consumer goods for an income tax will depend on factor elasticities, the burden being on the wage-earner if the supply of savings is taken to be infinitely elastic and on the interest recipient if the supply of labour is wholly elastic. This conclusion was reached in two steps. Step 1 was to argue that removal of the proportional income tax leaves relative positions unchanged. Step 2 was to argue that imposition of the sales tax will change relative positions depending upon factor elasticities.

   This argument overlooked the fact that, given factor supplies of varying degrees of elasticity, removal of the income tax will *not* leave relative positions unchanged. The conclusion reached, which was based on the contrary assumption, did in fact not describe the differential incidence which results when an income tax is replaced by a sales tax. Rather, it described something akin to the absolute incidence of a sales tax, the removal of the income tax being of no importance, as it was considered distributionally neutral.

   In the present paper I attempt to avoid this error by distinguishing carefully between problems 1 and 2 as stated in the text. A corrected interpretation of the earlier argument—that the absolute incidence of the sales tax depends on the elasticities of factor supplies—is entirely compatible with our present argument which says that (*a*) the absolute incidence of the income tax-financed budget depends on factor elasticities and (*b*) the result of substituting a sales for an income tax depends on the considerations outlined in the text discussion. An alternative approach, also compatible with the present procedure, would be first to determine the absolute incidence of a sales tax-financed budget and to proceed to the substitution of an income tax.

24. The present model is similar to the all-consumption model in that no balances are held. The relationship of money supply, total payments and the price level is the same in both cases. The principle demonstrated in Tables 12.2 and 12.3 above holds for both models.

25. This conclusion is reached on the assumption of pure competition but need not hold if market imperfections are allowed for. If we wish to argue, however, that the outcome is the result of pricing behaviour rather than of monetary policy, we pass over to the next model where liquidity preference is allowed for.

26. More correctly: the price of capital goods equals the discounted price of consumer-goods net of tax *and* net of the additional cost of direct labour input. Reference to the price of capital goods in the text is throughout to unripened capital goods, which is equal to the cost of the required labour input.

27. Factor payments remain unchanged in dollar terms, so that wage and interest incomes are unchanged. Disposable incomes of both wage and interest recipients rise at the same time as the income tax is removed. (Since factor supplies are held inelastic, no change in earnings will follow removal of the income tax in *this* case. See n. 23 above.) The wage rate and hence the price of capital goods is changed.

28. Factor payments and earnings are reduced by the amount of tax, but removal of the income tax leaves disposable incomes unchanged in dollar terms. As the money wage rate is reduced, the market price of capital goods will fall.

29. We need not in this case specify the sources of income for consumers and

savers as was necessary in the case of the discriminatory income tax. This is not required now because relative disposable incomes from various sources are left unchanged. Therefore we do not run into the difficulties of longer-run interpretation encountered in the case of the discriminatory tax on interest income. While there exists a direct causal relationship between present income uses and future earnings sources, there exists no such evident relationship in the reverse direction.

30. This is subject to the longer-run considerations to be noted presently.
31. The reader may find it helpful to think of the general income tax as a general spendings tax (on purchase of consumer or capital goods) so that substitution of the tax on consumer goods (which is the same as a tax on outlays for consumer goods) is equivalent to exempting capital good purchases from the spendings tax.
32. Suppose that A consumes and B saves his entire income. According to the potential consumption concept, relative positions are unchanged. The real income position (in terms of potential consumption) of both has worsened at an equal rate, as unchanged disposable incomes of both are deflated by higher consumer good prices! This, it seems to me, makes little sense.
33. The choice between these two interpretations comes down to essentially the same points as are involved in the old double taxation of savings controversy. See Musgrave [3].
34. It is not necessary for our purposes to specify whether the tax is assessed before or after the ripening process.
35. While the internal rate of discount (before tax) remains unchanged, only part of this return is now available to the suppliers of funds.
36. We may think of the interest recipient or saver as buying unripened capital goods from the producer of capital goods and of selling the ripened capital goods to the producer of consumer goods. If the tax is collected from the seller of unripened capital goods at the time of sale, the market price of such goods rises relative to the net price. Since the sales price of ripened capital goods has remained unchanged relative to the net price of unripened capital goods, the saver must absorb the tax through a reduction in this differential, which is his interest income. If the tax is collected from the saver when the ripened capital good is sold, he finds similarly that his net proceeds have fallen relative to his outlays.
37. This will tend to be the case because a larger part of interest income is received in higher income brackets. Also, it will be the case where at any given level of income there is a positive relationship between the ratio of interest to wage income and that of saving to consumption.
38. If we think of incidence in terms of changes in the bracket distribution of income, there might, however, be a fair degree of similarity between a tax the burden of which is distributed according to the distribution of wage income by brackets and a tax the burden of which is distributed according to the distribution of consumption expenditures by brackets.

REFERENCES

[1] Brown, H. G. (1939) 'The Incidence of a General Output or a General Sales Tax', *Journal of Political Economy*, 47.

[2] Hicks, J. (1936) 'Distribution and Economic Progress: A Revised Version', *Review of Economic Studies*, IV, 1.
[3] Musgrave, R. A. (1939) 'Double Taxation of Savings', *American Economic Review*, XXIX.
[4] ——(1953) 'General Equilibrium Aspects of Incidence Theory', *American Economic Review*, 43.
[5] Rolph, E. (1952) 'A Proposed Revision of Excise Tax Theory', *Journal of Political Economy*, LX, 2.

13 How Progressive is the Income Tax?*
1959

The outward appearance of the Federal income tax, with bracket rates ranging from 20 to 90 per cent, is exceedingly progressive. However, there are many features of the tax which counteract this progression. The purpose of this paper is to appraise who benefits from these features and to determine how progressive the tax really is.

That there exists a wide gap between nominal and actual progression is evident from even a cursory observation of the data given in 'Statistics of Income'. Take, for instance, taxpayers with adjusted gross income of from $50,000 to $100,000. In 1956, taxes paid by this group amounted to 37 per cent of their adjusted gross income. Yet by applying the nominal rate structure to the average income in this bracket, one arrives at a liability of about 50 per cent. Or, let us compare the taxes paid by taxpayers in the $100,000 to $150,000 bracket, with those paid in the $150,000 to $200,000 bracket. By taking the increase in average tax as a per cent of the increase in average income, we can compute what the 'bracket' or 'marginal' rate has been over this income range. Naive reference to the rate structure suggests that it should have been somewhere from 80 to 90 per cent, but the actual rate was only 53 per cent.

How can these differences be explained? The key does not lie in unlawful evasion, but results from specific features of the tax law. One explanation, especially important for our first comparison, lies in income splitting. For the case of joint returns, this provision means that bracket rates rise much more slowly, when moving up the income scale, than appears at first sight. Another explanation especially important for our second comparison, is found in the favourable tax treatment of capital gains. Thus, the array of special provisions, loopholes, or erosion of the tax base is important not only because it shrinks the base and reduces yield. It is important also because it punctures the pattern of progression provided for by the level of personal exemptions and bracket rates, and because it does so in an arbitrary and inequitable fashion.

---

* *Tax Revision Compendium*, Vol. 3. Committee on Ways and Means, Nov. 6, 1959. U. S. Government Printing Office, Washington, DC.

BASIS OF ESTIMATES

Our approach will be to compare, for various brackets of adjusted gross income, actual liabilities incurred in 1956 with such liabilities as would result if various specified changes in the tax law were made or if you wish, if various loopholes were closed. This will permit us to determine which income brackets are the primary beneficiaries of which provisions. By relating present liabilities to a revised concept of income without loopholes, we shall be able to see what the 'true' schedule of effective rates is like under present practice.[1]

The present pattern of liabilities, as given by payments for 1956, will be compared with estimated liabilities as they would be under three hypothetical plans of tax reform defined as follows:

Plan 1: Four major changes are made in this plan.
  (a) The rate advantage of income splitting is abolished and the rate structure now applicable to the single taxpayer is applied throughout.
  (b) Source withholding is applied to interest and dividend income.
  (c) Realised capital gains are taxed fully like other income.
  (d) A flat deduction of 10 per cent is substituted for present deductions.

Plan 2: This plan is similar to plan 1, with the only change that—
  (e) Deductions are disallowed.

Plan 3: This plan is similar to plan 2, with certain further changes:
  (f) Tax exempt interest and percentage depletion are abolished.
  (g) Unrealised gains at time of death are made taxable as if realised.
  (h) Wage supplements are included in taxable income.

In making the adjustments involved in (e), (f), (g), and (h) we first determine the total increase in adjusted gross income which results for each item. These totals are then divided between joint and single returns, and for each category are allocated among brackets of adjusted gross income by what seem appropriate patterns of distribution. In this fashion a computed distribution of adjusted gross income is obtained for each plan. By arriving at the corresponding value of average taxable income for each bracket, the average computed tax is determined and from this the various results shown in the following tables are readily obtained.[2] Since the estimated distributions are not necessarily the true distributions of the various items in question, these results are more or less rough estimates only.

RATIO OF ACTUAL TO COMPUTED TAX

Table 13.1 shows present tax liabilities as a per cent of computed tax liabilities under the three plans, and the same information is repeated for joint returns in Figure 13.1.

Table 13.1 Actual tax paid as per cent of computed tax

Returns with adjusted gross income of:	Joint returns			Single returns		
	Plan			Plan		
	I	II	III	I	II	III
$600 to $2,500	63	57	24	81	74	56
$2,500 to $5,000	76	68	57	88	79	76
$5,000 to $10,000	81	70	66	88	78	74
$10,000 to $15,000	73	64	62	81	70	64
$15,000 to $20,000	65	56	53	78	67	59
$20,000 to $25,000	61	52	50	75	64	58
$25,000 to $50,000	62	53	50	85	73	64
$50,000 to $100,000	61	55	45	71	62	49
$100,000 to $150,000	54	48	39	61	54	43
$150,000 to $200,000	52	46	37	57	49	40
$200,000 to $500,000	48	43	34	53	47	39
$500,000 to $1,000,000	44	40	31	45	40	33
$1,000,000 or more	39	35	26	39	39	32

Consider first the comparison of actual, with plan 1 liabilities. We find that actual payments in the $10,000 to $15,000 bracket exceed 80 per cent of the computed liabilities under plan 1, but that this ratio declines sharply as we move up the income scale, falling to about 40 per cent in the top bracket. Incomes in the range from $25,000 to, say, $100,000 benefit greatly from income splitting, while the preferential treatment of capital gains is of decisive importance in the higher brackets. Taxpayers at the lower end of the scale also show a lower ratio than does the $5,000 to $10,000 bracket. This reflects the impact of source withholding on capital income which, according to our estimates, carries significant weight in the low-income brackets.

This picture is more or less similar for plan 2, but the ratio of actual to computed tax lies lower at all levels. This is as may be expected since now deductions are disallowed.

The ratio of actual to computed taxes is reduced further under plan 3. Over the $5,000 to $50,000 range the pattern of the plan 3 curve shown in chart 13.1 is similar to that of plans 1 and 2. However, it now falls off even more sharply for higher incomes, dropping to a low of about 25 per cent at the upper end of the income scale. This reflects the full taxation of capital gains, including unrealised gains at death, provided for under plan 3. At the same time, the ratio now drops off sharply at the bottom end of the scale. This reflects the inclusion of wage supplements in the taxable income under plan 3.

In all, it appears that incomes between $5,000 and $20,000 are relatively close to their 'full' tax, while lower and especially higher incomes pay much

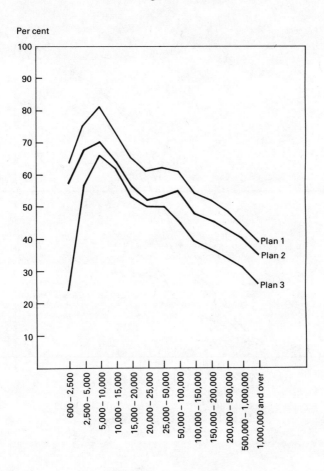

Figure 13.1

smaller shares thereof. As may be expected, the ratio of actual to computed tax is substantially higher for single than for joint returns, the difference being most pronounced over the range for which the benefits from income splitting are most important.

ACTUAL VERSUS COMPUTED EFFECTIVE RATES OF TAX

A comparison between actual effective rates and effective rates computed under our three plans is given in table 13.2. The information applicable to joint returns is repeated in Figure 13.2.

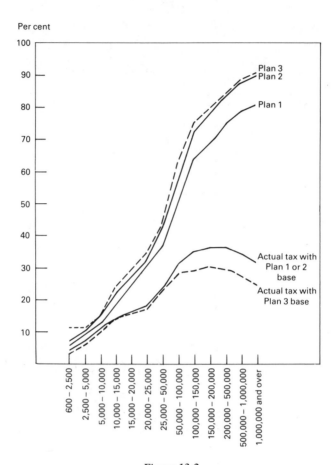

Figure 13.2

In the first column we show the effective rates of tax as usually thought of, that is, the ratio of tax paid to adjusted gross income as reported. We then show for each plan two sets of effective rates, one using the actual tax and the other using the computed tax, both divided by the computed value of adjusted gross income. The ratio between these two effective rates in turn equals the ratios shown in table 13.1. Table 13.2 thus repeats essentially the same information in somewhat different form.

We find that the major difference is not between the effective rates under plans 1, 2, and 3, but between any of these and the patterns of effective rates arrived at by using actual tax paid. This holds true even if reported adjusted gross income is used as base for the actual tax, but especially so if computed income is used as base.[3] In the latter case, note that the effective rate actually declines (the tax becomes regressive) for incomes above $150,000.

Table 13.2 *Actual effective rates compared with computed effective rates (joint returns)*

Returns with adjusted gross income of:	Plan I			Plan II		Plan III	
	Actual tax as per cent of adjusted gross income as reported	Actual tax as per cent of computed gross income	Computed tax as per cent of computed gross income	Actual tax as per cent of computed gross income	Computed tax as per cent of computed gross income	Actual tax as per cent of computed gross income	Computed tax as per cent of computed gross income
$600 to $2,500	4	4	6	4	7	3	11
$2,500 to $5,000	7	7	9	7	10	6	11
$5,000 to $10,000	11	11	13	11	15	10	15
$10,000 to $15,000	15	14	19	14	22	14	22
$15,000 to $20,000	17	16	25	16	29	16	29
$20,000 to $25,000	20	18	29	18	34	17	35
$25,000 to $50,000	25	23	37	23	43	23	44
$50,000 to $100,000	35	31	51	31	57	28	63
$100,000 to $150,000	41	35	64	35	72	29	75
$150,000 to $200,000	44	36	69	36	78	30	80
$200,000 to $500,000	47	36	75	36	84	29	85
$500,000 to $1,000,000	49	34	79	34	88	27	89
$1,000,000 or more	49	31	81	31	90	24	90

Table 13.3 Revenue gain by income bracket (In millions of dollars)

Returns with adjusted gross income of:	Joint returns			Single returns			Joint and single returns		
	Plan I	Plan II	Plan III	Plan I	Plan II	Plan III	Plan I	Plan II	Plan III
$600 to $2,500	62	81	330	214	330	736	276	412	1,066
$2,500 to $5,000	973	1,368	2,236	366	743	863	1,289	2,111	3,099
$5,000 to $10,000	2,459	4,496	5,391	175	363	412	2,635	4,859	5,803
$10,000 to $15,000	1,116	1,739	1,853	56	102	133	1,173	1,841	1,986
$15,000 to $20,000	717	1,064	1,164	38	69	97	756	1,134	1,261
$20,000 to $25,000	551	837	926	34	57	76	615	895	1,002
$25,000 to $50,000	1,619	2,294	2,608	52	106	165	1,671	2,401	2,773
$50,000 to $100,000	1,173	1,494	2,252	84	128	218	1,257	1,622	2,470
$100,000 to $150,000	507	660	944	48	65	100	554	725	1,044
$150,000 to $200,000	227	289	414	30	39	58	257	328	472
$200,000 to $500,000	474	584	844	74	93	132	548	677	976
$500,000 to $1,000,000	189	228	335	46	55	78	235	284	413
$1,000,000 or more	241	285	4,313	96	115	155	336	400	587
Total	10,290	15,421	19,731	1,315	2,266	3,224	11,542	17,686	22,954

GAIN IN REVENUE BY INCOME BRACKET

In table 13.3 we show the increase in tax liability which the three plans would impose on returns in the various income brackets. The estimated total gain would be $11.5 billion for plan 1, $17.6 billion for plan 2, and $23 billion for plan 3. It follows that an average reduction in tax rates of from 20 to 40 per cent would be possible while maintaining yield at present levels.

DETAILED VIEW OF PLAN 2

In table 13.4 we show, for various income brackets, how the increase in tax liabilities would be divided among the four major changes under this plan. In the low brackets the disallowance of deductions would be most important; in the $15,000 to $100,000 range the disallowance of income splitting is crucial; and for the higher incomes the full taxation of capital gains carries the major weight. Withholding on dividend and interest income is of importance not only at the upper end of the scale, but also at the lower end.

Table 13.4 Sources of increase in tax liability under plan 2 (joint returns) (In per cent)

Returns with adjusted gross income of:	Disallowing deductions	Disallowing income splitting	Full taxation of realised capital gains	Withholding on interest and dividends	Total
$600 to $2,500	83	0	0	17	100
$2,500 to $5,000	90	0	1	9	100
$5,000 to $10,000	81	11	2	7	100
$10,000 to $15,000	57	28	7	8	100
$15,000 to $20,000	42	32	14	12	100
$20,000 to $25,000	36	54	15	12	100
$25,000 to $50,000	32	44	20	5	100
$50,000 to $100,000	29	33	33	4	100
$100,000 to $150,000	28	23	47	2	100
$150,000 to $200,000	27	20	51	2	100
$200,000 to $500,000	26	12	59	2	100
$500,000 to $1,000,000	23	5	71	2	100
$1,000,000 and over	16	1	78	8½	100
Total	53	22	18	7	100

COMPARISON OF MARGINAL RATES OF TAX

A comparison of actual with computed marginal rates is given in table 13.5.

The first column shows the increment in actual average tax as a per cent of the increment in reported (actual) average adjusted gross income, as we move from the lower to the higher set of brackets. As noted before, the actual marginal rates fall far short of what is suggested by the pattern of statutory bracket rates. This result is accentuated in column 2, where the increment in actual tax is related to the increment in adjusted gross income as computed under plans 1 and 2.[4] Marginal rates now actually decline at the upper end of the income scale. Again this result is accentuated further in column 4, where the computed income for plan 3 is used as base.

In column 3, we show the marginal rates which would apply under plan 1, using the computed tax and the computed income for plan 1. This pattern generally resembles what one might expect by reference to the nominal bracket rates which are now on the statute books. Marginal rates for plan 2 are not shown separately as they are very close to those for plan 1. The picture for plan 3, shown in column 5, is also fairly similar to that for plan 1, except that rates are higher at the lower end of the scale.

Table 13.5   Actual marginal rates compared with computed marginal rates (joint returns)

Average to Average				1	2	3	4	5
$600–	$2,500 to	$2,500–	$5,000	20	15	20	14	23
$2,500–	$5,000 to	$5,000–	$10,000	20	17	22	16	28
$5,000–	$10,000 to	$10,000–	$15,000	22	18	29	19	36
$10,000–	$15,000 to	$15,000–	$20,000	26	20	40	19	48
$15,000–	$20,000 to	$20,000–	$25,000	31	25	50	23	57
$20,000–	$25,000 to	$25,000–	$50,000	40	33	60	31	63
$25,000–	$50,000 to	$50,000–	$100,000	52	39	72	34	76
$50,000–	$100,000 to	$100,000–	$150,000	61	38	86	31	89
$100,000–	$150,000 to	$150,000–	$200,000	64	39	90	31	91
$150,000–	$200,000 to	$200,000–	$500,000	65	35	91	28	91
$200,000–	$500,000 to	$500,000–$1,000,000		64	34	91	26	91
$500,000–$1,000,000 to	$1,000,000 and over			58	30	91	25	91

POLICY IMPLICATIONS

The preceding results show that there exists a vast gap between (1) nominal rates of tax as suggested by naive reference to the structure of bracket rates, assuming these to apply to a satisfactory concept of taxable income;

and (2) actual rates of tax, as computed by relating taxes paid to such a definition of income. If this gap was a fairly constant fraction for average incomes over all income brackets, its existence would not affect the degree of progression, but merely the level of rates;[5] and if the fraction was constant among taxpayers within any one income bracket, the gap would not conflict with the requirement that taxpayers with equal incomes should be treated equally. Given these assumptions, neither vertical nor horizontal equity would be affected by the existence of the gap. But in practice, neither condition applies.

With regard to effects on 'vertical equity', or the pattern of progression, our estimates show that the gap rises drastically for the average taxpayer in each income bracket as we move from the $5,000 to $10,000 bracket up toward higher brackets. This is so especially under plan 3, but the widening of the gap is substantial also under plans 1 and 2. Moreover, our estimates show that the gap rises as we move down from the $5,000 to $10,000 toward lower brackets, especially if plan 3 is taken as the standard. Now, it should be noted that these results are based on rather rough estimates. More detailed work of this sort is needed, and other items—such as imputed rent, expense accounts, executive pension plans, and so forth— might be brought into the picture. However, the general pattern of our results should be sufficiently reliable to tell the overall story.

It does not follow from our analysis that the effective rates implicit in plan 3 should be made to apply. The resulting yield would be much too large, and a substantial cut in the rate structure would be called for. What pattern this cut in rate structure should follow is a nice problem, but this is not at issue here. Our point is merely that actual and statutory rates should be brought together. The fiction of steep progression should be eliminated, if only as a matter of honesty in tax policy. The effective degree of progression, as it really comes about, should be made the explicit result of legislation with regard to personal exemptions and bracket rates and not the accidental (or worse: intentional but hidden) result of legislation for loopholes in the tax base and tricks such as income splitting.

Action along this line is needed, moreover, because the present system offends against the principle of 'horizontal equity', since taxpayers in any one income bracket are subject to widely varying effective rates of tax. The differential burden between taxpayers filing single and taxpayers filing joint returns has been mentioned already. In addition, there may be wide variations among taxpayers with equal incomes and within either category. In 1956, the effective rate for joint returns in the bracket of $50,000 to $100,000 was 31 per cent (using accrual tax and plan 1 base), but effective rates for individual taxpayers may range from less than 25 to over 50 per cent, depending upon the composition of their incomes. The nominal pattern of progression while fictitious on the average may be very real in particular cases, thus rendering the effects of the present system highly inequitable. Little is known about the degree of variation which exists in any one bracket, and I suggest that the committee request the Treasury Department to undertake some sample studies of this sort, especially with regard to the higher brackets. This will give an indication of how many taxpayers really pay what rates.

The particular packages of changes in the tax law included in our three plans are not the only possible combinations. Other groupings might be preferred, more refined adjustments will be needed, and additional ones may be called for. For instance, I do not recommend that all deductions be eliminated. Certain deductions, such as some allowance for emergency medical outlays are a sensible feature of an equitable income tax; others, such as certain kinds of contributions may be defended on valid grounds of public policy other than equity. However, there are further deductions, including interest and most taxes paid, the validity for which is much more dubious. In all, one can hardly deny that the present policy of deductions is much too generous.

Regarding our other adjustments, I see no argument whatsoever against source withholding on capital income, and find it most difficult to find convincing arguments against disallowance of percentage depletion and inclusion of tax-exempt interest. Also, I find the present system of income splitting thoroughly unsatisfactory. The additional burden on the single taxpayer is vastly above what might be justified by differentials in living costs; and for the bulk of taxpayers, the present arrangement merely permits the preservation of a fictitious picture of progression, which may easily mislead the public. If the rate structure applicable to joint returns is the one which Congress intends to apply, then let the single rates be repealed, and let the joint returns schedule be applied[6] to all returns, together with whatever adjustments in relative exemptions are needed to redress the balance between single and joint returns.

With regard to capital gains, finally, there is no question on equity grounds (based on the accretion concept of income) that capital gains should be taxed like other income and that unrealised gains at time of death should be treated as if realised. If the effects of such a change under the new pattern of bracket rates remains too detrimental to investment, ways should be found to provide preferential tax treatment to investment income where needed but to do so without puncturing the equity of the progressive income tax structure.

All this leaves open the question of how progressive the rate structure for a comprehensively defined income tax should be. This is a problem on which the preceding argument is quite neutral, our point being merely that the desired degree of progression, or lack thereof, should be arrived at in a direct, open, and horizontally equitable fashion. The problem of what the desirable structure of bracket rates should be, given such a tax, is important, but it is not to be dealt with in this paper.

APPENDIX

The analysis is based on table 13.4, parts 1 and 2, 'Statistics of Individual Income Tax Returns, 1956'. Joint returns and single returns not head of household are included but single returns of heads of household are disregarded. Taxable returns only are included.

In arriving at computed adjusted gross income under the various plans, the reported adjusted gross income is corrected first to include total realised gains, as given on pages 28 and 32 of 'Statistics of Income'. The further adjustments are as follows:

Source withholding of tax on interest income

The total amount to be added to adjusted gross income is $3,500 million. (See D. N. Holland, *Tax Revision Compendium*, p. 1551). This amount is distributed among returns falling within the thirteen brackets of adjusted gross income for joint and single returns, or twenty-six cells. Using the breakdown by broad brackets given by Holland as a base, the amounts are broken down further between the first brackets of adjusted gross income and between single and joint returns in proportion to the distribution of reported interest income.

Source withholding of tax on dividend income

The amount allocated is $1 billion. Sources and methods are the same as for interest income, using now the distribution of reported dividend income as our base for allocation.

Inclusion of tax-exempt interest

The total addition to adjusted gross income equals $600 million. (See J. A. Pechman, *Tax Revision Compendium*, p. 1479). It is assumed that tax-exempt interest accrues to the top six brackets of adjusted gross income. Allocation among single and joint returns and among these brackets is made in proportion to reported taxable interest income for the twelve cells to be included.

Disallowance of percentage depletion

The total addition to adjusted gross income equals $400 million. (See Pechman, *Tax Revision Compendium*, p. 1479). Allocation among single and joint returns and among the thirteen income brackets is by distribution of reported dividend income among the twenty-six cells.

Unrealised gains at death

The total addition, following Pechman in what seems a somewhat heroic estimate, is set at $5 billion. Next, a percentage distribution was computed for holdings of depreciable assets, based on R. Goldsmith, 'A Study of Savings in the United States', volume III, page 126. Depreciable assets are defined to include the Goldsmith categories of columns 3, 4, 7, 8, and 9. Since the Goldsmith distribution is for 1950, and in order to obtain a corresponding distribution for 1956, the bracket limits of the Goldsmith distribution were raised by the ratio of personal income in 1956 to personal income in 1950. This distribution was then adjusted to correspond to brackets given in 'Statistics of Income'. The fraction accruing to over $10,000 was broken down further, in proportion to the distribution of reported realised capital gains, among the twenty cells (ten brackets each for joint and single returns) over $10,000. For the six cells (three brackets each for joint and single returns) under $10,000, this method seemed inappropriate since the assets here are mostly residences. Instead, the breakdown was made in proportion to number of returns in the six cells.

Wage supplements

The total adjusted gross income equals $9.9 billion. (See Pechman, *Tax Revision Compendium*, vol. 1, p. 261.) From 'Study of Consumer Expenditures, Income and Saving', volume XI, University of Pennsylvania, 1957, pages 8 and 9, using data for 'Large Cities in North', we obtained the ratio of wage supplements to wage and salary earnings by income bracket. Wage supplements were defined to include the survey categories of public unemployment and social security benefits and pensions; public social assistance and private relief; military pay, allotments, pensions; etc. The ratios for income brackets up to $10,000 were then applied to wage and salary income reported in these brackets (using returns for all taxpayers), thus obtaining hypothetical amounts of wage supplements for each bracket. The percentage distribution of these amounts was then used to allocate the $9.9 billion of wage supplements among brackets under $10,000. The amounts thus allocated were split between joint and single returns in the ratio in which the total wage and salary income is divided between joint and single returns, the same ratio being used for all brackets under $10,000.

NOTES

1. The term 'effective rate' is used throughout to denote tax liability as per cent of income before exemptions. This is the relevant concept since exemptions should be considered a part of the rate structure.
2. For a description of statistical procedure, see appendix.
3. Since computed income is the same for plans 1 and 2, cols. 2 and 4, in table 13.2, are similar, and only 1 curve is drawn in chart 13.2 to represent both.
4. Adjusted gross income is the same under the two plans.
5. Such is the case if progression is measured as the ratio of percentage change in tax to percentage change in income.
6. If a requirement of mandatory joint returns is possible for constitutional reasons, other techniques accomplishing the same objective may be devised.

14 *Ad Valorem* and Unit Taxes Compared*
1953

A series of articles in the *Quarterly Journal of Economics* during 1939 and 1940 dealt with the comparative incidence of a unit and an *ad valorem* sales tax [4, 2, 5, 1]. This discussion analysed at length the comparative changes in price under a unit and an *ad valorem* tax which are, in some sense, matched in their relation to the initial (i.e. pre-tax) price. But little if any attention has been paid to what seems to us the more relevant comparison, namely that between unit and *ad valorem* levies which are equivalent in terms of final total tax yield. Also, the discussion has suffered from the use of a rather unwieldy diagrammatic technique.

In Section I we demonstrate the relationship between the prices resulting from equal-yield unit and *ad valorem* taxes. In Section II we show how certain conclusions from the earlier articles may be extended by reference to total yield conditions.[1]

I

Under pure competition it is obvious that unit and *ad valorem* taxes which result in equal yields will also result in equal final prices. The comparison of changes in monopoly price was made by Wicksell [7] nearly 80 years ago for the case of constant cost.[2] Wicksell argued that the increase in price would always be greater under the specific tax, which is therefore inferior to the *ad valorem* tax on welfare grounds. Unfortunately this discussion has remained almost entirely unnoticed. The following argument covers more or less the same ground, but is more general. For the monopoly case the following propositions apply:

1. The yield from any given unit tax is always smaller than the yield from the *ad valorem* tax which would result in the same final output and price.
2. The maximum yield which may be obtained from a unit tax is smaller than the maximum yield possible from an *ad valorem* tax.
3. If the same yield is obtained from a unit and an *ad valorem* tax, the final price will be higher (the output smaller) under the unit tax.

* With D. B. Suits (1965) *Quarterly Journal of Economics*, 57, 4.

Proof of Proposition 1. Suppose a tax of t dollars per unit has been imposed, with the result that the monopolist maximises profits at an output x_t and price p_t. At this output marginal production cost equals marginal revenue net of tax:

$$MC(x_t) = MR(x_t) - t.$$

Let the unit tax t be replaced by an *ad valorem* tax rate of r (fraction of gross revenue) which tax results in the same final price and output.[2] It must follow that marginal revenue net of tax still equals marginal production cost at output x_t:

$$MC(x_t) = MR(x_t) - r\, MR(x_t).$$

Equating the right sides of the two equations and solving, we obtain

$$r = \frac{t}{MR(x_t)}.$$

The yield of the unit tax is given as

$$Y_t = tx_t,$$

while the yield of the *ad valorem* tax is

$$Y_r = r\, p_i x_t = \frac{t}{MR(x_t)}\, x_t p_t.$$

The difference between the *ad valorem* yield and the yield of the unit tax will then be

$$Y_r - Y_t = tx_t \left(\frac{p_t}{MR(x_t)} - 1 \right).$$

Since the yield of the specific tax (tx_t) is positive and since price exceeds marginal revenue, the right side of the last expression is positive and the yield of the *ad valorem* tax exceeds that of the unit tax.[3]

Although proposition 1 is completely general, it may be illustrated for the linear case as shown in Fig. 14.1. Let OS be the marginal cost schedule, and FD and FA be the demand and marginal revenue schedules before tax. After imposition of a unit tax equal to KH, the net demand and marginal revenue schedules become EB and EL, respectively. The equilibrium output is OX and the tax yield, Y_t, is the area $RKHP$. For an *ad valorem* tax to result in the same price and output, the marginal revenue schedule net of *ad valorem* tax, AG, must pass through point T. The corresponding net average revenue schedule becomes GD. Average revenue net of tax is

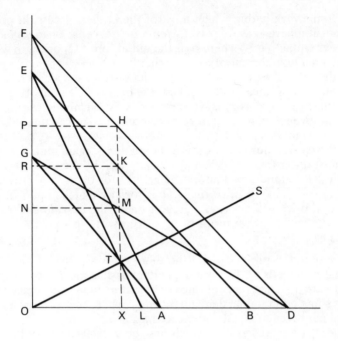

Figure 14.1

now XM (= ON) and tax yield is the area $NMHP$, which includes the area $RKHP$.

Proof of Propositions 2 and 3. Proposition 2 follows obviously from proposition 1. Since for every unit tax the *ad valorem* tax leading to the same price has a higher yield, this must be true also for that unit tax which gains the maximum possible unit tax yield.

To demonstrate proposition 3 we need merely recall that, up to maximum tax yield, the higher the yield is to be, the higher the final price will be. If an *ad valorem* tax results in a given yield, the unit tax which would result in the same price and output gives a lesser yield. To obtain the same yield with a unit tax, the resulting price must therefore be higher.[4]

It follows from this that the same welfare argument which shows a sales tax (either unit or *ad valorem*) to be inferior to an equal-yield income tax, also shows the unit sales tax to be inferior to the *ad valorem* tax [3;6].

II

We now return to the comparison of prices which result from *ad valorem* and unit taxes which are matched at the initial price. As noted before, this is the framework within which most of the earlier discussion proceeded. The question here is as follows: Given a unit tax rate t and an *ad valorem* tax rate r, equal to t/p_0, where p_0 is the initial (pre-tax) price, in which case will the final equilibrium price be higher?

For the sake of ease in presentation, let us call such a pair of tax rates a 'matched' pair of rates.[5] Let us denote the final equilibrium prices achieved under the two taxes as p_t and p_r, respectively. Symbolically the problem becomes: given a matched pair of rates r and t, what can be said about the relative magnitudes p_t and p_r?

For the case of pure competition the matter is again quite simple. Final price must differ from marginal production cost by the amount of tax paid per unit. This amount will always be greater for the *ad valorem* tax which increases (per unit) as price rises. Thus for any matched pair of rates the increase in price will always be greater under the *ad valorem* tax.

For the case of monopoly the following propositions can be demonstrated:[6]

4. For any initial pre-tax price, there are always matched pairs of rates, such that p_t exceeds p_r. This is independent of demand and cost conditions.
5. There are matched pairs of rates such that p_r equals or exceeds p_t only if there is some point on the demand schedule where the corresponding value of marginal revenue equals or exceeds p_0.
6. If there is a matched pair which has the special property that $p_t = p_r$, then for any matched pair of higher rates, p_r exceeds p_t and for any matched pair of lower rates, p_t exceeds p_r.
7. Assuming linear marginal cost and average revenue schedules, and under the presumption that tax rates are not pushed beyond maximum yield levels, for any matched pair of rates, p_t will always exceed p_r.

Proof of Proposition 4. For any unit tax t, marginal net revenue at the resulting price p_t equals marginal production cost:

$$MR(p_t) - t = MC(p_t). \tag{14.1}$$

If now we replace the unit tax with an *ad valorem* tax $r = t/p_0$, where p_0 is the initial price, then p_t is no longer necessarily an equilibrium price. We then have

$$MR(p_t) (1 - r) = MC(p_t) + k, \tag{14.2}$$

where k is the difference between marginal net revenue and marginal production cost under the *ad valorem* rate. Substituting the value of $r = t/p_0$ and subtracting (14.1) from (14.2) gives

$$t \left(1 - \frac{MR(p_t)}{p_0} \right) = k. \tag{14.3}$$

Since initial marginal revenue $MR(p_0)$ is less than p_0, it is always possible to select a value of t sufficiently small to keep $MR(p_t)$ smaller than p_0, so that k is positive. In this case, the marginal net revenue obtainable at p_t under the *ad valorem* rate will exceed the marginal cost of production at p_t. Hence output will be expanded and the *ad valorem* equilibrium price p_r will be lower than p_t.[8]

Proof of Propositions 5, 6, and 7. Propositions 5 and 6 follow directly from 4. To prove 5 we note that k can be zero or negative only if there is some price at which $MR(p)$ equals or exceeds p_0. If there is such a price, a unit tax can be imposed which will give this price as an equilibrium, and the previous argument now shows that p_r would equal or exceed p_t.

To demonstrate proposition 6 we need only note that k will be negative or positive as t, and hence p, exceeds or falls short of some value at which k equals zero.

The proof of proposition 7 follows from the readily demonstrated fact that with linear demand and cost schedules, the p_t corresponding to the unit rate which maximises total yield will also be that price at which marginal revenue is equal to p_0. By proposition 6, for any t less than this, p_t exceeds p_r.

The conclusion reached by previous writers has been that p_r may fall short of or exceed p_t, depending on the size of the levies and on cost and demand conditions. This is quite compatible with our propositions 4, 5 and 6. But for the linear case, our proposition 7 goes farther. By adding the perfectly reasonable assumption that rates are not raised beyond the level of maximum yield, we conclude that for any matched pair of rates the final price under the unit tax will *always* be higher.

In as much as linear functions provide useful approximations to reality, it follows that we may expect the price increase always to be greater under the unit tax, the more since sales tax rates, with some possible exceptions, are well below maximum yield.

The conclusion under conditions of monopoly is thus precisely the opposite of that under conditions of pure competition. But this does not imply that the welfare preference between the two taxes depends on the state of competition. On the contrary, such preference must be based entirely on the equal yield comparison of Section I: the choice between the two taxes is a matter of indifference under pure competition and the *ad valorem* tax is preferable under monopoly.

NOTES

1. Following the earlier discussion, this analysis is limited to the short-run adjustment and deals with the problem in a partial equilibrium setting only.
2. Throughout our discussion the *ad valorem* tax rate r is defined as a per cent of gross revenue. However, many tax laws are written so as to specify a rate which applies to gross revenue net of tax. Our propositions, of course, hold in either

case and the proofs are similar. If s is such a tax, we simply substitute r for s, where $r = s/(1 + s)$.

3. To be formally correct, it should be added, of course, that proposition 1 holds only for tax yields above zero.

   We may further note that the proof of proposition 1 also serves to prove the competitive case. If price always equals marginal revenue, the right side of the last expression is identically zero, and the yields are always equal.

4. This comparison, of course, holds only for *ad valorem* yields which do not exceed the maximum possible unit yield, and under the natural assumption that tax rates will not be pushed beyond the maximum yield point.

5. In section I we have compared tax levies which would give rise to equal final yields. In this section we compare levies which would give the same yield at the initial price. Thus a unit tax t is matched with a gross *ad valorem* rate of $r = t/p_0$, or with a net rate of $s = t/(p_0 - t)$.

   Due [1, ch. 5] defines two distinct problems. A: the comparison of 'two levies which impose the same burden at the old level of output' (p. 89); B: comparison between 'a specific tax and an *ad valorem* tax the rate of which is the ratio of the specific tax to the old price' (p. 90). If the *ad valorem* rate referred to were a gross rate the two cases would, of course, be identical. Since, however, Due adopts the net rate for his analysis, the two problems differ. In problem A, t is compared with s where $s = t/(p_0 - t)$. In B, t is compared with s (again a *net* rate) where $s = t/p_0$! (Given a unit tax of 10 cents on a commodity selling for $1, the liability of the matched *ad valorem* rate under A equals $1/10 \times 100 = 10$ for the gross, and $1/9 \times 90 = 10$ for the net definition. But under B the liability for the net *ad valorem* rate would be 100/9.

   In terms of welfare comparisons or optimal fiscal planning we believe the proper comparison should be between levies which give the same yield in final result. However, it seems to us that our (the usual) comparisons of Section II (Due's case A) are not irrelevant. Legislators may decide to levy a tax of x cents on a given article and then debate whether to use the unit or *ad valorem* tax. But we cannot conceive of a situation in which Due's case B would be of interest.

   Due's B formulation appears to have been thought a necessary counterpart of the 'net' legal definition of the *ad valorem* rate. As we have indicated, there is no such connection.

6. The essential elements of propositions 4–6 were demonstrated by Fagan and Jastram [2, p. 584, esp. notes 7 and 8] by diagrammatic analysis.

7. Note that proposition 7 is independent of whether marginal cost is increasing, constant or decreasing and depends only on its linearity. As a matter of fact, the proposition is valid for any marginal cost function whose slope does not decrease. Geometrically, that is, proposition 7 holds for any marginal cost curve that is linear or convex to the x axis.

8. The competitive case is a special case of the proof of proposition 4. Under competitive conditions marginal revenue at p_t always *equals* p_t, and (for t above zero) must exceed p_0. Thus k is always negative and the *ad valorem* tax results in a higher price.

REFERENCES

[1] Due, J. (1947) *The Theory of Incidence of Sales Taxation* (New York: King's Crown Press).

[2] Fagan, E. and Jastram, R. (1940) 'Tax Shifting in the Short Run', *Quarterly Journal of Economics*.
[3] Friedman, M. (1952) 'The Welfare Effects of an Income Tax and an Excise Tax', *Journal of Political Economy*.
[4] Gilbert, D. (1939) 'The Shifting of Sales Taxes', *Quarterly Journal of Economics*, 53.
[5] Higgins, B., Jastram, R., Due, J. and Gilbert, W. (1940) *Quarterly Journal of Economics*, 54.
[6] Little, I. (1951) 'Direct vs. Indirect Taxes', *Economic Journal*, 51.
[7] Wicksell, K. (1896) *Finanztheoretische Untersuchungen* (Jena: Fischer).

15   Growth With Equity*
1963

The novel issue in the current [1963] debate over tax reform lies in the interplay of equity and growth objectives. Were it not for the former, the certain way to avoid disincentive effects would be through adoption of a single-tax system, involving the use of a head tax only. The absurdity of such a 'solution' should leave no doubt that both objectives must be considered. The purpose of this paper is to examine how they may be reconciled.

I

Much depends on certain premises pertaining to the economics of growth. These need to be set forth before specific tax changes can be considered.

1. The nature of growth policy is sometimes seen in these terms: If there is to be more growth, there must be more capital formation, and if there is to be more capital formation, there must be more saving. More saving may be provided for by more extensive use of taxes which fall on consumption and less extensive use of taxes which fall on saving; therefore, the way to provide for more growth is to substitute taxes on consumption for taxes on saving. I see two objections to this argument.

The nature of our economy is such that provision for saving is a permissive, not a sufficient, condition for growth. That is to say, tax policy for growth cannot be conducted on the simple assumption of *ex ante* equality between saving and investment. However valid in other settings, such as India or the capital-starved post-war Europe of the 1950s, this premise does not meet our present case. Policies to increase the rate of saving without assurance of corresponding gains in investment would tend to retard the growth of the economy, not to raise it.

Moreover, even after provision for increased investment has been made and increased saving becomes called for, this increase may be provided better by raising the general levels of rates and yield from a given tax

---

* *The American Economic Review* (1963) vol. LIII, no. 2.

structure than by changing the tax structure with a given level of yield. The former approach is more flexible (which is important in view of fluctuating levels of investment) and avoids the heavy costs in tax equity inherent in the latter solution. Apart from substantial gains in business saving which may be obtained by reducing the weight of the corporation tax, extremely large changes in the tax structure towards regression would be required (short of a Kaldor-type progressive spendings tax) to raise personal saving by even a modest amount.[1] This is an unnecessary cost to incur. If all that has to be done is to secure a higher rate of saving, let the surplus be increased (or the deficit be reduced), and the funds thus gained be made available through debt retirement (or reduced borrowing) to the private capital market for investment. At the same time, let the composition of the tax structure be determined by equity considerations.

2. The primary and more difficult task, however, is to induce a higher level of investment, and this is a different matter. It cannot be accomplished in sufficient measure by reducing the general level of tax rates. Notwithstanding the current need for general rate reduction as a means of reaching full employment through raising the level of demand, the reduced rate level (if the cut is applied across the board) will still be sufficiently high to leave an incentive problem for growth purposes; and even though the yield from any given set of rates will rise as the economy grows, the outlook for future expenditure needs suggests that we shall be left with a high tax to GNP ratio for some time to come. In this situation, structural adjustment within a given yield total offers a much wider scope for action, and the issue of structural reform must be faced.

What these adjustments should be depends on how investors behave. While the issue of structural reform exists only to the extent that capital formation is not determined rigidly by an accelerator function—otherwise the problem is merely one of aggregate demand and may be handled by adjusting rate levels rather than tax structure—the proper remedy differs with the type of response, e.g. to changes in the net rate of return and/or changes in the internal flow of funds. Conflicts with tax equity are likely to be involved in either case, and the problem is how they may be minimised.

3. Given a need for tax reforms to provide investment incentives, must we reconsider the preceding conclusion that increased saving, when needed, should be provided through higher tax rates?

On economic grounds this is not a serious conflict, since a substantial gain in yield (and public saving) may be derived from slight increases in lower bracket rates which would still remain at levels not likely to pose a serious incentive problem, without demanding excessively high marginal rates at the end of the scale. On political grounds, it may be that incentive-type reforms are hard to come by and feasible only in a context of general rate reduction. But if this is the case, it will be even more difficult to secure the much more extensive structural changes which would be needed to raise saving by a substantial amount.

Given such a deadlock, fiscal policy for growth may require a reduction in the level of government expenditures of the consumption type, possibly at the cost of resulting distortion in resource use as between private and public consumption.

4. The other side of the coin is that tax incentives to investment must be accompanied by measures to assure a sufficient level of total demand. Unless this is done, increased capacity cannot be utilised and is wasteful, This is obvious, but there is the less evident point that structural tax changes to induce investment may affect the level of deficit or surplus needed for this purpose.

Since these structural changes may involve preferential treatment of profit income, they may well reduce the marginal propensity to spend (on investment plus consumption) i.e. raise the marginal propensity to save in the private sector. If so, this will require a decreased surplus (or increased deficit) on the public side. Suppose that the marginal propensity to consume out of wage income is 80 per cent and out of profit income 20 per cent. Substitution of $1 billion of taxes on wages for $1 billion of taxes on profits curtails consumption by $600 million. Also, suppose that it raises investment by $500 million. The change in tax structure thus raises planned saving by $600 million but investment by only $500 million. Hence, a fiscal policy aimed at raising the share of capital formation in a full-employment economy requires decreased government saving (or increased dissaving) of $100 million.

It follows that the association of higher growth with higher budget surplus or lesser deficit (the proposition that a fiscal policy for high employment and growth requires a larger surplus or lesser deficit than one for high employment only), which has become so widely popular in recent years, is by no means a logical necessity. It is an empirical proposition which, beyond the short-run context of a cyclical upswing, rests on what seems to me rather optimistic assumptions.[2] Its broad acceptance, reflecting the latent tendency for neoclassical economics to become ever more classical in its assumptions, needs to be reconsidered. This is the case especially in the present setting where easy money is limited by balance of payment considerations, and the brunt of investment-inducing policies is thrown on the tax system.

5. There remains the basic problem of by how much capital formation must be raised to achieve a given gain in growth. Suppose tax measures are taken which raise gross fixed business investment by 20 per cent, i.e. from about 10 to 12 per cent of GNP. With a GNP of $570 billion this means an increase in gross investment of over $10 billion and implies at least one-third rise in net investment. How much would we have accomplished? According to Solow [6], such a gain in investment would step up the growth rate by a full percentage point; but according to Denison [1], the gain would be only 0.2 of a percentage point, a doubling in the rate of capital formation being needed in order to gain a full point in growth.

These two conclusions spell vastly different lessons for tax policy. In the one case, feasible changes in the tax structure may make an important contribution to growth; in the other, the pay-off is so small that there is little point in disturbing equity considerations. The divergence, which results from different treatments of technical progress, is not easily reconciled, leaving tax policy for growth in a double state of ignorance. Neither do we know by just how much various tax adjustments will raise investment, nor do we know by how much a given rise in investment will increase growth. All that is known (more or less, at least) is the sign of the growth derivative which attaches to various tax measures. This is enough to go by if the growth measures carry no opportunity cost in reduced tax equity; but where they do, policy prescription is difficult since the terms of trade between equity and growth are largely unknown.

II

I now turn to some major areas of tax reform, and their implications for equity and growth. My equity criteria are: (1) that the index of equality should be defined in terms of accretion; (2) that people in equal position should be treated equally without discrimination by uses or sources of income—horizontal equity; and (3) that people in unequal positions should be subject to moderately progressive taxation—vertical equity. My concern with growth relates to investment (rather than saving) incentives. These incentives may be given either on the income sources side (preferential treatment of profit income) or on the uses side (preferential treatment of investment outlays). In either case, horizontal equity is interfered with. Profit income, moreover, is a more important source and investment outlay a more important use at high than at low levels of income, thus suggesting a conflict with vertical equity as well. Given the importance of both equity and growth objectives, what should and what should not be done by way of tax reform?

1. To begin on a negative note, I see little merit in the argument that growth policy calls for a large-scale change in the tax structure from direct to indirect taxes, including substantial replacement of the individual income tax by a sales tax. As noted before, such a substitution is not needed, in the context of the US economy, to increase the supply of saving. The objection, if any, is to income tax effects on work and investment incentives. Such effects, to the extent that they do exist, relate primarily to the higher bracket rates, my hypothesis being that the weight of the substitution effect rises relative to that of the income effect as the bracket rate increases. Since the higher bracket rates carry little significance from a revenue point of view—some 80 per cent of the total income tax yield of $45 billion is derived from the first bracket rate, while rates over 50 per cent contribute 1 per cent only—this problem can be met without changing significantly the weight of the income tax in the total tax structure and without weakening its vital role in securing a progressive tax distribution over the lower and middle income ranges.

2. Next, there is the question whether income tax progression should in fact be reduced.

As far as the upper brackets are concerned, we are faced with an anomalous situation of very high statutory rates which apply in a very spotty fashion only. For instance, the actual average or effective rate (ratio of tax liability to adjusted gross income, both as reported) ranges from about 40 per cent in the $100,000 to $150,000 bracket to about 50 per cent in the bracket above $1 million, as against a range of 50–80 per cent which a naïve view of statutory rates might suggest. If actual liabilities are related to adjusted gross income raised to include realised long-term gains at 100 per cent, as they should be for purposes of this analysis, effective rates for both brackets drop to about 30 per cent.

The picture is similar if marginal rates are considered. Including realised gains at full value in adjusted gross income, actual marginal rates (ratio of increment in liability to increment in income) reach 39 per cent in the $40–$75,000 range, and thereafter decline to 30 per cent in the above $500,000 range. These rates again stand in stark contrast to the 75–91 per cent rates which a naïve view of statutory rates would suggest [5].

From an equity point of view this situation calls for heroic reform. The answer is to lower the high bracket rates to levels which Congress is willing to enforce, and then to assure that they apply uniformly to the full income received. In the tradition of the accretion concept this requires constructive realisation at death and taxation of gains at full rates, allowing for appropriate averaging and corresponding treatment of losses.

From the growth point of view, the situation is not as clear-cut. While the present system of income taxation imposes a potential disincentive effect of high rates where paid, it also offers the incentive effects of exempting large parts of capital income (i.e. income received in the form of capital gains, especially if not realised) from the progressive income tax. Since the dividend income to which the high rates apply is more in the nature of a rent income, while entrepreneurial returns are more largely reflected in capital gains, the present [1963] system—bad though it is from the equity point of view—has attractions on growth grounds. Full taxation of gains, even if combined with a substantial cut-back of marginal rates, could well leave capital income in a less favourable state. There are, however, two factors which narrow the conflict between growth and equity considerations. One is that constructive realisation would largely remove the locking-in problem, the more so if it could be combined with a roll-over provision for realised gains during life; and the other is that taxation at death should be less of a disincentive than taxation during life. Depending on the weight of these factors, the investment effects of a heroic capital gains reform may not be disadvantageous on balance.

Two other upper-bracket problems might be mentioned, where both equity and growth considerations point in the same direction. One is the removal of tax exemption on state and local securities, which now offer a low-risk haven to potential risk capital, and substitution (if needed) of a more efficient technique of federal aid to state and local debt financing. The other is removal of barriers to executive mobility which now arise from various devices to cushion the impact of high marginal rates on executive compensation.

While venture-type investment largely originates in the upper brackets, subject to marginal rates of 50 per cent or more, total equity investment nevertheless derives a significant contribution from the middle and lower ranges. General rate reduction further down the line, however, is limited sharply by the much larger revenue loss involved; and rate reduction which is marked by an offsetting broadening of the base—highly desirable though it may be on grounds of horizontal equity and administrative simplicity—does not make a major contribution on growth grounds.[3]

There remains the possibility of granting preferential treatment to capital income or investment.[4] Since the distribution of capital income is much less equal than that of wage income, a vanishing capital income credit (illustrated in crude form by the dividend deduction) would permit an investment incentive without conflict with progression and without large revenue loss. At the same time, it would leave us with a new and, considering the tradition of earned income credit, particularly unhappy offence against horizontal equity. A less objectionable approach may be in the direction of inducements to investment, especially investment in education, e.g. provision for depreciation of education costs.

3. Turning now to the corporation profits tax and the corporate investment decision, we begin with a quite different premise. Whereas the individual income tax need be strengthened as the mainstay of an equitable structure, there is little place therein for an 'absolute' corporation tax.[5] If the tax falls on profits in the first instance, it discriminates against dividend income.[6] If shifted (in the sense of shortrun adjustments) into higher prices or lower wages, it is objectionable as a discriminating product or wages tax. Given these considerations, it is difficult to see why there should be so much concern with horizontal equity in the individual income tax if the corporation tax is to be accepted on purely pragmatic grounds. The best solution from an equity point of view would be to assure full taxation of capital gains (including constructive realisation at death) and then to forget about the corporation tax.[7]

Given preferential treatment of gains, some form of corporation tax need be retained. Corporate profits (whether retained or paid out) might be taxed to the shareholder as if he were a partner, a procedure which to me seems by no means as difficult as it is usually made out to be. Or, within the confines of a partial solution, the corporation may be given a dividend-paid credit while retained earnings are taxed at the corporate level.[8]

4. A comprehensive reform along these lines would be a gain in equity and, most likely, also on growth grounds. But the matter of shifting must be looked at more closely before adopting such a solution. It is usually assumed that the corporation tax, initially at least, falls on profits. But does it? Observation of the rate of return on capital invested in corporations shows that gross returns in the 1950s were nearly twice those of the 1920s, but that net returns (notwithstanding an increase in the corporate rate from 5 to 50 per cent) have remained about unchanged. While this observation is compatible with a hypothesis of full shifting, it is not conclusive since the effects of the corporation tax are not isolated from other factors, nor does

it tell us (which is crucial for purposes of this paper) whether shifting took the form of initial price wage adjustments, or whether it operated over the longer run through a reduction in capital input.[9] A recent attempt to isolate the tax from other effects, however, suggests that there has been a high degree of short-run shifting [3] and given the expansion in capital stock which did occur, it is indeed difficult to explain the constancy of the net rate of return without such an assumption.

If this is correct, and there has been a high degree of shifting in the short-run sense, the corporation tax did not have the disturbing effects on profitability and the flow of funds which it is alleged to have had. The offence against horizontal equity, similarly, was not by 'double taxation' of dividends but by sales or wage taxation. Given a symmetrical assumption of 'unshifting', repeal would be desirable on equity grounds, even though it would be of little significance on growth grounds.

But suppose that conditions with regard to shifting are asymmetrical, i.e. that the tax is passed on in the case of rate increase, but that there is no corresponding unshifting in the case of rate decrease. In this case (which also seems to have some support in our findings) repeal would be unjustified on equity grounds, as it would result in a transfer from other taxpayers to profits. At the same time, it would be effective as a profit subsidy and be helpful to growth. There would be much merit, however, in economising the scope of subsidy by rendering it most effective, i.e. by using a selective rather than overall rate reduction approach.

5. Let me now take a less heroic view and recognise that the corporation tax is accepted as an equitable part of the tax structure. One may then enquire what type of corporate tax relief would be most helpful on growth grounds, while requiring the least total reduction in the yield of the profits tax.

Taking the view that investment responds to the net rate of return, a comparison may be drawn between the profitability effects of rate reduction, accelerated depreciation, and the investment credit, assuming the revenue loss to the Treasury to be the same in all cases.[10] The result depends on how the condition of 'equal revenue loss' is defined,[11] but there is good reason to conclude that the credit approach, especially in the form of a marginal credit, is most effective. At the same time, these devices introduce an element of discrimination between corporations and their owners which conflicts with the criterion of equal treatment. In order to minimise the inequality which results from reducing the overall tax on profits (assuming that it is proper to begin with), a new inequality (relating to the relative treatment of various profit recipients) has to be taken into the bargain.

Much of the recent reasoning on the comparable effect of alternative devices on profitability implies that profitability—in the sense which is relevant for investor behaviour—is in fact reduced by the tax, and hence increased by rate reduction. It disregards the fact that a tax with loss offset reduces both losses and gains, with the result that an investor who responds to the rate of return on risk (the ratio of probable gains to losses) finds his reward unchanged.[12] Having some vested interest in this type of investor, the recent return to pre-loss offset thinking (and I plead guilty myself) bothers me. While the investment credit is still superior to rate reduction on these grounds,[13] the obvious remedy (if the loss offset line of reasoning were valid) would be neither a general rate reduction nor an investment credit, but an increase in the loss participation relative to the gain participation rate.

6. Apart from the profitability effect, reduction in the corporation tax may raise investment because the internal flow of funds is increased.[14] This result may be solicited most effectively by introducing a retained earnings credit along the line of the German practice in the early post-war years. Such a measure, however, is diametrically opposed to what needs to be done on equity grounds. The dividend paid credit in turn, while most desirable as a partial move towards integration on equity grounds, is undesirable (as far as the internal funds argument goes) on growth grounds. I am inclined, however, to discount the great weight frequently placed by the business community on this argument and to resolve this particular conflict on equity grounds.

My major conclusions are these. Starting from the premise that the problem of structural tax reform is one of equity and investment incentives rather than aggregate saving, there is no good case (except perhaps on grounds of tax politics) for reducing the weight of the individual income tax in the overall tax system. While equity and incentive considerations coincide regarding some cut-back in top-bracket rates, conflict may arise in the treatment of capital gains. A proper solution on equity grounds (taxation of gains at death with constructive realisation) would be economically helpful in eliminating locking-in effects, but the eventual taxation of hitherto untaxed (unrealised) gains might be harmful.

As for the corporation tax, the equity problem would be solved with full taxation of capital gains; but short thereof, a corporation tax with dividend paid credit is needed to include undistributed earnings in the tax base. From the incentive point of view, the most potent solution (and the one least in conflict with equity considerations) is given by the investment credit type of tax relief. In all, the conflict between equity and incentive considerations can be held in bounds, provided that a sufficiently comprehensive and courageous view of tax reform is taken.

NOTES

1. This conclusion is illustrated by the following estimates, showing the increase in saving (reduction in consumption) which would result from various tax substitutions, leaving total yield unchanged [5]:

Substitution	*Estimated gain in saving (million dollars)*
1. Reduce the high brackets of individual income tax to 50 per cent, substitute 2 per cent increase in other rates	+ 300
2. Reduce individual income tax rates by 10 per cent, substitute consumer tax of $5 billion	+ 600
3. Replace individual income tax with a flat rate tax on gross income	+ 3700
4. Replace individual income tax by sales tax	+ 5500

2. For similar reasons I am sceptical regarding the proposition that a tax cut will involve no net revenue loss since the initial loss will be recovered in the subsequent upswing. With investment constant this can be true only with a marginal propensity to consume larger than 1. With $c_m < 1$, the expansion must generate a substantial increase in investment, such that

$$\frac{t_0}{1 - c_m(1 - t_0)} (G + I_0) = \frac{t_1}{1 - c_m(1 - t_1)} (G + I_1)$$

and

$$\frac{\Delta I}{I_0} = \frac{G + I_0}{I_0} \left[\frac{n(1 - c)}{[1 - c(1 - t_0)] (1 - n)} \right]$$

where I_0 is the initial expenditure level, G is the level of government purchases, c_m is the marginal propensity to consume, t_0 is the initial tax rate and n is the proposed percentage cut in t_0. With $G = 100$, $I_0 = 50$ and $t_0 = 0.3$, a 20 per cent rise in investment is needed to neutralise the yield loss from a 10 per cent cut in tax rate.

3. Suppose that we combine base-broadening with rate reduction so as to leave total yield unchanged, the rate reduction taking the form of an equal percentage cut in all bracket rates. As a result, average as well as marginal rates will be reduced for each bracket of taxable net income, but the ratio of gross income to net income will be increased. On the average, the two factors will tend to wash out leaving the income as well as the substitution effect unchanged.

4. The problem is not solved by a progressive spendings tax since the need is for investment, not saving, incentives. A comprehensive solution, therefore, would require a progressive spendings tax plus a hoardings tax.

5. This is compatible with having the corporation (as well as unincorporated firms) pay a tax for services rendered by government. However, such a tax would be much smaller (especially at the federal level) and should take the form of a value added rather than a profits tax.

6. This is evident once it is recognised that the entire concept of horizontal equity relates to the individual as the bearer of tax burden. The corporation is a powerful unit from a social or economic point of view, but it does not follow that it has tax-paying ability of its own.

7. The net revenue loss from complete integration might be —$22 billion (corporation tax yield) + $7.7 billion (35 per cent personal rate on $22 billion gain in profits) + $3.5 billion (35 per cent on retained earnings of $10 billion) = $10.8 billion. Deducting further a service charge-type value added tax yielding, say, $3 billion (to be passed on to the consumer), and $3 billion due to capital gains reform, we would be left with a net loss of $5 billion, requiring an about 10 per cent average increase in income tax rates as offset.

8. Substitution of a value added tax for the corporation profits tax would not solve these problems. A value added tax is more or less similar to a general proportional gross income tax without exemptions. It is neither a means of integrating retained earnings into the existing income tax, nor a substitute for a profits tax.

9. If there is shifting of the latter type, depressing effects on growth result; if it is of the former type they do not. Similarly, if shifting operates through reduced capital formation, the double taxation argument remains valid; if shifting reflects a short-run adjustment with profits unchanged, it does not.

10. The catalogue of measures here given is by no means complete. As an alternative to a marginal investment credit, see Baumol's proposal for a tax subsidy scheme relating to growth in sales, which has the additional feature that it may be placed on a self-financing basis by penalising declining firms [8].

11. Reference may be to (a) receipts over a finite period. Or, it may be to (b) receipts pertaining to the effects over infinity of a change in the tax law applicable for a finite period. If accelerated depreciation is introduced in 1962 and discontinued in 1965, the revenue effect (assuming a maximum life of 20 years) will extend to 1985. The question is whether the positive 'tail' from 1965 to 1985 should be counted. Finally, reference may be to (c) receipts over infinity. Also, there is the question whether to define the loss of receipts in terms of (d) present value, or (e) independent of timing. Using assumptions (a) and (e), the investment credit is much superior to accelerated depreciation, especially if the period is brief (say, five years) and the economy is rapidly growing. Using (c) and (d), and assuming the Treasury's rate of discount to be the same as that of firms, the various approaches are equally effective.

12. Stated thus briefly, certain qualifications of the argument are overlooked, e.g. the tax is not truly general, and wages of management may be subsumed in profits [2]. Similar conclusions are reached if the risk is defined as the dispersion of the probability distribution of positive and negative yields [7].

13. Assume an investor who before the credit would have invested $100. Now a credit of 10 per cent is granted. Consider two possible reactions: (1) The investor continues to invest his own $100, but can now buy an asset worth $110. His gain prospects are increased by 10 per cent, while his loss prospects are as before. (2) The investor now invests $90.9 of his own funds, which with the credit of $9.09 purchases an asset of $100, and holds $9.1 in cash. His gain prospect is unchanged, but his loss prospect is reduced by 9 per cent.

14. Concern with tax effects on internal funds is quite compatible with our earlier conclusion that the supply of savings should not be dealt with through adjustments in tax structure. The flow of internal funds here enters not as a general supply of saving, but as an inducement to invest.

REFERENCES

[1] Denison, E. (1967) 'How to Raise the High Employment Growth Rate by One Percentage Point', *American Economic Review*, S. 57.

[2] Domar, E. and Musgrave, R. A. (1944) 'Proportional Income Taxation and Risk Taking', *Quarterly Journal of Economics*, 57, 4.

[3] Krzyzaniak, M. and Musgrave, R. A. (1963) *The Shifting of the Corporation Income Tax* (Baltimore: Johns Hopkins University Press).

[4] Musgrave, R. A. (1963) 'Effect of Tax Policy on Private Capital Formation', in Commission on Money and Credit, *Fiscal and Debt Management Policy* (New York: Prentice Hall).

[5] —— (1959) 'How Progressive is the Income Tax?', *Tax Revision Compendium*, vol. 3, Committee on Ways and Means, US Congress (Washington, D. C.).

[6] Solow, R. (1962) 'Technical Progress, Capital Formation, and Economic Growth', *American Economic Review*, S. 52.

[7] Tobin, J. (1958) 'Liquidity Preference as Behavior towards Risk', *Review of Economic Studies*, 25.

[8] Knorr, K. and Baumol, W. (eds.) (1961) *What Price Economic Growth?* (New York: Prentice Hall).

16 Effects of Business Taxes on International Commodity Flows* 1966

It is now [1966] widely argued that US business is at a disadvantage because European companies are permitted to deduct value added taxes from their profit tax base. The purpose of this paper is to examine this proposition and the effects of business taxation upon international commodity flows. From the point of view of efficiency, it is desirable to minimise such effects, and the question is what structure of international business taxation is best designed to serve this purpose. Though an important aspect of the broader problem of tax integration, this is by no means the entire story. Taxation effects on factor flows, which will be given little attention here, may be of equal or greater importance. Moreover, international business taxation poses equity problems regarding the treatment of the individual taxpayer as well as the distribution of tax bases between jurisdictions. The present discussion, therefore, covers but one aspect of a broader set of issues which arise if the principles of business taxation are reconsidered in the context of an open economy and assumes that exchange rates are fixed.

If taxes are to be neutral regarding product flows, the international price ratios of traded products at factor cost must equal those at market price. Taxes which enter into cost of production distort these ratios. Assuming the initial exchange rates to be proper, they give rise to an excess burden. Let us consider what changes in product flows result.

PRODUCTION TAXES

Consider countries A and B, producing products X and Y at pre-tax supply prices p_x^A, p_x^B, p_Y^A, p_Y^B respectively. We examine the imposition of various tax patterns, assuming fixed exchange rates to apply. It is also assumed for the time being that deficits or surplus on trade account are simply met by reduction or accumulation of reserves, without, however, affecting the money supply.

* In Krzyzaniak, M. (ed.) (1966) *Effects of Corporation Income Tax* (Detroit: Wayne State University Press).

Effects on relative prices

We begin with production taxes which are reflected in the cost of the taxed product, e.g. a value added, turnover or payroll tax. Such a tax may be imposed in a more or less general fashion.

1. We assume first that the tax is imposed on the production of X in A only. We than have $\hat{p}_X^A/\hat{p}_Y^A > p_X^A/p_Y^A$ where $\wedge$ indicates after tax. However, this change may involve an absolute rise in p_X^A, a decline in p_Y^A or a mixture of both.[1] As distinct from the closed economy case, this distinction is of importance. In the closed case, incidence is a matter of relative prices and absolute price changes have little importance. In the open case, what matters are relative international prices, and changes therein depend upon the movement of absolute domestic prices.

If p_X^A rises in absolute terms, we have $\hat{p}_X^A/p_X^B > \hat{p}_X^A/p_X^B$ and the result will be reduced exports or increased imports of X by A, depending on whether X was an export or import good. If p_Y^A falls in absolute terms, we have $\hat{p}_Y^A/\hat{p}_Y^B < p_Y^A/p_Y^B$, and the result will be increased exports or reduced imports of Y by A, depending on whether Y was an export or import good. Trade distortions (though at a different scale) occur in both cases, but (assuming price elasticities greater than 1) the balance of payment effects for A are unfavourable in the first and favourable in the second case.

2. Now let the production tax apply to both X^A and Y^A. If the absolute prices of the taxed products remain unchanged while factor costs fall, trade will be unaffected. If absolute prices rise, exports will decrease and imports will rise, the result being the same as that of exchange appreciation.

3. Next, assume that similar production taxes are applied to X^A and X^B. If the absolute price adjustments are symmetrical in A and B, trade is not affected. But what if absolute price changes diverge, e.g. if p_X^A rises while p_Y^B falls? We then have $\hat{p}_X^A/\hat{p}_X^B > p_X^A/p_X^B$ and $\hat{p}_Y^A/\hat{p}_Y^B > p_Y^A/p_Y^B$. In this case, A will export less (or import more) of X and import less (or export more) of Y. Trade patterns will change, there being no assurance that even a uniform tax policy (uniform, that is, between products but not countries) will be neutral in its trade effects.

4. Similar reasoning applies if the production tax is imposed on X^A and Y^B. Now a symmetrical price response to both taxes changes relative costs for both products, i.e. $\hat{p}_X^A/\hat{p}_X^B > p_X^A/p_X^B$ and $\hat{p}_Y^A/\hat{p}_Y^B < p_Y^A/p_Y^B$. This will be the case whether the prices of taxed products rise or the prices of tax free products fall. If adjustments are asymmetrical, relative price changes are limited to one product. For instance, if p_X^A rises while p_Y^B does not, p_Y^A/p_Y^B remains unchanged, while p_X^A/p_X^B rises even more sharply. Trade changes result in both cases, but the patterns differ.

5. Finally, let the production tax apply generally between products and countries, including X_A, X_B, Y_A and Y_B. No relative price changes will occur if the adjustment in the two countries is symmetrical. Hence trade patterns will not be affected. But changes result if the price level in A rises while that in B remains unchanged. A's exports will fall and imports will rise, and vice versa for B. The result (regarding both exports and imports)

will be precisely the same as that of appreciation in A's or depreciation in B's currency. Again we note that even a completely uniform tax policy (uniform, that is, between countries and products) need not be neutral in its allocation effects.

Neutralising adjustments

So far we have assumed that the tax does not provide for differential treatment of imports or exports. Certain adjustments in the treatment of international goods may be made which neutralise tax effects on commodity flows. Returning to the above cases, we find:

1. A tax on the production of X in A may be neutralised by an export rebate ER and a compensating import tax IT on the taxed product, provided that the tax is reflected in increased price; and by a compensating import rebate IR and an export tax ET on tax-free products, where the tax is reflected in reduced factor costs.
2. For a tax on X^A and Y^A the ER–IT adjustment is needed only in the case of price increase. The case of factor cost decline does not call for adjustments since there are no tax-free products.
3. For a tax on X^A and X^B, neutralising measures are needed in the case of asymmetrical adjustment only. They take the form of ER–IT adjustments to the taxed product in the country with price rise, and IR–ET adjustments to the tax-free product in the country with price decline.
4. For the taxes on X^A and Y^B, neutralising adjustment calls for application of ER–IT on the taxed product in the country in which the tax leads to price rise, and application of IR–ET on the tax-free product in the country in which the tax reduces factor costs.
5. For the case of asymmetrical adjustment (to a truly general tax) neutralisation is obtained by applying ER–ID in the country with price rise.

CONSUMPTION TAXES

We now turn to a similar analysis of consumption taxes. As before, we begin with a general view, excluding equalising adjustments, and then consider what adjustments are called for to neutralise trade effects.

Effects on relative prices

Similar reasoning may now be applied to the case of consumption taxes, say, a retail sales tax. By its very nature, such a tax applies to the sale of home-produced as well as imported products.

1. Suppose that the tax is imposed on the sale of X in A. If the price of X rises by the amount of tax, trade effects will be neutral. If the tax is reflected in reduced factor cost, this will not be the case. Exports of Y will increase, since $\hat{p}_Y^A/\hat{p}_Y^B < p_Y^A/p_Y^B$, the cost of producing Y in A being reduced relative to that in B. Moreover, imports of X will fall, since the reduced net

price will reduce competition from *B*'s exporters who did not share the reduction in factor costs.

2. If the tax applies to the sale of both *X* and *Y* in *A*, and is reflected in higher prices, trade effects will again be neutral. If it is reflected in reduced factor costs, exports will rise and imports will fall, the effect being similar to that of exchange *de*preciation. The difference with the corresponding case 2 for the cost tax is thus twofold: In the cost tax case the equivalence to exchange rate adjustment arose with price rise and was compared with appreciation; in the retail sales tax case it arises with factor-cost decline and is compared with depreciation.

3. Turning to a tax which applies to the sale of *X* in both *A* and *B*, trade distortions will result only if the adjustment for the two countries is asymmetrical, analogous to the preceding case 3 result.

4. For a tax on *X* in *A* combined with a tax on *Y* in *B* relative price changes result, as in the corresponding case for the production tax, even if the adjustment is symmetrical. But again the distortion is limited to one product in the asymmetrical case.

5. This leaves the general retail tax, applying to both countries and both products. As for the general production tax, the result is neutral for the symmetrical adjustment, but not so for the asymmetrical case. The country with rising product prices now experiences effects equivalent to depreciation, while that with falling factor costs experiences appreciation. The adjustment direction has the opposite implication as in the cost-tax case.

Neutralising adjustments

As in the case of cost taxes, certain adjustments may be introduced to neutralise trade effects.

1. For the case of reduced factor cost, neutralisation is obtained by applying *ET* to all exports and by granting *IR* to tax-free goods.

2. If the tax on X^A and Y^A leads to reduced factor cost, *ET* is applied to exports but no *IR* is needed since there are no tax-free goods.

3. For the case of asymmetrical adjustment to a tax on the sale of *X* in both *A* and *B*, the country which experiences reduced factor cost proceeds as under 1. No adjustment is needed for the country with increased prices.

4. The adjustment to a sales tax on *X* in *A* and *Y* in *B* is as under 3.

5. For the case of asymmetrical adjustment to a general sales tax in both countries, *IT* is applied in the country which experiences price rise, while *ET* is applied in the country which experiences declining factor costs.

PROFITS TAX

So far we have dealt with production taxes of various sorts, and with a retail sales tax. Imposition of such taxes on product *X* but not on *Y* may be expected to raise the gross price of *X* relative to that of *Y*. This follows because variable factor inputs demand the same return in both uses, but the price of X must include the tax cost as well. The rest of the analysis follows from this initial proposition of relative price change.

In the case of the corporation tax, such a change will not come about unless there is shifting in the 'short-run' sense of the term, i.e. the tax is not reflected fully in reduced profits but its effect is cushioned by administered price or wage adjustments. In the absence of such adjustments, no immediate trade effects will result. But if there is short-run shifting on domestic sales—and I am somewhat committed to this hypothesis—the situation is quite similar to that of the outright cost taxes. In this case, the profits tax qualifies for an *ER–IT* adjustment, provided that the shifting takes the form of absolute price rise. While determination of appropriate *ER–IT* rates is more complicated than in the case of a cost tax, the basic rationale is the same. At the same time, *ER–IT* is not called for if the adjustment operates via wage reduction. The Krzyzaniak–Musgrave results [2] are silent on this point. Thus, even if the shifting hypothesis is accepted, our results do not tell us whether *ER–IT* is called for or not.

But let us assume that the tax is shifted forward on domestic sales so that the *ER–IT* adjustment is called for. If the adjustment is not made, trade effects on the import side will result at once, as imports would become cheaper relative to home products. Export effects will result with some delay to the extent that in the short run, capital previously used to produce for exports cannot be promptly used for home production, so that the return to such capital is in the nature of a rent income. Thus, the analogy to a tax on variable cost has to be qualified in this respect. But in the longer run, capital will move from production for exports to production for domestic sales so as to equalise net returns, and exports will decline.

Finally, it is conceivable (though unlikely) that the tax may be shifted on foreign as well as on domestic sales. If such is the case, no change in the domestic capital structure occurs, and *ER* is inappropriate. However, the *IT* adjustment is still called for.

NEUMARK COMMITTEE VIEW

It follows from the above that various tax patterns may give rise to a variety of results, depending on the absolute directions of the price adjustments. Matters are much simplified if one is willing to assume that (a) cost increases due to tax must be reflected in absolute price rise, and (b) the profits tax is not shifted in the short-run sense. This is the view which underlies the Neumark Report, GATT practices,[2] and more or less the entire discussion of tax integration in the Common Market.

Given this assumption, the underlying set of principles is very simple. Profits taxes are neutral regarding commodity flows. Production taxes upon X imposed at differential rates by A and B are non-neutral. A general production rate, imposed by

1. A general cost tax, imposed in one country only, is similar to appreciation, if reflected in rising prices;

2. A general retail sales tax, imposed in one country only, is similar to depreciation, if reflected in falling factor costs;

3. A general cost tax, imposed in all countries, is similar to appreciation for countries which experience rising product prices, and to depreciation in countries which experience falling factor costs;

4. A general retail sales tax, imposed in all countries, as above is similar to depreciation in countries where product prices rise, and to appreciation in countries where factor costs fall.

Obviously, there can be no equivalence of exchange rate changes which are inherently general with tax rate changes which are applied to particular products only. Moreover, the tax changes noted under 1–4 are neutralised if the proper *ER–IT–ET–IR* are applied, so that the equivalence with exchange rate changes disappears.

'DIRECTION' OF ADJUSTMENT

Given the strategic importance which the absolute changes in product or factor prices occupy in a fixed exchange rate setting, it is well to enquire upon what factors these absolute changes depend.

To begin with, we should note that this issue must not be confused with a quite different question, traditionally considered in the closed economy context, whether a business tax is 'shifted forward' in the sense of passing the real burden on to consumers; or 'backward', in the sense of passing the real burden on to wage-earners. Forward shifting in this real incidence sense can come about with or without an absolute rise in product prices, just as backward shifting may occur with or without a fall in factor prices. The issue, in this traditional context of shifting analysis is one of relative prices; the issue in the present context, is one of change in absolute prices.

To illustrate, consider the case of a value added tax of the income type, which may be expected to be reflected in a proportional reduction in factor incomes. This result may come about via an increase in product prices with factor incomes constant, or a decline in factor costs with product prices constant. Or consider a corporation profits tax and assume market forces to be such that the tax is shifted forward (in the real burden sense) upon the consumer. Again, the adjustment may take the form of rising product prices with wages and profits after tax unchanged, or it could take the form of falling wages and profits after tax (though the latter decline would be much less than in the non-shifting case) with product prices unchanged. Similarly, backward shifting in the real burden sense could take the form of declining wages with profits after tax and prices unchanged, or of a rise in profits after tax and prices with wages unchanged. The forces which determine these relative price changes, i.e. where the real burden of the tax comes to rest, evidently depend upon the competitive (or lack thereof) market structure. There remains the question of how the absolute price changes are determined.

Obviously, the answer depends upon the macro nature of the system in which the tax change operates, not to speak of the nature of the particular tax change, e.g. whether it is accompanied by an expenditure increase, a tax substitution, and so forth. To simplify, let us assume here that we deal with a tax substitution. To begin with, consider a flexible system of the classical type, in which full employment is maintained automatically, and the money supply is held constant. The absolute price adjustment, inherent in any tax change may then be said to depend upon 'monetary' factors, such as effects of changes in the structure of payments upon income velocity or the operation of the real balance effects, and the extent to which the latter differentiates between holdings of transaction and asset money. However this may be, there is nothing in the operation of the pricing system which tells us what the nature of absolute price change will be. Turning now to a more realistic setting, the nature and degree of price rigidities, as well as the behaviour of monetary policy becomes of paramount importance.

Consider the following five policy settings:

1. Wages flexible; monetary policy permissive
2. Wages downward rigid; monetary policy permissive
3. Wages flexible; monetary policy stabilises product price level
4. Wages downward rigid, monetary policy stabilises product price level
5. Wages flexible, monetary policy stabilises factor price level

and the possible patterns of absolute price change in response to a tax change, e.g. imposition of a value added tax. Under 1 we are back to the general monetary forces noted in the preceding paragraph, with either adjustment pattern being possible. Under 2 the tax must either be reflected in higher product prices or be absorbed in reduced profits. Under 3 it must be either reflected in reduced money wages or be absorbed in reduced profits. Under 4 only absorption in profits is possible, while under 5 the situation is the same as under 2.

Looking at this schema, one is tempted to conclude that case 2 is the most realistic one, and that, therefore, absolute price increase is the most likely result. This conclusion, however, is qualified somewhat if the problem is looked at in a dynamic context. With economic growth, the tax change may depress money wages not in the absolute sense but in the relative sense of limiting the increase which otherwise would have occurred. This is compatible with the hypothesis of downward rigid money wages, yet for purposes of the present discussion has the same implications as would result from an actual wage decline.

EMPIRICAL ASPECTS

Let us now leave this theoretical discussion and consider to what extent the US balance of payment position may have been affected by differences in the US and European tax structures. The relevant comparison for our purposes is not the composition of the tax structure (per cent of total from various taxes) but the relative (or even absolute) level of tax rates. Assuming that 'shifting patterns' are the same for various countries, the relevant factor (as noted before) is the different level of rates. As a first approximation, this may be looked at in terms of tax to GNP ratios, although this may be somewhat misleading since the composition of GNP (and hence the level of particular tax rates corresponding to a given tax in GNP ratio) differs among countries. Even though a number of tax comparisons have been made recently, there is no readily available table which puts matters into a form which conveniently serves present purposes. Table 16.1 takes a rough stab at this.

Table 16.1 Tax revenue as per cent of GNP (1961)

	US	Germany	UK	France	Italy
1. Personal income tax	9.2	7.6	7.1	3.9	4.9
2. Employee Contribution to National Insurance	1.2	4.6	1.8	3.2	0.8
3. 1 + 2	10.4	12.2	8.9	7.1	—
4. Corporation tax	4.4	3.0	2.9	2.3	(2)
5. Sales tax, etc.	11.1	17.4	9.2	14.0	15.0
6. Employer contribution to National Insurance	1.9	5.0	1.1	11.5	3.8
7. 5 + 6	13.0	23.4	10.3	25.5	18.8
8. Property taxes, etc.	3.5	1.2	0.3	....	....
9. Other	0.7	−3.8	+6.6	0.1	3.5
10. Total	32.0	35.0	29.0	35.0	28.0

The level of *direct personal* taxes in the US falls between that of the UK and Germany, and tends to be higher than that of continental countries. But as noted before, it may be assumed that this has no direct price effects. In comparing the income tax ratios shown in Table 16.1 note that the relative level of US rates is greatly exaggerated by comparing rates at similar absolute income levels. A more meaningful comparison would be between equal relative (e.g. mean, limits of decile) income positions. Also, for European countries, the weight of NI contributions is higher relative to the income tax.

The *corporation profits tax* ratio as recorded in Table 16.1 is substantially higher for the US, but the more relevant indicators are the tax to profit ratios. Here we have the following picture:

Table 16.2 Profits tax rates

	Profits tax rates				Direct taxes on profits and proper- ty as proportion of net profits	
	Statutory		*Effective*			
	(a)	*(b)*	*(a)*	*(b)*	*(a)*	*(b)*
France	.50	.50	.46	.46	50	50
W Germany	.56	.32	.53	.30	70	53
Italy	.36	.36	.32	.32	45	45
UK	.54	.24	.39	.18	54	24
US	.47	.47	.43	.43	50	50

(a) Undistributed; (b) Distributed.

It appears that the US rate on undistributed profits is pretty well in line with, and in some cases substantially below, foreign rates. However, the US rate on distributed profits is higher.

The *sales tax* pattern shows a substantially higher ratio for continental Europe than for the US, with a large part of the difference accounted for by turnover tax in Italy and Germany, and value added tax in France.

Employer NI contributions show also considerably higher ratios in continental Europe. However, it may be noted that company-type contribution systems are higher here and that these should perhaps be included into the comparison.

Empirical evaluation
The evidence of Table 16.1 boils down to three conclusions:
(a) The weight of personal taxes (line 3) may be somewhat higher in the US than in most European countries excluding West Germany; (b) the corporation tax to GNP ratio (line 4) is relatively high in the US, but the difference is rather slight if the tax to profit ratio is considered; (c) the 'cost taxes' to GNP ratio (line 7) is distinctly lower in the US than in continental Europe. From what has been said before, (a) is not very relevant in this connection. The main factor is (c) and to some extent (b).

Cost Taxes. As far as the US is concerned, let us assume (due to wage rigidities) that cost taxes are reflected in higher prices. The central question then is whether the higher 'cost taxes' in Europe have been reflected in higher prices, lower wages or squeezed profits. Considering European profit rates over the 1950s, the latter does not seem likely. The main alternative would appear to be relatively lower wages or higher prices.

Suppose the adjustment in Europe was via wage reduction while in the US it was via price increase. This would place Europe at an advantage for both the line 5 taxes where *ER–ID* applies, and the line 6 taxes where it does not apply. The advantage in the line 5 case is measured by the absolute level of European rates, while in the line 6 case it relates to the absolute level of US rates. If the adjustment is towards higher prices in Europe as well, the line 5 taxes are neutral, independent of rate levels, while the line 6 taxes give an advantage to the US as the lower rate country, the advantage being related to the rate differential.

One way of evaluating what happened is by general appraisal of the European scene during the 1950s. With regard to Germany (and this is the only country on which I shall venture a general impression), the fact is that wage rates did lag during, say, the first two-thirds of the 1950s, but the explanation hardly lies in the turnover tax. Other factors, such as labour influx, union attitudes, etc. seem a much more plausible explanation. This is reinforced by the fact that the tax factor did not prevent a more rapid rise in the wages in recent years. As to the monetary policy restraint, it is again true that German monetary policy was on the restrictive side, although perhaps less so than usually assumed. However, the policy objective was hardly that of maintaining a fixed price level. Rather, it was one of curtailing the expansionary influence of export surplus on money supply.

Moreover, it is important to note that the high indirect tax rates were introduced even before the currency reform. This poses the question whether the price level set at the time of the currency reform was higher because of these taxes—a query impossible to answer with precision, but it seems unlikely. Beyond this, there is the question whether the existence of the given rate level was a retarding factor in wage increases. An affirmative answer would imply that the tax was absorbed into wages gradually as productivity rose by retarding corresponding wage increases—a possibility which, it seems to me, is again unlikely. While one could not say that the German situation was altogether that of our policy setting in case 1, it would be mistaken as well to interpret the situation in terms of case 3.

Apart from such general speculation about the various countries, what indices are there by which to test what has happened? Various hypotheses, not all of which are helpful, may be considered:

(1) If countries with high indirect tax rates exhibit a low ratio of export prices to domestic prices this is evidence that the adjustment to the tax was backward. I do not think this is correct. Whether the value added tax raises prices or lowers wages, it will always raise the ratio of market price to factor cost. If export prices are defined net of rebate, they equal factor cost. Therefore, the tax must always lower the ratio of net export to domestic prices. Thus, a finding regarding relative prices tells us nothing about the direction of the absolute price adjustment, and it is only the latter that matters.

(2) If net export prices in high tax rate countries are high relative to those in low tax rate countries, this suggests that the tax adjustment was

favoured. The trouble with this is that the comparison involves the use of exchange rates which may not be (and indeed are not) equilibrium rates. Moreover, many other factors, e.g. productivity differences enter.

(3) If in any one country frequent tax rate changes could be observed, these might be related to wage rate or price changes. In this way, it might be possible to determine a causal influence which would solve our problem. Unfortunately, tax rate changes are usually too few (and other influences too powerful) to permit such analysis.

(4) Perhaps it might be possible to observe wage rate changes relative to productivity in various countries, and to test the hypothesis that wages have lagged more in high-rate countries. Probably the result would differ greatly for the earlier and later part of the 1950s.

The general conclusion is that rigorous empirical tests would be very difficult.

Corporation Tax. With regard to the profits tax there is the further question whether it is to be considered a 'cost tax', posing more or less the same problems just noted, or whether it may be expected to be absorbed in profits, leaving wages and prices unaffected.

While the traditional view has been that the profits tax does not lead to short-run changes in prices and wages, the proposition (derived from short-run profit maximisation) has become dubious. Theoretically, many situations can be imagined where shifting occurs. Superficial empirical evidence shows that the net rate of return has changed little from the 1920s to the 1950s (which supports shifting), and that the gross profits share has remained stable (which may support non-shifting). However, these overall observations are of little value since too many factors (other than tax rates) varied as well. Recently there has been some statistical work in this area, with one study suggesting full shifting (3) and the other zero shifting (2). Having been associated with the former, I am persuaded that short-run shifting is an important factor. However, in the present context two additional questions arise.

First, it must be decided whether the absolute adjustment was in wages or prices. The first of the above studies, though concluding that there was shifting, does not pronounce on this crucial point. However, considering the US setting, let us assume that prices rose. Query: if the post-war price inflation reflected a delayed real balance effect, was this secondary adjustment not curtailed because of the previous tax-induced price rise? and if so, which of the two was the causal factor?

This leaves the further question whether a symmetrical shifting assumption can be made for European profits taxes. If yes, the US disadvantage (arguing as before regarding cost taxes with *ER–ID*) is measured by the relatively minor rate differential; but if the European tax was not shifted, our disadvantage relates to the absolute US rate level. The observation that European firms tend to be less competitive (if correct) does not prove that they were in a better position to shift. To the extent that they are in a better position to act as pure monopolists, the opposite would follow.

Quite possibly, different assumptions are in order for the US and Europe—but if they are made the case for international tax integration vanishes in a morass of special situations.

Policy conclusions

Finally a word about the policy conclusions (or questions) which this discussion implies.

Should a frontal attack be made on GATT rules? This could be done on two grounds:

With regard to 'cost taxes', GATT policy (by permitting *ER–ID*) is based on the notion that the tax adjustment in all countries takes the form of absolute price rise. Present practice is distorting rather than neutralising if adjustments are asymmetrical. Prevailing asymmetry is likely to be pro-Europe.

With regard to the profits tax, GATT rules (by excluding *ER–ID*) are based on the assumption that there is no wage price adjustment. Present practice is distorting if the tax raises price. Given this assumption for the US and Europe, the prevailing rate differential is slightly pro-Europe; given the assumption for the US only, the situation (measured by our absolute rate level) is distinctly pro-Europe.

Some argument can be made along these lines, but one hesitates: What would be a workable alternative to GATT rules if asymmetrical adjustments were introduced? What would be done about the crediting of foreign profits taxes (presumably it would have to be replaced by deduction) if *ER–ID* is applied to the profits tax?

2. Obviously, introduction of a value added tax *per se* would not help us if 'over-rebating' is ruled out. Substitution of such a tax for the profits tax would help to the extent that the latter did increase price, as a 'cost tax' without *ER–ID* would be replaced by one with *ER–ID*. However, one hesitates to consider such a change as long as the taxation of capital gains remains so inadequate.

3. Selective export incentives under the corporation tax may be preferable, and may stand a better chance to be applied unilaterally.

4. In addition, it may well be that tax measures aimed at the capital account would be more feasible.

NOTES

1. To simplify, we consider throughout only the extreme cases of no price rise and price rise by the full tax. Obviously, the real situation may fall between these extremes.
2. No clear-cut statements of these principles can be found in the GATT Articles, but practices have consistently followed these lines.

REFERENCES

[1] Klein, L. R. (1962) 'Statement of L. R. Klein', *Measures of Productive Capacity*, Hearings before the Sub-committee on Economic Statistics of the Joint Economic Committee (May 14, 22, 23 and 24), p. 59.
[2] Krzyzaniak, Marian and Richard A. Musgrave (1963) *The Shifting of the Corporation Income Tax*. (Baltimore: The Johns Hopkins University Press).
[3] Lerner, Eugene M. and Eldon S. Hendriksen (1956) 'Federal Taxes on Corporate Income and the Rate of Return on Investment in Manufacturing, 1927 to 1952', *National Tax Journal*, IX.
[4] Phillips, A. (1963) 'An Appraisal of Measures of Capacity', *American Economic Review*, Suppl., May, p. 275.

17 In Defence of an Income Concept*
1967

In his recent piece [2], Professor Bittker launched a frontal attack on income tax reform aimed at realising a closer approximation to the accretion concept. He felt that the accretion concept of income had little normative value, and gives little help in the practice of income definition. In fact, we were told that nothing is to be gained by trying to define a generalised income concept. Rather, treatment of particular income items should be considered provision by provision, with each item dealt with on its merits. The drive towards a comprehensive (i.e. consumption plus accretion) base is rejected as leading to undesirable results, and should be replaced by an *ad hoc* approach.

Bittker's discussion is helpful in examining technical issues and in noting that implementation of a normative income tax is not that simple. There is a place for the sceptic, but he greatly over-states his case. His counsel of despair is unjustified and damaging to income tax reform. While the accretion concept does not answer all problems (and what policy rule ever does?) it points to the solution of most specific issues of income definition; and though the concept has to be qualified in application by considerations of administrative feasibility, and equity must give way at times to other policy objectives, construction of a fair income tax is well-nigh impossible without the guidance of a basic income concept.

I. PRINCIPLES

While Bittker's argument is largely in terms of specific points of income definition, the basic theme is that there is no need for a general income concept on which to build a rational income tax system. This, I believe, is an untenable position.

* R. Musgrave (1967) *Harvard Law Review*, vol. 81. Copyright © 1967 by the Harvard Law Review Association.

Income vs. consumption as an index of equality

Everyone will agree that taxation should not be used as a punitive device to damage one or another group of the population. Taxation should not be a tool of personal discrimination. This minimal condition for equitable taxation could be met by a random, lottery-type distribution of the tax burden, but no intelligent observer would be satisfied with this. An equitable distribution of the tax burden is more than a non-arbitrary one. It is necessary that the tax bill be allocated according to an equitable and positively-defined pattern.

Two requirements follow. First, people in equal position should pay equal amounts of tax; second, people in unequal position should pay different amounts related in a meaningful fashion to difference in position. These two requirements are referred to respectively as *horizontal* and *vertical* equity. While vertical equity remains controversial,[1] few would disagree with the horizontal equity rule, and I assume that Bittker as well accepts this norm. The question, however, is how the concept of equal position—the 'index of equality'—is to be defined. This choice of index is not a purely objective matter. It depends on what society considers to be equitable, and how it wishes to pose the problem. At the same time, it does not follow that anything goes. Certain criteria are more meaningful than others, and any one criterion must be interpreted consistently once it is chosen. In particular, two approaches must be distinguished.

The most obvious approach is to look for a general index of economic well-being which broadly measures a person's capacity to contribute or to 'sacrifice' on behalf of government. This is the tradition of taxation according to ability to pay.[2] In colonial times, gross produce of land served as a more or less meaningful measure of well-being, and other simple proxies, such as the number of windows, are cited by tax historians. But today's economic society is too complex to permit so simple a solution. A more comprehensive criterion is needed, and income is the most appropriate choice.

Alternatively, one might argue, following Hobbes, that the taxpayer should contribute in line with what he 'takes out of the pot', and not what he 'contributes to society'. The tax in effect becomes a fine on consumption (the sin of non-accumulation) with equal taxes being paid by equal sinners. This view has considerable merit in the context of growth policy, provided that full employment is assured, but it seems less plausible as an equity rule. Certainly it is inferior to income if equality is to be defined in terms of general economic capacity.[3]

Nevertheless, there is no absolute standard by which the choice between the income or consumption index can be made. Reasonable men may differ on whether equal position should be defined in terms of capacity (income) or consumption. The choice is essentially one of value judgement. But whichever view is taken, the equitable tax should be a personal tax, assessed in global fashion on the taxpayer's total base. Thus, the proper counterpart to the personal income tax is not a sales, but a personal expenditure tax, and quite parallel problems (e.g. the need for a central concept) arise in its implementation [6].

Income as a measure of ability to pay

Fortunately, the choice between income and consumption is not at issue in this discussion. Historical development, if not logic, has made the choice in favour of income. I have no complaint about this, and Bittker seems satisfied as well to proceed on this basis. Our ways part, however, when it comes to the question of how income should be defined and, indeed, whether it should be defined at all.

Whereas the choice between income and consumption as the appropriate tax base involves value judgement, there is a clear case for Simons' income definition once the income alternative is chosen. It is this definition on which the case for a comprehensive income tax is based. Bittker's impression [2, p. 931] that the advocates of the comprehensive base waver between various income concepts—including aggregate gross income minus certain expenses, personal income as defined by the Department of Commerce, as well as the accretion concept—is mistaken. As the literature clearly shows, it is the accretion concept which people have in mind, and not the other two, which have no normative value.

According to this definition, income equals gain in net worth plus consumption during a given period.[4] What matters is *total* income thus defined. No distinction is to be made between either sources or uses of income. Gains may be factor earnings (e.g. wages, interest, rent) in the economist's sense, or they may be mere transfers (e.g. gifts or gambling gains); they may be expected or unexpected, irregular or regular, accrued or realised from business or accident, and so on and so forth. All that matters is that there exists a gain which gives rise to consumption or to increase in net worth. Similarly, it is left to the recipient whether he wishes to use his gain for one or another type of present consumption, or whether he wishes to postpone consumption and save.[5]

While income thus defined (net worth gain plus consumption) equals the concept of income as used in economic analysis of capital theory, this is not what gives it legitimacy as an index of equality in the equity context. Indeed, the sum of individual incomes as defined under accretion exceeds national income in the economist's sense. National income excludes transfers, but gifts are accretion to the donee without reducing the income of the donor. The defence for the accretion plus consumption concept as an index of equality must rest on its superiority as an equity concept, not as a tool of economic theory. The most the economist can claim is that the meaning of accretion as an equity concept is appreciated more fully if the economic analysis of income is understood.

The merit of the concept may be demonstrated by considering two of the more popular arguments for discrimination. Traditionally a case has been made for taxing 'unearned' (capital) income more heavily than 'earned' (labour) income. Based initially on the labour theory of value, whereby labour only earns enough to sustain itself and hence cannot pay taxes, it was reformulated later with reference to the disutility of labour which presumably is absent in the earning of capital income. Tax-paying ability, in other words, was to be defined as income earned minus the value of sweat expended. This view was more convincing with an 80 than a 35 hour week, and would call for other adjustments as well, including differentiation between work incomes (miners vs. professors) and an allowance for psychic income (work utility). Surely this would not be a workable concept or a very sensible one. Nor can much credence be given to the proposition that capital income should pay more because it carries higher capacity to pay since it is joined with the presence of a capital reserve. This overlooks the fact that the choice between consumption and savings is open to recipients of both work and capital income, and that (under the proper accretion system) initial acquisition of capital through transfer is also subject to tax.

Next, it is frequently argued that unrealised capital gains do not constitute income. This position is untenable. Suppose I continue to hold an investment which has appreciated in value instead of realising the gain. This is equivalent to my realising the gain and reinvesting in the same asset. To tax gains only when realised is to make the tax contingent on the technicality of portfolio shifts rather than on the incidence of gain. Nor can it be argued that the unrealised gain should be exempt because it has not been withdrawn for consumption. If such were the position all income which is saved should be exempted and a consumption tax substituted for the income tax.[6] It is clear conceptually that unrealised gains constitute income, and a taxable income concept which in principle considers unrealised gains as non-income is not a valid equity concept.[7] To be sure, administrative difficulties do not permit full implementation of this principle, but recognition of what should be done in principle—temporarily disregarding administrative difficulties—is crucial in choosing between alternative feasible solutions.

We conclude that the sum of increase in net worth plus consumption is the superior measure of tax-paying ability, once the income (as distinct from consumption) view has been chosen. Whereas the latter choice is a matter of value judgement, the accumulation plus consumption view of income follows as a matter of consistent thinking once the income approach has been decided upon.

The *ad hoc* approach

Let us backtrack briefly and once more ask whether a generalised concept of tax base is needed to obtain an equitable solution. Leaving aside the evident political fact that loophole pressures are difficult to meet without reference to a basic income concept, is it analytically possible to define an equitable solution in its absence? This, it seems to me, is the basic question which has to be faced in dealing with Bittker's position.

To be sure, people with equal characteristics can be treated equally, and personal discrimination can be avoided, without resort to a generalised concept of tax base. Thus, all left-handed people may be asked to pay twice the head tax contributed by all right-handed people; all buyers of white bread may be taxed, while all buyers of dark bread are not, and so forth. But as noted before, absence of discrimination in this sense is not enough. Reasonable men will also demand that the taxable characteristics be chosen in a meaningful fashion. This means that the tax base should be chosen to give a 'fair' result, which requires an explicit concept of fairness, such as asking for contributions in line with ability to pay, or in line with unwillingness to save and add one's earnings to the community's capital stock. Either concept, and perhaps still other criteria may be chosen, but I find it exceedingly difficult to visualise a standard of fairness which deals piecemeal with each specific characteristic of households (including various aspects of income, consumption and other features), asking in each case whether it does or does not constitute a proper tax base, and doing so without the guidance of a general principle by which to relate specific decisions.

But even if the possibility of such an approach were granted, and I doubt whether it can be, it would surely lead to a broad bundle of taxes, and not to an income tax *per se*. If the problem of income taxation is discussed, and this is to what Bittker addresses himself, the income components of the wide range of possible tax bases must be identified. And to do so, an income concept is needed.

We thus arrive at the conclusion that a pure *ad hoc* approach is not tenable on analytical grounds. A generalised concept of taxable capacity and taxable income is needed if there is to be a meaningful discussion of the equity aspects of tax reform. Short of this, one may discuss what treatment Congress intended to apply when present Statutes were enacted and what interpretation the Courts have given to the Statutes, without asking whether Congress was correct in so intending in the first place. This, to be sure, is an essential step in the detailed implementation of tax policy, but it is not a basis for tax reform—the essence of which is consideration of change in existing Statutes, including change of legislative intent—and, I gather, not the ground on which Bittker's comments proceed.

Vertical aspects of base imperfections

Defective definition of taxable income results in horizontal inequities because taxpayers in equal position (equal, that is, in terms of consumption plus accretion) do not pay equal tax. At the same time, it would be naive to overlook the fact that these horizontal inequalities are not random from a vertical point of view.

Some aspects of tax base definition are of primary concern to the lower and middle-income groups. This includes such items as the treatment of imputed income from housing, of social security benefits, of interest paid on mortgages and consumer loans, and of various fringe benefits. Certain other omissions from the tax base, which should be included under a proper definition of income, relate to forms of income which are important primarily in the upper-income brackets. These include interest received from tax-exempt securities, certain types of executive compensation, and—much the most important—capital gains.

As is well known, the income tax, though it has highly progressive bracket rates, ceases to be progressive above a certain level of income and in fact turns regressive. This is due very largely to the effects of taxing capital gains at a maximum rate of 25 per cent. The situation is thus one where steeply progressive rates apply to a limited group of high-income taxpayers, while much of the income received in the high brackets is subject to a modest proportional rate. The result is not only horizontal inequity among high income recipients but also vertical inequity in that the progression expressed in statutory rates does not apply. Even if it is argued that these rates are too high, this is hardly the way of dealing with the matter. Obviously, equity would be served better if a more modest rate structure were applied uniformly over a more complete income base. This is precisely what the proponents of a comprehensive tax base have proposed. The fact that various income omissions or preferential treatments—and I have no hesitation in referring to them as tax loopholes—have such vertical implications adds to their distorting effects. At the same time, it serves to explain why they exist, and how political pressures in their favour come about.

Other objectives

Before turning to cases, let us note that equity is not the only criterion of tax policy. While of great importance, it must give way on occasion to other objectives. For instance, it may be desirable to encourage investment via an investment credit, and even to limit such inducements to particular industries or types of assets. Or it may be desirable to encourage charitable donation by tax exemptions. Either measure is inequitable, but the cost in equity may be justified if the gain from the competing policy objective is the greater, and if other means of achieving the competing end are distinctly inferior.

It may be argued, of course, that any preferential treatment to achieve particular objectives is in fact a subsidy, and that it would be better to pay such subsidies on an explicit basis, without clouding their true nature by disguising them in the form of tax reductions. The problem here is essentially a political one. If the cash subsidy would be the same as the tax reduction, the result (in its economic and equity effects) is identical whichever technique is used. The tax relief is simpler, as it avoids the process of collection and payment. The situation differs, however, if the technique of tax relief leads to subsidies which Congress would not be willing to give in explicit form. In this case, faith in the democratic process suggests that the subsidy approach is superior.

However this may be, the proponent of a proper income definition (or opponent of loopholes) need not commit himself to an all-out opposition to tax remissions as an incentive device. Contrary to Bittker's intimation [2, p. 954], acceptance of the investment credit does not require abandonment of a properly-defined income base. All that need be recognised is that such incentives involve an equity cost, and that this cost must be taken into consideration when deciding on the incentive policy. The fact that equity considerations are not always controlling does not imply, as Bittker seems to suggest, that equity standards are a mirage.

Base broadening vs. improvement

As Bittker points out, much of the discussion has been in terms of 'broadening' the tax base, with the promised reward that once the base is broadened, lower rates of tax will suffice to furnish the same yield[1] [2, p. 926]. I have never been happy with this emphasis on base *broadening* rather than *improvement*. Since the proper base (i.e. the base corresponding to the accretion concept of income) is broader than the actual base, tax reform will involve base-broadening; but this broadening is an incidental result, not the objective of the reform. If it were, a gross income tax using the entire GNP as base would surely be better than a net income tax; and a turnover tax would be better than a gross income tax. But equity is reduced if lower rates are traded against an undue expansion of the base to include items that are not components of accretion; and equity demands that the base be narrowed should there be instances where non-accretion items are included. But having made this clear, the fact remains that existing departures from the proper concept are very largely in the form of omissions, and that the needed reform is, therefore, one of broadening rather than restricting the base.

II. CASES

I now turn to a brief consideration of some of the special problems of income definiton which according to Bittker demonstrate the uselessness of the basic income concept. I find, on the contrary, that the concept points a clear way to the proper answer in most instances; and if it must then be modified by considerations of administrative feasibility, this does not destroy the importance of recognising the proper solution. Among feasible solutions, some are much closer to the proper measure than others, and the results—if second best—will be far better than what can be done without the guidance of a normative concept. While Bittker's analysis of some of the technical difficulties is helpful, his all-or-nothing position is thoroughly unjustified.

Exclusions from gross income

Government Transfers and Public Services. Advocates of the accretion concept have urged that transfers such as social security benefits and veterans' payments should be included in the tax base. Professor Bittker argues that if this is done, there logically should also be inclusion of all other benefits (in cash or kind) received from public services [2, p. 935]. If fellowships are taxed, why not also tax income in kind received through free (or subsidised) education; in fact, why not impute income from all public services derived free of direct charge?

A distinction needs to be drawn between benefits from contributory insurance, cash subsidies and income in kind from public services. Regarding insurance benefits, there should be tax-free recovery of contributions, but taxation of interest earnings from the investment of insurance funds. Regarding cash subsidies, the choice between lower but tax-exempt, or higher but taxable subsidies is essentially a political and administrative question. If the net result (in terms of after-tax income) is the same under both procedures, both policies are equivalent and, while tax reduction is simpler, either method is acceptable. But the results may not be the same. A more explicit, 'out in the open' policy determination may be preferable, in which case transfers should be taxed.

Ideally, imputed benefits from public services would be considered in the same way as transfers.[9] The accretion concept includes all gains, whether they be in cash or kind, obtained through market transactions, as gifts or as imputed gains. The principle is clear, but as Bittker points out, the difficulties of imputation would be insurmountable [2, p. 936]. Feasibility suggests, therefore, that inclusion be limited to cash grants.

Personal Exemptions. Professor Bittker suggests that the personal exemption is inconsistent with the idea of a comprehensive tax base. If the purpose is to protect minimum incomes, it would be better to combine full taxation with cash subsidies [2, p. 940]. This again raises the question of how subsidies should be handled. But, more basically, I do not think that this properly interprets the role of exemptions.[10] The exemption, above all, should be looked upon as a matter of rate progression (vertical equity) rather than income definition. That is to say, the exemption merely sets a zero rate bracket and, under a negative income tax system, would be replaced by a set of negative (subsidy) rate brackets.

In addition, differential exemptions are a way of allowing for differences in the ability to pay of taxable units of unequal size. This adjustment, which also might be made through differential rates, is surely needed in any meaningful ability-to-pay concept. Leaving aside certain technical improvements which, as Bittker notes, are in order, (e.g. replacing the exemption by a credit), I see no conflict between such an allowance and the case for a comprehensive tax base.

Gifts and Bequests. Professor Bittker notes that the accretion concept of income requires inclusion of bequests and gifts in the recipient's income [2, p. 945]. He is correct in so stating, as evidenced by the Carter Commission report [1] which recommends inclusion of such transfers.[11] At the same time, inclusion of bequests and gifts in the income of the recipient leaves open the question whether society wishes to impose a prior tax on the donor or the decedent, a tax which would be outside the income tax system.

Imputed Rent. Professor Bittker criticises proponents of the comprehensive tax base for demanding inclusion of imputed rent in taxable income, without extending the same principle to imputed income from other assets [2], p. 947]. The answer again is that in principle all imputed income (including even income from cash-holding) should be taxed, but that it is not a feasible procedure. Taxation of imputed rent, on the other hand, is feasible. The inequity between owners and renters, which results from the present practice of deducting mortgage interest while not taxing imputed rent, is unfair, especially at the lower end of the income scale, and could be improved even by a rough approximation to imputed rent.

Personal deductions

Professor Bittker points to the allowance of personal deductions by the advocates of a comprehensive tax base as further evidence that the generalisation of a comprehensive tax base cannot be accepted as the prime criterion [2, p. 950]. Here a distinction should be drawn between (1) deductions which allow for disaster expenses, be they medical costs, disaster losses or what not, and (2) deductions which are granted to induce certain uses of income such as charitable donations.

I see no conflict whatsoever between group (1) deductions and the concept of a comprehensive income base. The purpose is not to exclude specific income sources but to allow for situations where taxpayers with equal incomes and family size have strikingly different needs. The logic of the case points to combining such 'disaster' items, and to rendering the joint deduction subject to a floor. By allowing for disaster situations, the equity goal, far from being offended, can be achieved more fully.

Deductions of type (2) are a different matter. Though they clearly offend against equity they may be in order if the rival policy objectives such as encouraging charity are worth the equity loss, and provided that tax deduction is a superior way of achieving these objectives. In the case of charitable contributions in particular, the question arises whether Congress would be willing to adopt a system of subsidising charitable gifts such that the subsidy rate (as is implied in the deduction system) rises with the taxpayer's income; and, indeed, whether Congress would be willing to appropriate amounts (corresponding to the revenue loss) for such purposes at all.

Personal-business borderline

Professor Bittker makes much of the difficulty of drawing a line between outlays which constitute business expenses and should be deducted to obtain net income, and others which bestow personal benefits and thus should not be allowed [2, p. 952]. And he holds that the accretion concept does not help in drawing a line.

Again the case is presented as if all aspects of the problem were equally difficult and arbitrary. Thus insurance against occupational accidents is cited in the same sentence with entertainment expenses. As I see it, the former is clearly eligible as deduction, while the latter should be viewed with great suspicion. The reason is that such expenses can be used to bestow income so as to avoid personal income tax, and that this is in fact done to a substantial degree. This, above all, is an area where reference to an income concept is needed. Such reference is helpful because it tells us that consumption is part of accretion. Therefore, business costs under-taken to give consumption benefits constitute income to the recipients. Granted that there are situations in which consumption benefits are derived as a truly necessary part of doing business, the present rules (after some tightening in response to the administration proposal for more drastic revision in the Revenue Act 1962) still leave the margin of error heavily in the direction of excessive allowance.

Business deductions

Professor Bittker argues that if percentage depletion is to be classified as a preference, so should the investment credit or accelerated depreciation for wartime production facilities [2, p. 954]. As noted before, he overlooks the fact that tax policy must balance between various objectives. While both adjustments are inequitable, the investment credit serves the explicit purpose of encouraging general capital formation and economic growth. The depletion allowance, on the other hand, does not serve such an objective.

It has been defended traditionally on equity grounds, i.e. as compensa-tion for the 'using-up' of natural resources. This argument was proved fallacious because there is no case for permitting recovery (even if the loss of value were measured properly as a percentage of gross income) over and above the exploitation costs which are already expensed. The case for depletion then shifted to an argument based on national defence needs; and, more recently, the greater riskiness of such investment has been emphasised. Neither case is convincing, and even if there were a case for special aid, such aid is not granted effectively as a tax subsidy to gross income.

The cases of depletion and investment credit, therefore, are very different. While the investment credit offers a substantial policy advantage to be weighed against the equity loss, the depletion provision does not do so.[12]

Problems of timing

Finally, let us consider various aspects of the timing problem. Here, as in other parts of the discussion, Bittker makes the problem appear rather more complex and unwieldy than it really is [2, p. 958]. There are three basic propositions to be made:

(1) Ideally, tax liability should become due when accretion occurs. This follows from the very approach to accretion as a measure of ability to pay. The present value of tax payments is reduced if tax payments are postponed. Therefore, horizontal inequities arise if different taxpayers are granted different periods of postponement.[13] While this difficulty is

avoided if everyone pays, say, 13 years after accretion occurs, it should not be too difficult to agree, on common sense grounds, that concurrent incidence of the liability is to be preferred.[14]

(2) Obviously, it is not feasible to define concurrent on an 'every minute' basis. While the choice of the accounting year is arbitrary, common sense suggests that use be made of an annual accounting period followed by business firms or the government.

(3) Most important is the fact that under a progressive income tax, liabilities differ depending on the time-path of income. This distorts the intent of tax equity, thus calling for averaging of income. The same holds for the carry-over of losses or unused credits under a flat rate tax.

Given these principles, which are wholly in line with the accretion approach, I do not follow Bittker's complaint that provision for carry-over of losses should have been criticised as an undue 'preference' [2, p. 961]. On the contrary, income is to be defined in net terms, and failure to permit carry-over would impose a penalty on taxpayers with irregular income, while favouring those with a steady income flow.

The case for income averaging is essentially the same. Professor Bittker comments that he has seen no analysis of the implications of the Haig–Simons definition for income averaging [2, p. 963]. Again the principle of the matter seems quite clear. Ideally, all income would be taxed on an accrual basis. The tax would become due concurrent with the accretion of income. Thus gain from tax postponement, or penalties from tax anticipation would be avoided. At the same time, averaging would be applied to avoid the inequitable impact of rate progression upon irregular incomes. Ideally, averaging would apply annually and be over a lifetime period. For reasons of administrative feasibility, such averaging has to be applied from time to time and is limited to a period of, say, five years, but this does not change the principle involved.

Similarly, recognition must be made of the fact that income is not taxed on an accrual basis, but that (again for reasons of administrative feasibility) the tax becomes due at actual or (under the proper system) constructive realisation. Such being the case, averaging involves the averaging of realised (actually or constructively) rather than of accrued income. The principle of the matter is clear, and there is no issue of preferences in the application of a general averaging rule.

Unrealised gains

Finally, there is again the question of unrealised appreciation. Bittker rightly notes that complete compliance with the accretion concept would call for annual taxation of accrued gains [2, p. 967]. He recognises the difficulty of annual valuation but wonders why advocates of the accretion concept have not favoured annual valuation of at least those assets which permit the assessment. I see no objective to this, although I doubt whether it can be done readily over a wide range of assets. Moreover, advocates of the accretion concept, from Simons on, have favoured 'constructive realisation', e.g. taxing of accrued gains at death or transfer. Thus, valuation would be needed at a much reduced scale only, and the administrative task would be greatly simplified. Bittker is quick to point out that this is no perfect solution as it would leave capital gains income with the advantage of tax postponement [2, p. 970]. This is correct, but the preference would be on a much reduced scale, and the remaining advantage could be approximately offset by applying an interest charge when the tax becomes due.[15] While stressing the difficulties of fully taxing capital gains, Bittker leaves us uncertain whether he himself believes that unrealised gains are income, and hence should be taxed. Yet this is the crucial issue, and one which cannot be solved without reference to a systematic income concept.

Taxable unit: family relations

As Bittker points out, the problem of formulating the taxable unit is not solved by the income concept. [2, p. 974]. Yet this task is not unrelated to which 'index of equality' is chosen. Indeed, the definition of taxable unit has its logic—derived again from the underlying concept of ability to pay—and is not as arbitrary a matter as Bittker suggests.

Clearly, the relative treatment of taxable units of different size should relate to the cost of maintaining households of different size, and clearly the present split-income system over-taxes single relative to married units, especially over the $25,000–70,000 income ranges. Which technique is best to meet the problem (separate rate schedules for single and married with mandatory joint returns, etc.) is a different matter, but the present pattern can clearly be improved upon.

Also, the definition of the taxable unit needs to be designed to forestall tax avoidance through allocation of property income to minor children. Again the [present] law is far from satisfactory in this respect, giving substantial preference to capital as against wage income. While solutions of these problems do not follow directly from the income concept, reasonable standards can be developed which are in line with the basic rationale of the accretion approach. Surely the problem is not as wide open as Bittker suggests.

Taxable unit: business

Bittker notes correctly that the accretion concept requires the shareholder to be taxed on gains in the value of his shares, whether or not the underlying profits are distributed in the form of dividends [2, p. 977]. Short thereof, he notes that retained earnings might be imputed to the shareholder. In fact, both should be done, allowing the share base to be written up for retention when computing capital gains. Having done so, the corporation tax (except as a withholding device) should be dropped.

So far so good. But instead of concluding that this avenue points to a reasonable and practicable solution of the problem, as developed in the Carter Commission Report [1], Bittker proceeds to ridicule the principle by asking what then should be done about discretionary trusts, or the employer's contribution to qualified pension plans. My answer is: (1) much would be gained if the taxation of corporate profits could be integrated if the individual income tax, even if these other and comparatively minor issues remained unsolved; and (2) appropriate answers to these issues may be given as well. As to discretionary trust, Bittker himself notes the proper solution—interim taxation of fiduciary with subsequent adjustment when the party in interest becomes identifiable. As to employer contributions to qualified pension plans, such contributions and the earnings on them should be taxable to the recipient, with the tax (subject to interest for postponement) payable when benefits are received.

In concluding, I believe that Bittker's message is wrong in both principle and application. His principle—that matters of income definition should be decided on an *ad hoc* basis—is mistaken. A generalised income concept is needed as an analytical tool if an equitable income tax base is to be defined. In application, his position—that the income concept is useless because it does not solve all problems and must be moderated by administrative feasibility—is also in error. In most situations, the concept points to the equitable solution, and administratively feasible measures can usually be found which approximate the proper result to a fair degree. We should, therefore, not heed his message, and get on with the task of tax reform, aimed at reforming the tax base in accord with the norm provided by the accretion concept. Considering the disappointing record of accomplishment after two decades of public (and Congressional) discussion—especially the backsliding in the tax legislation of 1966, after modest progress in 1964—everybody's, and surely Bittker's, help is needed.

NOTES

1. The more controversial problem of vertical equity is left aside in this discussion. Whether taxes should be regressive, proportional or progressive (and how much so) depends essentially on society's view as to the desirable state of income distribution. Such at least is the case in the context of the 'ability to pay' approach to taxation, which underlies this discussion. While we shall note that the definition of the tax base has important bearing on the vertical distribution of the tax burden, we need not consider here what the 'proper' vertical distribution would be.
2. This discussion, like the current debate over income tax reform and Bittker's paper, is in terms of a 'fair' distribution of the tax burden, as developed by the 'ability to pay' school of thought. Thus the problem is dealt with independently of the expenditure side of budget policy. Alternatively, taxes could be considered as payment for public services rendered. This 'benefit' approach has its advantages for purposes of economic analysis as it relates to both sides of budget policy [7, Parts I, II]. However, the allocation function of tax policy, i.e. allocating the opportunity cost of public services, must then be supplemented by the distribution function, which provides for corrections in the

distribution of income. In the latter context the basic issue of ability to pay re-emerges. If the 'fair' tax distribution is disassociated from expenditure benefits, it becomes simply a matter of distribution.

3. To tax consumption is to tax income while exempting saving. But why should saving be excluded from the measure of economic capacity? A person's choice between consumption and saving, after all, is his own decision. If X and Y both receive an income of $10,000, they may both choose between consuming or saving $10,000, as they wish. While their choices may differ, this does not void the equality of their prechoice position and hence their ability to pay taxes.

4. This concept was first proposed by Schanz [11] and introduced into American discussion by Haig [4]. It was developed systematically by Simons [12, 13]. See also Pechman [9] which laid the foundation for the subsequent discussion of a comprehensive tax base. Alternatively, income may be defined as potential consumption, i.e. actual current consumption plus consumption foregone, as reflected in increased net worth. See Simons [12], where accumulation is deflated by consumer goods price increases.

5. The equal treatment of income independent of source and use suggests that the income tax has the further advantage of being neutral in the sense of not distorting economic decisions. This is true to a degree, but the same can be claimed—and under certain assumptions, more persuasively—for a general consumption tax. The consumption tax is neutral between present and future consumption, while the income tax discriminates against future consumption. This fact has been used mistakenly by Fisher [4] to argue that the income tax is inequitable because it 'double-taxes' savings. The point is that equity and neutrality are not the same thing. If income is chosen as the equity base, the consumption tax is inequitable because it undertakes saving, and this is the case even though it may not be neutral. See Musgrave [7, chs. 8, 12].

6. Still another, if less meaningful, criterion would be to define the tax base as consumption plus increase in liquid balances, in which case exemption should be given for investment from liquid balances, as well as for continued investment of unrealised gains.

7. Of course such gains must be in real terms without reflections of change of price level. Similarly, the 'good' income tax should allow for creditor losses and debtor gains due to inflation.

8. Bittker argues, in line with the second-best theorem in welfare economics, that where a number of imperfections exist, adjustment of any one partial defect towards the norm may only worsen matters. Rather, the optimal solution may be approached better by introducing offsetting imperfections. Thus, if industries A, B and C are monopolistic while D and E are competitive, the competitive norm may be served better by making D monopolistic than by forcing C to become competitive.

While instances might conceivably exist where the tax distribution under accretion could be approximated more closely by adding deletions so as to balance existing loopholes, I find it difficult to construct an illustration. Surely, under-taxation of capital gains is not 'balanced' in terms of *horizontal* equity by exclusion of imputed rent, and depletion is not 'balanced' by exclusion of fringe benefits.

Such balancing might occur after a rough fashion with regard to *vertical* equity, but this would surely be a poor solution. Vertical equity can be accomplished (in principle at least) by applying the desired rate structure to an income base defined so as to secure horizontal equity.

To be sure, the nature of fiscal politics may be such that certain vertical equity goals can be secured only by trading horizontal inequities. A choice may then have to be made, but to do so intelligently, the cost in terms of horizontal inequity must be known, and an income concept will again be needed.

9. The reader will recall (see note 3) that this discussion is in ability to pay terms, disregarding benefit aspects. If benefits were to be imputed, only net benefits or burdens could properly be included in computing income.

10. Proponents of the comprehensive tax base have invited the critique of exemptions by listing income loss due to exemptions in tables showing the various sources of base erosion [9].

11. See [1]. Bittker, however, does not favour this inclusion, partly because of the distortions in transfer patterns to which it would give rise. I find this ironical, given the degree of distortion now resulting from estate tax avoidance. A redefinition of the taxable unit as proposed by the Carter Commission, together with inclusion of transfers, would reduce rather than increase such distortions.

12. Usually the choice is not between wholly abandoning equity and wholly forgoing desired economic effects, but a reasonable compromise may be worked out. See Musgrave [8].

13. Simons, as Bittker notes [2, p. 958], de-emphasised the importance of tax postponements. However, Simons failed to realise that the gains thus derived could be very substantial.

14. This is desirable also on fiscal policy grounds, as concurrent payments increase the effectiveness of the tax structure as an automatic economic stabiliser.

15. Bittker [2, p. 958] notes correctly that the interest aspect was unduly minimised by Simons, but that it has been emphasised by later writers. He then emphasises distortions which may result if the wrong interest rate is chosen, and that borrowing rates for individual taxpayers will differ. Without entering into the question as to which is *the* proper interest rate (and a good case can be made for using the Treasury rate), the fact of the matter is that constructive realisation with interest would leave us vastly closer to an accretion concept solution than does the present procedure. This is what matters, and not whether a completely perfect solution can be secured.

REFERENCES

[1] Carter, K. L. (1966) *Report of the Royal Commission on Taxation* (Ottawa: Queen's Printer).

[2] Bittker, B. (1967) 'A Comprehensive Income Tax Base as a Goal of Income Tax Reform', *Harvard Law Review*, 80.

[3] Bittker, B. I., Galvin, C. O., Musgrave, R. A. and Pechman, J. A. (1968) *A Comprehensive Income Tax Base? A Debate* (Branford, Conn.: Federal Tax Press).

[4] Fisher, I. (1939) 'Double Taxation of Savings', *American Economic Review*, 29.

[5] Haig, R. (1921) *The Federal Income Tax* (New York: Haig).

[6] Kaldor, N. (1955) *An Expenditure Tax* (London: Allen & Unwin).

[7] Musgrave, R. A. (1959) *The Theory of Public Finance* (New York: McGraw-Hill).

[8] —— (1963) 'Growth with Equity', *American Economic Review*, 53.

[9] Pechman, J. (1957) 'Erosion of the Individual Income Tax', *National Tax Journal*.

[10] —— (1957) 'Individual Income Tax Provisions of the Revenue Act of 1964', *Journal of Finance*, 260.

[11] Schanz, G. (1896) 'Der Einkommensbegraff und die Einkommensteuergesetze', *Finanz Archiv*, I.

[12] Simons, H. (1938) *Personal Income Taxation* (Chicago: University of Chicago Press).

[13] —— (1950) *Federal Tax Reform* (Chicago: University of Chicago Press).

18 The Distribution of Fiscal Burdens and Benefits*
1974

This study updates earlier attempts [2, 5, 6, 7] at estimating the distribution of tax burdens and benefits to 1968 levels and explores some new variants of such estimates. As in the earlier studies, patterns arrived at reflect assumptions regarding burden or benefit incidence. These assumptions are stated explicitly and cover a wide range of hypotheses, depending on how one interprets the functioning of markets and the behaviour of firms. Thus, the sensitivity of the results to alternative assumptions may be explored.

TAX BURDENS

Measuring the distribution of tax burdens involves three major steps, including (1) the allocation of tax burdens by household income brackets, (2) a corresponding allocation of income, and (3) the determination of effective rates as the ratio of tax to income in each income bracket. In step 1 the crucial problem is to determine what incidence assumptions are to be made. These assumptions are then implemented by allocation of the tax burden in line with a distributive series which reflects each assumption. In step 2 consideration must be given to what constitutes the proper income base for determining effective rates. In step 3 burdens are taken as a per cent of income. For purposes of this analysis, use is made of a broad income concept, including transfers, retained earnings of corporations, capital gains and wage supplements.

The various incidence assumptions used in this analysis are listed in Table 18.1 and representative distributive series on income and consumption are then applied to arrive at corresponding burden patterns.[1] Corresponding patterns of effective rates are shown in Table 18.2.

Federal taxes
The major progressive component of the federal tax structure (Table 18.2, line 2) is the personal income tax. Following the usual practice, its burden

---

* With Karl E. Case and Herman Leonard (1974) *Public Finance Quarterly*. July. Reprinted by permission of Sage Publications, Inc.

is assumed to fall on the payee. Excises, the burden of which is assumed to fall on the consumer, are progressive at the lower and regressive at the upper end of the scale. For the case of the corporation tax, alternative incidence assumptions are used. Allocation by dividends (line 8) gives the most progressive pattern with allocation by all capital income (line 7) next but much less progressive at the upper end of the scale. Allocation by consumption (line 10) makes for a regressive burden distribution. A mixed assumption with one half on all capital income and one half on consumption (line 9) renders the tax more or less proportional, a result which is changed but little if wages are substituted for consumption (line 6). The burden of the payroll tax (lines 11 and 12) is somewhat progressive at the lower and regressive at the upper end of the scale. Except for the bottom of the scale, the results are fairly similar whether the employer contribution is assumed to be borne by the employee (line 11) or to be shifted to consumers (line 12).

In combining federal taxes, distributions based on the various shifting assumptions were grouped into a number of packages, including one combining the most progressive assumptions (line 13), one combining the more regressive assumptions (line 14), a set of 'benchmark assumptions' allowing for some degree of shifting (line 15), and one using the assumptions most appropriate for perfectly competitive markets (line 16). The benchmark package (line 15) shows slight progression up to a total income of say $6000, a more or less proportional pattern over the $6,000–$17,000 range, and progression thereafter. The competitive package in turn (line 16) shows more moderate progression at the lower end, an essentially similar pattern over the middle range, but sharper progression at the top.[2] The pattern at the upper end, of course, depends on how detailed a bracket breakdown is given. With further breakdown of the top bracket (here defined as exceeding $92,000), somewhat increased progression would be shown. However, as is well known from income tax analysis, the rate level flattens off rapidly above the $100,000 range as capital gains and other preferred income sources become the major income component.

State and local taxes

The corresponding pattern of state and local taxes is shown in Table 18.2, lines 17–35. State and local income taxes, again assumed to be borne by the payee, are progressive except for the upper end of the scale where exclusion of capital gains and other forms of income render them regressive. Excise and sales taxes again assumed to be borne by the consumer, are now regressive throughout. The corporate tax pattern varies as in the federal case. As with the corporation tax, the property tax pattern is shown for a variety of incidence assumptions. If the tax is allocated in line with all capital income (line 31), the burden distribution is progressive at both ends of the income scale and proportional over the middle range. This picture is not changed greatly if the tax on owner-occupied residences is imputed to owners (line 30). Assignment of the tax on rental housing to tenants increases regressivity at the lower end (line 33). If the tax on business

Table 18.1 Tax-shifting assumptions

Tax	Burden assumed to fall on
Federal personal income	Taxpayer
State personal income	Taxpayer
Excises	
Tobacco	Consumers of tobacco
Alcohol	Consumers of alcohol
Gas, oil, tyres, tubes:	
Business portion (1/3)	Consumers in general
Household portion (2/3)	Households with auto.op.exp.
Automobiles:	
Business portion (2/3)	Consumers in general
Household portion (2/3)	Purchasers of automobiles
Trucks	Consumers in general
Gift, estate and death	Households with capital income whose total income exceeds $25,000
General sales	Consumers of taxable items
Motor vehicle licences:	
Business portion	Consumers in general
Household portion	Household with auto. op. exp.
Customs and duties	Consumers of taxable items
Corporate income:	
Case A	1/3 Consumers
	2/3 Dividend recipients
Case B	1/2 All capital income
	1/4 Wage and salary-earners
Case C	1/4 Consumers
Case D	All capital income earners
Case E[b]	Dividend recipients
Case F	1/2 All capital income earners
	Consumers in general

a. Two-thirds allocated to households on the basis of estimated petrol consumption by private passenger cars as a per cent of total consumption (including lorries, buses, taxis, and the like); data are taken from United States Federal Highway Administration, *Highway Statistics*. See also *Statistical Abstract of the United States* (1972), Table 898, p. 549.
b. Benchmark case.

property is assumed to be passed to consumers, that on rental property to be paid by tenants, and that on homeowners to be borne by owners, the burden distribution (line 32) becomes regressive throughout. Under the benchmark assumptions (line 29), this is modified by assuming one half of the tax on business property to be borne by capital income. Accordingly, regressivity at the lower end is reduced and progression reappears at the top.

Table 18.1 continued

Tax	Burden assumed to fall on
Property:	
Case A[b]	
Commercial	1/2 All capital income earners
	1/2 Consumers
Residential, owner occ.	Homeowners
Residential, rental	Renters
Case B:	
Commercial	All capital income earners
Residential, owner occ.	Homeowners
Residential, rental	All capital income earners
Case C:	
Commercial	All capital income earners
Residential, owner occ.	Homeowners
Residential, rental	All capital income earners
Case D:	
Commercial	Consumers in general
Residential, owner occ.	Homeowners
Residential, rental	Renters
Case E:	
Commercial	All capital income earners
Residential, owner occ.	Homeowners
Residential, rental	Renters
Contributions for social insurance:	
Case A[b]	
Employer portion	Consumers in general
Employee portion	Employee
Case B:	
Employer portion	Employee
Employee portion	Employee

Combining state and local taxes we again compute four burden packages. The benchmark package (line 38) reveals a moderately regressive pattern throughout the scale while the competitive package (line 39) shows a more or less proportional pattern up to a total income of about $23,000 with moderate progression thereafter.

Table 18.2 Tax burden as a per cent of total income[a]

		Total income brackets (000s of dollars)										
		Under 4	4–5.7	5.7–7.9	7.9–10.4	10.4–12.5	12.5–17.5	17.5–22.6	22.6–35.5	35.5–92.0	Over 92.0	Average
Federal												
1. Personal		2.0	2.8	5.9	7.1	7.9	10.1	10.6	12.7	14.8	18.5	9.9
2. Excises		2.1	2.4	2.7	2.6	2.5	2.3	1.8	.9	.8	.6	2.0
3. Gift and estate		.0	.0	.0	.0	.0	.0	.0	.6	2.0	2.7	.4
4. Customs		.4	.4	.4	.4	.4	.4	.3	.2	.1	.0	.3
5. Corporate:	Case A	5.5	5.1	3.8	3.0	2.9	3.5	3.5	4.9	5.9	17.6	5.0
6.	Case B	3.9	5.6	5.1	4.7	4.4	4.7	4.6	5.6	5.4	6.8	5.0
7.	Case C	3.2	5.7	3.7	2.9	2.6	3.5	4.3	7.2	9.3	12.7	5.0
8.	Case D	4.7	4.4	2.7	1.4	1.3	2.4	2.7	5.8	8.2	26.1	5.0
9.	Case E	5.1	6.1	5.0	4.6	4.3	4.6	4.8	5.1	5.3	6.6	5.0
10.	Case F	7.1	6.6	6.2	6.2	6.0	5.8	5.3	3.1	1.3	.6	5.0
11. Soc. Ins.	Case A	5.5	6.3	7.0	6.9	6.7	6.1	5.2	4.2	1.5	.6	5.2
12.	Case B	2.1	5.1	7.0	7.1	7.0	6.4	5.3	5.0	1.4	.3	5.2
Total federal taxes												
13. Progressive assumptions[b]		11.2	15.0	18.7	18.6	19.0	21.4	20.6	25.3	27.3	48.2	22.7
14. Regressive assumptions[c]		17.1	18.3	22.1	23.2	23.3	24.5	23.1	21.8	20.5	23.0	22.7
15. Benchmark assumptions[d]		15.2	17.9	20.9	21.6	21.6	23.4	22.6	23.8	24.5	29.1	22.7
16. Competitive assumptions[e]		9.7	16.3	19.7	20.1	20.3	22.5	22.2	26.7	28.4	34.8	22.7
State and Local												
17. Personal income		.0	.1	.3	.6	.7	1.1	1.4	2.3	1.6	1.3	1.0
18. Excises		1.4	1.6	1.7	1.6	1.5	1.3	1.0	.5	.4	.3	1.1
19. General sales		3.4	2.8	2.5	2.3	2.2	2.0	1.7	1.0	.5	.3	1.8
20. Gift, death		.0	.0	.0	.0	.0	.0	.0	.2	.6	.8	.1
21. Other		.9	1.0	1.1	1.0	1.0	.8	.6	.3	.3	.2	.7
22. M.V. licence		.4	.4	.5	.4	.4	.4	.3	.2	.3	.1	.3
23. Corporate:	Case A	.4	.4	.3	.2	.2	.3	.3	.4	.5	1.4	.4

24.	Case B	.3	.4	.4	.4	.3	.4	.4	.4	.4	.5	.4
25.	Case C	.3	.4	.3	.2	.2	.3	.3	.6	.7	1.0	.4
26.	Case D	.4	.3	.2	.1	.1	.2	.2	.5	.6	2.0	.4
27.	Case E	.4	.5	.4	.4	.3	.4	.4	.4	.4	.5	.4
28.	Case F	.6	.5	.5	.5	.5	.5	.5	.2	.1	.0	.4
29. Property:	Case A	6.7	5.7	4.7	4.3	4.0	3.7	3.3	3.0	2.9	3.3	3.9
30.	Case B	3.5	4.4	3.2	3.0	3.1	3.3	3.5	4.6	5.4	7.1	3.9
31.	Case C	2.5	4.4	2.9	2.3	2.0	2.7	3.3	5.6	7.2	9.9	3.9
32.	Case D	8.0	6.1	5.3	5.0	4.7	4.1	3.4	2.1	1.2	.8	3.9
33.	Case E	5.4	5.3	4.1	3.5	3.3	3.3	3.2	3.9	4.5	5.8	3.9
34. Soc. Insur.	Case A	.2	.5	.8	1.2	1.1	1.0	1.0	1.0	.2	.1	.8
35.	Case B	.2	.5	.8	1.2	1.1	1.0	1.0	1.0	.2	.1	.8
Total state and local taxes												
36. Progressive assumptions[f]		9.1	11.1	9.9	9.4	8.9	9.4	9.6	11.8	11.7	15.0	10.3
37. Regressive assumptions[g]		14.8	13.1	12.6	12.4	12.0	11.1	9.9	8.0	5.1	3.9	10.3
38. Benchmark assumptions[h]		13.4	12.6	11.9	11.6	11.1	10.6	9.7	9.1	7.1	6.9	10.3
39. Competitive assumptions[i]		9.0	11.2	10.0	9.5	9.0	9.5	9.7	11.9	11.8	14.0	10.3
Total taxes												
40. Progressive assumptions		20.3	26.1	28.6	27.9	27.0	30.8	30.2	37.1	39.0	63.2	33.0
41. Regressive assumptions		31.9	31.4	34.7	35.7	35.3	35.6	33.0	29.8	25.6	26.9	33.0
42. Benchmark assumptions		28.5	30.5	32.8	33.1	32.8	33.9	32.4	32.9	31.6	35.9	33.0
43. Competitive assumptions		18.7	27.5	29.7	29.6	29.3	32.0	31.9	38.6	40.2	48.8	33.0
Total taxes net of social security tax (benchmark assumptions)												
44. Federal		9.7	11.6	13.9	14.7	14.9	17.3	17.4	19.6	23.0	28.5	17.5
45. State and local		13.2	12.1	11.1	10.6	10.1	9.6	8.6	7.9	6.9	6.8	9.5
46. Total		22.9	23.7	25.0	25.3	25.0	26.9	26.0	27.5	29.9	35.3	27.0

a. See Table D below for translation of bracket limits into alternative income concepts.
b. Includes lines 8 and 12.
c. Includes lines 10 and 11.
d. Includes lines 9 and 11.
e. Includes lines 7 and 12.
f. Includes lines 26, 31 and 35.
g. Includes lines 28, 32 and 34.
h. Includes lines 27, 29 and 34.
i. Includes lines 25, 31 and 35.

Total taxes

The burden incidence of the total (federal, state and local) tax structure is given in lines 40–3. Under the package containing the most progressive assumptions (line 40), effective rates rise from 20 per cent at the bottom to 63 per cent in our top bracket. For the packaging containing the most regressive assumptions (line 41), the pattern is bell-shaped, rising from 32 per cent at the bottom to 36 per cent in the middle and then declining to 27 per cent for the upper bracket. The benchmark assumption (line 42) yields a pattern rising from 28 per cent to 36 per cent while the competitive package (line 43) rises from 19 per cent at the bottom to 49 per cent at the top. Notwithstanding these differences at the two ends of the scale, the regressive, benchmark and competitive assumptions all show a more or less proportional pattern over the $6000–$25,000 income range, a range which in 1968 included about 70 per cent of all households.

The total patterns for federal, state and local taxes under the benchmark assumptions are also shown in Fig. 18.1. Under all assumptions it is evident that the federal structure is much more progressive than the combined state and local structure. Whether or not there is a major difference between its state and local components depends greatly on the shifting assumptions for the property tax.

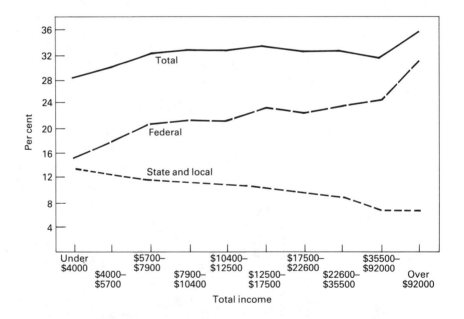

Figure 18.1 Total taxes at all levels as a percentage of total income (benchmark assumptions)

Differential incidence

It remains to note a number of qualifications.[2] In the preceding discussion we have examined the burdens which result from the imposition of various taxes, but no allowance was made for the expenditure side of the budget. But the introduction of taxes without allowing for expenditures or removal of taxes while holding expenditures constant is not a very meaningful mental experiment; and unless the changes involved are assumed to be so small as to be of little policy interest, the resulting macro effects (deflationary in the first and expansionary in the second case) can hardly be overlooked. Two ways out of the dilemma present themselves. One is to consider the net result of changes in tax burdens and benefits, referred to as 'balanced budget incidence'. Another is to limit analysis to the tax side of the budget but to formulate the problem in terms of 'differential incidence'.

Leaving budget incidence for later consideration, we begin with the distributional changes which result if one set of taxes is replaced by another of equal revenue. In Table 18.3 we thus consider the change in burden distribution which would result if the actual tax structure (using the benchmark and competitive patterns of lines 42 and 43 in Table 18.2) was replaced by a wholly general flat-rate income tax, yielding a proportional burden distribution. Under the competitive pattern (line 4) we find differential incidence to be heavily negative at the bottom of the scale, becoming decreasingly so as we move up the income scale and turning positive for the two top brackets. The resulting gains to low-income and losses to high-income households reflect the progressive nature of the estimated burden distribution under the actual tax structure. Under the benchmark assumptions (line 3) the effective rates for differential incidence are lower and the resulting gains and losses at the two ends of the scale are dampened. This reflects the less progressive distribution of the actual burden.

Viewing the problem this way, the general equilibrium setting of tax incidence comes closer to being allowed for, while public expenditures are held constant so that concern need be with the tax side only. Moreover, the differential approach gives a realistic reflection of the issues considered in actual tax policy where legislative consideration deals typically with the choice between alternative revenue sources. As long as the problem of tax burden distribution is to be considered independent of expenditure benefits, differential incidence is clearly the superior approach.

Changes in earnings patterns before tax

At the same time, it cannot be claimed that general equilibrium relationships are fully allowed for. While tax burdens are imputed to households in given income brackets, the distribution of pre-tax earnings is assumed to remain unchanged and to be independent of the tax structure. Thus, no allowance is made for such distributional changes in pre-tax earnings as may result from changes in the *pattern* of demand subsequent

Table 18.3 Differential incidence, total income base

	Total income brackets (000s of dollars)									
	Under 4	4– 5.7	5.7– 7.9	7.9– 10.4	10.4– 12.5	12.5– 17.5	17.5– 22.6	22.6– 35.5	35.5– 92.0	Over 92.0
Proportional pattern	33.0	33.0	33.0	33.0	33.0	33.0	33.0	33.0	33.0	33.0
Actual pattern										
1. Benchmark[a]	28.5	30.5	32.8	33.1	32.8	33.9	32.4	32.9	31.6	35.9
2. Competitive[b]	18.7	27.5	29.7	29.6	29.3	32.0	31.9	38.6	40.2	48.8
Differential incidence										
3. Benchmark[a]	−4.5	−2.5	−0.2	+0.1	−0.2	+0.9	−0.6	−0.1	−1.4	+2.9
4. Competitive[b]	−14.3	−5.5	−3.3	−3.4	−3.7	−1.0	−1.1	−4.4	+7.2	+15.8

a. Line 42, Table 2.
b. Line 43, Table 2.
− indicates differential gain.
+ indicates differential burden.

to changes in the tax structure. This remains a problem even under the differential incidence formulation where total pre-tax earnings may be assumed to stay constant.

While it must be granted that distributional changes in pre-tax earnings will result, the hypothesis underlying this approach is that their systematic impact on the state of distribution (e.g. the Gini coefficient) is not likely to be of major importance. Holding total output constant, substitution of a more for a less progressive income tax will increase the output of products purchased by low-income households while reducing that purchased by households with high incomes. There is, however, no evidence that earnings originating in the production of the former are distributed more (or less) equally than are earnings originating in the production of the latter, thereby strengthening (or weakening) the equalising effect generated by the resulting change in income tax burdens. Similarly, substitution of a progressive product tax (i.e. a tax on products bought by high-income consumers) for one on products bought by low-income consumers will clearly involve a shift in burdens on the uses side of the household account. Again, the change in product mix may affect factor prices and the distribution of earnings, but once more the presumption is that there will be no correlation between the distribution of products by income levels of consumers and the distribution of earnings. While the analyst should allow for systematic earnings effects in those instances in which they are known to occur, it seems reasonable that they be disregarded in a general analysis of this sort.[3]

EXPENDITURE BENEFITS

While the distribution of tax burdens has been dealt with repeatedly since the 1940s, that of expenditure benefits has come to be considered only later [3]. No particular difficulty arises with regard to allocating the benefits from transfer payments. Such payments may be viewed as negative taxes and no difficulties arise which are not encountered on the tax side. The distribution of benefits generated by goods and services expenditures, however, poses new problems. These problems are severe, but it can hardly be argued that they are beyond comprehension.

Some public services are such that the resulting benefits may be imputed to particular individuals or groups thereof. While the measurement of benefit levels may be difficult, some form of imputation to particular households is feasible. This we refer to as the group of 'allocable expenditures'.

Other expenditures, however, do not lend themselves to this procedure. Being in the nature of social goods, the benefits which they generate come to be enjoyed 'by all'. Here no specific imputation to particular groups is possible. If an allocation is to be made, it must be based on a general distribution formula. For purposes of this analysis, $142 billion dollars out of total 1968 expenditures of $271 billion were considered such as to permit specific allocation, with the allocable share higher at the state-local than at the federal level. The division here drawn is admittedly rough. On the one side, expenditures such as education are allocated entirely to the student while external benefits are disregarded; on the other, expenditures for general public services such as municipal outlays for fire protection are treated as unallocable, even though more detailed study might permit partial allocation among income groups.

Expenditures subject to specific allocation

In determining the benefit incidence of specifically allocable expenditures, the case of transfer payments is straightforward. A dollar of transfer payments provides a dollar's worth of benefits to the recipient, transfer payments being similar in this respect to taxes. The only question is whether such benefits are shifted or 'snatched away'. As shown in lines 10–13 of Table 18.4, we assume that this is not the case, with full benefits imputed to the recipient.

With regard to benefits from expenditures involving purchases of factors or of products, we are faced with two problems. One is to determine who benefits, and the other is to determine its value to the recipient. Regarding the former, our assumptions, which parallel the shifting assumptions of Table 18.1, are shown in Table 18.4. Regarding the latter, we follow the simplifying procedure of allocating outlays made or costs incurred 'on behalf of' various beneficiaries. Thus, in the case of education, we considered the building or salary *cost* which may be imputed to the students attending a particular school. We did not attempt to estimate the *benefit* which the particular student derives therefrom. In the case of highways we imputed the construction and maintenance cost incurred on behalf of the users of particular highways, without trying to estimate the benefits which they derive therefrom. This procedure has the advantage that total benefits are equated with total costs or expenditure, just as on the tax side of the analysis total tax burden is equated with total revenue.

Though attractive for reasons of simplicity, allocation by 'costs incurred on behalf of' by-passes the valuation problem and may introduce significant distortions into our benefit pattern. Among the items specifically allocated, consider, for instance, the allocation of education expenditures, here assigned to students. To the extent that the return on education is lower for the poor than for the well-to-do, our procedure tends to overstate the benefits for low-income households. To the extent that external benefits result, the pattern of these externalities would have to be determined. To the extent that education merely assigns positions in a queue; benefits to A are offset by losses to B and no net benefits to the group occur, but distribution is affected. All these difficulties are disregarded here by following the 'costs incurred in behalf of' formula.

The resulting patterns of benefit distribution are shown in Table 18.5. Beginning with federal expenditures (lines 1–14), we find the effective benefit rate for elementary and secondary education to be regressive (a

Table 18.4 Benefit shifting assumptions

Expenditure	Benefit assumed to fall on
1. *Allocable expenditures*	
1. Education, higher	Families of students enrolled
2. Education, elem. and sec.	Families of students enrolled
3. Highways:[a]	
4. Business portion (1/3)	Consumers in general
5. Household portion (2/3)	Households with auto. op. exp.
6. Health and hospitals:	
7. Public health	All families and unrelated indiv. equally
8. Hospitals	Patients in funded hospitals
9. Agricultural expenditures	Farm proprietors
10. Public assistance	Public assistance recipients
11. Social insurance and retirement	Recipients of social insurance and retirement payments
12. Unemployment ins. benefits	Recipients of unemployment benefit
13. Veteran disability and pension	Recipients of veteran's disability and pension
14. Interest[b]	
15. Portion paid to individual	Households earning interest income
16. Portion paid to institutions	Holders of equity in recipient institutions
II. *Other expenditures*	
17. Assumption a	Families in proportion to total income
18. Assumption b	Families in proportion to taxes paid
19. Assumption c	All persons equally

a. Two-thirds allocated to households on the basis of estimated gasoline consumption by private passenger cars as a per cent of total consumption (including, e.g. trucks, buses, taxis); U.S. Federal Highway Administration, *Source: Highway Statistics*. See also *Statistical Abstract of the United States* (1972) Table 898, p. 549.
b. Line 15 includes interest paid to individuals and governments. Line 16 includes interest paid to banks (including mutual savings banks), corporations, insurance companies, and other. Estimates of debt ownership based on US Department of the Treasury, *Treasury Bulletin and Statistical Abstract of the United States* (1972) Table 635, p. 398.

term which now connotes pro-poor), while that for higher education proves bell-shaped. Interest payments show a U-shaped distribution, while highway benefits are proportional except for regression at the upper end. Agricultural expenditures are distributed in a progressive (pro-rich) pattern except for the top bracket. Benefits from health and hospital expenditures are regressive. Transfer payments are heavily concentrated at the lower end of the scale and are regressive throughout. The same holds for the distribution of total allocable expenditures (line 14), which is dominated by the transfer pattern.

The corresponding benefit patterns for state and local expenditures are given in Table 18.5, lines 15–22. The combined picture for all levels of government (line 23) remains one of sharp regression at the lower end of the income scale and moderate regression over the middle range.[4] A

Table 18.5 Allocable benefits as per cent of total income

	Total income brackets (000s of dollars)										
	Under 4	4– 5.7	5.7– 7.9	7.9– 10.4	10.4– 12.5	12.5– 17.5	17.5– 22.6	22.6– 35.5	35.5–92.0	Over 92.0	Average
Federal											
1. Total education	.6	1.1	1.1	1.0	.7	.6	.4	.3	.2	.1	.6
2. Elem. and secondary	.4	.6	.6	.5	.4	.3	.1	.1	.1	.0	.3
3. Higher	.0	.2	.2	.2	.2	.1	.1	.1	.1	.0	.1
4. Interest	2.1	2.0	1.2	.6	.6	.8	1.0	1.8	2.3	6.3	1.5
5. Highways	.6	.8	.9	.8	.8	.7	.6	.3	.2	.1	.6
6. Agriculture exp.	.0	.2	.3	.4	.3	.4	.8	1.8	2.6	.8	.7
7. Health & hospitals	1.9	1.8	1.0	.5	.3	.2	.1	.1	.0	.0	.4
8. Total transfers	78.3	19.8	8.8	4.3	2.6	2.1	1.5	1.2	.2	.2	6.2
9. Public Asst.	14.2	1.5	.6	.2	.1	.0	.0	.0	.0	.0	.7
10. Soc. ins. & ret.	52.5	14.5	6.2	2.8	1.7	1.4	1.1	.8	.2	.2	4.2
11. Unemployment	.8	.9	.6	.4	.3	.2	.1	.1	.1	.0	.3
12. Veterans dis. & pen.	5.8	1.6	.8	.6	.4	.3	.2	.2	.0	.0	.6
13. Other	5.0	1.2	.6	.3	.2	.1	.1	.1	.0	.0	.4
14. Total	83.5	25.7	13.3	7.6	5.3	4.7	4.3	5.3	5.5	7.5	10.00
State and local											
15. Total education	5.5	9.9	10.4	8.7	6.7	5.4	3.1	2.7	1.5	.5	5.2
16. Elem. and secondary	4.7	7.8	8.0	6.4	4.9	3.7	1.8	1.6	.8	.3	3.7
17. Higher	.4	1.5	1.7	1.8	1.4	1.4	1.1	1.0	.5	.2	1.2
18. Interest	.1	.1	.0	.0	.0	.0	.0	.0	.1	.2	.0
19. Highways	1.2	1.6	1.9	1.8	1.7	1.5	1.2	.6	.5	.3	1.3
20. Health & hospital	5.7	5.6	2.9	1.5	.9	.5	.4	.2	.1	.0	1.1
21. Public assistance	14.5	1.6	.6	.2	.1	.0	.0	.0	.0	.0	.7
22. Total	27.1	18.7	15.8	12.2	9.4	7.4	4.8	3.6	2.2	.9	8.4
All levels											
23. Total	110.6	44.4	29.1	19.8	14.7	12.0	9.1	8.9	7.7	8.4	18.4

comparison between the federal and state local benefit patterns shows less difference than was found to prevail for tax allocations. While the federal pattern is more regressive at the very bottom of the scale, the state local pattern is somewhat more regressive thereafter. Some of the major limitations of this type of analysis discussed in connection with tax burden distribution again apply and will not be repeated here.

Expenditures not subject to specific allocation

With regard to general expenditures, i.e. expenditures not subject to specific allocation, a general allocation formula must be resorted to if a distribution pattern is to be obtained. For present purposes three hypotheses were used, including allocation (a) in proportion to total income, (b) in proportion to tax burdens, and (c) on a *per capita* basis. Some rationale may be developed for each of the three.

Assumption (a) may be taken to reflect the traditional view of the state as a protector of private property, or to rest on the hypothesis that the benefits derived from the consumption of social goods are complementary to those derived from private goods. More subtly, assumption (a) may be interpreted as reflecting the recipient's evaluation of social goods, based on the hypothesis that income and price elasticities of demand for social goods are equal, in which case application of a 'Lindahl pricing rule' calls for a proportional benefit tax.

Assumption (b) implies an interpretation not of hypothetical but of actual taxes as conforming to a benefit rule. This is questionable for two reasons. For one thing, it can hardly be assumed that actual legislation conforms to a normative rule. For another, this interpretation overlooks the fact that the total tax structure (even in the normative case) consists of an 'allocation' and a 'distribution branch' component, with only the former subject to the benefit rule. To impute benefits in line with the pattern of benefit taxation, the tax structure must thus be divided into its two components, and the burden pattern of only the allocation branch component must be applied. Since this is not observable as a separate component, hypotheses must be established on the basis of which it can be deduced. The above interpretation of assumption (a) as conforming to a Lindahl pricing rule is one such attempt, and others can be made as well. Such procedures, however, are of more theoretical than practical interest and will not be pursued here.

Assumption (c), finally, reflects a view of social goods as consumed equally by all, but it does not allow for differences in the value placed on such equal consumption due to differences in income. Among the various cases considered, assumption (a) thus seems the least unreasonable, although it may be expected to overstate the benefit share received by low- and to understate that received by high-income recipients.[5]

The effective general benefit rates resulting under the various assumptions are shown in Table 18.6, lines 1–9, with total income again being used in the denominator of the ratio. Assumption (a) yields a proportional pattern, while assumption (b) repeats the pattern previously shown for tax burden distribution, with use being made of the benchmark case. Since the tax burden distribution was more or less proportional over most of the range, the results under the two assumptions are rather similar. Assumption (c), by its very nature, gives a regressive (pro-poor) schedule. Using assumptions (a) and (c) the same patterns apply for the various levels of government, with the ratios differing in average level only. Pattern (b) differs by level of government, since different tax burden distributions apply.

Total expenditure benefits

The lower part of Table 18.6 shows total benefits, combining the results of Table 18.5 for specifically allocable expenditures with those for expenditures subject to general benefits only. The federal benefit distribution (lines 10–12) remains heavily regressive or pro-poor. Under assumptions (a) and (b) regressivity is dampened throughout by the inclusion of general benefits (as compared to Table 18.5, line 14) while it is increased at the bottom of the scale under assumption (c).

The distribution of total benefits at the state and local level (lines 13–15) also remains regressive or pro-poor under assumptions (a) and (b). Indeed, the total benefit pattern does not differ greatly from that given before (Table 18.5, line 22) but assumption (c) once more significantly increases regressivity at the lower end of the scale.

Combining all levels of government, the benefit distribution (lines 16–18) continues highly regressive (pro-poor) at the lower end of the scale. While inclusion of general benefits again dampens regressivity (cf. Table 18.5, line 23) under assumptions (a) and (b), the regressive or pro-poor distribution at the lower end of the scale is once more accentuated under assumption (c).

NET BENEFITS OR BURDENS

Finally, the burden and benefit sides of the fiscal equation may be combined to arrive at the distribution of net benefits or burdens. The net effective rate for any particular bracket may be negative or positive depending on whether burdens outweigh benefits, or vice versa. The case for considering the resulting net pattern is evident since, in the end, it is the combined distributional effect of the tax and expenditure side of fiscal policy that matters. As noted before, this formulation also has the further advantage (shared with the differential approach to tax or expenditure incidence) of permitting the problem to be viewed in general equilibrium terms. Such at least is the case where the budget is balanced, so that the revenue and expenditure totals equal each other.

Net benefits or burdens as per cent of total income

The ratio of net benefits or burdens to total income is shown in Table 18.7.

Table 18.6 General and total benefits as per cent of total income

					Total income brackets (000s of dollars)						
	Under 4	4– 5.7	5.7– 7.9	7.9– 10.4	10.4– 12.5	12.5– 17.5	17.5– 22.6	22.6– 35.5	35.5– 92.0	Over 92.0	Average
A. General benefits²											
Federal											
1. Assumption A	13.6	13.6	13.6	13.6	13.6	13.6	13.6	13.6	13.6	13.6	13.6
2. Assumption B	9.0	10.7	12.5	12.9	12.9	13.9	13.5	14.2	14.6	17.3	13.6
3. Assumption C	56.6	26.5	23.4	17.0	14.7	11.5	9.1	6.1	3.7	1.2	13.6
State and local											
4. Assumption A	3.2	3.2	3.2	3.2	3.2	3.2	3.2	3.2	3.2	3.2	3.2
5. Assumption B	4.1	3.9	3.7	3.6	3.4	3.3	3.0	2.8	2.2	2.1	3.2
6. Assumption C	13.2	6.2	5.5	4.0	3.4	2.7	2.1	1.4	.9	.3	3.2
All levels											
7. Assumption A	16.7	16.7	16.7	16.7	16.7	16.7	16.7	16.7	16.7	16.7	16.7
8. Assumption B	13.2	14.6	16.1	16.4	16.3	17.2	16.5	17.0	16.8	19.5	16.7
9. Assumption C	69.8	32.7	28.9	21.0	18.1	14.2	11.3	7.5	4.6	1.4	16.7
B. Total benefits											
Federal											
10. Assumption A	97.0	39.2	26.9	21.1	18.9	18.2	17.9	18.9	19.1	21.0	23.5
11. Assumption B	92.5	36.3	25.8	20.4	18.2	18.6	17.8	19.5	20.1	24.8	23.5
12. Assumption C	140.1	52.1	36.7	24.6	20.0	16.2	13.5	11.5	9.3	8.6	23.5
States and local											
13. Assumption A	30.2	21.9	19.0	15.4	12.6	10.5	8.0	6.7	5.3	4.1	11.6
14. Assumption B	31.2	22.6	19.4	15.8	12.8	10.6	7.8	6.4	4.4	3.0	11.6
15. Assumption C	40.3	24.9	21.2	16.2	12.8	10.0	6.9	5.0	3.0	1.2	11.6
All levels											
16. Assumption A	127.3	61.1	45.8	36.5	31.4	28.8	25.8	25.6	24.4	25.1	35.1
17. Assumption B	123.7	58.9	45.2	36.3	31.1	29.2	25.6	25.9	24.5	27.8	35.1
18. Assumption C	180.4	77.0	57.9	40.8	32.8	26.2	20.4	16.5	12.3	9.8	35.1

a. For explanation of assumptions, see Table 19.4, lines 17–19.

Since the estimated benefit distribution for specifically allocable expenditures is less problematic than the hypothetical distributions for general benefit expenditures, net benefits are shown on two bases, one including specific expenditures only and the other covering total expenditures.

In showing net benefits with specifically allocable expenditures only (lines 1–3), a judgement must be made as to what part of tax revenue is to be matched with these outlays. As a simple but somewhat arbitrary solution, each dollar of expenditures is financed by drawing on the average tax dollar. Thus, benefits from specific federal expenditures are matched with burdens corresponding to an equal amount of taxes distributed in line with total federal taxes. The same procedure is followed at the state-local level, using now the overall pattern for state local taxes. The benchmark tax-shifting assumptions are used throughout.

As will be seen from the table, the federal net benefit pattern (line 1) is highly regressive, which in this case means again pro-poor. Moreover, this net pattern is somewhat more regressive than was the case for benefits only (see Table 18.5, line 14) since it combines the regressive (pro-poor) benefit pattern with the progressive (pro-poor) tax pattern. However, the major contribution to the pro-poor result comes from the benefit side. The net pattern for state and local finances (line 2) is also regressive throughout the scale, but considerably less so than at the federal level. The combined pattern for all levels of government (line 3) falls between the two sub-patterns, with the breakeven point occurring at a total income of about $10,000.

In the lower half of Table 18.7, general and specific benefits are combined, with results again shown separately for the three general benefit assumptions. Under assumption (a) the pattern becomes somewhat more regressive (pro-poor) than with specific benefits only. Under (b) the results remain unchanged with the benefit and tax additions to the numerator cancelling out. Under assumption (c), however, the regressivity of the net ratios (redistribution toward lower end) is sharply increased. This, of course, results from the regressive (pro-poor) nature of the *per capita* benefit distribution.

The net patterns under assumption (b) are also plotted in Figure 18.2. We note that the breakeven point for the federal system falls at about $8500. At 1968 levels of income, this divided the population about equally between gainers and losers, a result which is not uninteresting from the point of view of voting theory. The mythical 'median voter', it appears, strikes even.

Introduction or removal of fiscal system?

Following the usual practice in presenting effective rates of tax burden, the ratios of Table 18.7 show net gains or burdens from expenditures and taxes as a per cent of 'total income'. As noted previously, this view of the tax ratio, with its asymmetrical treatment of expenditures in the denominator, is inconsistent with the question to be examined. Similar problems arise with increased importance in the analysis of net burden. Here, two

Table 18.7 Net budget incidence: benefits net of taxes paid as a per cent of total income

	Total income brackets (000s of dollars)									
	Under 4	4– 5.7	5.7–7.9	7.9– 10.4	10.4– 12.5	12.5– 17.5	17.5– 22.6	22.6– 35.5	35.5– 92.0	Over 92.0
I. Specifically allocable expenditures only										
Federal										
1. Federal	76.7	17.7	4.1	−1.9	−4.2	−5.6	−5.6	−5.1	−5.1	−5.1
2. State and local	15.7	8.2	5.9	2.7	.2	−1.4	−3.2	−3.6	−3.4	−4.4
3. All levels	92.4	25.9	10.0	0.8	−4.0	−8.0	−8.8	−8.7	−8.5	−9.5
II. Specific and general expenditures										
Federal										
4. Assumption A	81.0	20.5	5.1	−1.3	−3.6	−5.9	−5.6	−5.7	−6.1	−8.7
5. Assumption B	76.7	17.7	4.1	−1.9	−4.2	−5.6	−5.6	−5.1	−5.1	−5.1
6. Assumption C	124.0	33.4	14.9	2.2	−10.0	−13.1	−16.9	−21.1		
State and local										
7. Assumption A	14.6	7.4	5.4	2.2	−.1	−1.5	−3.0	−3.2	−2.3	−3.2
8. Assumption B	15.7	8.2	5.9	2.7	.2	−1.4	−3.2	−3.6	−3.4	−4.4
9. Assumption C	24.6	10.4	7.7	3.0	.2	−2.0	−4.0	−4.9	−4.6	−6.1
All levels.										
10. Assumption A	95.6	27.9	10.5	.9	−3.7	−7.4	−8.6	−8.9	−8.4	−11.9
11. Assumption B	92.4	25.9	10.0	.8	−4.0	−7.0	−8.8	−8.7	−8.5	−9.5
12. Assumption C	148.7	43.8	22.6	5.3	−2.3	−9.9	−13.9	−18.0	−20.5	−27.2

Note: Assuming all expenditures out of general revenues and benchmark tax-shifting assumptions hold. Totals are total benefits minus government receipts accounting for charges and deficits. For unallocable expenditure assumptions, see Table 18.4, lines 17–19.

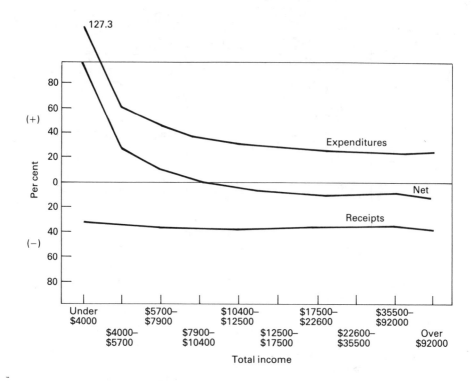

Figure 18.2 Total receipts and expenditures as a percentage of total income (taxes, benchmark assumptions; general expenditures allocated by total income).

questions may be asked or mental experiments made. The first deals with what would happen to the state of distribution if the fiscal system were to be introduced into a setting without a public sector. The second deals with what would happen to the state of distribution if the fiscal system were to be withdrawn from a setting with an existing public sector. The ratios of Table 18.7 answer neither question.

(1) If our concern is with considering the net benefits and burdens which particular income groups derive from the *introduction* of the fiscal system, we should measure these relative to income as it would be in the pre-fiscal state. The numerator of the ratio should include transfers plus real expenditure benefits minus taxes, while the denominator should include total income minus transfers. The ratios given in Table 18.7 should thus be corrected to exclude transfer payments from the denominator.

The corrected ratios are shown in Table 18.8, lines 1–3. All expenditures and all levels of government are included, so that comparison is with Table 18.7, lines 10–12. As a result of this revision, we find the net benefit ratios at the very bottom of the income scale to be vastly increased, with little

Table 18.8 Net benefit or burden ratios resulting from establishment or removal of the fiscal system (all levels of government, all expenditures, benchmark assumptions)

				Total income brackets (000s of dollars)						
	Under 4	4– 5.7	5.7–7.9	7.9– 10.4	10.4– 12.5	12.5– 17.5	17.5– 22.6	22.6– 35.5	35.5– 92.0	Over 92.0
I. Establishment[a]										
1. Assumption A	1,333.3	35.4	11.6	1.0	−3.8	−7.6	−8.7	−9.0	−8.4	−11.9
2. Assumption B	1,283.7	32.7	10.9	0.7	−4.2	−7.1	−8.9	−8.7	−8.3	−9.2
3. Assumption C	2,074.3	55.7	25.0	5.5	−2.4	−10.2	−14.2	−18.2	−20.5	−27.2
II. Removal[b]										
4. Assumption A	−88.0	−25.7	−10.2	−0.9	4.0	8.2	9.5	9.8	9.1	13.5
5. Assumption B	−84.8	−23.8	−9.7	−0.7	4.3	7.5	9.7	9.5	9.1	10.4
6. Assumption C	−137.0	−40.5	−22.2	−5.4	2.5	10.9	15.5	20.0	22.4	31.0

a. Numerator of ratio equals transfers plus real expenditure benefits minus taxes. Denominator equals total income minus transfers.
b. Numerator of ratio equals taxes minus real expenditure benefits. Denominator equals total income plus real expenditure benefits minus taxes. In considering both, note that total income includes transfers.

change over the rest of the income scale. This reflects the fact that welfare and social security benefits to the very poor are a large multiple of their other earnings. In the absence of transfers, households in this bracket would be close to a zero income level. Even though the ratio of transfers to earnings is high, total income remains very low relative to the average. Putting it differently, one may view the difference between Tables 18.7 and 18.8 as indicative of the scope of redistribution or of the abysmal poverty which would prevail in its absence.

(2) If our concern is with considering the distributive effects of *removing* the fiscal system, the numerator of the ratio must be defined as taxes, minus transfers, minus benefits from real expenditures. The denominator now should record the household's income position with the fiscal system in existence (i.e. include total income which already contains transfers) plus benefits from real expenditures. The difference with Table 18.7 is now that benefits from real expenditures are included in the denominator. This corrected ratio is shown in Table 18.8, lines 4–6.

We now find the pattern of lines 1–3 reversed. Lower-income house-holds lose while upper-income households gain. The percentage loss is highest at the bottom, becomes zero toward the middle of the scale, and then turns into a gain. Lines 4–6 may also be viewed as inverting the patterns given in Table 18.7, lines 10–12, but apart from this, the change in pattern is relatively slight. The results of the conventional (Table 18.7) approach do not differ greatly from those of system removal (Table 18.8, Part II), but the distribution toward the bottom is vastly greater for system introduction (Table 18.8, Part I). The reason, to repeat, is that the share of the bottom bracket in the pre-budget distribution, which forms the denominator in case I, is much smaller than in the post budget distribution which is used in II. Both comparisons are valid, and to the informed observer they will make the same point; but, as usual, statistics may be misleading if the formulation of the problem is not understood.

NOTES

1. Description of the underlying series contained in the original paper is here omitted.
2. Further issues, discussed in the original paper include (1) whether indirect taxes should be added back into the income base, (2) whether the denominator of the burden ratio should be defined as money income only or, as done here, as total income; and (3) whether the use of distributive series based on cross-section rather than life-time data is permissible. Also there is the question whether the burden of payroll taxes can be considered without allowing for benefit payments.
3. Since this paper was written, estimations based on general equilibrium models have appeared. These models have the advantage of allowing for second round effects, but the results are based on the assumption of perfectly competitive markets. See also ch. 20 below, where results under the two procedures are compared. The difference, it appears, is not substantial.

4. The reader should not be surprised that the ratio in the bottom bracket exceeds 100 per cent. This is readily possible since the concept of 'total income' which is used in the denominator does not include benefits from government purchases other than transfers and interest.
5. Aaron and McGuire, [1] have argued that allocation in line with a Lindahl benefit rule calls for a division of benefits from general expenditures such that the product of benefit share and marginal utility of income is the same for all consumers. Experimentation with simple utility functions or use of a marginal utility of income elasticity of −1.5 [4] leads to a benefit allocation which slightly tips the net benefit pattern of assumption (a) as given in Table 18.7, line 10, in favour of higher incomes. Using Maital's formulation, the new range is from about 90.0−−4 per cent. Since high-income consumers are willing to pay more, their net burden is reduced.

REFERENCES

[1] Aaron, H. and McGuire, M. (1970) 'Public Goods and Income Distribution', *Econometrica*, 38.
[2] Bishop, G. (1973) *Tax Burdens and Benefits of Government Expenditures by Income Class, 1961 and 1965* (New York: Tax Foundation).
[3] Gillespie, W. (1965) 'Effects of Public Expenditures on the Distribution of Income', in R. A. Musgrave (ed.), *Essays in Fiscal Federalism* (Washington, D.C.: Brookings Institution).
[4] Maital, S. (1973) 'Public Goods and Income Distribution: Some Further Results', *Econometrica*, 46.
[5] Musgrave, R. A., Carroll, J. J., Cook, L. D. and Frane, L. (1951) 'Distribution of Tax Payments by Income Groups: A Case Study for 1948', *National Tax Journal*.
[6] Pechman, J. A. and Okner, B. (1974) *Who Bears the Tax Burden?* (Washington, D.C.: Brookings Institution).
[7] Tarasov, H. (1972) 'Who Does Pay the Taxes?', *Social Research*, Suppl. 4.

19 ET, OT and SBT*
1976

1. INTRODUCTION

The normative theory of taxation has a long history, with the concept of a 'good tax structure' developed along two lines. One is the ability to pay or sacrifice approach, the other that of benefit taxation. The ability to pay school takes a 'taxation-only' view of the problem. While transfers can be included as negative taxes, the design for a good tax structure is drawn apart from the provision for social goods. Taxes should be equitable (i.e. in line with ability to pay) whatever the revenues are used for. In this respect, the traditional theory of equitable taxation (henceforth referred to as ET) resembles the new writings on optimal taxation (henceforth referred to as OT). Both incorporate transfers *qua* negative taxes, but do not provide an analytical link between the provision for social goods and the determination of the tax structure by which they are financed. OT and ET are both inferior in this respect to the benefit tradition. This tradition, especially in its Wicksellian version, has the great advantage of linking the tax to the expenditure side of the problem and of emphasising the integral role of taxation in the provision for social goods.[1] Both ET and OT, to use my terminology, are essentially theories of the distribution branch, without inclusion of allocation branch taxes. Nevertheless, it remains convenient in some respects to consider the tax transfer process in isolation and, for purposes of this paper, I shall follow the ET–OT pattern in this respect.

2. THE ET CONCEPT OF HORIZONTAL EQUITY

The ET view of the good tax structure rests on the central proposition that the tax system should be equitable. More specifically, it should meet the double criteria of horizontal and vertical equity.[2]

---

* *Journal of Public Economics*, (1976) 6.

The role of 'equal position'

Horizontal equity calls for equal tax treatment of people in equal positions. ET holds this to be a basic requirement for a good tax structure. It is called for by the principle of equal justice under the law and is accepted as a value judgement or ethical axiom, not as a proposition in economic efficiency. Vertical equity calls for a meaningful pattern of differentiation between people in unequal positions, related to society's evaluation of various states of well-being. Both concepts are interrelated and neither has priority over the other. In the absence of vertical equity norms, the case for horizontal equity is reduced to providing protection against malicious discrimination, an objective which might be met more simply by a tax lottery. Vertical equity in turn cannot be defined without horizontal equity norms, as it must deal with differential treatment of people who, to begin with, have been grouped on horizontal equity grounds.

Horizontal equity calls for equal treatment of people in equal positions. The general rule is plausible, but how should one define 'equal position' and 'equal treatment'? The basic meaning of 'equal position' must be that people enjoy equal levels of welfare, somehow defined; and that of 'equal treatment' that people in equal pre-tax positions should also be left in post-tax equality. But this is only a statement of the problem, not its solution. As a first step, operational meaning must be given to the concept of equal position. One must devise an 'objective' index of welfare before addressing the problem of how to compare levels of welfare derived by people in unequal positions.

ET writers have tended to define economic position in terms of income, and to interpret equal treatment of people with equal income as calling for equal amounts of tax. The Edgeworth–Pigou-type sacrifice theory [3, 5] was developed in terms of sacrifice incurred when surrendering income, just as the Schanz–Haig–Simons tradition [6] of tax-base definition proceeded to interpret income in terms of accretion. ET writers, in following up this lead, adapted the accretion concept to the complexities of economic institutions [1, 7, 8] and arrived at some normative findings for the direction of income tax design. These include: (1) capital gains should be treated as ordinary income, whether realised or not, provided that appropriate allowance is made for averaging and loss offset; (2) gifts and bequests should be treated similarly; (3) corporate source income should be integrated into the individual income tax base, whether or not distribution occurs, without a separate or 'absolute' tax being imposed on corporate income; (4) appropriate treatment of home-owners calls for the taxation of imputed rent, combined with deduction of depreciation and mortgage interest; and (5) income should be defined in real terms, thus calling for inflation adjustment. While these and other rules may have to be modified in application, they nevertheless offer criteria for applying horizontal equity norms and provide guidance to tax policy. Leaving aside these matters of application, which have been discussed at length, we here turn to certain more basic difficulties inherent in the definition of equal position—difficulties which have not been scrutinised sufficiently. This is surprising, since the concept of equal position is at the heart of horizontal equity, and horizontal equity is central to the entire ET approach.

In order to derive an acceptable measure of equal position or equal welfare, we consider consumers who may choose between the consumption of two commodities X and Z and leisure L, with L defined as the use of time for non-income earning activity, be it sleeping, playing or the enjoyment of literature. We also introduce a variable P which stands for psychic income or the pleasure or displeasure associated with particular jobs. To simplify matters, we begin with a one-period model so that the distinction between income and consumption may be disregarded for the time being. The definition of equal position is now examined under various assumptions regarding the equality or inequality of available options and preferences.

Equal preferences and options

No problem arises if all people have both equal options and preferences. Individuals A and B will be confronted with the same set of options (consumption packages of X, Z, and L) as given by the surface DCE in Fig. 19.1. Since they also have similar tastes, they will locate at the same

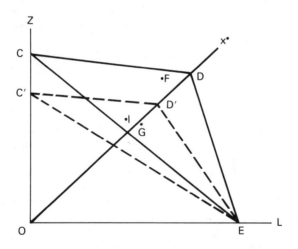

Figure 19.1.

point, say at F. It is a matter of indifference in this case how economic position is measured, whether in terms of X, Z, L or some composite expression. Indeed, there is no problem of defining equal position since all people choose the same mix of X, Z and L. Horizontal equity being met by any of the various indices of taxable capacity, the choice of tax base may be made on efficiency grounds. In this simplest case, taxes may be imposed in poll tax form, thus avoiding any problem of dead weight loss. The same holds if differences in P are allowed for. Since the same job is chosen and the same P is experienced by all, the problem of its measurability does not arise.

Nevertheless, one difficulty must be noted. While rates of substitution between X, Z and L are similar across individuals in this simplest case, the 'level' of utility which A and B derive from the same bundles of X, Z and L may differ. If some absolute comparison could be drawn, they may prove to be in dissimilar positions. Since individuals vary in most other respects, such would not be a surprising finding. But no operational test is available (utility comparisons based on risk-aversion are of no help since they address the slope, not the level of utility schedules) so that the best society can do is to adopt the hypothesis that the 'ability to enjoy' consumption (be it of X, Z or L) is the same for all. Justice is taken to call for treating individuals as if they were the same in this respect, i.e. derived equal welfare from similar baskets. Given this initial hypothesis, the conclusion for the equal option equal preference case remains that people should pay the same amount of tax.[3]

Equal preference with unequal options

Next we allow for differences in available options while retaining the assumption of equal preferences or utility functions. Suppose first that P is the same for all jobs, so that only differences in earning capacities need be considered. In this case, individuals $(A_1, A_2, ...)$ may be confronted with the opportunity set given by CED in Fig. 19.1, while individuals $(B_1, B_2, ...)$, who earn less, confront the lower set $C'ED'$. Since they have the same utility functions, all members of A group will choose the same mix, say F, located on CED while all members of the B group choose a mix, such as I, located on $C'ED'$. The As may then be grouped as equals and so may the Bs, following our earlier rule that people with identical baskets are considered to be in equal positions. As in the equal options case, horizontal equity is met equally well whether we choose X, Z, L or a composite as base.

But now there arises the additional problem of vertical equity. On what basis are we to conclude that the Bs are better-off than the As? If L, X and Z are all superior goods, the baskets of individuals with a superior option set will contain more of each X, Z and L, and they can be ranked accordingly. But such will hardly be the case. Even though the opportunity set of the As is higher, they may consume less of some good. We must therefore be satisfied with saying that the Bs are in a better position because their opportunity set lies above that of the As, without insisting that they have more of each commodity. A higher opportunity set in turn means that a higher level of welfare can be achieved. This level may be measured in terms of income defined broadly to include the imputed earnings from leisure (or consumption broadly defined to include the consumption of leisure) and individuals may be ranked accordingly.

Income thus defined is given by $Y_b = wK$, where w is the *observed* wage rate and K is a constant such as 16 or 24 hours. Or, we may write $Y_b = Y+wL$, where $Y = wH$ is earnings (or income as usually defined) and $H = K-L$ is hours worked. With leisure thus allowed for, wK becomes an operational measure of options and is clearly superior to Y or outlays on $X+Z$. Horizontal equity calls for people with equal values of wK to pay the same amount of tax. The tax base accordingly is to be defined as wK, which is also the optimal base on efficiency grounds.

Assuming the value of P to be the same for all jobs, a person will choose the job with the highest wage rate. The observed wage rate, therefore, equals the potential wage rate and $Y_b = wK$ is an operational concept. But matters are more difficult if a variable P is allowed for. Options now differ regarding P as well as w and a person's observed wage rate no longer reflects a unique potential wage rate. This is no trivial matter since Ps do in fact vary widely. Moreover, differences in options with regard to P are a major form in which job discrimination occurs. Using only one commodity Z, the choice between Z, L and P is now given by a surface such as *HIM* in Fig. 19.2. Assuming this to reflect the options available to the As, they

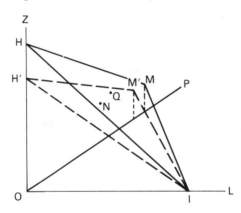

Figure 19.2.

might choose a point such as Q on the plane *HIM*. The set of options available to the Bs might be given by the lower plane *H'IM'*. They might then choose a point such as N. The difference in the position of the As and Bs is no longer reflected correctly by wK (with w the observed wage rate) because w differs with P. The definition of Y_b needs to be expanded to $(w+\alpha)K$, where w is the observed wage rate and α (which may be positive or negative) is the supplementary psychic wage rate. Since α is not given by observable market behaviour, the correct definition of Y_b ceases to be operational. This being the case, the quest for an index of horizontal equity has to be satisfied with a second-best solution. Treating people with equal

wKs as equals now involves a discrimination against the person whose option set is limited to lower values of P.[4]

Unequal preferences with equal options

Consider now a setting where available options are the same but preferences differ. The P variable is disregarded to begin with. People confronted with the same choice set on surface CED in Fig. 19.1 now select different positions. A may choose point F while B chooses G. The criteria of equal baskets no longer yields a measure of equal position. While wK remains an operational measure of equal options, it is no longer obvious that the equal option criteria can be taken as index of equal position. To do so now involves more than our earlier hypothesis that individuals with similar baskets derive equal satisfaction. We must now accept a broader and intuitively less plausible hypothesis that people with equal options but different baskets derive the same satisfaction. Differences in welfare which result from difference in tastes (with similar options) are to be disregarded. While one feels uneasy with this construction, it seems the best that can be done in deriving an operational measure of economic position. Horizontal equity once more is satisfied by using wK as the tax base, with equity and efficiency considerations again in accord. No substitution effects result and individuals with equal options, in paying the same amount of tax, may also be taken to receive equal treatment, i.e. to bear the same burden.

Matters are more complex as P is allowed for. Even if options are similar, differences in preferences with respect to P will result in different job choices. The proper tax base $(w+\alpha)K$ is not an operational measure since the values of α, applicable to A and B respectively, are not observable. If the tax is imposed on wK only, A and B will experience the same change in their option set but it would be difficult to argue that they experience the same burden. Depending on their preferences, they pay more or less tax, with the person who values goods highly relative to job satisfaction bearing the heavier burden. An even greater bias results if the tax is limited to wH, where an equal change in options benefits the individual with high leisure preferences. Whereas equal pre-tax positions (given acceptance of the broad hypothesis) can be defined in terms of equal options, equal treatment evidently can no longer be defined in terms of equal changes in options. As a second-best solution, equal tax treatment (among pre-tax equals) might be measured in terms of equal changes in real income, with the consumption pattern (pre- or post-tax) for each taxpayer used as weights. But if this were done, different tax formulae would have to be applied to pre-tax equals; different amounts of tax would be paid by them, and the equal option criteria (though applicable to the pre-tax setting) could no longer be used to define equal post-tax positions.

As unequal options are combined with unequal preferences it becomes difficult to distinguish the impact of the two on actual behaviour. Difficulties of defining equal pre-tax position are compounded with those of defining equal tax treatment. In all, it is evident that the concept of horizontal equity requires more scrutiny and careful thought than it has been given in the literature. Not only is α unobservable, but differences in preferences make it difficult to define pre-tax equality and equal treatment consistently. This, I hasten to add, does not mean that the search for horizontal equity should be abandoned: an orderly tax system has to be placed on a reasonable index of equality; and many of the departures therefrom can be identified as such even though certain aspects of the equality concept remain short of precise specification.

3.   TIME DIMENSION OF HORIZONTAL EQUITY

Thus far the concept of horizontal equity has been viewed in the context of a one-period model, thus by-passing the distinction between income and consumption. We now allow for a time dimension, and with it the choice between income and consumption as the proper index of equality. Around seminar tables the debate has been over whether or not the income tax involves 'double taxation of savings'. In the political forum, the issue has been less ethereal. The debate has been basically one over progressive taxation, since the income base has developed historically as the instrument of progressive taxation while the consumption base has been associated with the use of regressive taxes. We are here concerned with the former issue only, keeping in mind that the consumption base (through a personalised expenditure tax) could be rendered progressive. Specifically, what does the equal option approach tell us about the appropriate choice between the income and consumption base?

In addressing this topic, a distinction needs to be drawn between asking (1) which base is preferable on efficiency grounds, and (2) which offers the more meaningful index of equality in the ET context. Under highly simplified assumptions, a clear case can be made for the consumption base on efficiency grounds. A tax on income discriminates against future consumption, whereas the tax on consumption is neutral. Under more realistic assumptions, this conclusion need not follow, but in any case this line of reasoning, which pertains to efficiency only, does *not* tell us which of the two bases is preferable on equity grounds, i.e. as an index of equal position in the ET context.

To view the problem in its simplest setting, we assume leisure to be fixed and consider two individuals, A and B, who receive a given endowment or initial accretion M at the beginning of period 1. We may think of this as a gift, bequest or as wage income which will not reoccur. They may use their M for consumption in period 1 or they may save, receive interest and enjoy increased consumption in period 2. All income is consumed in the course of lifetime (the two-year period), with bequests excluded for the time being. To simplify matters, we further assume that A consumes his entire M in period 1 while B saves and consumes in period 2 only.

Period-by-period view

One approach is to apply the standard of horizontal equity to each period separately, without continuity between periods. Thus, in period 1 both *A* and *B* receive an endowment (or wage income) of *M* which they may consume or save. They therefore have the same option and should pay the same tax. This they do if the tax is on *M* but not if it is on consumption since, in that case, only *A* would pay. Equal treatment, therefore, calls for a tax on *M*, i.e. an income tax. In the next period, *A* receives no income and has no consumption, while *B* receives interest income. The two are in unequal positions and the entire tax should be paid by *B* since only he receives income. Again this is accomplished by an income tax. While it is evident for period 1 that *B* prefers the consumption tax and *A* the income tax (with both indifferent in period 2), it does not follow that *B* suffers 'double taxation' under the income tax. With each period considered by itself, *B*'s period 2 income presents a new option and he is properly taxed thereon.

Table 19.1

	Period	(α) Accretion	(β) Change in net worth	+	Consumption	= Total
A	1	M	–		M	M
	2	–	–		–	–
B	1	M	M		–	M
	2	$i(1-t)M$	$-M$		$[1+i(1-t)]M$	$i(1-t)M$

This reasoning holds whether income is defined (α) as accretion, i.e. additions to a person's net worth before counting withdrawals for consumption, or (β) as the change in net worth (additions minus withdrawals) plus consumption. Under the (α) concept, the period 1 tax base equals M for *A* and *B*, while the period 2 base equals zero for *A* and $i(1-t)M$ for *B*. Under the (β) concept, the period 1 base for *A* equals consumption of M (with change in net worth of zero), while that for *B* consists of increase in net worth by M (with consumption zero). The period 2 base equals zero for *A*, who has neither a change in net worth nor consumption. B's base in turn combines a reduction in net worth of M with consumption of $[1+i(1-t)]M$, which nets out to $i(1-t)M$. Thus, the bases under the (β) concept equal those recorded under the (α) concept. The two formulations of the income concept lead to identical results. What matters is not whether the income tax is interpreted under the (α) or (β) concept. What matters is whether a tax is to be imposed on income or on consumption.

Lifetime view

Though implicit in most of the literature on income tax, the above differs from the economists' view of income, based on Fisherian capital theory, as permitting a consumption stream, present and future. Having received equal initial endowments in period 1, A and B have the same consumption options over time, i.e. the two periods combined. This is what matters, not how each chooses to distribute his consumption over his lifetime. Since the present value of lifetime consumption is the same whatever the timing, both should pay the same present value tax for the period as a whole. This condition is met by a currently collected tax on consumption, where A pays t_cM in period 1 and nothing in period 2, while B pays $t_c(1+i)M$ in period 2, the present value of which (as viewed in period 1) is again t_cM.

Relating the lifetime view to the concept of income tax as commonly understood, no difficulty arises with regard to taxpayer A, whose income base is M in period 1 and zero in period 2. The present value of his tax base equals M under both the income and consumption tax. Turning to B, the present value of his consumption tax base again equals M, but the present value of his income tax base,

$$\left[1 + \frac{i(1-t)}{1+i} \right] M,$$

is larger. For the present value of the income tax base to equal M, accretion (or change in net worth) would have to be measured so as to exclude interest income, or the entire tax would have to be assessed at the end of the period.

Conclusion

Both the period-by-period and lifetime views can be made compatible with the equal option criteria, and it is not obvious which of the two offers the more meaningful base in the context of tax equity. However, if the lifetime view is chosen, it becomes essential to revise the assumption that all income is consumed during the entire period and to allow for bequests. The leaving of bequests offers an alternative option and therefore should be included in the tax base along with consumption. Since bequest rates differ among people with equal lifetime incomes, this is of obvious importance for horizontal equity; and since the ratio of bequests to lifetime income appears to rise with lifetime income (a matter on which little data are available) it is of importance for vertical equity as well. The definition of an equal options tax base must thus include bequests along with consumption. The rationale for this is not that bequeathing constitutes consumption, but that both uses of funds are alternative options. It is somewhat misleading, therefore, to refer to our 'equal options tax' as a consumption tax. Given such a restatement of the consumption tax base, the distinction between it and the income tax base is greatly reduced. While A will still prefer the income tax, whereas B prefers the consumption tax, the remaining difference merely relates to their chosen time path of disposal.

The argument so far has been based on the assumption that the utility of income derives from consumption, including the leaving of bequests. But savings may be for the sake of security, social position or power rather than for future consumption. If so, should not a tax on holding of wealth be added to that on consumption? Evidently a person will save more, in response to a given rate of interest, if he values the holding of wealth as well as future consumption. Moreover, the benefits from holding of wealth accrue currently as wealth is held, and thus suffer less from discounting. Do these factors justify an additional tax being imposed on the holding of wealth? We believe not, since gains from both sources will be equated at the margin with the rate of interest and will thus be captured by discounting the value of future consumption or accumulation. Individuals whose savings motivation leans largely on the benefits from accumulation will derive a higher consumer surplus, due to the earlier accrual of accumulation benefits, than those whose savings motivation is directed mainly toward future consumption. This, however, does not seem to justify an extra tax on accumulation, as it reflects the more general problem of differences in consumer surplus which arises once differences and preferences are allowed for.

Finally, note should be taken of the fact that the lifetime model as here discussed is based on the assumption that consumers are free to arrange their timepaths of consumption within their lifetime budget constraint. Given the fact that the availability of borrowing and lending facilities may differ among individuals, the consumption base may impose hardships by imposing the heaviest taxes when taxpayers can least afford to pay, a consideration speaking in favour of the income option.

4. EQUITY AND EFFICIENCY: ET AND OT COMPARED

The preceding discussion of ET has been in terms of horizontal equity, with little emphasis on efficiency aspects. We now consider how efficiency fits into ET analysis and how the equity norms of ET can be related to OT.

Efficiency and horizontal equity

ET literature, preoccupied with the quest for horizontal equity, has gone light in allowing for efficiency considerations. But this is not inherent in the horizontal equity concept. Proper interpretation of 'equal treatment of equals' calls for the imposition of equal burdens, measured not simply by tax dollars paid but by welfare losses incurred. This means inclusion of losses of consumer surplus or excess burden suffered. Moreover, it is only reasonable that the requirement of ET thus defined should be supplemented by the further requirement that excess burdens be minimised.

Just as efficiency considerations do not suffice without allowance for equity (in which case the ideal tax would simply be a poll tax), equity considerations cannot be dealt with without allowance for efficiency aspects. This is obvious enough, but the question is whether both goals can be met at the same time.

If utility functions were the same for all individuals, the same tax formula would impose equal excess burdens on *A* and *B*. People in equal positions (confronted with equal options) would incur the same burden when exposed to the same tax formula. But if preferences differ, a uniform formula, short of one which covers the entire vector of options, will not minimise burdens and also equalise them among individuals. Different formulae would have to be used, with each person's formula tailored to his particular preference set. This, however, is not an operational proposition. Tax theory, to be relevant to tax policy, must accept the constraint that the same tax base or formula is applied to all individuals; but closer consideration shows that there is no single formula that will be wholly satisfactory in both respects. A tax formula designed to avoid inefficiency will discriminate against products with low elasticities of substitution, whereas one designed to avoid inequities will discriminate against products whose share in consumer budgets (at given levels of income or consumption) shows a low degree of dispersion. The two sets of products will hardly be the same.

This being the case, a trade-off between equity and efficiency becomes necessary, and to carry it out two tasks of measurement arise. First, it is no longer sufficient to rank taxes by efficiency cost. The absolute cost of various tax formulae must be determined. Secondly, the quality of various formulae in terms of horizontal equity must be measured [9] and evaluated so that it can be balanced against excess burden incurred or avoided. Solving for the good tax structure is to strike this balance but even then, only a second-best solution (SBT) can be found.

Seen in this perspective, the essential difference between ET and OT is not merely that the former has been more closely related to the institutional setting of taxation while the latter has been more abstract and technical in its reasoning. It lies in the fact that ET has been preoccupied with horizontal equity at the cost of neglecting efficiency, while OT (especially in its commodity tax branch) has been concerned primarily with efficiency while neglecting horizontal equity. As I see it, horizontal equity has been defined out of existence by assuming all individuals to be subject to identical utility functions. Essentially, the problem is viewed in terms of a one-consumer economy, with taxes tailored to *his* particular preference function, thereby eliminating the distinction between using a generally applicable tax formula and the tailoring of tax bases in line with the preferences of different individuals. The ET and OT approaches thus move in quite different conceptual worlds. They come together only if it is realised that efficiency must be accounted for more fully by ET, while the horizontal equity issue must be faced by OT. The heart of the matter is how to apply equal treatment to a world of unequals, and OT will be of little help to policy-makers until this is recognised. My OT friends tell me that the allowance for differential tastes would render the problem too unwieldy for a neat solution, but I shall leave it to their ingenuity to find it.

5. EFFICIENCY AND VERTICAL EQUITY

We have noted that horizontal and vertical equity are closely linked concepts. Without criteria for differential treatment of unequals, there is little reason for worrying about the treatment of equals. ET writers have tended to interpret vertical equity in terms of equal sacrifice which (as applied to people in unequal positions) was taken to call for progressive taxation. Closer consideration, however, showed that this may or may not be the case, depending on the shape of the marginal income utility schedule and on how equal (absolute, proportional or marginal) sacrifice is defined. Moreover, the very assumption of objectively measurable, comparable and similar utility schedules became subject to increasing criticism. Eventually, the entire approach was replaced by a socially-postulated marginal income utility schedule with all individuals treated *as if* they were subject thereto.[5] Cognisant that progressive taxation aggravates the problem of deadweight loss, ET writers have hastened to add that vertical equity considerations in support of progression must be tempered by an allowance for adverse efficiency effects, a call for penance dating back to Edgeworth and Pigou. In all, the argument was left in a murky state and no clear conclusion emerged, with vertical equity analysis giving way to concern with horizontal equity.

OT, in its optimal income tax branch, has brought new life to the old issue of vertical equity. In postulating a utility function which specifies the taxpayer's choice between goods and leisure, his responses to tax or transfer rates are determined; and in postulating a social welfare function which permits alternative states of distribution to be ranked, an optimal structure of income tax is deduced (assuming a given distribution of earnings capacities) which will maximise social welfare under that function. Making the distribution of the tax transfer burden progressive results in a social welfare gain since the high-income loss is valued less heavily than the low-income gain. But the higher marginal tax and transfer rates needed to accomplish this also impose an efficiency cost or welfare loss. The optimal degree of progression is reached where the former gain at the margin falls short of the latter loss. The model may then be applied not only to the optimal distribution of a given tax bill but also to the broader problem of redistribution through the inclusion of taxes and transfers in the context of a negative income tax. As distinct from the theoretical aloofness of the OT work on commodity taxes, this branch of OT has arrived at specific conclusions, results which place narrower limits on progressive taxation than might have been expected. The results, however, depend in large part on the underlying assumptions, including the stipulated utility function as well as the particular social welfare function which is assumed [2]. While the analysis is superior to the old sacrifice approach, one's view as to the optimal tax structure remains in substantial part a matter of value judgement.

Most important in our context, identical utility functions are again applied to all individuals. This assumption not only eliminates the horizontal equity issue but thereby by-passes an essential aspect of the redistribution problem. Since in fact people have different income leisure preferences, any solution which assigns roles in the redistribution process (whether as taxpayer or as transfer recipient) in terms of actual earnings discriminates against persons with high goods preference and in favour of persons with high L and P preference. Thus vertical equity (defined in terms of X and Z but without regard for L and P) is implemented at the cost of violating horizontal equity. Inequities, moreover, are to be found throughout the capacity scale, as persons with high income preference stand to suffer discriminatory treatment under the OT model. The OT standard, by postulating equal utility functions, offends horizontal equity and falls short of being optimal, as I would use the term. The scholar who likes to think of himself as pursuing the higher things of life (rather than money income) may be inclined to overlook this defect, but the public at large may not. It is not surprising that, in the end, the failure to choose a satisfactory index of equality proves to be troublesome in the derivation of vertical as well as horizontal equity norms.

NOTES

1. It is ironic that this inherent advantage should have been lost in the modern theory of social goods. In integrating social goods into the Paretian efficiency system, the problem has been viewed as one of deriving the efficient set of allocation between private and social goods in a de novo, predistribution state, where all preferences are known to an omniscient referee. As a result, taxation remains outside the model, except in its most barren form of lump-sum transfers. Yet, taxation is an essential part of the fiscal problem in the real-world setting, where a resource transfer from the private to the public sector is called for, where consumer preferences for social goods are not known and where there exists a distribution of income to which effective preferences must be related. As Wicksell had stressed to begin with, it is through coordinated decisions on taxes and public services that consumers and voters must be induced to reveal their preferences, thus giving a central role to taxation. The suitability of various taxes in serving this revelation function then becomes an important normative criterion for what constitutes a good tax structure, just as allowance for the political process of preference determination becomes an integral part of a positive theory of the public sector.
2. Without using the terms 'horizontal' and 'vertical' explicitly, this distinction is drawn clearly by Simons [6, p. 30], who states that 'tax burdens should bear similarly upon persons whom we regard as in substantially similar circumstances, and differently where circumstances differ.'
3. While most people will accept this way of short-circuiting the 'differences in capacity' problem, there remains the question of whether certain differences in

need should not be accounted for. This includes the obvious issue of size of taxpaying unit, as reflected in the granting of differential exemptions under the income tax. Beyond this, one may argue that an allowance should be made for extra costs resulting from such handicaps as blindness. The latter may not only affect earnings abilities (this being allowed for automatically by reducing the level of taxable income) but also give rise to additional costs (the seeing-eye dog). A good case can be made in the ET context that such a cost should be allowed for. In other words, A and B should be considered in equal position if they consume equal bundles of X, Z and L, while B is allowed the additional cost of a seeing-eye dog. Of course, it is difficult to decide just what disabilities should be allowed for, and no clear line can be drawn. It does not follow, however, that the issue should be dismissed. A degree of arbitrariness is inevitable whenever normative concepts are applied to complex institutions.

4. If the opportunity sets, such as given by HIM in Fig. 19.2, were revealed, the psychic wage rate might be measured by the difference between a person's hourly earnings at his chosen job and at the highest-paying job available to him. This position could then be measured in terms of potential earnings at that job. The difficulty arises because potentially available (as distinct from chosen) wage rates are not observable. Further difficulties may arise even in the absence of psychic income, since the leisure income choice will frequently be constrained by institutional arrangements. Assuming that a person would like to consume less leisure than arrangements permit, valuation of leisure as wL is an overstatement.

5. As the slope of the schedule remains unknown, so is the degree of progression called for to secure equal sacrifice. While efforts have been made to reverse the problem by deriving the shape of the utility function from the existing income tax, this would seem an excessively optimistic procedure [4].

REFERENCES

[1] Bittker, B. I., C. O. Galvin, R. A. Musgrave and J. A. Pechman (1968) *A Comprehensive Income Tax Base? A debate* (Branford, C. T.: Federal Tax Press).

[2] Cooter, R. and E. Helpman (1974) 'Optimal Income Taxation for Transfer Payments under Different Social Welfare Criteria', *Quarterly Journal of Economics*.

[3] Edgeworth, F. Y. (1897) 'The Pure Theory of Taxation', *Economic Journal*, 7.

[4] Mera, K. (1969) 'Experimental determination of relative marginal utilities', *Quarterly Journal of Economics*.

[5] Pigou, A. C. (1951) *Studies in Public Finance*, 3rd edn (London: Macmillan).

[6] Simons, H. (1938) *Personal Income Taxation* (Chicago: University of Chicago Press).

[7] —— (1940) *Federal Tax Reform* (Chicago: University of Chicago Press).

[8] Vickrey, W. (1947) *Agenda for Progressive Taxation*.

[9] White, M. and A. White (1965) 'Horizontal Inequity in the Federal Income Tax Treatment of Home Ownership and Tenants', *National Tax Journal*, September.

20 Estimating the Distribution of Tax Burdens: A comparison of different approaches
1980

1. INTRODUCTION

The problem of tax burden distribution is an illustration, *par excellence*, of the difficulties facing policy-oriented economists. On the one hand, it is evident that firm scientific judgement regarding the distribution of tax burden, or the distributional implications of alternative tax measures, is exceedingly difficult to come by. Approached in rigorous terms, the problem involves fully-fledged general equilibrium analysis with all its difficulties. On the other hand, it is no less evident that distributional considerations are (and properly so) a prime factor in the formulation of tax policy. Policy-makers *will* make assumptions regarding the burden distribution of various taxes and the question for the tax economist is whether or not to help in formulating them. Proceeding on the premise that even defective information is better than a random choice, economists have provided answers, based on rather simplified assumptions, and a methodology which falls far short of a genuine general equilibrium approach. These studies, several of which have appeared over the last three decades,[2,11,12] have been used widely for policy judgement and for assessing the quality of the tax structure in distributional terms.

The purpose of this paper is to compare the outcome of the simplifying approach underlying these studies, with that of two possible general equilibrium models: a simple, two-sector analytical model designed to reflect a general equilibrium formulation of the problem, and a larger-scale, empirical general equilibrium model developed by Fullerton, King, Shoven and Whalley[3,4] (hereafter referred to as FKSW). First, we point

* With D. Fullerton and S. Deravajan (1980) *Journal of Public Economics*, 13.

out the methodological assumptions of the traditional approach and note the hypotheses to be tested. In Section 2 we present the analytical model and identify conditions which lead to rejecting these hypotheses. In Section 3 we test the hypotheses for four different taxes in the framework of the empirical, general equilibrium model. Section 4 concludes the analysis by summarising its salient points and discussing interpretations of the results. In an addendum, we examine the importance of price-change (uses) effects versus income (sources) effects in the context of the FKSW model.

We begin by briefly describing the major steps typically involved in the traditional approach to incidence studies as followed by Pechman[12], Musgrave[11] and others (hereafter referred to as PM). The objective of these studies is to allocate tax burdens by income groups. This is done for each tax by taking the total amount collected and imputing the resulting burden to households grouped by income classes. The total burden for each tax equals revenue collected.

The procedure is to *stipulate* the specific response of the economy to various taxes, based on theoretical analysis and market structure specifications, and then to allocate the burden by income groups. Thus, it is stipulated that excise and sales taxes will be borne by the consumers of the taxed products and that the income tax is borne by the taxpayer. For some taxes alternative assumptions are explored. The burden distribution of the corporation tax may be examined assuming that the tax is borne by shareholders, that it falls on all capital income, or that the burden is spread to wage-earners or to consumers of corporate products. Similarly, alternative assumptions may be examined for the property and payroll taxes.

This procedure has the advantage that it can be implemented readily, that the underlying assumptions are visible, and that the implications of alternative hypotheses can be appraised. It also has the weakness that the nature of incidence is stipulated rather than empirically derived. Furthermore, this stipulation is limited to only partial responses of the economy. Thus, taxes on products are taken to affect households from the uses side of their accounts only, the burden being distributed in line with the distribution of consumer expenditures. Further effects on factor prices, which may affect the position of households from the sources side, are disregarded, as are second-round effects on relative commodity prices. Thus, it is concluded that a sales tax on a luxury item will be progressive whereas one on a necessity will be regressive. Similarly, taxes on factor income such as the income tax are taken to affect household positions from the sources side only, the burden being distributed in line with earnings subject to tax. Further effects from the uses side, brought about by changes in relative prices, are disregarded.

To be sure, this procedure is not altogether arbitrary. The underlying argument is that the burden distribution of a tax which initially impacts from the sources side will be dominated by sources-side effects, because secondary effects operating from the uses side have no systematic relation to sources effects.[1] Thus, a progressive income tax is taken to be progressive. Similarly, it is postulated that the effects of a tax which initially impacts from the uses side will be dominated by uses-side effects, while further effects which result from the sources side due to changes in earnings will have no systematic relation to the uses side. The following discussion aims at testing these hypotheses.

In comparing the results of the PM methodology with those obtained from the FKSW model, we can ascertain the magnitude and direction of the change caused by allowing general equilibrium interrelationships. At the same time, we do not mean to imply that the model's results do indeed provide the 'true' answers. The model represents a first step in reproducing these real-world effects, but, by necessity, it employs simplifying assumptions of its own. This being the case, we attempt to gain further insights into the interaction of several key variables in terms of a simple, two-sector analytical model.

2. THE ANALYTICAL MODEL

Since Harberger's [5] pioneering work, several authors have developed general equilibrium models to analyse the effects of taxation.[2] Their contributions are surveyed in McLure [6] and a particularly simple illustration is given by McLure and Thirsk [7]. Our model is essentially based on theirs. However, as with most writers in this field they focus on the general equilibrium effects of a tax on resource allocation and the functional distribution of income. Since we are concerned with the allocation of tax burden between individuals, we extend the McLure and Thirsk model to include two consumers with different endowments of each factor. Our model is structured to investigate the impact of a tax allowing for all general equilibrium effects. The purpose is to identify the strategic variables which determine the outcome. We consider a selective sales tax in this illustration, although the model can also be used to illustrate the effect of other taxes.

Description of the model
Since the two-sector model is familiar to most readers, we treat it very briefly here. Cobb–Douglas assumptions are made in order explicitly to solve for large tax changes. We consider an economy with two goods (X, Y) each of which is produced by a Cobb–Douglas production function, using only capital and labour, which are available in fixed total supply, K and L:

$$X = K_X^\alpha L_X^{1-\alpha}, \tag{20-1}$$

$$Y = K_Y^\beta L_Y^{1-\beta}, \ \alpha, \ \beta > 0. \tag{20-2}$$

There are two consumers (A, B) who derive utility by consuming goods X

and Y in the Cobb–Douglas utility functions

$$U_A(X_A, Y_A) = X_A^\gamma Y_A^{1-\gamma}, \tag{20-3}$$

$$U_B(X_B, Y_B) = X_B^\delta Y_B^{1-\delta}, \; \gamma, \delta > 0. \tag{20-4}$$

Each consumer makes his purchasing decision by maximising his utility subject to a budget constraint derived from his endowments of capital and labour. If we let I^A be consumer A's income; R, W the price of capital and labour, respectively, and λ, μ his share of the economy's capital and labour supplies, then

$$I_A = \lambda RK + \mu WL \tag{20-5}$$

Because this economy has only two consumers,

$$I_B = (1 - \lambda)RK + (1 - \mu)WL \tag{20-6}$$

Throughout the analysis we assume all agents are price-takers, producers maximise profit, consumers maximise utility, and all factors are mobile across sectors. Initially, there are no taxes in the system.

Equilibrium with a sales tax

We assume the economy is initially at an equilibrium with quantities normalised so that all prices are unity. We now impose a tax t on sales of good X. In order to keep the analysis as simple as possible, we assume, as do McLure and Thirsk [7], that the government spends the tax revenue to replace exactly the loss in private demand in each sector from tax-induced income losses.[3] That is, nominal national income is constant before and after the imposition of the tax. Thus, if we denote with primes the prices and quantities in the new, cum-tax equilibrium, we have

$$P_X'X' = P_X X = X; \; P_Y'Y' = P_Y Y = Y. \tag{20-7}$$

But, from our Cobb–Douglas assumptions we know that factor payments command a constant share of net revenue in each industry. In other words,

$$R'K_X' = \alpha(1 - t)P_X'X' = \alpha(1 - t)X = (1 - t)K_X \tag{20-8}$$

and

$$R'K_Y' = \beta P_y'y' = K_Y. \tag{20-9}$$

Note that P'_X denotes the new gross of tax price of X. We now have an expression for R', the new net rental price for capital services, from (20-8) and (20-9) and the fixed factor supply assumption ($K'_X + K'_Y = K$):

$$R' = \frac{(1 - t)K_X + K_Y}{K}.$$ (20-10)

Similarly, it can be shown that

$$W' = \frac{(1 - t)L_X + L_Y}{L}.$$ (20-11)

In the same way one can solve for all the new quantities, prices and incomes. For brevity, we only state the latter two:

$$P'_X = \frac{R'^\alpha W'^{1-\alpha}}{1 - t},$$ (20-12)

$$P'_Y = R'^\beta W'^{1-\beta},$$ (20-13)

$$I'_A = \lambda R'K + \mu W'L$$ (20-14)

$$= I_A - t(\lambda K_X + \mu L_X L_X),$$

$$I'_B = I_B - t[(1 - \lambda)K_X + (1 - \mu)L_X].$$ (20-15)

It can be shown that this new equilibrium satisfies certain conditions which appeal to intuition:

(1) If the tax is imposed on a capital-intensive commodity, the price of capital falls relative to the price of labour. That is, $R'/W' < 1$. By 'capital-intensive', we mean that the taxed industry's capital:labour ratio (K_X/L_X) exceeds the economy's (K/L).
(2) A tax on the capital-intensive commodity will result in a greater percentage loss in nominal income to the consumer with the more 'capital-intensive' factor endowment. For example, if $\lambda/\mu > (1 - \lambda)/(1 - \mu)$, A's endowment is more capital intensive than B's, so that

$$(I'_A - I_A)/I_A < (I'_B - I_B)/I_B.$$

(3) The gross of tax price of the taxed commodity increases relative to the price of the untaxed commodity. In our notation $P'_X > P'_Y$.

From now on, therefore, we assume that X is the more capital-intensive commodity, and A is the consumer with the more capital-intensive endowment.

Testing the PM hypothesis

The PM estimate of the distribution of tax burden undoubtedly will not coincide with that of the general equilibrium approach, but we might ask whether the *ordering* of burdens to the groups of taxpayers can be reversed. The variables which determine the ordering will *a fortiori* determine relative income disparities.

As a commodity tax is imposed on X the PM method would compare the proportion of income spent on X by the two consumers to determine who bears the greater burden, defined as the ratio of tax paid to income. In our example this amounts to comparing γ and δ. Suppose $\delta > \gamma$, so that B is hurt more than A by the tax in the PM framework. We then look at the percentage change in real income from the general equilibrium calculation, and try to identify conditions under which the scales will tip the opposite way, with A registering a greater proportional loss in real income than B.

In general, if P'_A is some measure of the price level facing A in the new equilibrium (where P_A is unambiguously one), his percentage change in real income would be

$$\frac{I'_A/P'_A - I_A}{I_A}.$$

P'_A will depend on which market basket (the old or the new) is used for quantity weights. We compute both Laspeyres and Paasche versions of P'_A since they serve as bounds to the true measure of real income loss.

The Laspeyres price index (LPI) is defined as the change in prices weighted by old quantities. For A,

$$LPI_A = \gamma P'_X + (1 - \gamma)P'_Y.$$

Similarly,

$$LPI_B = \delta P'_X + (1 - \delta)P'_Y.$$

For A to suffer a greater real income loss than B, in proportional terms, it must be the case that

$$\frac{\dfrac{I'_A}{\gamma P'_X + (1 - \gamma)P'_Y} - I_A}{I_A} < \frac{\dfrac{I'_B}{\delta P'_X + (1 - \delta)P'_Y} - I_B}{I_B} \qquad (20\text{-}16)$$

Letting $I_{AX} = \lambda K_X + \mu L_X$ and $I_{BX} = (1 - \lambda)K_X + (1 - \mu)L_X$ stand for the incomes derived from industry X by A and B, respectively, we have, by rearranging, the inequality

$$\left(\frac{P'_X}{P'_Y} - 1\right)\left[\delta\left(1 - \frac{tI_{AX}}{I_A}\right) - \gamma\left(1 - \frac{tI_{BX}}{I_B}\right)\right]$$

$$< t\,\frac{L_X}{L}\,\frac{\left(\dfrac{\lambda}{\mu} - \dfrac{1 - \lambda}{1 - \mu}\right)\left(\dfrac{K_X}{L_X} - \dfrac{K}{L}\right)}{\left(\dfrac{\lambda K}{\mu L} + 1\right)\left(\dfrac{1 - \lambda}{1 - \mu}\dfrac{K}{L} + 1\right)} \qquad (20\text{-}17)$$

Real income changes evaluated with the Paasche index lead to a similar inequality:

$$\left(1 - \frac{P'_Y}{P'_X}\right)\left[\delta\left(1 - \frac{tI_{BX}}{I_B}\right) - \gamma\left(1 - \frac{tI_{AX}}{I_A}\right)\right]$$

$$< t\,\frac{L_X}{L}\,\frac{\left(\dfrac{\lambda}{\mu} - \dfrac{1 - \lambda}{1 - \mu}\right)\left(\dfrac{K_X}{L_X} - \dfrac{K}{L}\right)}{\left(\dfrac{\lambda K}{\mu L} + 1\right)\left(\dfrac{1 - \lambda}{1 - \mu}\dfrac{K}{L} + 1\right)} \qquad (20\text{-}18)$$

These inequalities can now be interpreted. Consumer A, even though he spends a smaller fraction of his income on the taxed commodity, can be hurt more by the tax the greater are

$$\left(\frac{\lambda}{\mu} - \frac{1 - \lambda}{1 - \mu}\right)$$

and

$$\left(\frac{K_X}{L_X} - \frac{K}{L}\right);$$

that is, the more capital-intensive are his endowment and the taxed industry. Furthermore, since $P'_X/P'_Y - 1 > 0$, $\delta > \gamma$ and since $I_{AX}/I_A > I_{BX}/I_B$ from (21-4), (21-5), and condition 2, the left-hand side of (21-7) or (21-8) will be smaller the greater is the discrepancy between I_{AX}/I_A and I_{BX}/I_B. In other words, the more A relies on industry X for his income (relative to B), the more likely he is to lose from the tax.[4]

A numerical illustration
We can use the relationships developed above to study the relative importance of various parameters, such as capital:labour ratios, capital:la-

bour intensities of endowments, etc. in reversing the pattern obtained by a PM calculation.

First, we estimate inequality (20-6) for a tax on housing, because this sector has by far the highest capital:labour ratio, a parameter which seems to be significant in altering the PM pattern. As data, we use the benchmark equilibrium of the FKSW model, collapsing their twelve consumer types into two, where A represents the six high-income groups, and B is the six low-income groups. We let X be the housing sector and Y an aggregate of all the other sectors. The FKSW data give the following values, where factor incomes equal quantities since units are defined as the amount which sells for $1 net of taxes:

$$K_X = 56,832; \qquad K = 181,974,$$

$$L_X = 7,782; \qquad L = 643,040,$$

$$\alpha = 0.84; \qquad \lambda = 0.81;^5 \ \gamma = 0.12,$$

$$\beta = 0.20; \qquad \mu = 0.80;^5 \ \delta = 0.17.$$

Now, inequality (21-6) is equivalent to

$$\frac{1 - tI_{AX}/I_A}{1 - tI_{BX}/I_B} < \frac{\gamma(P'_X/P'_Y - 1)}{\delta(P'_X/P'_Y - 1)} \tag{20-19}$$

since $I'_A - I_A = tI_{AX}$, etc.

From the above data,

$$I_{AX} = \lambda K_X + \mu L_X = 52,260; \qquad I_{BX} = 12,345,$$

$$I_A = \lambda K + \mu L = 661,830; \qquad I_B = 163,183.$$

We consider the effect of a 50 per cent tax on the gross price of X, or $t = \frac{1}{2}$.

Thus, the left-hand side of (20-19) is 0.998. To calculate the right-hand side, we first estimate the new price ratio P'_X/P'_Y from eqs. (20-10)–(20-13). This value is 1.7, so the right-hand side of (20-19) is 0.965. Thus, even for the industry with the highest capital:labour ratio, the general equilibrium effects do not reverse the burden distribution pattern given by a PM or partial equilibrium calculation. On the other hand, the factor intensities of the two consumers' endowments were nearly equal which may explain the non-reversal. It is possible that more divergent parameters, on both sources and uses sides, could lead to results which conflict with the PM calculations. Sensitivity analysis shows that changing the endowments λ and μ to 0.9 and 0.7, respectively, still leaves the general equilibrium ordering the same as that obtained under partial equilibrium analysis. Increasing the capital:labour ratio of the taxed industry may lead to reversal, but the ratio used in the illustration is already quite high.

Conclusion

It goes without saying that this two-sector/two-consumer model is a highly simplified view of the world. For one thing, changes in A's and B's relative positions hide further changes that occur within the two halves of the distribution. For another, using only two sectors and two factors oversimplifies the process of substitution which affects both sources and uses sides. Furthermore, the potential advantages of the general equilibrium over the PM approach are not properly tested by asking whether the *orderings* can be reversed, since policy decisions must consider *magnitudes* and not only directions of change. Nevertheless, our formulation has the virtue of helping to identify the parameters which offset the partial equilibrium pattern. For instance, the capital:labour ratio of the taxed industry plays an important role because it affects both sides of inequality (20-19); the capital-intensity of a consumer's factor endowments, on the other hand, appears only on the left-hand side. Finally, we have here considered only a sales or product tax. A similar analysis may be performed for an income tax or a factor tax.

3. COMPARISONS WITH THE EMPIRICAL MODEL

An outline of the FKSW model

The empirical model developed by Fullerton *et al.* [3,4] uses 1973 data from the *National Income Accounts*, the *Consumer Expenditure Survey*, and the Treasury Department's merged tax file. The solution procedure employed is Merrill's algorithm similar to the well-documented Scarf [13] technique. We present here only a brief sketch of the model, a full description of which can be found elsewhere [see 3,4].

There are 19 industries that use capital and labour in constant elasticity of substitution production functions and also use the outputs of other industries as intermediate inputs through an input/output matrix with fixed coefficients. Each of these 19 producer goods are used directly by government, by foreign traders, and for investment goods, but indirectly for consumption through a fixed coefficient G matrix of transition into 16 consumer goods with suitable definitions for consumer demands. There are 12 consumer groups, differentiated by income class, each with an initial endowment of capital and labour and each with a set of preferences over the 16 consumer goods. Government collects taxes on many of these transactions and uses the revenue in a balanced budget to purchase producer goods via Cobb–Douglas demand functions, and to make direct transfer payments to consumers.

Through their interaction, these utility-maximising consumers and profit-maximising producers are assumed to reach a competitive equilibrium where all profits are zero and supply equals demand for each good and factor. Starting with data on endowments, budget patterns by income groups, taxes, and production parameters, we use the algorithm to calculate prices that satisfy these conditions. By first calculating an equilibrium that replicates our data and then altering some tax rule or parameter in order to calculate a simulated equilibrium, we can estimate the economic effects of such a change. Since the counter-factual equilibrium solution provides a complete set of prices and quantities, we can estimate the change in national income, utility or income changes for each group, and all new factor allocations among industries.[6]

While an economic model necessarily abstracts from reality, the FKSW model captures three features which are especially relevant to the analysis of tax incidence, namely variations in demand patterns across income groups, variations in capital:labour ratios in production, and variations in ratios of consumer factor endowments. On the other hand, in the neoclassical tradition the present version of the FKSW model assumes full employment of two homogeneous factors, each in fixed supply. It assumes perfectly competitive markets with no externalities, no quantity constraints, and no barriers to factor mobility.

To analyse a tax in this model, the institutional setting must be converted into model-equivalent terms. The corporation income tax and property tax, for example, are treated in combination as a tax on capital use by industry.[7] The assumption of perfectly competitive behaviour then determines how these burdens are transmitted through the system. Finally, note that the model is essentially comparatively static, so that each equilibrium can be thought to represent a world where all adjustments have already taken place.[8] Moreover, by holding the capital and labour stocks fixed, growth effects are disregarded. Undoubtedly, because of these simplifying assumptions the model overlooks other aspects of the economy which have a bearing on the result. FKSW are currently extending their model to relax some of these assumptions.

Table 20.1 shows the industry and consumer good aggregations used in the model and their capital:labour ratios derived from the data. The two classifications are related by the fixed coefficient transition matrix. For example, the appliances commodity would require some machinery, some chemicals and rubber, some trade, and some transportation: its capital:labour ratio is a weighted average of the producer's capital:labour ratios.

Table 20.2 shows the income side for consumer groups by level of annual gross income. Column I displays the ratio of capital to labour income. Column II shows capital income as a share of total income (which includes earnings and transfers). The marginal tax rates, shown in column III, were averaged over individuals in each group from Treasury Department data. The high share of capital earnings to total earnings in the low-income

Table 20.1: Classification of industries and consumer goods, with capital:labour ratios

Industry I	K/L ratio II	Consumer goods III	K/L ratio IV
1. Agriculture, forestry, fisheries	1.893	1. Food	0.125
2. Mining	0.241	2. Alcoholic beverages	0.077
3. Crude petroleum and gas	0.987	3. Tobacco	0.077
4. Construction	0.020	4. Utilities	0.203
5. Food and tobacco	0.107	5. Housing	5.354
6. Textiles, clothing, leather	0.062	6. Furnishings	0.106
7. Paper and printing	0.143	7. Appliances	0.095
8. Petroleum refining	2.922	8. Clothing and jewellery	0.070
9. Chemicals and rubber	0.202	9. Transportation	0.239
10. Lumber, furniture, stone	0.243	10. Motor vehicles	0.154
11. Metals, machinery, and misc.	0.118	11. Services	0.116
12. Transportation equipment	0.012	12. Financial services	0.233
13. Motor vehicles	0.322	13. Recreation, reading, and misc.	0.122
14. Transportation, communications, utilities	0.224	14. Nondurable household items	0.107
15. Trade	0.075	15. Gas and other fuel	0.379
16. Finance and insurance	0.239	16. Savings	0.105
17. Real estate	7.303		
18. Services	0.113		
19. Government enterprises	0.515		
Total	0.283[a]	Total	0.272[a]

[a]Total K/L ratios differ because some of the producer goods are not used for consumption, and because consumers own some capital that is used by government and not by industry. A unit of each factor is defined as that which sells for $1 net of factor taxes but gross of personal income taxes.

brackets reflects a high proportion of retired persons who have no current labour income, but only capital income, largely in the form of imputed rents. The ratio of capital to labour income shown in column I is strongly U-shaped. This is less so in column II because transfers make up a high share of total incomes in the low brackets.

Experiments with the model

The experiments with the model involve the introduction of various taxes, where it is assumed that the revenue is returned to the taxpayers in the

Table 20.2: Classification of consumer groups, capital:labour ratios, and marginal tax rates

Consumer groups by $ thousand of AGI	Ratio of capital to labour income I	Capital share of total income[a] II	Marginal tax rate III
1. 0– 3,000	0.708	0.23	0.0100
2. 3– 4,000	0.436	0.19	0.0608
3. 4– 5,000	0.293	0.16	0.1019
4. 5– 6,000	0.263	0.17	0.1228
5. 6– 7,000	0.230	0.16	0.1346
6. 7– 8,000	0.193	0.15	0.1570
7. 8–10,000	0.159	0.13	0.1813
8. 10–12,000	0.159	0.14	0.2078
9. 12–15,000	0.137	0.13	0.2215
10. 15–20,000	0.143	0.14	0.2618
11. 20–25,000	0.180	0.16	0.2897
12. 25+	0.549	0.43	0.4067
Total	0.233	0.20	

[a]'Total income' includes transfers, labour and capital incomes. Capital income for each consumer group includes the sum of their interest, dividend and rent receipts, realised capital gains, some unincorporated income and imputed net rent of owner-occupied homes.

form of a transfer, made in proportion to after-tax income received prior to the change. The transfer is treated as non-taxable. Thus viewed, the experiments may be seen to measure budget incidence, i.e. the combined effects of a tax and expenditure change. Alternatively, the experiments may be viewed as combining the various tax increases with corresponding equal yield and income tax reductions in proportion to after-tax income. Thus seen, the experiments may be taken to measure differential tax incidence.[9]

The model has been estimated for four experiments, including (1) a progressive increase in income tax, (2) a tax on housing services, (3) a tax on clothing and jewellery, and (4) a tax on gasoline.[10]

Within the categories used, housing is clearly the most capital-intensive consumer good, as seen in Table 20.1, since it uses mostly the real estate industry's output. Clothing and jewellery is the most labour-intensive consumer good, but its K/L ratio is still higher than the minimum for producer goods since it is a weighted average of several of those goods. It includes mostly textiles, with the lowest K/L ratio. In Table 20.3 we show the expenditure patterns on our three commodities by income group.[11] It can be seen that housing behaves much like a necessity, making up a relatively larger proportion of the low income consumer's budget. Clothing and jewellery behaves more like a luxury good. These characteristics help explain the choice of these commodities for an analysis of the product tax.

Table 20.3: Expenditures on housing, petrol, and clothing and jewellery as a proportion of after-tax income for each consumer group

Consumer group	Housing	Petrol	Clothing and jewellery
1	0.22	0.029	0.054
2	0.20	0.028	0.062
3	0.18	0.032	0.059
4	0.17	0.030	0.067
5	0.15	0.032	0.064
6	0.15	0.034	0.067
7	0.14	0.033	0.067
8	0.14	0.033	0.070
9	0.13	0.034	0.068
10	0.12	0.031	0.072
11	0.12	0.024	0.073
12	0.10	0.019	0.067

Gasoline is also chosen since its characteristics are much closer to the average of all commodities.[12]

In determining the magnitudes of the tax changes for our experiments, it is useful for the approach taken in Section 3 that the taxes yield more or less the same revenue prior to the proportional redistribution. However, to design a set of tax rates which, after allowing for general equilibrium adjustments, would raise precisely the same revenue, would require extensive simulation with the FKSW model. Instead, we use an approximation technique which employs the revenue raised by increasing the tax on gasoline to 100 per cent as a benchmark. We determine tax rates on income and on various commodities needed to yield the same revenue, or $9,893 million, assuming that expenditures on the commodities remain unchanged. The resulting levels of revenue obtained by applying these rates to the FKSW model, as shown in Table 20.4, fail to equalise, but to economise on computation these rates were used in the subsequent analysis.[13]

Table 20.4 also shows the percentage change in the relative price of capital and the welfare gain or loss for each experiment. The latter is defined as the change in real national income, as measured by the geometric mean of the Paasche and Laspeyres measures. We would normally expect that a large 'distortionary' tax on only one commodity would result in a welfare loss, but only in a world with no other distortions. The natural advantage of this model is that all taxes are included, particularly taxes on the use of capital by industry. The corporate income tax represents a large distortionary tax on the use of capital by many industries other than the housing/real estate industry. A new high rate of tax on housing output is essentially a tax on capital in housing since this industry is so capital-intensive. It tends to equalise the levels of capital tax rates across industries and cause a welfare gain in this second-best world. Taxes on the other commodities cause net distortions and welfare losses.

Table 20.4: *Summary of the experiment*

	Existing tax I	Additional tax II	PM yield[a] III	FKSW yield[a] IV	FKSW change in return to capital V	Welfare gain[a,b] VI
Income tax	—	—	9,893	9,906	0.03%	−4
Housing tax	0	8.52%	9,893	7,699	−1.52%	500
Clothing and jewellery tax	7.32%	19.3%	9,893	7,926	0.49%	−194
Petrol tax	29.51%	70.49%	9,893	5,752	−0.33%	−228

[a]In millions of 1973 dollars.
[b]Welfare gain is defined as the geometric mean of Paasche and Laspeyres measures of the change in real national income.

Comparison for Single Experiments

We now compare the results obtained under the model with those of the PM procedure. For this purpose, the revenues obtained from the model procedure as given in column IV of Table 20.4 are allocated according to the PM-type approach for each tax increase, using the incidence assumptions as specified below.

Increase in Income Tax. The progressive increase in income tax is shown in Table 20.5. In column I we show the increase in tax burden which arises under the PM procedure which, in this case, simply allocates the burden in

Table 20.5: *Progressive increase in income tax*

Consumer type	PM procedure		FKSW model % real income change (Laspeyres and Paasche) III
	Tax paid I	Net tax II[a]	
1	−0.018	+1.02	+1.03
2	−0.15	+0.89	+0.89
3	−0.34	+0.69	+0.70
4	−0.45	+0.59	+0.59
5	−0.50	+0.53	+0.54
6	−0.65	+0.39	+0.39
7	−0.80	+0.24	+0.24
8	−0.99	+0.05	+0.05
9	−1.07	−0.03	−0.03
10	−1.31	−0.27	−0.27
11	−1.38	−0.34	−0.34
12	−1.47	−0.43	−0.42

All figures are percentages of real after-tax income.
[a]Rebate calculated as 1.04% of each group's original after-tax income.

line with statutory liabilities. This result is not comparable with that of the model because the latter shows the net outcome of the combined tax transfer measure. To permit comparability, we allocate the transfer in proportion to disposable income, prior to the change thereby obtaining column II, with the difference between I and II equal to 1.04 per cent throughout the income scale. (This figure of 1.04 per cent represents the ratio of the tax revenue to disposable personal income. Since the revenues are rebated according to each consumer group's disposable income, the transfers amount to 1.04 per cent across the board.) Column II may then be compared with column III, showing the model estimate of the resulting change in real income. Note that column II necessarily contains plus and minus items, since the underlying amounts (net taxes or net transfers) add to zero. This need not be the case, for the model results since the stipulated changes in tax structures may raise or lower the efficiency cost of the system and hence lower or raise the level of real income.

As will be seen by comparing columns II and III, the results under the two procedures are almost identical. The burden distribution of the income tax in the model appears to be dominated entirely by the distribution of the initial liabilities and transfer claims. Secondary effects due to changes in earnings and relative prices seem negligible.

One might expect a pro-poor shift in disposable income to increase the relative price of necessities versus luxuries in the short run, counteracting on the uses side the pro-poor effect of the sources side. The FKSW model includes constant returns to scale, however, so that long-run higher prices of necessities can only occur if these goods are produced by a process which is particularly intensive in one factor, and the price of that factor rises.[14] This effect is not noticeable, so the results of the model sustain the PM procedure of allocating a change in income tax liabilities to the statutory base.

Tax on Housing. The patterns become more divergent, however, as we turn to the other taxes. Table 20.6 shows the comparison for a tax on housing. A first relevant characteristic of housing services is the high capital:labour ratio in the provision of such services. The distributional significance of this is shown in Table 20.2, indicating that the share of capital income follows a U-shaped pattern. Another, as shown in Table 21.3, is the regressive consumption pattern, with housing expenditures declining as a share of income when moving up the income scale.

The results under the PM procedure are shown in Table 20.6, columns I and II. In column I the tax is viewed as falling on housing consumption and is allocated accordingly. In column II the tax is viewed as a selective tax on capital income which, in the process of adjustment, comes to be distributed and hence is allocated in line with capital income from all sources. The burden distribution in column I is thus regressive, while that in column II is U-shaped. These are the two extreme alternative incidence assumptions generally used in the PM procedure. Columns III and IV give corresponding results after adding back gains from the corresponding transfer, equal

Table 20.6: *Tax on housing*

Consumer group	PM procedure				FKSW	
	as consumer tax I	*as capital tax* II	*I as net tax*[a] III	*II as net tax* IV	*Laspeyres* V	*Paasche* VI
1	−1.34	−0.93	−0.54	−0.13	−0.29	−0.19
2	−1.22	−0.77	−0.42	+0.03	−0.16	−0.07
3	−1.10	−0.65	−0.30	+0.15	−0.08	+0.01
4	−1.04	−0.64	−0.24	+0.16	−0.09	0
5	−0.92	−0.65	−0.12	+0.15	−0.03	+0.05
6	−0.92	−0.61	−0.12	+0.19	0	+0.07
7	−0.85	−0.53	−0.05	+0.27	+0.03	+0.11
8	−0.85	−0.57	−0.05	+0.23	+0.07	+0.14
9	−0.79	−0.55	+0.01	+0.27	+0.13	+0.20
10	−0.73	−0.57	+0.07	+0.23	+0.15	+0.21
11	−0.73	−0.65	+0.07	+0.15	+0.14	+0.21
12	−0.61	−1.75	+0.19	−0.95	0	+0.05

[a]Rebate: 0.8% of income. All figures are in percentage of real after-tax income.

in this case to 0.8 per cent of disposable income. Since the transfer distribution is proportional, the incidence, measured as the income elasticity of tax burden between any two points, becomes less regressive.

The results for the model include effects emerging from both the uses and the sources side. Over the lower half of the income scale both are regressive and mutually reinforcing, whereas over the upper half they work in opposite directions. The results are shown in column V for the Laspeyres and in column VI for the Paasche index. We note that the net effect of column VI is one of gain almost throughout the scale. This, in part, reflects the rise in total income because of the welfare gain from a housing tax, as described in the previous section. The 'true' income changes would presumably lie between the Paasche and Laspeyres measures, with losses to low-income groups, gains to high-income groups, and a net increase in the total.[15]

Comparing columns III and IV on one side and V on the other, it appears that the monotonically regressive (pro-rich) pattern of III is more similar to V than is that of IV. This suggests that the PM procedure, based on treating the housing tax as a consumption tax, is more in line with the FKSW result than treating it as a tax on capital income.

Tax on Clothing and Jewellery. Clothing and jewellery reflects a commodity group with a capital:labour ratio well below the average and a rising consumption to income ratio when moving up the income scale. However, the category represents an aggregate of too many commodities

Table 20.7: Tax on clothing and jewellery

Consumer group	PM procedure		FKSW	
	Tax paid I	Net tax[a] II	Laspeyres III	Paasche IV
1	−0.66	+0.17	+0.26	+0.41
2	−0.76	+0.07	+0.11	+0.28
3	−0.72	+0.11	+0.05	+0.21
4	−0.82	+0.01	−0.12	+0.07
5	−0.78	+0.05	−0.12	+0.05
6	−0.82	+0.01	−0.22	−0.04
7	−0.82	+0.01	−0.26	−0.08
8	−0.86	−0.03	−0.31	−0.12
9	−0.83	0	−0.31	−0.13
10	−0.88	−0.05	−0.35	−0.15
11	−0.89	−0.06	−0.34	−0.14
12	−0.82	+0.01	−0.15	−0.04

[a]Rebate: 0.83% real income. All figures are in percentages of real, after-tax income.

to exhibit distinct luxury characteristics. Columns I and II of Table 20.7 accordingly show a somewhat progressive burden distribution under the PM approach, dampened somewhat in the net distribution of column II. A stronger progressive pattern is shown by both the Laspeyres index of column III and by the Paasche index of column IV. The more highly progressive burden distribution derived from the model is in line with expectations. The low capital-intensity of the taxed product, combined with the U-shaped pattern of the capital income share, should be expected to highlight the progressive nature of the real income change over the lower end of the scale. However, it should be expected to dampen it over the upper end, where the last two consumer groups also have higher than average capital-intensity of income. This effect can be seen at the bottoms of columns III and IV.

Tax on Petrol. The relevant characteristics of gasoline are its approximately average capital:labour ratio in production and its bell-shaped distribution in consumption. The ratio of gasoline expenditures to income rises over the lower and falls over the upper part of the income scale. As shown in Table 20.8, column I, this translates to a U-shaped burden allocation under the PM procedure since the table records estimated changes in real income from the tax. This pattern is repeated in the net burden distribution of column II. The model results for both Laspeyres and Paasche also show a U-shaped pattern, with both measures recording a decline in real income throughout the scale. As expected, because of the average K/L ratio in production, model results differ more by price index than they differ from the PM pattern. The pattern set by the initial impact on the uses side appears to dominate the complete result.

Table 20.8: *Tax on gasoline*

| Consumer group | PM procedure | | FKSW | |
	Tax paid I	Net tax[a] II	Laspeyres III	Paasche IV
1	−0.59	+0.01	−0.55	+0.14
2	−0.57	+0.03	−0.55	+0.11
3	−0.66	−0.06	−0.82	−0.07
4	−0.61	−0.01	−0.84	−0.13
5	−0.66	−0.06	−1.01	−0.26
6	−0.70	−0.10	−1.22	−0.42
7	−0.68	−0.08	−1.21	−0.42
8	−0.68	−0.08	−1.22	−0.43
9	−0.70	−0.10	−1.31	−0.50
10	−0.64	−0.04	−1.09	−0.36
11	−0.59	+0.01	−0.95	−0.28
12	−0.39	+0.21	−0.50	−0.04

[a]Rebate: 0.6% real income. All figures are in percentage of real, after-tax income.

Cross-experiment comparisons

Continuing our comparisons between the results obtained from the empirical model with those arrived at under the PM procedure, we now focus on the distribution of losses and gains which result as one tax is substituted for another. Assuming equal yields are obtained in all cases, this leaves transfers unchanged, and the incidence of any one replacement becomes independent of the transfer pattern. In this case only the tax difference would matter. Since, for previously noted reasons, the equal revenue criterion is not entirely met by our experiments, the transfer pattern continues to affect our outcome, but only to a minor degree.

Table 20.9 shows the substitution of the three commodity taxes for the income tax. Replacing a progressive increase in income tax by a tax on housing services may be expected to be regressive in its impact; this is shown in column I for the PM (using burden distribution by consumption) and the columns II and III for the model results. The same also holds for the clothing and jewellery tax, although less so, reflecting the difference in patterns previously shown in Table 20.7. Substitution of an increase in the gasoline tax, as may be expected, falls between the two preceding cases in its effect. Not surprisingly, the PM and FKSW results appear closer in these cross-experiment comparisons than with the single experiments.

4. CONCLUSION

In this paper we described a simple approximation method for estimating the distribution of tax burdens (the PM procedure), and compared its results with two alternative approaches. The first, an analytical two-sector general equilibrium model, helped identify the parameters which are crucial in causing the outcome of the PM procedure to diverge from the general equilibrium outcome. The second, a medium-scale, empirical model (the FKSW model) gave estimates of tax incidence which allow for general equilibrium effects and enabled a direct comparison with estimates of the PM procedure for four tax changes and three tax substitutions.

The PM and FKSW approaches give strikingly similar results for the case of the income tax. For the other cases we leave it to the reader to judge the degree of similarity. As may be expected, the similarity is greater for taxes on products whose capital:labour ratios are close to the average. Also, the cross-experiments come out closer than the single experiments.

There remains the question of how similarity, or lack thereof, should be interpreted. Similarity may be taken to validate the PM procedure if it were assumed that the FKSW outcome is the 'true' one. It is evident, however, that the FKSW model still represents a highly simplified and overly aggregative picture. As the model is further refined, the results may well change and differ more from those of the PM procedure. For example, factor supplies might be rendered elastic. Also, if the model were more disaggregated, it would presumably show certain consumers with factor endowment ratios that were further from the average. This would cause stronger sources effects of a product tax. Similarly, consideration of heterogeneous factors, especially those factors specific to certain industries, would show strong short-run losses on the earnings side of a product tax.

Finally, we have compared the PM and FKSW approaches only with regard to estimating the burden distribution of a given tax revenue. We have not used any traditional or partial equilibrium procedures to estimate the revenue of a given tax rate, to estimate excess burdens, or to analyse other major taxes such as the payroll or corporate income tax.

5. ADDENDUM ON THE SEPARATION OF USES AND SOURCES EFFECTS

As noted earlier, the PM approach allocates product taxes in line with their initial impact on the uses side of the household account while allocating factor taxes on the sources side, either in line with their initial impact or as otherwise specified. With regard to product taxes, this neglects the resulting changes from the sources side, as well as further feedback effects from the uses side. With regard to factor taxes, it neglects resulting changes from the uses side as well as further feedback effects from the sources side. The underlying hypothesis is that initial uses and sources effects are controlling in determining incidence, while the neglected effects bear no systematic relationship to the pattern which emerges from these primary effects.

Table 20.9: Comparison across experiments

	Progressive increase in income tax replaced by:								
	Housing tax			Clothing tax			Gas tax		
Consumer group	PM^a	Laspeyres FKSW	Paasche	PM	Laspeyres FKSW	Paasche	PM	Laspeyres FKSW	Paasche
	I	II	III	IV	V	VI	VII	VIII	IX
1	−1.32	−1.32	−1.22	−0.64	−0.76	−0.61	−0.57	−1.86	−1.17
2	−1.07	−1.05	−0.96	−0.51	−0.78	−0.61	−0.42	−1.67	−1.01
3	−0.76	−0.77	−0.69	−0.38	−0.64	−0.48	−0.32	−1.69	−0.95
4	−0.59	−0.68	−0.59	−0.37	−0.71	−0.52	−0.15	−1.55	−0.85
5	−0.42	−0.57	−0.49	−0.28	−0.66	−0.49	−0.16	−1.65	−0.89
6	−0.32	−0.39	−0.32	−0.17	−0.61	−0.43	−0.09	−1.66	−0.86
7	−0.05	−0.20	−0.13	−0.02	−0.49	−0.31	+0.12	−1.47	−0.68
8	+0.14	+0.02	+0.09	+0.13	−0.36	−0.17	+0.31	−1.27	−0.49
9	+0.28	+0.16	+0.23	+0.24	−0.27	−0.09	+0.37	−1.24	−0.45
10	+0.48	+0.42	+0.48	+0.43	−0.08	+0.12	+0.65	−0.78	−0.05
11	+0.65	+0.48	+0.54	+0.49	−0.00	+0.20	+0.79	−0.56	+0.12
12	+0.86	+0.43	+0.47	+0.65	+0.28	+0.38	+1.04	+0.01	+0.42

[a]Housing tax is viewed as a consumption for the PM calculations. All figures are in percentage change in real, after-tax income.

The general equilibrium approach of the FKSW model differs in that it is designed to account for total effects, primary as well as feedback, and covering both uses and sources side for all types of tax. Nevertheless, these overall results may be divided into two components: (1) sources effects which reflect changes in nominal income, and (2) uses effects which reflect changes in price. This decomposition of the overall result is of interest because it indicates the relative importance of uses and sources characteristics of various households, as they bear on their burden under a particular tax. Moreover, it may throw further light on the reliability of the PM approach. However, a word of caution is warranted here. If it turned out that the FKSW approach shows the incidence of product taxes to be dominated by effects recorded on the uses side, while that of factor taxes is dominated from the sources side, this does not necessarily lend justification to the PM procedure of benign neglect. While some degree of support might be inferred, the answer is not at all clear-cut. This is the case because the PM concepts of sources and uses effects include primary effects only, while the sources and uses effects as recorded by the FKSW procedure are total, i.e. include playback effects.

The FKSW decomposition is also interesting because of its intuitive appeal. A general equilibrium result can be more easily comprehended by considering one part at a time. For any given consumer we define a real income change in the manner of Section 2 for the Laspeyres and Paasche price indices. The proportional change in his real income is given by

$$\frac{I_1/PPI - I_0}{I_0} \text{ or } \frac{I_1/LPI - I_0}{I_0}.$$

Note that the initial, nominal, after-tax income I_0 is equal to $\Sigma Q_0 P_0$, the sum of original expenditure at original cum-tax prices, and final after tax income I_1 is equal to $\Sigma Q_1 P_1$.[16] Since the proportional change under the Laspeyres measure is equivalent to $(I_1 - I_0 \cdot LPI)/(I_0 \cdot LPI)$, we have the operational relationships of Table 20.10 for the numerators of these bounds. By either index, the uses and sources sides sum to the total change

Table 20.10: Operational definitions of the uses side, sources side, and total change in real income

Index	Total effect: change in real after-tax income	Sources side: from changes in factor prices and income taxes	Uses side: from changes in gross of tax expenditure prices
Laspeyres	$I' - I^0 \cdot LPI$ $= \Sigma Q_1 P_1 - \Sigma Q_0 P_1$	$I' - I^0$ $= \Sigma Q_1 P_1 - \Sigma Q_0 P_0$	$I^0 - I^0 \cdot LPI$ $= \Sigma Q_0 P_0 - \Sigma Q_0 P_1$
Paasche	$I'/PPI - I^0$ $= \Sigma Q_1 P_0 - \Sigma Q_0 P_0$	$I' - I^0$ $= \Sigma Q_1 P_1 - \Sigma Q_0 P_0$	$I'/PPI - I'$ $= \Sigma Q_1 P_0 - \Sigma Q_1 P_1$

in real after-tax income. Heuristically, the sources side is the change in nominal income, the uses side is the effect of price changes (using either quantities as weights), and real income is the change in quantities (using either prices as weights).[17]

An unavoidable feature of this split between uses and sources effects is that it is not unique with respect to a shift from direct to indirect taxation. If an income tax were replaced by an equivalent tax on all consumption and investment commodities, these definitions would register a gain to the sources side and a loss to the uses side. The important aspect of this division, however, is the relative change accruing to different consumers. For brevity, only the Laspeyres calculations of the FKSW model are shown in Table 20.11.

(1) The progressive change in the income tax appears to concentrate its impact on the sources side. The magnitudes of the uses (price change) effects are almost negligible. However, the directions of the changes displayed by the two effects are interesting.

The price change effect alone is uniformly regressive, since prices of capital-intensive products, including many necessities, have risen. The net effect on real after-tax incomes is clearly progressive, but certainly less progressive than intended by the change in income tax rates. Commodity price changes serve to moderate the desired change in progressivity.

(2) The housing tax is fairly clear in its distributional effect. The uses side, or cum-tax expenditure price changes, are regressive as expected, since the proportion of income to housing is monotonically decreasing. The income or sources effect is progressive. We might have expected a U-shaped loss pattern since the relative price of capital falls 1.5 per cent, but the income tax rebates make all sources effects positive. The regressive uses side and progressive sources side combine to a net regressive change in real after tax income.

(3) The 'clothing and jewellery' aggregate good behaves most like a luxury good, as seen in Table 20.3. The uses side of a tax would have progressive effects on consumer welfare, but again the sources side might counteract. Since this is the most labour-intensive product, a lower demand for clothing would imply a higher demand for capital relative to labour, and gains to capital-endowed individuals. As Table 20.11 shows, price change effects are progressive as anticipated. Sources side gains are mostly U-shaped, according to K/L ratios of endowments, and total effects are mostly progressive, but somewhat U-shaped. A major point, however, is that the expected price change effect is substantially altered by the income effect and the latter cannot be ignored.

(4) The consumption tax on petrol would be expected to have the predicted (uses side) effect since the capital:labour ratio in its production is close to the economy's ratio. As a result of the tax, the price of capital falls relative to that of labour by a minuscule 0.3 per cent. With almost no change in the factor price ratio, we expect no sources effect. Indeed, the only income effect to be noticed from Table 20.11, part C, is from original transfers (social security, welfare), which make up a larger portion of the

Table 20.11: Uses, sources, and total effects of each tax change, in percentage terms, for Laspeyres index only

Consumer no.	Laspeyres index	Real after-tax income	Price change effect	Income effect
A. Income tax change				
1	1.000	1.026	−0.009	1.035
2	1.000	0.889	−0.009	0.898
3	1.000	0.696	−0.009	0.705
4	1.000	0.590	−0.009	0.598
5	1.000	0.537	−0.008	0.546
6	1.000	0.389	−0.008	0.397
7	1.000	0.237	−0.008	0.245
8	1.000	0.048	−0.008	0.056
9	1.000	−0.033	−0.008	−0.024
10	1.000	−0.271	−0.008	−0.263
11	1.000	−0.338	−0.008	−0.330
12	1.000	−0.424	−0.007	−0.416
B. Tax on housing				
1	1.013	−0.292	−.1326	1.034
2	1.012	−0.164	−1.149	0.985
3	1.010	−0.077	−0.986	0.909
4	1.009	−0.085	−0.923	0.839
5	1.008	−0.031	−0.828	0.797
6	1.008	−0.002	−0.769	0.767
7	1.007	0.034	−0.744	0.778
8	1.007	0.066	−0.693	0.759
9	1.006	0.131	−0.619	0.750
10	1.006	0.147	−0.604	0.751
11	1.006	0.143	−0.567	0.710
12	1.004	0.003	−0.392	0.395

first consumer's income used for consumption. The model scales up these transfers by the price index to preserve their value in real terms, while factor incomes do not get scaled up. The total effect follows the price change pattern, where greater losses are made by middle-income groups.

NOTES

1. More precisely, the PM considers *either* uses effects only *or* sources effects only. Whether a particular tax is considered as having uses or sources effects depends on market structure assumptions. For instance, if markets are competitive, an employer payroll tax is treated in terms of its sources effects on

Table 20.11 continued

Consumer no.	Laspeyres index	Real after-tax income	Price change effect	Income effect
C. Tax on clothing and jewellery				
1	1.012	0.263	−1.201	1.464
2	1.014	0.113	−1.334	1.447
3	1.013	0.052	−1.286	1.338
4	1.014	−0.115	−1.424	1.309
5	1.014	−0.121	−1.364	1.243
6	1.014	−0.224	−1.416	1.191
7	1.014	−0.258	−1.426	1.167
8	1.015	−0.310	−1.479	1.168
9	1.015	−0.311	−1.439	1.128
10	1.015	−0.347	−1.515	1.167
11	1.016	−0.341	−1.534	1.193
12	1.014	−0.145	−1.415	1.270
D. Tax on gasoline				
1	1.020	−0.553	−1.914	1.362
2	1.019	−0.552	−1.817	1.265
3	1.021	−0.817	−2.071	1.255
4	1.020	−0.836	−1.944	1.108
5	1.021	−1.010	−2.096	1.086
6	1.023	−1.220	−2.255	1.035
7	1.023	−1.205	−2.209	1.003
8	1.023	−1.218	−2.203	0.986
9	1.023	−1.306	−2.263	0.958
10	1.021	−1.091	−2.043	0.951
11	1.019	−0.952	−1.876	0.925
12	1.013	−0.501	−1.251	0.750

wage income; if markets are imperfect so that the tax is added to product price, the PM analysis considers its uses effects on consumers of labour-intensive products.

2. A similar analysis was developed earlier by Meade [8] in the context of tariffs and international trade.

3. This procedure ignores the excess burden of the tax, so that the sum of net gains and losses to consumers equals the yield of the tax.

4. Instead of comparing percentage changes in real income, the utility functions can be used to calculate compensating or equivalent variations. Because the functional forms imply constant marginal utility of income, the ratio of the equivalent variation to income in this case is equal to the percentage change in utility for each consumer. Reconsider the tax on X where B buys more of it ($\delta > \gamma$), X is the capital-intensive good, but A has capital-intensive income. Under what conditions is it true that

$(U'_A - U_A)/U_A < (U'_B - U'_B)/U_B?$

After some manipulation it can be shown that this inequality is equivalent to

$$\frac{1 - tI_{AX}/I_{AX}}{1 - tI_{BX}/I_{BX}} < \left(\frac{1}{1 - t}\right)^{(\gamma-\delta)} \left(\frac{1 - tL_X/L}{1 - tK_X/K}\right)^{(\gamma-\beta)(\delta-\gamma)}$$

   Thus, the greater the discrepancy between I_{AX}/I_A and I_{BX}/I_B, the greater is the chance that the PM trend will be reversed. Turning to the right-hand side of the inequality, since $(\gamma - \delta) < 0$ and $1/(1 - t) > 0$, the wider gap between γ and δ, the more difficult it will be to reverse the PM calculations. However, the second term on the right-hand side gets larger as the capital intensity of industry X grows, so a high K_X/L_X (relative to K/L) could offset the PM pattern. Because PM use no utility functions, we proceed to a comparison between real income changes in the two approaches. See note 6 for a discussion of compensating and equivalent variations in the FKSW approach.

5. Our model has no transfers whereas the FKSW model, and therefore its data, contain transfer payments. In calculating the capital and labour intensities of consumers' endowments, we treat transfer income as additional labour income. The surprising similarity of these capital:labour ratios is due to the high proportion of retired individuals in low-income groups.

6. In comparing the PM and FKSW approaches, we use Laspeyres and Paasche measures of changes in real income. As an alternative measure of individual welfares the model calculates compensating variations, defined as the additional income at new prices required to attain old utility levels. We use only the real income changes, partly because they are easier to interpret, and partly because of complications in the model's utility functions: the individual chooses between future consumption and present consumption based on the current rate of return to savings. The utility level would be higher if the return to capital were higher and no other real changes occurred.

7. While assuming that existing tax instruments can be modelled as *ad valorem* tax rates applied to sales of a good or factor, the FKSW model does not assume the incidence of the tax. For example, a tax on one use of capital might come to burden consumers *or* recipients of capital income depending on behavioural reactions described by the elasticity parameters.

8. Although the data consider several types of capital income, it should be noted that the FKSW model aggregates these to one type of capital before calculations. One result of this procedure is that a tax on housing injures all capital, including the capital owned by the high-income consumer. Thus, the model does not consider the short-run effects on individuals who own capital specific to some industry, but instead concentrates on the long-run equilibrium effects, after capital has adjusted to the hypothetical tax, and earns the same return in all industries.

9. Under either interpretation, the government maintains enough tax revenue to purchase the same commodities as it did in the benchmark equilibrium, thus preventing a higher level of government purchases from interfering with the general equilibrium effects of the tax change alone.

10. Other experiments involving factor taxes could also be undertaken.
11. While our groupings are by gross income brackets, the consumption ratios relate to after-tax income.
12. It should be noted that these expenditure patterns reflect the use of cross-section data and are thus based on annual, rather than lifetime, consumption behaviour.
13. This differential is troublesome only for the cross-experiment comparisons in Section 3 since the PM incidence is estimated for the FKSW yield in the single experiment comparisons of Section 3.

    By its nature, the PM procedure's patterns are invariant to changes in the size of the tax rate, which of course is a highly questionable notion. It is interesting to note, though, that the pattern of the model's distributional results, even though it depends on the level of taxation, does not change significantly for variations in the magnitude of the tax. For example, the percentage changes in real, after-tax income (using a Laspeyres price index) for the twelve consumer groups from a 8.52 per cent increase and a 100 per cent increase in the housing tax are:

Consumer group	1	2	3	4	5	6	7	8	9	10	11	12
8.5 tax	−0.29	−0.16	−0.08	−0.09	−0.03	0	+0.03	+0.07	+0.13	+0.15	+0.14	0
100% tax	−6.6	−5.8	−5.3	−5.5	−5.1	−5	−4.7	−4.4	−3.8	−3.6	−3.5	−3.7

The welfare gain, however, does change significantly up from $500 to $3340 million per year.

14. In fact, low-income groups tend to purchase goods that are somewhat more capital-intensive, and an increase in their disposable income tends to raise the price of capital and therefore the prices of these commodities. The higher price of capital also has second-order effects on the sources side of income. Note from Table 20.4, however, that this experiment changes R by a mere 0.03 per cent. Without an effect on factor prices there can be no change in consumer prices. Hence, the sources side dominates.
15. The net gain comes about notwithstanding the fact that in designing the model, the transfer is made in lump-sum form, and thus the level of taxes which can create efficiency costs is increasing.
16. Savings in the FKSW model are fed through directly to investment purchases. Thus I_1 is the numerator of the *PPI*, and I_0 is the denominator of the *LPI*.
17. As an index for real income, it is well known that the Laspeyres is a lower bound since it understates gains and overstates losses, and Paasche is an upper bound since it overstates gains and understates losses. This can be seen in Table 20.10 where the Laspeyres change, $\Sigma Q_1 P_1 - \Sigma Q_0 P_1$, puts a lower weight $(P_1 < P_0)$ on the quantities that have increased $(Q_1 > Q_0)$. It puts a higher weight $(P_1 > P_0)$ on quantities that have decreased $(Q_1 < Q_0)$. Similar arguments exist for the Paasche index. In this manner, we can also see how these indices represent bounds on the uses side alone. In Table 20.10 the Laspeyres uses side is $\Sigma Q_0 P_0 - \Sigma Q_0 P_1$, where a greater weight $(Q_0 > Q_1)$ is put on prices that have risen $(P_1 > P_0)$, and a lower weight $(Q_0 < Q_1)$ on prices that have fallen $(P_1 < P_0)$.

REFERENCES

[1] Bishop, C. A. (1953) *Tax Burdens and Benefits of Government Expenditures by Income Class* (New York: Tax Foundation).

[2] Colm, G. and H. Tarasov (1940) *Who Pays the Taxes?*, Monograph 3, Investigation of Concentration of Economic Power, 76 Congress, 3rd Session (Washington, D.C. US Govt. Printing Office).

[3] Fullerton, D., J. B. Shoven and J. Whalley (1978) *A General Equilibrium Analysis of US Taxation Policy, 1978 Compendium of Tax Research, US Treasury Department, Office of Tax Analysis* (Washington, D.C.: US Govt. Printing Office.)

[4] Fullerton, D., A. I. King, J. B. Shoven and J. Whalley (1979) 'Corporate and Personal Tax Integration in the US: Some Preliminary Findings from a General Equilibrium Analysis' in R. Haveman and K. Hollenbeck (eds.), *Microeconomic Simulation* (Madison: Institute for Research on Poverty).

[5] Harberger, A. C. (1962) 'The Incidence of the Corporate Income Tax', *Journal of Political Economy*, 70, 215–40.

[6] McLure, C. E. (1975) 'General Equilibrium Incidence Analysis: The Harberger Model after Ten Years', *Journal of Public Economics*, 4, 125–61.

[7] McLure, C. E. and W. R. Thirsk (1975) 'A Simplified Exposition of the Harberger Model I: Tax Incidence', *National Tax Journal*, 28, 1–27.

[8] Meade, J. E. (1955) *Mathematical Supplement to Trade and Welfare* (Oxford: Oxford University Press).

[9] Musgrave, R. A. (1959) *The Theory of Public Finance* (New York: McGraw-Hill).

[10] Musgrave, R. A. *et al.* (1951) 'Distribution of Tax Payments by Income Groups: A Case-study for 1948', *National Tax Journal*, 4, 1–53.

[11] Musgrave, R. A., K. E. Case and H. Leonard (1974) 'The Distribution of Fiscal Burdens and Benefits, *Public Finance Quarterly*, 2, 259–311.

[12] Pechman, J. A. and B. A. Okner (1974) *Who Bears the Tax Burden?* (Washington, D.C.: Brookings Institution).

[13] Scarf, H. E. with T. Hansen (1973) *The Comptation of Economic Equilibria* (New Haven, Conn.: Cowles Foundation Press).

21 The Nature of Horizontal Equity and the Principle of Broad-based Taxation: A Friendly Critique* 1983

This paper examines three questions: (1) Given that a broad-based tax is desirable to implement horizontal equity, in terms of what should the base be defined? (2) How do considerations of feasibility and efficiency square with the requirement of comprehensive base and the norm of horizontal equity? (3) Should the index of equality, underlying the horizontal equity concept, be applied to pre- or post-tax positions? Following consideration of these issues on a rather purist level, I conclude with a few reservations on their policy application.

1. WHICH BROAD BASE?

The question of base determination may be approached in two ways. One grows out of the requirement of horizontal equity, i.e. the principle that people in equal position should be treated equally. 'For what reason ought equality to be the rule in matters of taxation?', so J. S. Mill [13] asked, and responded: 'For the reason that it ought to be so in all matters of government.'[1] The other approach is efficiency-based, calling for taxes to be imposed so as to cause the least burden or sacrifice. Both formulations intertwine, but let us begin with the equity rule.

Here the issue reduces to defining what I like to call the appropriate index of equality. In respect to what characteristic of their economic position do two people have to be similar to declare them 'equal' for tax purposes? In particular, should the index be measured in terms of income or consumption?

---

* From *Taxation Issues of the 1980 s* (1983) John C. Hind (ed.), Australian Tax Research Foundation.

Income vs. Consumption

The index should be such as to group as equals individuals who have the
same ability to pay tax, i.e. who enjoy the same level of welfare. The index
should thus offer a meaningful measure of pre-tax welfare. The traditional
front-runner has been income, but (gaining lately) consumption now
claims a strong second.

Income in the Schanz–Haig–Simons tradition has been defined as
accretion, including all gains which a person derives during a period.[2] All
forms of accretion or gain are to be included, independent of the particular
source from which they come or the use to which they are put. This total of
'incoming' may then be divided between consumption and saving, so that it
may be defined (viewed from the uses side) as consumption plus saving, or
consumption plus increase in net worth. But observation of this particular
division is not central to defining income. It does not affect the income
total, as the basic income concept is defined from the sources side. This
concept is designed to describe a particular recipient's gain in economic
power and thus to serve as index of equality for purposes of taxation. It is
not meant to define a category suitable for other purposes, such as national
income accounting or the principles of capital theory.

Those of us (a few specimens of whom are still in circulation and even
present) who have grown up and worked in the Schanz–Haig–Simons
tradition have tended to take it for granted that income thus defined is *the*
best criterion by which to measure ability to pay. Income accordingly was
to be *the* index of equality in the context of horizontal equity analysis.
People with equal incomes were to be treated as equals and to be taxed
equally. This has obvious intuitive appeal.[3] Income is the more comprehensive measure as it includes saving as well as consumption and thus
seems to provide a better measure of economic power than does consumption only. But broadness of base in itself is not decisive, as otherwise gross
receipts would be preferred. A more searching foundation of the base
concept is needed.

To be sure, a great deal of work has been done on refining the
broad-based income concept and exploring how it should be applied in
practice. This work, led by the basic contribution of Henry Simons,[4] has
addressed such issues as the deduction of depreciation and other costs
needed to derive net income, the treatment of capital gains and the
integration of corporate source income into the personal tax base. While it
had to be granted that a fully comprehensive concept of accretion cannot
be achieved in practice, an operationally meaningful concept of broad
income has nevertheless emerged. This has been a major accomplishment,
as it has provided a compass by which to judge the detailed provisions of
the income tax code. But income tax theorists have been less successful in
explaining just why accretion (assuming that it can be implemented) should
be the best index of equality. Instead, its superiority has been taken largely
for granted.

Opponents of the income base, on the other hand, have been vociferous in their critique. The essential proposition, as presented first by J. S. Mill, has been that

the proper mode of assessing an income tax would be to tax only the part of income devoted to expenditure, exempting that which is saved. For when saved and invested . . . it henceforth pays income tax on the interest or profit which it brings, notwithstanding that it has already been taxed on the principal. Unless, therefore, savings are exempted from the income tax, the contributors are twice taxed on what they save, and only once on what they spend . . . The law ought not to disturb, by artificial interference, the natural competition between the motives for saving and those for spending. But we have seen that the law disturbs this natural competition when it taxes savings, not when it spares them. [13, p. 813]

Alfred Marshall [11, p. 350] similarly criticised the income tax for interfering with the choice betwen consumption and saving, but thought a progressive tax on all consumption, though correct in principle, difficult to accomplish. Irving Fisher [6, p. 56], the most persistent critic of the income base, held that in taxing income 'a tax on the savings is added to a tax on the fruits of savings' so that 'essentially the same thing is taxed twice'. To avoid such double taxation, saving should be exempted from the base (while including interest); that is, the tax should be on consumption. Unfortunately, and responsible for much subsequent confusion, Fisher then insisted on referring to such a tax as an income tax. More to his credit, he was also the first to propose a cash flow approach to its determination, thus moving the expenditure tax towards an operationally meaningful concept. Pigou [12, p. 135] similarly held that, in a continuing system of taxation, the income base discriminates against saving and in favour of consumption. Arguing on efficiency grounds, he concluded that this offends the requirement of least sacrifice. Unless demand elasticities for the two uses of income are shown to differ, the two uses of income should be taxed at the same rate, and he notes that this can be accomplished either by exempting saving or by exempting interest from the base [12, pp. 138, 148]. Kaldor's case for the expenditure tax, finally, was based not so much on concern with double taxation of capital income as on the opposite difficulty of reaching such income under the income tax.[10]. To reach the rich, a progressive expenditure tax is needed.

Given this formidable array of critics, how did the proponents of the income base respond? While Simons [18, p. 89] addressed the problem at length, he saw it largely as a terminological issue. Confusion had been caused by applying the same term 'income' to Fisher's concept of yield and to the quite different Schanz–Haig–Simons concept of accretion. Moreover, even if Fisher's concept was correct for purposes of capital theory (and Simons even questioned this), it need not also be right for the context of horizontal equity. Simons was correct in this complaint. But to note that the two concepts differ and serve different uses does not tell us which offers the appropriate index and why. Nor is the case for the consumption base defeated (as we shall see below) by noting that saving is undertaken for many reasons, including the advantage of wealth-holding as well as postponing consumption. In the end, Simons arrived at the rather pragmatic position that income is the better base because it has come to be the accepted index and it is too late for a change [18, p. 98].

It thus remains necessary to test the rationale for the income base in a more systematic fashion. If this is to be done in the equity context, the Pigovian case, based on the distorting announcement effects of the income tax, need not be decisive. Equity and efficiency considerations need not coincide. Another criterion of judgement is needed. For this purpose, we shall proceed from the premise that two people are to be considered in equal positions and should therefore be treated equally if they are confronted with the same *options*.

Given this rule, consider first the case for income. Two people who obtain the same income within a given period have the same options to consume or save. Therefore, it is only fair that they be treated equally, and be called upon to pay the same tax. To exempt saving would be an undue preference. As Pigou noted, this makes good sense if we take a one-period view. But the tax system, certainly on an ideal basis, should have a longer perspective. Under the income tax A, who saves in period I and consumes in period II, pays a higher present value tax than does B who consumes his entire income in period I. Is this unfair? Has not A enjoyed an additional period II accretion which, by the accretion standard, justifies an additional tax? Yes, provided that accretion (or in a multi-period model, the sum of accretions) is *the* basic index. But should it be? Suppose that there are no bequests, with all income consumed during the recipient's lifetime. The purpose of current accumulation then is to sustain future consumption. If so, equals should be defined as people who have the same option of present and future consumption, i.e. who can sustain the same present value consumption stream. Equal treatment of equals thus defined is accomplished by the consumption tax which imposes the same present value of tax on two people whose initial accretion permits them to dispose over the same present value consumption stream. It is not accomplished by the income tax, which imposes higher present value tax on A, the late consumer. While I have grown up with the income tax tradition (one of my first publications defended its base), I now find this reasoning rather persuasive, and have come to feel uneasy with the traditional defence of the income tax base.[15]

At the same time, this conclusion in favour of the consumption base rests on a rather purist model. It involves a host of assumptions which may be quite unrealistic. (1) A first assumption is that present and future consumption are the only options for income use which, as we shall see presently, is not the case. (2) The underlying Fisherian model assumes that all individuals have access to perfect capital markets and face the same discount rate, which they do not. (3) The essence of the case for the consumption base is that horizontal equity be viewed in the context of an extended multi-period, preferably a lifetime, perspective. The need for averaging (due to progressive rates) thus becomes even more important than under the income tax. Moreover, changing tax rates should be allowed for by continuous recalculation of past liabilities. (4) There is the massive question of how to deal with the transition problem, i.e. the case of tax reform as against *de novo* design. What protection should be given to past savers who, having paid income tax, are now about to dissave and consume? [16,21,12]. (5) There remains the question of administrative feasibility. The consumption base avoids certain difficulties of the income tax, especially as related to unrealised gains and depreciation, and it is less open to distortion by inflation. At the same time, it also poses new and as yet untested problems in defining consumption. This is important to keep in mind, lest the comparison is drawn between the existing imperfect income tax and an idealised loop-hole-free expenditure tax.

If the expenditure tax were to be tried, this need not involve a complete replacement of the income tax from the outset. As a matter of prudence a more limited trial would be called for. This would best take the form of partial substitution of an expenditure tax for income tax at high levels of income, combined with the necessary estate tax adjustment. What should *not* be done is to move the income tax towards an expenditure tax by 'going easy' (1) on capital income from the sources side and (2) on saving from the uses side. Such a course, which seems to reflect US trends, leads to a tax covering consumption out of wage income only, surely not an acceptable base definition.

Further options
The central theme of my approach has been that people with equal options should be treated equally. So far the only two options allowed for were present and future consumption. We must now allow for the evident fact that other options also enter.

Bequests. It is convenient but unrealistic to assume that all income is consumed during the recipient's lifetime. Bequests and gifts are made. How are they to be allowed for in the context of our equal option rule?

One line of reasoning suggests that bequests be excluded from the tax base [3]. A person has three options, i.e. (1) to consume now, (2) to consume later, and (3) to leave a bequest. He derives utility from all three, which in the case of (3) takes the form of pleasure which the testator derives from the heir's consumption. Since this pleasure relates to the heir's consumption net of heir's tax, inclusion of the bequest in the testator's base, with subsequent taxation of the heir's consumption, would discriminate against the leaving of bequests. Thus equal treatment requires that bequests be excluded.

Two considerations speak against this conclusion. To begin with, consider what happens if the heir does not consume, with the wealth passed on along subsequent generations. Exclusion of bequests then means that there will never be a tax. Moreover, if the heirs do not consume, they must prefer to hold the wealth because they derive satisfaction therefrom.

This being the case, the testator's satisfaction must also be in his knowledge that the heirs can hold wealth. But if this is the case, exclusion of the bequest from the testator's base discriminates in favour of leaving bequests. Thus, bequests should be included.

A further concern applies even if the heirs will consume. It may well be argued that considerations of horizontal equity should relate to the satisfaction which individuals receive from their own use of income, and not from that of their heirs. The leaving of bequests is then viewed as an own use, equivalent to consumption.[5] This seems to me preferable to extending the equity concept across generations, thus placing it on a dynastic basis. Where heirs do consume, this may discriminate against bequests, but I would pay the price of this efficiency cost so as to keep the criterion of horizontal equity on a lifetime basis.

Wealth-holding. Even in a world without bequests, it is relevant to note that saving not only adds to a person's future consumption, but also gives the pleasure (security, power, prestige) which goes with being wealthy. Thus the question arises whether an additional tax is needed to reach the utility which the saver derives from holding wealth.

Looked at from the perspective of an accretion-based approach to the income tax, the answer is no. As has been pointed out by Simons and others, postponing consumption is but one among many savings motivations.[18, p. 96] All these motivations are accounted for in determining the desired rate of saving relative to the available return. The value of property being equal to the capitalised return thereon, taxing property would impose an additional tax on that part of accretion which is derived from property income.

The pleasure of wealth-holding, however, becomes a more potent factor if seen in the context of our equal option or neutrality approach. In a world without holding pleasure, introduction of a consumption tax leaves the return to saving unchanged. But, as recently noted, this may not be the case in a setting where holding pleasure applies [4].[6] Here the tax reduces current and future consumption but may be taken to exempt that part of the reward to saving which accrues in the form of holding pleasure. Thus postponement is favoured relative to current consumption. To offset this bias, a tax on wealth-holding, in line with the holding pleasure, is in order. Or, viewing the correction in terms of a tax on interest rather than on capital, a supplementary income tax on capital income would be needed.

All this, of course, leaves open the question whether society should impose a tax on wealth on other grounds. Thus, a case for a wealth tax might be made in the context of benefit taxation [4, p. 386][7]. Or society may wish to impose a progressive tax on large wealth-holdings, so as to counter what are considered adverse social implications of excessive concentration. Such a tax may or may not be desirable, but this is not an issue in the definition of horizontal equity or efficiency analysis. Moreover, if such a tax was called for, it might well take the form of a tax on gross rather than net worth, as social control is linked more directly to the former.

Leisure. The preceding discussion was based on the assumption that leisure is fixed, the choice being between present consumption, future consumption, and bequeathing. As leisure is allowed to be variable, consumption of leisure becomes a further option. Both income and consumption now become deficient indices of equal position, as individuals with a high leisure preference are favoured. Equal options are now enjoyed by individuals confronted with equal wage as well as interest rates. But an index of equality defined in terms of equal wage rate (or rather, potential wage rate × 8 hours, equal to potential daily income) is hardly practicable. In addition, there is the complication that any one individual may choose between jobs of differing disutility or pleasurability, carrying different wage rates.

Given that the practical choice has to be between second-best measures such as income and consumption, how does variability of leisure affect the comparative merits of these two indices? The answer hinges on the substitutability between present consumption and leisure, as compared with that between future consumption and leisure. If future consumption is complementary to leisure while present consumption is rival, then the income tax may well be preferable. Its bias against present consumption may substitute for a tax on leisure. Or the opposite may be the case if the reverse substitutability conditions apply. Which is the more likely hypothesis is an interesting topic but not one to be explored here.

2. CHALLENGES TO THE NORM

The objectives of horizontal equity and of global base, which we have taken for granted in the preceding pages, have been criticised in various ways, and these must now be considered.

Is a truly global base feasible?
In practice, so the critics of the broad-based rule say, there is no neat way of measuring total accretion, and they stress that the tax laws fail to do so properly. The income of house persons, for instance, is neglected. Therefore, had we not better abandon the pretension that there is some underlying and meaningful income concept? What is or is not to be taxed must be decided pragmatically, point by point.[2] This has been essentially the British tradition as against the German and US (Schanz–Haig–Simons) school. I am not persuaded. No economic concept can be applied neatly, hardly in theory and certainly not in practice, so that if one wishes to be purist enough, nothing that is real will make sense. This position, however, overstates the difficulties involved. There are, to be sure, shortfalls and inconsistencies in application, but their presence does not deny the meaningfulness of a central concept. On the contrary, the messier is reality the greater the need for a focal point or measuring rod by which to decide specific issues. Otherwise, there is no check to arbitrariness and political corruption. Needless to say, I am not proposing that any criterion (e.g. the

weight or birthdate of taxpayers) would be better than none, if only to fight off the forces of evil. While a random distribution of taxes might be preferable to malicious discrimination, no such retreat is needed. The comprehensive base concept, be it in income or consumption terms, gives a generally meaningful measure of economic capacity, and its approximation (even if imperfect) is a worthwhile second-best solution.

Efficiency and the global base

A more serious challenge to the comprehensive base as a norm of tax policy is posed by the requirement that taxes should be imposed so as to incur the least efficiency cost. In fact, this challenge not only extends to the broad base concept, but also encompasses the very idea of horizontal equity.

Suppose taxation is to be on the consumption base. The tax could then be implemented as a general retail sales tax. The globality requirement would be met, as all goods are included. This, however, offends against the requirement that taxes be imposed so as to minimise efficiency cost. Proposed first by Pigou [27], and developed in recent years under the banner of optimal taxation, commodity taxation calls for a uniform *ad valorem* rate only in the very special case where leisure is fixed and the demand elasticity for all products is the same. If elasticities differ, so should tax rates in inverse proportion thereto. If leisure is variable and elasticities differ, the Ramsay rule (simplified) calls for tax rates to vary so as to reduce outlays on various commodities by the same proportion, and so forth [20, ch. 12].

Precisely the same argument applies to the case of the income tax. If some factor supplies or services are more elastic than others, differential rates of tax are called for so as to minimise efficiency cost, contrary to the globality requirement of the accretion principle, where income from all sources is to be included and treated alike. It is thus evident that an efficiency cost-minimising system of taxation departs from the broad base principle and its requirement of uniform treatment of all income uses or sources.

Efficiency and horizontal equity

To make matters worse, efficiency requirements may conflict not only with the broad base doctrine, but also with the more basic goal of horizontal equity. No conflict arises if there is one taxpayer only, for the simple reason that horizontal equity is a non-problem in a single taxpayer setting. The same still holds in a situation with two taxpayers and similar utility functions. While the broad base principle is qualified by the efficiency rule, the condition of equal treatment remains intact as the same differential rates are appropriate for and applied to both taxpayers. Since this is the case typically dealt with in optimal taxation theory, it is readily seen why the theory has developed without contact with the horizontal equity tradition. But the two lock horns once different preferences are allowed for. Suppose that A's labour supply is fixed independent of the wage rate while B's supply is elastic. The efficiency considerations of optimal taxation theory then call for the entire revenue to be drawn from A, subject only to such vertical equity considerations as may be introduced by application of a social welfare function. Assuming society to be neutral in this respect, the entire revenue will be drawn from A. This contradicts the requirement of horizontal equity. With A and B confronted by the same options, they should be treated equally. Both should contribute. The same principle holds for the consumption base. By concentrating on the case of equal utility functions, optimal taxation theory has by-passed an important part of the problem. Recently efforts have been made to bring the two issues together, but much remains to be done in this respect.

The horizontal equity doctrine, however, is also at fault. Its usual practice has been to interpret equal treatment as calling for *equal dollar amounts* of tax liability, thus overlooking the fact that tax burden includes not only the tax dollars paid but also the excess burden which is suffered in the process. Horizontal equity, properly interpreted, thus calls for the tax burden to be distributed between A and B so as to impose *equal welfare losses*, i.e. tax dollars *plus* the 'triangle' of excess burden. Given their different utility functions, A will be called upon to pay more than B, not the same amount.

But even though the 'equal treatment' concept is corrected in this way, the requirement of horizontal equity still conflicts with the efficiency rule. Aggregate efficiency cost will not be minimised since B shares part of the burden. Efficiency is not only incompatible with the global base criterion, but with the very requirement of horizontal equity. Given two incompatible policy goals, a trade-off between the two must be made. That is to say, horizontal equity must be entered as a separate argument into the social welfare function. It must be quantified and its price be determined. Society must then decide how much or little thereof it wishes to buy.

Single rate structure

Without extending this discussion unduly, it remains to note the restraint imposed by the need to apply a single rate structure to all taxpayers. In the purest of pure theory, optimal taxation as well as (redefined) horizontal equity would call for different patterns of tax rates (be they on the consumption or the income base) to apply to individuals with different preferences. The patterns of base differentiation would have to differ with the pattern of preferences.

Average patterns. In practice this is not possible. The same rate system, involving the same pattern of base differentiation, must be applied to all taxpayers. This means that base differentiation should reflect some sort of average preference pattern. What does this second-best constraint do to our preceding conclusions?

Beginning with the consumption base, people with the same potential for consumption should incur the same welfare loss. This would require taxation of commodities for which various individuals have a more or less *uniform demand elasticity*. But the set of commodities with this characteristic may not be the same as the set for which demand (on the average) is *relatively inelastic*. Selection of base differentiation in line with horizontal equity considerations therefore does not lead to the same result as base differentiation in line with considerations of minimum efficiency cost. Thus there arises a further trade-off problem, calling for further evaluation of the efficiency cost which it is worth undertaking to secure horizontal equity.

Once more, the same applies to the income base approach. Horizontal equity calls for taxation of factor supplies for which individuals with similar income potential have more or less *similar supply elasticities*, whereas efficiency calls for concentration on factors which (on the average) are *inelastic in supply*. The same further trade-off conflict arises as with commodity taxation.

Vertical equity. Matters are complicated further as considerations of vertical equity are added. Beginning with the consumption base, vertical equity, we assume, calls for burdens (tax plus loss of consumer surplus) to rise with total expenditures as prescribed by the social welfare function. This objective may be implemented by taxing products with low income elasticities at lower rates and commodities with high income elasticities at higher rates. Given the need to apply a generally applicable rate structure, this involves four conflicting criteria by which to choose commodities, i.e. price elasticities of demand, which relates to efficiency; income elasticities of demand, which relates to vertical equity; dispersion of price elasticities at given levels of income, which relates to horizontal equity; and dispersion of income elasticities for particular commodities, which once more bears on horizontal equity.

Alternatively, vertical equity might be implemented by applying progressive rates to total consumption, thereby forgoing the efficiency gained from differentiating between products but (possibly) gaining on horizontal equity grounds. Given that the difficulties of multi-dimensional differentiation may be forbidding even in terms of a theoretical solution, the latter may appeal as the more practicable, though theoretically inferior, outcome.

As before, the same record plays for the income base. Vertical equity might favour heavier taxation of capital and lower taxation of wage income, which, since Adam Smith, has been the reason for granting preferences to earned income. But efficiency considerations might not support this conclusion. Once more, it may be that the combination of a broad base with progressive rates offers the more attractive and practicable solution.

In conclusion, it appears that the constraint of applying the same rate and base system to all taxpayers, combined with allowing for vertical equity, tips the argument back in the direction of a broad base approach.

Moreover, the tipping may also be towards an income base. Such at least would be the case if we can assume that factor supply elasticities (among people with equal potentials) are less differentiated than product demand elasticities.

3. PRE- AND POST-TAX EQUITY

We have argued that horizontal equity calls for equal treatment of people in equal positions, where equal position was defined in terms of equal options. Our approach has been to begin with the requirement that equal treatment be given to people in equal pre-tax positions. But if the treatment is to be equal, they will also be left in equal positions thereafter. Horizontal equity may thus be defined either as (1) equal treatment of people in equal pre-tax positions, or (2) taxation so that people who were equal prior to tax will also be equal after tax. While the former version has been used traditionally, the latter has now come to be preferred, but there is no difference.[5]

To illustrate actual income tax practice, consider two taxpayers A and B with labour supply schedules S_a and S_b, respectively. Their pre-tax wage rate is w and their post-tax wage rate is $w(l-t)$. Their gross income, after the tax is imposed, equals ODEG, their tax equals CDEF and their net income equals OCFG. People with equal gross income *after* imposition of the tax are treated equally in the sense that they pay the same amount of tax and

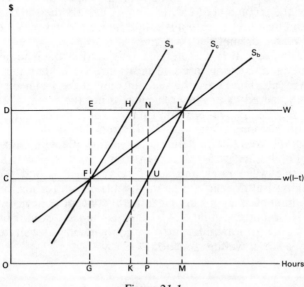

Figure 21.1

are left with the same net income. But their *total burdens* are not the same, with B's burden of CDLF exceeding A's burden of CDHF. If equals are defined in terms of their gross income after imposition of tax, they are treated equally in terms of tax, but not in terms of welfare loss. Equal treatment in terms of *tax plus loss* would call for a lower rate to be applied to B. But if this was done, they would no longer have the same gross income after tax.

There is the further question whether equals should be defined in terms of A and B (who share the same gross income *after* the tax is instituted) or in terms of B and C (whose supply schedule equals S_c) who share the same income *before* the tax is introduced. B and C pay taxes of CDEF and CDNU, respectively, with C paying more. Their respective welfare losses are CDLF and CDLU, with C's loss exceeding A's by FLU. Once more C would have to be given a lower rate to equate welfare losses, but this would not contradict their common position in absence of tax.

In short, if we define equals as A and B, equal tax treatment gives equal tax liabilities but unequal welfare losses. If we define equals as B and C, equal rates give both unequal tax liabilities and unequal welfare losses. To equalise welfare losses differential rates would be required in both cases. Choosing rates so as to apply equal welfare losses on B and C would meet the condition that B and C who enjoy similar incomes in the absence of tax are in a similar position after tax. This follows because they suffer the same welfare loss. The logic of the argument thus points to the proper solution as involving differential rates which impose equal burdens on B and C. This being the case, actual procedure is in double error: it errs in equalising liabilities rather than welfare losses, and it errs in equalising liabilities among the wrong people. This, to be sure, is placing unfair blame on the architects of the income tax (and, of course, exactly the same would hold for an expenditure tax) since point L and hence the pairing of C and B is not an observable datum. Sad, but true.

On closer consideration it even becomes questionable whether C and B should be defined as being in equal positions. While they face the same options (wage rates) and have the same income in the absence of tax, their welfare, as measured by producer surplus, is not the same. C is better off than B and may be in equal position (in terms of producer surplus) with D whose pre-tax income differs due to different hours or wage rate. The utopian solution would be to define as equals people with equal producer surplus in the absence of tax and then to impose tax rates which (given their respective wage rates and supply elasticities) would reduce their surplus equally. But this, alas, is an impossible dream (or nightmare). The problem of implementing a truly meaningful concept of horizontal equity, it appears, is beyond feasibility. And such is the case even if one is quite willing (as I am) to draw interpersonal comparisons of welfare losses as weighted by a social welfare function.

4. FROM THEORY TO POLICY

In conclusion, it is evident that the pure theory of tax base determination and horizontal equity is extremely complex. Judged on efficiency grounds alone, the best solution calls for a complex set of varied rates on different parts of the base. This solution in turn conflicts with the set of rates which would be best in terms of horizontal equity. Policy must thus strike a balance between two 'best' solutions. This task is complicated by the practical fact that a single rate system has to be applied to all taxpayers. Seen against this full complexity, the traditional case for the income base and its corollary of broad-based taxation becomes rather shaky. But pure theory is one thing and applied tax policy is another. While it is essential (and the central task of tax theory) to determine what would be the correct solution if properly applied, it is also necessary to consider how various formulations will operate in practice.

Looking at the tax scene, it is evident that existing departures from the broadbase rule are widespread. It is evident also that they have not been introduced in line with implementing efficiency or horizontal equity considerations. They are the outcome of tax politics rather than reflecting a central scheme of efficient and equitable taxation. It is quite likely, therefore, that a shift to a broad base would do more good than harm, and do so on grounds of both efficiency and horizontal equity. It would also carry the advantage of permitting the same revenue to be obtained at a lower rate. Considerations of tax politics similarly make one wonder whether advocacy of the consumption base will lead to enactment of a comprehensive expenditure tax, or rather provide occasion to further dismantle the income base. Such are the disturbing facts of life which, however deplorable to the theorist, render tax counsel a subtle art rather than a firm science.

NOTES

1. See Mill [13, p. 804]. With Mill, we take this to be a primary principle of social justice, the validity of which does not rest on its being derivable from utilitarian premises. Nor is its validity removed by demonstration that it may under certain circumstances be incompatible with utilitarian doctrine. See Stiglitz (1982).
2. See Simons [18] where the extensive literature (largely German) is reviewed.
3. See Goode [8, p. 52] who suggests that the increase in a person's power to consume market output has greater intuitive appeal as an indicator of ability to pay than the exercise of the power to consume has. Goode also notes that the income tax reaches differences in power associated with the accumulation of wealth whereas a consumption tax does not. See Goode [7, p. 24].
4. See Simons [19] where a pragmatic application of the earlier findings is considered. This is the volume which, for decades to follow, became the essential blueprint for tax reformers in the United States.

5. By the same token, the accretion concept calls for the inclusion of bequests in the income tax base of the heir. See Simons [18, p. 57]. In either case, an exception may be made for limited transfers within the close family.
6. Note that Brennan and Nellor [4] consider the case where the utility of wealth holding is a function of saving in period *I*. Alternatively, and more realistically, it might be viewed as a function of wealth held by period *II*, thus allowing for interest accumulation. Viewed this way the conclusion (that the consumption tax favours saving) still holds *provided* that wealth utility is a function of wealth holding *gross* of such period *II* tax as becomes due when the wealth is consumed. If wealth utility is considered a function of holdings *net* of period *II* tax, then the consumption tax becomes neutral. The argument thus depends on how wealth-holding enters the utility function. If viewed as *anticipation* of future consumption pleasures, the consumption tax is neutral. If viewed as enjoyment of economic and social power, the consumption tax is non-neutral. I am indebted to Ronald Grieson for discussion of this point.
7. It should be noted that Hobbes' primary reason for the consumption tax is on benefit grounds, with the benefit of public protection strangely seen to apply to consumption rather than wealth. The proposition that the consumption tax prevents the Commonwealth from being 'defrauded by the luxurious waste of private men' appears only at the very end of the section.

REFERENCES

[1] Atkinson, A. B. and J. E. Stiglitz (1982) *Lectures on Public Economics* (New York: McGraw-Hill).
[2] Bittker, B., C. Galvin, R. A. Musgrave and J. Pechman (1968) *A Comprehensive Income Tax Base?* (Federal Tax Press).
[3] Brennan, H. G. (1978) 'Death and Taxes: An Attack on the Orthodoxy', *Public Finance*, 33, 201–24.
[4] Brennan, H. G. and D. Nellor (1982) 'Wealth, Consumption and Tax Neutrality', *National Tax Journal*, 35, 427–36.
[5] Feldstein, M. (1976) 'On the Theory of Tax Reform', *Journal of Public Economics*, 6, 77–104.
[6] Fisher, I. and H. W. Fisher (1942) *Constructive Income Taxation* (New York: Harper).
[7] Goode, R. (1976) *The Individual Income Tax* (Washington, D.C.: Brookings Institution).
[8] Goode, R. (1980) 'The Superiority of the Income Tax', in J. A. Pechman (ed.), *What Should be Taxed: Income or Expenditure?* (Washington, D.C.: Brookings Institution), pp. 49–113.
[9] Hobbes, T. (1968) *Leviathan*, C. B. McPherson (ed.), (London: Penguin Books).
[10] Kaldor, N. (1955) *An Expenditure Tax* (London: George Allen & Unwin).
[11] Marshall, A. (1925) 'Social Possibilities of Economic Chivalry', in A. C. Pigou (ed.), *Memorials of Alfred Marshall* (London: Macmillan).
[12] Meade, J. E. *et al.* (1978) *The Structure and Reform of Direct Taxation* (London: Institute for Fiscal Studies).
[13] Mill, J. S. (1849) *Principles of Political Economy*, W. J. Ashley (ed.) (1921) (London: Longmans, Green).

[14] Musgrave, R. A. (1939) 'A Further Note on the Double Taxation of Savings', *American Economic Review*, 39, 549–50.

[15] Musgrave, R. A. (1976) 'ET, OT and SBT', *Journal of Public Economics*, 6, 3–16.

[16] Pechman, J. A. (ed.) (1980) *What Should be Taxed: Income or Expenditure?* (Washington, D.C.: Brookings Institution).

[17] Pigou, A. C. (1928) *A Study in Public Finance* (London: Macmillan).

[18] Simons, H. C. (1938) *Personal Income Taxation* (Chicago: University of Chicago Press).

[19] Simons, H. C. (1950) *Federal Tax Reform* (Chicago: University of Chicago Press).

[20] Stiglitz, J. E. (1982) 'Utilitarianism and Horizontal Equity: The Case for Random Taxation', *Journal of Public Economics*, 13, 1–33.

[21] U.S. Treasury Department (1977) *Blueprints for Basic Tax Reform* (Washington, D.C.: US Government Printing Office).

Part III
Fiscal Policy

22 The Nature of Budgetary Balance and the Case for the Capital Budget* 1939

The budget serves the twofold function of providing for the planning of the revenue expenditure process over the coming fiscal period and of supplying an instrument of parliamentary control over the public finances. From the point of view of either objective, it is desirable that the partial revenue and expenditure proposals should be arranged and formulated into one comprehensive plan, so as to indicate most clearly the short-run as well as the long-run implications which the programme involves. The specific form in which the budget should be arranged is a technical issue, however, and depends upon the kind of information the budget is supposed to supply as well as upon the nature of the fiscal programme which is to develop. The validity of the principle of budgetary unity—i.e. the requirement that the budget should not be divided into independent parts, but that all items should be included in one total revenue and expenditure balance—depends therefore upon the significance attributed to the particular type of information which the unitary budget supplies and upon the planning efficiency which it permits. The case for a double budget system, as suggested in the proposal for the separation of the budget into a current and a capital one, similarly depends upon its respective merits as a tool of fiscal planning. The evaluation of the capital budget scheme must therefore be preceded by a discussion of the different planning considerations which the budget may be expected to express. On the basis of such clarification a proper distinction between various arguments in favour of the capital budget scheme is facilitated.

Although alternative arrangements of the budget refer to distinctly separate issues, they have the formal similarity of referring to some type of budgetary balance. In distinguishing the separate issues we may therefore distinguish between various types of budgetary balance. In the following,

---

* *American Economic Review* (1939) vol. XXIX, 2. June.

four major interpretations of budgetary balance are presented: (1) liability balance, (2) monetary balance, (3) hedonistic balance, and (4) long-run planning balance. Further alternatives may be conceivable, but need not concern us here.[2]

Liability balance

By confronting total governmental cost payments with total tax revenues it is shown whether an addition to or an amortisation of outstanding obligations (not considering the alternative of a cash balance depletion or accumulation) proves necessary to provide a formal balance.[3] The usual inclusion of non-governmental cost payments on the expenditure side distorts the balance from the liability point of view. The significance attributed to the state of liability balance is based on the alleged or real implications of public debt accumulation.

Monetary Balance

By balancing the income-increasing effects of public spending with the income-decreasing effects of revenue collection, the total direct effects of the revenue expenditure process upon the monetary income of the community as a whole are determined. The determination of monetary balance is thus concerned not with the confrontation of revenue and expenditure items as such, but with their effects upon the flow of monetary income. For an examination of these effects a detailed analysis of the revenue and expenditure items proves necessary. The significance of the state of monetary balance, as distinct from the liability balance, lies in the field of compensatory fiscal policy. The failure to recognise the simultaneous reduction in monetary deficit and the continuation of the liability deficit during 1937, due to the introduction of the social security taxes, was a case in point.

Hedonistic Balance

By confronting the cost of public services with the benefits derived therefrom, information concerning the rationality of the revenue expenditure process is obtained. The formal confrontation of revenue and expenditure items constitutes a mere tautology from the point of view of hedonistic balance. To render the balance significant in the hedonistic sense, the monetary items have to be corrected for errors in the planning as well as in the execution of the suggested programme. Public economy being a continuous institution, the determination of benefits and losses must furthermore be concerned with the consideration of future as well as current effects. While the concept of hedonistic balance is a complex one, it is nevertheless considered basic for the problem of economic planning and the development of a theory of public economy. Although the state of hedonistic balance is under any given set of conditions determinately related to the other types of balance, this relationship is too intricate to permit a simple hypothesis.

Long-run Planning Balance

Although related to liability balance, planning balance is a broader concept. It is concerned with both the currently suggested programme and its relation to a possible long-run programme. Non-fulfilment of spending obligations imposed upon the current budget by the long-run programme will cause a planning balance deficit, independent of the possible existence of liability balance. Current borrowing, on the other hand, if allowed for in the long-run programme, will not disturb the planning balance, although a liability balance deficit may result. The concept of planning balance may be applied regarding various types of long-term programmes, e.g. the maintenance of public capital equipment, the carrying out of long-run investment programmes or the execution of redemption schemes extending over a period longer than the one covered by the current budget. We proceed to examine the capital budget scheme from the point of view of the various concepts of budgetary balance.

II

If the budget is to supply information regarding the state of *liability balance*, the demand for budgetary unity clearly follows. The first argument for the capital budget system which we are to consider rests, however, with the contention that the traditional concept of liability balance is valueless, from both the theoretical and practical point of view. The determination of a liability balance by way of confronting *all* expenditures with *all* non-loan revenues, it is argued, fails to recognise that the economic significance of borrowing depends upon the nature of public outlays. Although applicable to the case of loan finance of *current* expenditures, the concept of liability balance is, the argument continues, entirely inapplicable to the case of *investment* expenditures, i.e. expenditures which create additional 'assets' to be registered as an offset against additional liabilities. Traditional objections to the accumulation of public debt can therefore be directed against the case of loan finance of current expenditures only; loan finance of investment expenditures is considered an altogether different issue. It then follows that the budget should be arranged so as to indicate the state of liability balance in the revised sense of the term, i.e. as applied to borrowing for the financing of non-investment expenditures only. This requirement in turn is complied with by a division of the budget into a current and an investment budget. New investments will, by their very nature, be loan-financed; but the capital budget will be balanced nevertheless from the 'revised' liability balance point of view. The current budget, on the other hand, may at times show a liability balance deficit in the traditional sense of the term.[4] Although loan-finance of investment outlays appears entirely acceptable from this point of view, liability balance deficits on the current budget are considered permissible only as a temporary device and have to be made up in the years succeeding the deficit period.[5]

If the alleged difference between the respective issues arising from the loan-financing of current or of investment expenditures could be accepted as basic, the above case for the capital budget would be a strong one. In stating the liability balance in the 'revised' sense, the budget would indicate more clearly the economic significance of the revenue-expenditure programme suggested, for both the future status of government finances and the remaining sectors of the economy. The present case for the capital budget thus rests with the validity of the contention that borrowing for purposes of public investment offers, due to creation of offsetting assets, no deficit problem in the traditional liability sense. There are additional difficulties that may seriously impair the practical usefulness of the capital budget system, e.g. the problem of evaluating public assets and the treatment of obsolescence. From the theoretical point of view they are, however, of secondary importance. If the argument in favour of the capital budget, based on the theory of the 'revised' concept of liability balance, were fundamentally valid, agreement might be reached regarding these subsequent points.

There can be no disagreement that possible deterring effects, resulting from a given addition to the public debt, will be less severe the greater the increase in national income accompanying the borrowing process. The argument in favour of the capital budget is, however, not concerned with the secondary effects of public spending upon the private employment of resources: effects of this kind may just as well result from a liability deficit on the current budget as from borrowing for purposes of investment expenditures. The specific justification for loan-finance of investment spending is supposed to lie in the supply of durable goods—consumers' goods or capital goods—the benefits of which continue to be derived *after* the borrowing/spending process has occurred. It is the supply of these durable goods, or the benefits derived therefrom, which are supposed to constitute the addition to the national income against which the current liability of debt service is offset.

The validity of the argument greatly depends upon the type of investment expenditures to which we refer. The case is weakest for those expenditure projects the benefits of which may be enjoyed independent of individual contributions to the cost of providing them. Regarding investment outlays of this non-self-liquidating type, the practice of offsetting the debt liability with the 'asset' of public investments is fallacious. The assets with which the debt liability ought to be confronted lie in the taxable capacity of the economy and not in the highways or playgrounds which have been constructed with the loan funds. The addition to taxable capacity, necessitated by the increased obligation of debt service, is far from identical with the addition to the national income in the form of an increased supply of transportation and recreation facilities.

Although a public auditorium adds to the real income of the community, it fails to create additional objects of taxation or to increase existing tax bases. This holds for the auditorium as such, as well as for the real income derived from its use. The auditorium, the services of which are supplied 'free of charge' and are financed out of general revenue, is obviously no object of property taxation. The real benefits derived from the auditorium in turn cannot be traced to the individual income receiver and hence cannot be assessed as taxable personal income.[6] Increased tax revenue, and cost of maintenance must therefore be assessed on the old tax base, thus resulting in an increased tax burden.

But cannot the monetary authority provide a corresponding increase in taxable monetary income, sufficient to offset the burden of the additional tax collection? The success of such a policy will depend upon the effects of credit-creation on the level of employment. Notwithstanding the importance of these effects for the problem of loan finance in general, they need not be considered in this more specific discussion of the distinction between loan finance of spending on durable goods and loan finance of current outlays. The difficulties in the way of the indicated monetary approach to the tax burden problem are similar for both cases. In either instance the increase in monetary income needed to offset the increased tax burden will be considerably larger than the additional tax sum[7] and thus exceed the amount absorbed in the circular flow from the interest taxpayer to the Treasury and back to the bond-holder. The further effects of income-creation upon prices and the level of employment will be the same in both cases. It cannot be maintained that in the case of spending upon durable public goods an increase in the monetary income by an amount equal to the additional tax collection will be sufficient to offset the additional tax burden. This follows from the compulsory nature of taxation and the problem of friction resulting therefrom. If taxes were voluntary price payments, no problem of friction would exist; the existence of tax friction in turn proves the compulsory nature of the tax intervention.[8] Tax frictions not only prevail during the period of adjustment to a newly-introduced tax. Fluctuations in the economic system continuously result in changes in the objects of taxation as well as in the economic position of taxpayers. Due to the technical characteristics of the tax system, these changes necessitate adjustments which give rise to tax frictions similar to those resulting from direct alterations in the tax structure. The effects of taxation upon the supply and the allocation of resources, moreover, continue to operate after the change has occurred.

The interest payment aspect of the debt problem thus continues to demand consideration, whether the loan funds are applied for the public supply of currently consumed or of durable goods. The other aspects of the debt problem, especially the effects of borrowing upon the capital market for private investments, similarly continue to exist whether the spending of the loan revenue is or is not directed into the supply of durable goods. These considerations do not express a judgement upon the desirability or undesirability of loan-finance, or upon the social usefulness of non-self-liquidating public investments. The issue under consideration merely refers to the alleged distinction between the problems of loan finance arising in case of alternative spendings of the loan sum.

Regarding investments of a clearly self-liquidating nature, the fee income from which may be pledged for debt service on outstanding obligations, the case differs. Here the analogy to corporate assets and the case for a capital budget is justified. Fee payments are of a voluntary nature and thus unaccompanied by the frictional effects resulting from compulsory tax collection. Failure of the fee income to cover the cost of debt service would furthermore signal the necessity for a corresponding reduction in the capital value of the debt and for partial redemption.[9] Serious difficulties of assessing the capital value, similar to the problem encountered in utility regulation, would remain; but the basic theoretical objection against the special treatment of borrowing for purposes of public investments would disappear.

Actual investments falling clearly into the self-liquidating group are limited. There remains, however, a considerable field of public investments which to some degree might be rendered self-liquidating. An illustration is provided by the financing of highway debt out of petrol taxes; the taxes may be considered as fees, paid voluntarily in proportion to the use of highway services. Possibilities of this sort might be numerous and worth consideration; but the effects which such reorientation of the tax structure in the direction of the benefit principle would have upon other aspects of fiscal policy must not be overlooked. There is also little doubt that the difficulties of capital evaluation and the difficulties of corresponding debt management would greatly increase in regard to this group of semi-self-liquidating investments.[10]

With the exception of application to clearly self-liquidating investments, the above argument in favour of the capital budget is, we conclude, not acceptable. The argument implies, to be sure, an element of truth: given the alternative spending of loan revenue for the public supply first of non-durable goods and second of durable goods, it follows that—not considering secondary effects upon the private employment of resources—future national income will be greater in the second instance; and hence the deterring effects of the debt will be smaller. This element of truth must not, however, be magnified into the erroneous contention that in the case of loan-finance of investment expenditures no debt problem exists. A division of the budget into capital and current budgets is apt to misrepresent the actual state of liability balance and thus offend against the primary function of the budget to supply an unambiguous presentation of the fiscal programme, a prerequisite for any intelligent parliamentary decision on public policy.[11] Arrangement of the unitary budget so as to determine liability balance in the traditional sense is less ambiguous and in no way excludes a subsequent evaluation of the liability balance deficit as it appears in view of the possible creation of truly offsetting assets on the expenditure side.

Although theoretically the case for the capital budget is unrelated to the case for the extraordinary budget, the past experience with the latter as a means of camouflaging the actual state of the liability balance deficit must not be overlooked. The cases in which the capital budget method is clearly applicable are limited as yet. This applies to the sphere of federal finances in particular, where there are a number of projects which may or may not be eligible. The merits of each case should be considered carefully before any inclusion in a capital budget is decided.[12]

III

Further aspects of the capital budget, referring to other types of budgetary balance remain to be considered. From the point of view of *monetary balance* it is apparent that the capital budget scheme would complicate rather than clarify the issue; the problems of monetary balance and capital budget are unrelated. Concerning both hedonistic and planning balance the case is, however, different.

IV

From the *hedonistic balance* point of view the following questions arise:

(a) Does not the heterogeneity of specific revenue and expenditure items forbid the formation of a general aggregate and hence invalidate the principle of budgetary unity?
(b) Is the capital budget desirable for purposes of efficient planning and accounting of capital charges?
(c) Does the capital budget system provide for a more realistic allocation of costs and benefits over time?

These points are considered in turn.

(a) Specification and classification of revenue items on the one side, and expenditure items on the other side of the budgetary balance is entirely compatible with the principle of budgetary unity and essential for parliamentary control over public finances. The very practice of classification indicates that specific revenue and expenditure items can be placed into distinguishable groups. Whether these distinct characteristics render the items heterogeneous so as to forbid the formation of an aggregate, however, depends upon the interpretation of the sum totals. The private householder, when arranging his monthly budget, will allocate his funds between various alternative forms of expenditures and in so doing will have to refer to revenue and expenditure totals. This same allocation applies to the public household; in either instance the formation of aggregates is valid. Objections arise only if the aggregate figures come to be considered a complete statement of the revenue expenditure process; such interpretation would, as indicated previously, be tautological. Information regarding the monetary revenue and expenditure items and their sum total provides but a stepping stone for further analysis; if recognised as such, there is no objection against the formation of revenue or expenditure aggregates.

(b) Careful planning and accounting of capital charges is undoubtedly necessary. Recognition of the cost of maintenance is a prerequisite for a rational decision regarding the desirability of continued maintenance of durable public goods, producer or consumer goods. Recognition of obsolescence, due either to changes in the evaluation of services rendered or to changes in the technique of providing such services, is similarly a prerequisite for a rational choice between maintenance, replacement or net reduction in capital value. The authorities, trusted with the management of durable public goods, should consider these factors in preparing the expenditure programme. For this purpose they will have to maintain a statement of the existing public goods, the cost of their maintenance and the alternative cost of possible replacement with similar or superior facilities. Only then will they be in a position to suggest a rational expenditure programme and corresponding appropriations.

While careful capital accounting of this sort is considered altogether desirable, its appropriate place is not in the central budget but in the financial statements of the various governmental departments. The budget, presenting the summarised revenue and expenditure programme for the coming fiscal period, is the result of a large number of planning considerations, only one of which deals with the problem of capital charges. The separation of the budget into a current and a capital budget, where the latter would include all capital charges, is thus unnecessary for the achievement of efficient planning and accounting of capital outlays.

(c) Benefits derived from public investments are distributed over a period of time which continues after the initial investment expenditures have been made. This being the case, it might be objected that the picture of the present budget will be distorted if burdened with the entire cost of benefits to be enjoyed in both the present and the future. The objections fail to consider that the monetary items of the budget as such do not supply a sufficient basis for hedonistic judgement. To determine the balance in a hedonistic sense, aggregate discounted future benefits must be confronted with the total capital cost, or present benefits with current interest and depreciation cost. The budget obviously cannot, without further correction, be interpreted as a statement of current public consumption.

But does not the inclusion of the entire capital outlay in the present budget, and the subsequent inclusion of depreciation charges in the future budgets, involve an error of double counting? This issue arises only if the series of short-term budgets were to be added up into a long-term budget. Such summation is neither permissible nor necessary. The budget for any given period should be related to a long-run plan of public finance; but this long-run programme is not identical with the aggregate of successive short-term budgets. If a summary of fiscal activity over several budget periods were to be derived from a series of successive short-term budgets, the latter would naturally have to be adjusted so as to avoid double counting. No valid objection against the unitary budget system arises from the point of view of hedonistic balance.

V

We finally turn to the case for the capital budget as related to *planning balance*. From the obvious desirability of long-term fiscal planning it follows that the determination of the revenue expenditure programme for a budget period should be correlated with previous decisions on long-term policies. There is, however, no need for a division of the budget into one part which is optional for present planning and another part which has been predetermined by past decisions. Although the formulation of the short-term plan should be preceded by and adjusted to a definite long-term policy, the budget as a statement of the short-term programme should not be rendered ambiguous by making it a medium for the expression of long-term policies.

At times the argument is heard that tax finance of investment expenditures would be unfair to the present generation since actual investment benefits will be derived in the future. Loan-finance of investment outlays is proposed as a means of spreading the burden over time. A spreading of the burden over time can, however, from the point of view of the community at large, be achieved only in the sense that frictional effects of taxation are postponed to a future period. In a real sense each generation pays for its own investments. From the point of view of state or local governments the argument is nevertheless of broader validity: collection of funds from outside the tax jurisdiction and gradual repayment out of tax revenues will permit a spreading of the burden. From the point of view of the community at large, the more important consideration would be that the immediate tax financing of an entire investment programme—which in itself cannot be carried out piecemeal—would result in more serious frictional effects than those resulting from initial borrowing and gradual redemption of the debt out of tax revenue collected over a longer period of time.

The long-term programme may thus, for various reasons, propose loan-finance of investment expenditures and at the same time provide for the financing of debt charges and eventual redemption of the capital sum out of current tax revenues. Redemption might, for example, be desirable within the lifetime of a public auditorium—not, we note, for reasons of the erroneous 'asset analogy', but because it may seem unfair to burden future generations with the frictional effects of charges on a debt, the benefits from which have ceased. There is the further consideration that if future generations decide to replace the auditorium and correspondingly increase their debt, the frictional effects per dollar of tax-financed interest payment will—assuming the national income to have remained constant—have increased.

Having already dealt with the problem of planning of depreciation charges, the method of redemption remains to be considered. Will the capital budget system provide a redemption mechanism superior to the traditional sinking-fund policy? Under the assumption that the sinking-fund arrangement decided upon is actually carried out, the scheme is found satisfactory. But in fact, this assumption rarely holds. The difficulty is a political one and lies in the enforcement of the execution of whatever redemption scheme has been decided upon, rather than in the construction of the scheme itself. Without such enforcement the separation of capital charges and outlays into a capital budget would be equally ineffective as a redemption mechanism.

Much can be said in favour of concentrating long-run investment expenditures during depression periods, but supplementary depression spending of a more current nature, e.g. for relief, is likely to remain necessary. The advisability of loan-finance and of various redemption schemes will differ in the two instances, although the nature of the resulting debt problem will be much the same. Redemption of the investment debt might, as pointed out, be linked to the lifetime of the auditorium; or redemption of the 'current' depression debt might be desirable over the cycle period. If any such policy of applying different redemption schemes to loan funds collected for different purposes were to be accepted as a 'principle of sound finance'—and good arguments may be made in favour of such policy—an arrangement of the budget so as to permit evaluation of the suggested revenue expenditure programme in the light of the principle would be advantageous. The various redemption schemes could be developed within a unitary budget system; this would be but one application of the general rule of adjusting short-term budgets to long-term policies. A double budget system would, however, have the comparative advantage of expressing such 'principle of sound finance' more clearly. By dividing loan revenues and outlays in accordance with the type of redemption policy provided for, the position of the budget as a whole (including both current and capital budget) in respect to long-run policies would be set in bold relief.[13] In this respect a good case for the capital budget exists.

The general budget can be presented in one form only—a decision has hence to be made in favour of either the unitary or the double budget scheme. The two advantages of the capital budget scheme which have been recognised—the case of clearly self-liquidating public investments and the application of different redemption schemes for different types of borrowing—have to be weighed against the danger of presenting a distorted picture of the state of liability balance. First, the advantages of redemption schemes distinguishing between different types of borrowing are available (though not quite as effective) within the framework of a unitary budget system. Second, there is a severe danger of misrepresentation of the state of liability balance if the capital budget system is applied. There is also the further disadvantage of the encouragement which the capital budget may give to the notion that durable public goods can be considered the equivalent of corporate assets.[14] As far as these two points are concerned the disadvantages outweigh the advantages. Third, the strictly self-liquidating nature of public investments must be proven in any specific instance before inclusion in a capital budget is justified. Regarding strictly self-liquidating assets there is, subject to the technical difficulties indicated, a strong case for the capital budget.

The budget is but a final presentation of the revenue-expenditure programme and the outcome of multiple-planning considerations. The unitary budget system is not only compatible with the development of supplementary types of financial statements, but supplementary statements are in themselves necessary for purposes of efficient planning.

NOTES

1. The principle of 'budgetary unity' should not be confused with that of 'budgetary comprehensiveness'. While comprehensiveness merely requires that 'all government expenditures and revenues must be subject to the budgetary mechanism and must enter into the recognised budgetary procedure' [7], unity requires that all revenues and expenditures should be included in one total balance. A multiple-budget system, while incompatible with unity, is thus quite compatible with comprehensiveness. The principle of 'budgetary comprehensiveness' is, as a matter of theory, hardly a controversial issue. The budgeting of semi-independent government-owned corporations raises certain problems, e.g. the choice between gross or net budgeting, which need not be dealt with in this connection.

2. We are not dealing in this connection with the so-called balance sheet of public investments in which previous investments are balanced against outstanding obligations. Our discussion is concerned with the short-run budget, covering the fiscal programme for a strictly limited period of time.

3. The distinction between revenue receipts and non-revenue receipts on the one hand, and cost payments and non-cost payments on the other, is derived from the same concept of liability balance. Cf. Fairchild [7].

4. Interest service and depreciation allowance for the public investments is to be financed out of the current budget. The capital budget for any given budget period thus includes new investments, interest service on old obligations and maintenance of old investments on the expenditure side, and new loan revenue plus transfers from the current budget on the revenue side.

   The policy of rendering the investment budget elastic while stabilising the current budget, which follows from the acceptance of borrowing in the one and rejection of borrowing in the other case, may easily result in an undesirable curtailment of useful, 'ordinary' expenditures, at a time at which depression spending is directed into more questionable 'emergency' channels.

5. Cf. Myrdal [5] for a discussion of the Swedish budgetary system.

6. Not considering the determination of specific benefit shares, the following problem arises. The real income of an individual increases with an increase in the 'free' supply of public services, assuming his net income received in monetary form to have remained constant. It may then be argued that the friction resulting from the imposition of a given tax upon an individual will vary inversely with his real income, whether received in monetary form or not. The psychological issues upon which this proposition depends cannot be considered here. It appears, however, that the real income derived from the 'free' public

services will, in so far as taxable capacity is concerned, be no full substitute for the money income which the individual would have lost had he made a tax contribution sufficient to cover the cost of the services consumed. To maintain that the former is a full substitute for the latter implies the fallacious interpretation of taxes as voluntary price payments.

7. As a first approximation we suggest that a percentage increase in taxable money income, equal to the percentage increase in tax revenue collected, is necessary to 'offset' the additional burden. Further approximations would have to consider the resulting changes in the relative taxable capacities of various tax objects and corresponding changes in the tax structure.

8. For a discussion of the interpretation of taxes as voluntary price payments, see Musgrave [4].

9. To avoid frictional effects of debt redemption, amortisation as well would have to be financed out of the fee income.

10. In so far as the determination of cost (original or replacement) is concerned, the problem is analogous to that of public utility evaluation. Additional difficulties may arise regarding the allocation of joint costs, public investments being more likely to serve several purposes at the same time.

    The market value of utilities, itself a function of the rates charged, is useless for purposes of rate-making. The reaction of demand to rate variations does, however, supply some information concerning the desirability of maintenance or replacement. This information is not available in case of public investments which are not clearly self-liquidating.

11. If it is held that legislative inhibitions against borrowing should be cured, the capital budget argument as discussed above may constitute a valuable tool of persuasion, but then it should be recognised as such.

12. An enumeration of possible cases is to be found in the President's budget message of 5 January 1939 (*New York Times*, 6 January 1939, p. 10) under the rather unsatisfactory heading of 'Extraordinary Expenditures'.

13. The Swedish budget provides for redemption of the 'current' debt within a period not longer than five years after the initial borrowing. To assure compliance with this requirement, unfulfilled redemption obligations of the present current budget are carried forward to the next year's current budget. [5, pp. 140, 142].

14. The differences between corporate assets and durable public goods are neglected, for instance, in Gilbert *et al.* [3, p. 63].

    Attention may also be called to their proposition (p. 43) that the borrowing programme during 1932–37 'paid for itself handsomely' because tax revenues at the end of the period were $4.4 billion higher than at the beginning of the period, while annual interest charges had increased by only $258 million. Once the *future* cost of interest charges and possible *future* downward fluctuations in national income are considered, the proposition as presented becomes untenable.

REFERENCES

[1] Fairchild, F. R. (1935) 'An Analysis of the Government's Financial Reports, with Special Reference to the Deficit', *American Economic Review*, 25.

[2] Gayer, A. D. (1938) 'Fiscal Policies', *American Economic Review*, 5, 28.

[3] Gilbert, R., *et al.* (1938) *An Economic Program for American Democracy*.

[4] Musgrave, R. A. (1939) 'The Voluntary Exchange Theory of Public Finance', *Quarterly Journal of Economics*, 53, 1.
[5] Myrdal (1938) 'The Swedish Budget System', *Fortune Magazine*.
[6] Smith, D. T. (1938) 'An Analysis of Changes in Federal Finances', *Review of Economics and Statistics*, 20.
[7] Sandelson, J. S. (1935) 'Budgetary Principles', *Political Science Quarterly*, 50.

23 A Stable Purchasing Power Bond*
1941

In this paper a plan for a 'constant purchasing power' government bond is presented. The essential feature of such security would be its redeemability in terms of an amount of dollars representing a stable amount of purchasing power rather than a constant amount of dollars. At this juncture such a security would provide a helpful technique of defence finance, while in a post-war economy it might contribute to a social security programme and exert stabilising effects on business fluctuations.

Stable purchasing power bonds may prove a helpful contribution to the Treasury's endeavour to restrict the net income contributing effects of defence financing, since the offering of such bonds promises to increase the extent to which Treasury borrowing may syphon funds from the active income stream into defence outlays. For the individual income receiver, hesitant to engage in security speculation, a general anticipation of price rise places a premium on current spending and a penalty on cash saving or investment in bonds. Instead, saving takes the form of economically undesirable investment in durable consumer goods. If, however, stable purchasing power bonds were available for investment his choice between spending and saving would be much less affected by anticipated price level changes. Investment in government bonds would be rendered more attractive; less savings would be devoted to 'forward buying' of durables. At the same time the new-type security would little appeal to banks.

In addition to providing an incentive for money-saving, the availability of purchasing power bonds might provide an inducement for the investment of present cash balances in government securities. Absorption of such balances is desirable since in response to inflationary anticipation they may sooner or later be transformed into equity holdings or commodity hoards, accentuating inflationary tendencies. Finally, by imposing upon the government a contingent liability dependent on its failure to check price inflation, the flotation of stable purchasing power bonds may exert a wholesome pressure upon Congress to adopt aggressive anti-inflationary policies.

The technical details of such a stable purchasing power bond would be

---

* With G. L. Bach (1941) *American Economic Review*, vol. XXXI.

relatively simple. The essence of the plan is that the bond would be redeemable at maturity for that number of dollars which would provide the same purchasing power as the issue price of the bond at the issue date.[1] This would involve redemption in a larger number of dollars if the price index used had risen, in a smaller number of dollars if it had fallen. Whether or not interest payments should also be put in terms of stable purchasing power is a secondary and separate question. For simplicity it would seem desirable to use the present form of interest, at least at the outset.

A cost of living index appears to be the best choice for a 'constant purchasing power' guide, especially in view of the primary appeal of this sort of security to individual savers to whom the cost of living is apt to be the major factor in 'constant purchasing power' considerations. Of course, there is no 'the cost of living' and if there were, it would still be a far from perfect indicator of the value of money. But a cost of living index does represent a workable purchasing power concept for the purpose envisaged with this bond. It should be evident that the particular index chosen is a secondary consideration; in view of its governmental source, its long standing, and its general acceptance there is a strong presumption in favour of the B.L.S. index. The important consideration is to find a roughly satisfactory indicator and one which can be protected as much as possible from pressure groups which would gain from having it 'tinkered' with.

Such constant purchasing power securities would presumably be of fairly long maturity, though no particular long period appears to have a unique advantage over others. Correlative with the question of maturity are those of negotiability and redeemability before maturity. In view of the special appeal of the bonds there is a strong presumption in favour of non-negotiability, the more so since the resulting lack of liquidity could be removed by providing for optional redemption before the maturity date. It would be desirable, however, to impose some penalty before the maturity date. It would surely be desirable, however, to impose some penalty on pre-maturity redemption lest widespread speculation in the securities should develop.

In view of the special guarantee offered by these bonds, the interest rate on them should be considerably less, say by 50 per cent, than on regular Treasury issues of comparable maturity. The rate chosen would depend to some extent on how widespread an appeal it was desired for the bonds to make. As their interest rate approached that on ordinary securities, there would be an increasing incentive to shift to the new type bonds, though for large groups of institutional investors, especially banks and insurance companies, the securities would have no particular advantage. Of course, to assume a shift into constant purchasing power securities presumes that investors are not primarily interested in speculating on governments as a real income gain in an expected falling price period. At the moment, certainly, price expectations are strongly upward.

Lastly, in introducing constant purchasing power bonds it would probably be desirable to offer to convert any outstanding Treasury issues into them at the market price of the old securities or the current redemption value of Savings Bonds. It is now essential to avoid any unnecessary liquidation of governments in the market.

Certain broader implications of the stable purchasing power bond for a peacetime economy are worth brief mention.

At present, in view of widespread price level fluctuations, there is no really 'safe' investment for the person or institution seeking primarily security of capital in terms of purchasing power with only secondary emphasis on yield. The constant purchasing power bond would offer this sort of security for persons wanting to provide for old age, future schooling for children, contingencies, etc. The bond would be primarily, though by no means exclusively, attractive to small savers. Even though the government fails to recognise its proper responsibility for providing a relatively stable value for the dollar, surely the demands of such savers constitute a legitimate aspect of an overall security programme.

The virtues of such securities in widening the non-banking market for governments, in reducing the 'hoarding' of consumers' durables, and in putting some anti-inflationary pressure on Congress[2] have already been noted for the present juncture. Related considerations apply to all boom cases, and the lessening of speculation in commodities has special potentialities as a stabilising cyclical influence. In boom periods, the availability of such a security would tend to draw 'hoarding' away from commodities into securities. In depression periods these securities, liquidated through redemption as the cash need for purchases increased, would provide the mechanism for a flow of government funds into consumers' hands at the most appropriate time. These implications become much broader if one assumes that widespread government use forced corporations to adopt the same type of security.[3] Then corporate maturities to be faced during depressions would be greatly eased by the lowered cash requirements; maturities during boom periods would generally be harder to meet, providing a stabilising influence in both cases.[4]

Assuming a balance between periods of rising and falling prices, the purchasing power bond would result in a reduced burden of debt service due to its lower rate of interest. If, on balance, periods of rising prices predominate, this advantage might be offset by the need for redeeming or refunding at a higher amount of dollars than the issue price. The Treasury, however, would then find itself in a position to meet such need without difficulty since, together with the rise in living costs, there would probably have occurred a rise in money income, so that larger amounts of loan funds or tax receipts could be drawn from an enlarged base. Indeed, such increase in the dollar payments would appear desirable from an equity point of view unless it were maintained that debt repudiation through currency depreciation constituted an equitable process.

It would be easy to overrate the potentialities of the purchasing power bond. None the less it does appear to be capable of playing a very real role in the defence programme, and in general its implications for a more 'normal' world are attractive. On balance, it appears worthy of trial in Treasury financing.

NOTES

1. Turning to the history of this proposal, most interesting are a short statement by J. M. Keynes before the Colwyn Committee, suggesting this type of security to the British Treasury, and a statement by Alfred Marshall before the Royal Commission on Depression of Trade and Industry favouring by implication the same plan.
2. The political implications of the bond might be detrimental in a period where 'inflationary' policy is desirable.
3. The brief experience of Rand Kardex with this type of corporate security is well known. Unfortunately, the experience was so brief as to be of little value.
4. The use of interest rates varying according to purchasing power changes would provide a further stabilising effect along this same line.

24 Alternative Budget Policies for Full Employment*
1945

During the 1930s fiscal theorists were interested primarily in the effects of deficit-spending, that is, changes in overall income resulting from an increase in public expenditures above the level of tax yields. Recently, attention has been drawn to an alternative approach to deficit finance under which the deficit is brought about by a reduction of tax yields below the level of expenditures. Both techniques may be considered at the same time and be combined with other approaches not directly concerned with the size of the deficit. The level of private consumption and investment expenditures may also be affected by adjusting the *kind* of taxes and public expenditures included in the budget totals, and under certain conditions public expenditures may provide for a net addition to national income, even though there is no deficit and the level of private expenditures does not increase.

Adjusting the level of expenditures relative to tax yields is thus only one among several approaches. If fiscal policy is to provide for a given dollar addition to the national income, this may be accomplished through a number of alternative budgets, providing for varying tax, expenditure and deficit totals and for varying revenue and expenditure structures [1, p. 182; 2, p. 244; 3;4;8].

I

The interrelationships between the major variables of budget policy may be presented in a simplified form, somewhat similar in nature to the statement of monetary variables in the equation of exchange. Suppose that with a given federal budget overall income falls substantially short of the potential output at full employment. What adjustment in the budget can be

---

* *American Economic Review* (1945), vol. XXXV, 3.

made to raise income to the full employment level? Any adjustment in the budget will do which meets the condition

$$G = E_1 + k\,[\alpha(E_1 + E_2) - \beta T] + kI \qquad (24\text{-}1)$$

where G is the required increase in income, E_1 is the *additional* public expenditure on currently produced goods and services, E_2 is the *additional* public transfer expenditure, T is the *change* in tax revenue ($+$ or $-$), α is the marginal propensity to consume (out of income after tax) of the recipients of additional government expenditures, β is the marginal propensity to consume (out of after-tax income) of the taxpayers meeting the changed tax bill, I is the induced change in private investment expenditures ($+$ or $-$) and k is the multiplier applicable to an extra dollar of private expenditures on consumption or investment, based upon the community's marginal propensity to consume out of income after tax and independent of a given tax rate. Expression (24-1) shows that, for the budget adjustment to be successful, the required increase in income must be matched by the proposed increase in public expenditures on currently produced goods and services plus the resulting net increase in private consumption and investment expenditures. These variables will be examined briefly.

The *required increase in income* (or G) is the gap between the income which is realised 'in absence' of an active fiscal policy—defined, for purposes of this discussion, as a situation where the budget is balanced at a minimum level—and the income that can be reached at full employment. For the gap to be filled without a change in public expenditures or tax yields (allowing, however, for reduced tax rates), there would have to be an autonomous increase in private investment or consumption by an amount equal to G/k.

The *increase in public expenditures on currently produced goods and services* (or E_1) is the first leverage factor. E_1 is here written as a separate term, distinct from E_2, because real expenditures on currently produced goods and services are in themselves a direct addition to national income. Transfer expenditures make no such direct addition; they enter into national income only when respent by private income recipients.[1]

An increase in public expenditures on currently produced goods and services will thus result in a net addition to overall income unless offset by reduced private expenditures. Suppose the government spends $100,000 on a soil conservation project and increases taxes to cover the cost. The national income will then be increased by public expenditures of $100,000. Now suppose that those paying $100,000 of additional taxes reduce their consumption expenditures by $50,000 while those receiving $100,000 of additional income payments from the government increase theirs by $50,000. As a result, the level of private consumption expenditures is unchanged. Assuming private investment to be unchanged, the $100,000 worth of soil conservation is a net addition to national income.[2] For private consumption expenditures to remain unchanged, in this illustration, there must be no lag between the public outlay on the conservation project, the reduction in the taxpayers' consumption expenditures and the increase in consumption expenditures of the project workers; that is to say, there must be an increase in income velocity. If there is a lag in the public disbursement of the additional tax yield or in the respending of the additional income received by the project workers, the direct contribution of the real public expenditure may be offset in part or fully by reduced private expenditures, measured in the second term of expression (24-1). If such lags apply, this result may be avoided if the initial public outlay is financed out of credit or taxes drawn from idle balances. For purposes of present analysis, we assume that no lag exists [7, p. 81].

The *increase in private consumption expenditures*, resulting from adjustments in public expenditures and taxes, is the second leverage factor. The total increase is equal to $k \times$ the initial net increase. The initial net increase in turn equals the initial increase in expenditures by those receiving additional income from the government $-$ ($+$) the initial decrease (increase) in expenditures of those paying additional (or reduced) taxes. The initial increase in expenditures by those receiving additional government payments is defined as $(E_1 + E_2)$, i.e. the marginal propensity to consume (α) of those receiving the additional payments, $\times$ the total increase in public expenditures, including transfer as well as real expenditures. The initial decrease (increase) in expenditures of taxpayers is defined as $\pm \beta T$, i.e. the marginal propensity to consume (β) of those who meet an increased (decreased) tax bill, $\times$ the *change* in tax yield, $\pm T$.

It is a major point of this analysis that E_1, the initial public expenditure on currently produced goods and services, is singled out as the first term, while the multiplicand to which k is applied is defined to include the initial increase in *private* expenditures only.[3] This permits us to differentiate between the marginal propensity to consume of income recipients in the economy at large, which underlies k, and the marginal propensity to consume of those who receive additional income from the government (α), or of those who meet a changed tax bill (β).[4] This is of considerable advantage. During a depression, for instance, fiscal planning calls for taxes which are drawn from taxpayers whose marginal propensity to consume is low relative to that of income recipients as a whole, and for expenditures going to recipients whose propensity to consume is high relative to that of the community as a whole. The opposite tends to hold during a period of inflation. If the specific propensities of taxpayers and expenditure recipients are not allowed for, i.e. the marginal propensity to consume of all groups is assumed to be the same, the number of variables is reduced.[5] However, this simplified formulation of the problem is not very useful for our purpose since it implies the assumption that resulting changes in consumption expenditures are independent of the type of public expenditure or tax adjustment. Only changes in revenue or expenditure totals are accounted for, and thereby an important part of the problem is assumed away.[6]

The marginal propensities to consume of those receiving additional income from the government (α) or of those meeting a changed tax bill (β) are weighted averages. They greatly depend upon the kind of policy by which adjustments in the expenditure or yield levels are brought about. The α applicable to transfer expenditures may exceed or fall short of the α for real expenditures. Thus, if the additional expenditures are relief payments, α may be close to one; if they are for debt redemption, α may be close to zero. If the expenditures qualify for inclusion in E_1, it is likely that α will fall somewhere in between these extremes. Similarly, if the change in tax yield is in the sales tax yield, β may be close to 1; if the estate tax yield is involved, β may be close to zero. The β applicable to the corporation tax depends upon its incidence. To the extent that the tax is reflected in higher prices or lower wages, β will be relatively high; to the extent that the tax is reflected in reduced dividends, β will be less, and where the tax is reflected in the retention of less earnings, β will be equal to zero. By defining the revenue item as $\pm\beta T$, the implicit assumption is made that the β applicable to borrowing is equal to zero. This assumption is not entirely realistic, even for the case of depression borrowing, but is made to simplify the problem.

The *change in tax yield*, or $\pm T$, includes all changes in yield, whether due to changes in the tax base (brought about by increased consumption, investment and public expenditures) or to changes in tax rates. When government expenditures ($E_1 + E_2$) increase and the tax rate remains unchanged, T will be positive since a part of the additional income received from the government will be returned to the Treasury in taxes. Having defined T in this way, α is defined as the marginal propensity to consume out of income after tax but is applied to ($E_1 + E_2$), the full initial addition to private income, before allowing for additional taxes. In other words, with respect to the term $\alpha (E_1 + E_2)$ it is assumed that no additional taxes are paid by the recipients of the additional government payments. The fact that additional taxes are paid by this group and that the net increase in their expenditures falls short of $\alpha (E_1 + E_2)$ is allowed for in deducting βT, where T covers all additional tax yield.

Changes in tax yield are here considered the primary planning factor, the necessary changes in tax rates being determined by the changes in yield and income. The opposite approach could be taken but would be less useful.[7] As a matter of fiscal planning, yield adjustments are the primary objective and changes in tax rates the means to accomplish them. In planning rate adjustments to bring about the desired change in yield, secondary changes in yield due to changes in the level of income and hence in the tax base must not be neglected. As a matter of legislation, action is taken in terms of rate adjustment but the final purpose is adjustment of tax yields.

The change in yield (or T) may be positive or negative, depending on whether the yield provided for in the adjusted budget falls above or below the initially assumed level. T is equal to zero if the yield level is unchanged. It should be noted that $\pm T$ refers to increments or decrements in tax yield only, so that βT does not allow for changes in private expenditures brought about by changing the sources from which the initially assumed amount of tax yield is drawn, as, for instance, by changing from excise to income taxes.[8]

The *multiplier k* is here applied to initial changes in private expenditures on consumption or investment. It is based on the marginal propensity to consume of the community at large, not on α or β which reflect the consumption habits of certain groups only. Usually, k is based on the community's marginal propensity to consume out of income before tax and thus allows for leakages from additional tax payments, in this paper it is based on consumption out of income after tax. Since the multiplier is based on the community's marginal propensity to consume out of income after tax, k will remain constant when tax rates fall and/or when tax rates rise. This avoids considerable difficulties which can only be mentioned here. If, for instance, expenditures are increased to sustain a higher level of income and the tax *rate* is held constant, the initial increase in expenditures must be sufficiently high to allow for the fact that tax yield will be increased at the higher level of income and the deficit be smaller. This is allowed for in our formulation of the problem where the deduction from βT will be positive. If, instead, the tax *yield* is held constant, this leakage will not be present and T will be equal to zero. However, the implied reduction in tax rates means that the marginal propensity to consume out of income before tax payments will be larger at the higher level of income. Under our definition k remains unaffected by such changes.

The final leverage factor is kI, the change in private expenditures on investment and consumption due to $\pm I$, the *induced change in private investment*. It is not related to changes in E_1, E_2 or T in any simple multiplier fashion as is the case for consumption expenditures. Specifically, I is defined to include both such changes in investment as may accompany *any* overall increase in income, brought about by fiscal or other policies, and such changes as may result from the impact of quite specific revenue or expenditure policies. If fiscal policy can be successful in assuring a high and stable level of income, this very assurance will undoubtedly contribute to a higher level of private investment. Also, private investment may be stimulated directly through developmental programmes (power development, urban redevelopment, and so forth). Well-selected reductions in tax rates may give further incentives to private investment. On the other hand, higher tax rates, public expenditures which compete with private enterprise, and psychological repercussions of an increased budget or of a rising debt may work in the opposite direction.

II

The interrelationship between the contribution of the budget to overall income and the major variables of budget policy may now be illustrated with reference to hypothetical post-war magnitudes. The quantitative results, of course, are illustrative relationships, not forecasts or policy data.

Like the equation of change, our formula presents questions rather than answers, but it may serve as a 'table of contents' for some functional relationships involved.

For purposes of these illustrations the familiar concept of GNP may be used as the overall measure of income, even though theoretically the net product would be the better concept. GNP for the year 1950 is widely estimated at about $200 billion under conditions of full employment. Now suppose that the outlook at the close of 1949 indicates a prospective GNP of $170 or $180 billions only, both estimates being based on the assumption that the federal budget is balanced at a level of $10 billions.[9] This exceedingly low initial budget level is assumed for analytical reasons, not because it is felt that expenditures could or should be reduced that far. Under such conditions, what adjustments in the budget can be made that will raise total income by $30 or $20 billions for the two assumptions, respectively?

In answering this question, attention will be concentrated on three variables: the size of the budget, the size of the deficit and the consumption impact of the tax structure. First we shall consider the required level of public expenditures if given amounts of deficit are incurred and then the required size of the deficit if public expenditures are at given levels. In both cases the results will be observed for varying values of β.

Size of Required Budget as a Function of the Deficit and Tax Structure

It will be convenient to make certain substitutions in expression (24-1) as follows: E_1 the total increase in expenditures may be written for $(E_1 + E_2)$; rE may be written for E_1, where r is the fraction of additional budget expenditures in the form of real expenditures; $E - D$ may be written for T, where D is the deficit. Because the effects of specific revenue and expenditure policies upon private investment cannot be appraised without a much more detailed analysis, they will be neglected in the following illustrations *and the term kI in expression (24-1) will be omitted.*[10] Specific investment effects will be reconsidered in the concluding paragraphs. Solving expression (24-1) for E, we have

$$E = \frac{G - k\beta D}{r + k(\alpha - \beta)} . \tag{24-2}$$

To concentrate on the more important variables, let us assume constant values for r, k and α. Values of .75 for r, 2 for k, and .70 for α may be reasonable.[11] Substituting in (24-2) for the larger of the two gap assumptions, i.e. for a gap of $30 billion, we have

$$E = \frac{30 - 2\beta D}{2.15 - 2\beta} . \tag{24-3}$$

Fiscal Policy

To obtain total budget expenditures, the initially prevailing expenditure amount of $10 billion is added to E; if E is equal to zero, total expenditures are equal to $10 billion. Similarly, if the level of tax yield, or $E + 10 - D$ falls below $10 billion, tax yields are reduced from their initial $10-billion level.

Table 24.1. Required size of budget under alternative fiscal policies[a] (bn dollars)

						Deficit—billion dollars							
β^b	0	1	3	5	7	9.3	10	13	13.9	15	16	18	20
						G = $30 billion[c]							
0	23.9	23.9	23.9	23.9	23.9	23.9	23.9	23.9	23.9	23.9	23.9	23.9	23.9
.2	27.1	26.9	26.5	26.0	25.5	25.0	24.9	24.2	23.9	23.7	23.5	23.0	22.6
.4	32.2	31.6	30.4	29.3	28.1	26.7	26.3	24.5	23.9	23.3	22.7	25.6	20.3
.5	36.1	35.2	33.5	31.7	30.0	28.0	27.4	24.8	23.9	23.0	22.2	24.0	—
.6	41.6	40.3	37.8	35.3	32.7	29.8	29.0	25.1	23.9	22.6	21.4	18.8	—
.7	50.0	48.1	44.4	40.7	36.9	32.6	31.3	25.7	23.9	22.0	20.1	—	—
.9	95.7	90.6	80.3	70.0	59.2	47.9	44.3	28.9	23.9	18.6	—	—	—
						G = $20 billion[c]							
0	19.3	19.3	19.3	19.3	19.3	19.3	19.3	19.3	19.3	19.3	19.3	19.3	—
.2	21.4	21.2	20.7	20.3	19.8	19.3	19.1	18.5	18.3	18.0	17.7	—	—
.4	24.8	24.2	23.0	21.9	20.7	19.3	18.9	17.1	16.6	15.9	—	—	—
.5	27.4	26.5	24.8	23.0	21.3	19.3	18.7	16.1	15.3	—	—	—	—
.6	31.0	29.8	27.3	24.7	22.2	19.3	18.4	14.6	13.5	—	—	—	—
.7	36.7	34.8	31.1	27.3	23.6	19.3	18.0	—	—	—	—	—	—
.9	67.1	62.6	51.7	41.4	31.1	19.3	15.7	—	—	—	—	—	—

Notes:
[a] Effects of specific revenue and expenditure policies on private investment are disregarded.
[b] Fraction of marginal tax dollar reflected in reduced consumption expenditures.
[c] Deficiency in income if budget were balanced at $10 billion.

Proceeding from these assumptions, Table 24.1 shows the size of the budget total required to raise overall income by the deficiency G if selected values of D and β apply. For each combination in the table, the required increase in expenditures (E) is obtained by deducting $10 billion, from the budget total. The required change in tax yield (T) is obtained by deducting $10 billion from the yield total, i.e. from the total budget minus the deficit. The results are shown for values of G equal to $30 and $20 billion. The table is to be read like a mileage chart. It shows, for instance, that with a deficit of $5 billion and a β equal to .6, an increase in expenditures from $10 to $35 billion would be required under the $30-billion gap assumption.

Moving *down* each column, Table 24.1 shows that, for low levels of deficit, the required budget will be the larger the higher the value of β, whereas for high levels of deficit the opposite is the case. At the deficit level of \$13.9 billiion for the \$30-billion gap assumption (\$9.3 billion for the \$20-billion gap assumption), the size of the required budget will be the same for all values of β. This must be the case because at that point E is equal to D so that T or $E - D$ is equal to zero.[12] Since the tax yield remains unchanged, the value of β does not matter. If the deficit falls short of \$13.9 billion, it appears that $E - D$ is positive, i.e. tax yield must be increased above the initial level because required expenditures are relatively high and the deficit is relatively small. If the deficit exceeds this figure, $E - D$ is negative, i.e. the tax yield can be reduced from the initial level because required expenditures are relatively low and the deficit is large. While the change in yield is upward, the budget must of course be the larger the heavier the pressure of the additional taxes on consumption. If a reduction in tax yield occurs, this will be the more stimulating and hence the budget may be smaller the heavier the prior burden of the tax yield upon consumption.

Moving down the deficit columns, the required budget figure ($E + 10$) is carried to the point at which the size of the budget falls to the level of the corresponding deficit. Combinations which would require a smaller budget are not very meaningful and are indicated in Table 24.1 by dashes.[13]

Moving *across* each row, Table 24.1 shows how the required budget will be the smaller for any positive value of β the larger the deficit. If β is equal to zero, the required size of the budget will be the same for all values of D since there will be no difference between tax and deficit finance. Moreover, if β is equal to zero, the required budget level will be the same as in the preceding case where the budget level was the same for all values of β.[14] By increasing D for the higher values of β we again reach a point at which the entire budget is deficit financed and beyond which a further increase in the deficit would be meaningless.[15]

Table 24.1 obviously does not provide us with ready-made prescriptions for post-war budget policy. A number of arbitrary assumptions are involved and, most important, effects of specific tax and expenditure policies upon private investment are neglected.[16] It will be of some interest, however, to consider what ranges of Table 24.1 may be relevant and what, if any, significance the results may have for post-war fiscal policy.

The value of β will undoubtedly depend upon the amount of tax yield relative to the level of income. If the tax yield were very small, say \$5 billion out of a GNP of \$200 billion, β might be held to a very low level; a very substantial part of the tax yield might be obtained out of middle to high bracket income taxes. But if the tax yield were to be larger, say \$10 or \$15 billion, this would be more difficult. If the yield were \$20 or \$25 billion a substantial burden on consumption would be inevitable. A β of close to .5 might be the best that can be expected for a \$20-billion level. If the level of tax yield were still higher, say \$30 billion or more, β would hardly be below .6 and possibly substantially more.[17]

If this is the case, the currently popular proposition that full employment can be readily reached through a large balanced budget may be dismissed as of little practical interest. Assuming a β of .6, the balanced budget needed to fill the $30-billion gap would be about $42 billion; for a β of .7, the result would be $50 billion, levels of expenditure which would seem out of question for the peacetime economy. If, as is altogether likely, such an exceedingly high level of taxation should depress private investment below the assumed level, the required budget would be still higher, which in turn might depress private investment still further and so on. The result might be expected to be more favourable if a higher value for α is assumed. Thus, with α equal to .9 and β equal to .6 the required budget would be $32 billion instead of $45 billion, but only on the assumption that r remains at .75. This, however, is unlikely, since the increase in α to .9 would require that almost all the additional expenditures be for cash subsidies to low-income consumption. If we allow for this and assume r to fall to .1, while keeping α at .9, the required budget rises to $53 billion, or above the level required under the initial assumption. More reliance on consumption subsidies, therefore, does not render the 'large and balanced' budget approach more feasible.

Size of Required Deficit as a Function of the Expenditure Level and Tax Structure

There is much to be said in favour of an alternative approach under which the desired size of the budget is taken as the independent variable, while the size of the deficit is obtained as a function of the predetermined expenditure level and of the best possible value for β. If this approach is taken, expenditure planning will be guided more largely by considerations of resource allocation and there will be less need for 'made-work' projects. To illustrate this approach, expression (24-2) might be rewritten as

$$D = \frac{G + Ek(\beta - \alpha) - rE}{k\beta} \tag{24-4}$$

Retaining r at .75 and α at .7, we have, for the $30-billion gap assumption,

$$D = \frac{30 + E(2\beta - 2.15)}{2\beta} \tag{24-5}$$

Table 24.2 shows the required levels of deficit corresponding to selected levels of public expenditures ($E + 10$) and values of β. Again the results are shown for both the $30-billion and the $20-billion gap assumptions and again Table 24.2 is to be read like a mileage chart. Thus for the large-gap assumption and a budget of $28 billion (where $E = 18$), the required deficit is somewhat below $11 billion if β is equal to .6.

The general picture provided by Table 24.2 is very similar to that of Table 24.1. Moving *down* each column we now find that the required deficit will increase or decrease with a rising value of β, depending on

Table 24.2: Required size of deficit under alternative fiscal policies[a] (bn dollars)

	$G = 30$[a]				$G = 20$[c]			
	Total budget expenditures							
β[b]	28	23.9	20	15	28	20	19.3	15
0	*	d	—	—	*	*	d	—
.1	*	13.9	—	—	*	2.5	9.3	—
.2	*	13.9	—	—	*	6.3	9.3	—
.3	3.5	13.9	—	—	*	7.5	9.3	—
.4	7.1	13.9	—	—	*	8.1	9.3	—
.5	9.3	13.9	18.5	—	*	8.5	9.3	14.3
.6	10.8	13.9	17.1	—	2.4	8.8	9.3	12.7
.7	11.8	13.9	16.1	—	4.6	8.9	9.3	11.6
.8	12.6	13.9	15.3	—	6.3	9.1	9.3	10.8
.9	13.2	13.9	14.7	—	7.6	9.2	9.3	10.1
.95	13.4	13.9	14.5	15.0	8.2	9.2	9.3	9.9
1.0	13.7	13.9	14.3	14.72	8.7	9.3	9.3	9.6

Notes:
[a] Effects of specific revenue and expenditure policies on private investment are disregarded.
[b] Fraction of marginal tax dollar reflected in reduced consumption.
[c] Deficiency in income with balanced budget of $10 billion.
[d] If $\beta = 0$, it is a matter of indifference whether the budget is tax- or loan-financed. Hence, the deficit may assume any value between zero and total budget expenditures.

whether the adjusted yield falls above or below the initial level, i.e. whether T is positive or negative. Again the required deficit is the same for all values of β when E is equal to D so that the level of tax yield is unchanged.[18] Moving *across* each line, we now find at all values of β that the required deficit is the larger the smaller the size of the budget.

Again certain combinations of E and β are ruled out because they imply either (a) an excess of deficit over total expenditures, or (b) a negative deficit. In the case of (a) we have a situation where the proposed increase in expenditures is relatively small, so that a decrease in tax yield is required to obtain the necessary leverage. The heavier the consumption incidence of the initially obtained tax yield, i.e. the higher β, the more stimulus is provided by a dollar's worth of tax reduction and hence the smaller is the required tax reduction or necessary deficit. If the β of the decrement in tax yield falls to a certain point, the required deficit will be so large as to necessitate the repeal of all taxes. If β is still smaller, we have the situation indicated by dashes in Table 24.2 where the scheduled increase in expenditures is insufficient to provide the required leverage, even though the entire budget is deficit-financed. The leverage cannot be increased further without raising expenditures, and this is not possible because a given budget level is assumed. With respect to (b) the opposite situation prevails. There the scheduled increase in expenditures is relatively great, so that tax yields must be raised to avoid inflation. The lower the value for

β, the higher will the increase in tax yield have to be and the smaller is the permissible deficit. If the β of the increment in tax yield falls to a certain point, it will be necessary to balance the entire increase in expenditures with increased tax yield, so that D is equal to zero. If β is still smaller we have the situation indicated by asterisks in Table 24.2, where the scheduled increase in expenditures is too high to avoid inflation, even though a balanced budget is retained.[19]

Table 24.2 indicates that, within the range of feasible adjustments, the size of the required deficit may be considerably reduced, or the extent of permissible tax increase be considerably increased, if β can be held to a low level. Taking the $28 billion budget, for instance, the necessary deficit for the large gap assumption will be $7 billion if the β for the additional taxes can be held to .4 and nearly $12 billion if the β rises to .7. For the small gap assumption the same budget can be balanced only if β can be held down to .52. But whatever their relative impact upon consumption, all additions to tax yield are more or less restrictive. As shown in Table 24.2, the size of the deficit will have to remain the major variable of budget policy if the initial gap in the level of overall income is large, whether the deficit be brought about by raising expenditures more than tax yields, as under the large budget assumptions, or by raising expenditures while lowering tax yields, as under the small budget assumptions.

Specific revenue and expenditure effects on investment are included in expression (24-1) but have been neglected in its experimental application to possible post-war magnitudes. Since the picture might be quite different if such effects on private investment are accounted for, this greatly limits the usefulness of our illustrations. The effects of fiscal policy upon private investment are a complex matter and sufficiently familiar to render any brief enumeration superfluous; a detailed discussion would greatly exceed the limits of this paper.

Even cursory examination of the problem suggests, however, that private investment is likely to be the lower, *at any given level of total income*, the higher the level of taxation and (with the exception of stimulating developmental programmes) the larger the government budget. If the initial deficiency in overall expenditures is large, we have seen that the balanced budget approach will require exorbitantly high levels of expenditures and taxation, both of which will tend to depress private investment. If, as a result, private investment expenditures are depressed, budget figures even higher than those shown in Table 24.2 are needed. If the unfavourable reaction of private investors is violent, tax-financed additions to expenditures when carried beyond some point may well lower rather than increase the overall level of income.

All this points to the conclusion that a substantial deficit will be needed unless we succeed by non-fiscal means to narrow down the initial deficiency in the overall expenditure level to much below the illustrative figure of $30 billion used in the preceding discussion. If a large deficiency remains to be filled through fiscal measures, after other policy approaches have been exhausted, it will be neither desirable nor feasible to make expenditures sufficiently large to balance the budget at full employment. Instead, a thoroughly worthwhile expenditure budget should be provided including expanded social security and adequate developmental programmes stimulating to private investment, but excluding made-work projects. On the basis of such an expenditure programme the level of taxation should then be set sufficiently low to leave such deficit as the economic situation may require in the average year. After the budget is thus adjusted to the longer-term needs of the economic situation, short-term variations in underlying conditions and localised relief needs remain to be met by a flexible expenditure programme and an elastic tax system, including flexible income tax rates.

NOTES

1. Pigou [5, p. 19] defines as 'exhaustive' or real expenditures those expenditure items which involve surrender of real resources and are made to secure the production of goods and services. Placed on a current basis, this definition meets our requirements although there are numerous borderline cases.
2. This, of course, involves the assumption that public projects, valued at cost, can be added on to privately produced goods, valued at market price. For present purposes this assumption is accepted.
3. No double counting is involved by including E_1 as a separate first term, because the multiplicand to which k is applied in the second term includes only such fraction (α) of $(E_1 + E_2)$ as is initially respent.
   Alternatively, E_1 might be omitted as a separate term, in which case k would apply to $(E_1 + E_2)$ as a whole and E_2 would be deducted in the first round.
4. As pointed out below, α and β also differ from the community's propensity to consume upon which k depends in that they refer to consumption of particular groups, whereas the latter refers to consumption of the community at large.
5. We have in this case $\alpha = \beta = \gamma/(1-t)$, where γ is the community's marginal propensity to consume before tax and t is the marginal tax rate. In this case

   $$k = \frac{1}{1 - \alpha} \text{ and expression (24-1) reduces to:}$$

   $$G = E_1 + \frac{\alpha (E_2 + E_1 - T) + I}{1 - \alpha}$$

   For a discussion of the relationship between multiplier and tax rate, see Samuelson [6, p. 584].
6. Ideally, we should apply different multipliers to $E_1 + E_2$ and T, respectively, instead of assuming different marginal propensities to consume in the first round of private spending, while applying the general multiplier thereafter. But this is impracticable. Within the limitations of any multiplier analysis based upon the marginal propensity to consume of the community as a whole, the formula should give a reasonably good approximation.

7. An alternative approach would be to define α as the propensity to consume out of income before tax and T as such addition to tax yield as results from an autonomous increase in tax rates only, excluding such additional yield as results from an increase in the tax base. The net result, in terms of the addition to total income, would be the same for both approaches.

8. The lower the initially assumed yield level, the less serious is this defect. At the cost of some complication it may be remedied by adding another term to expression (24-1).

The difficulty might be avoided by redefining G to be the deficiency in income on the assumption of a zero (rather than a balanced minimum) budget. This would have the advantage of making T identical with the overall yield level, so that changes in the β for the total tax yield would be accounted for. But this would be more than offset by the disadvantages of this approach, in particular (a) it would pose the altogether unrealistic problem of having to estimate G for the assumption of zero public expenditures, and (b) it would exclude the analysis of budget adjustments involving a reduction in tax yield.

9. The underlying situation might be as follows: Given a balanced federal budget of $10 billion and a similar budget for state and local governments, consumers' expenditures corresponding to a GNP of $200 billion might amount to $142 billion. With real public expenditures of $17 billion, the remaining quota for private investment would be $41 billion. Assuming housing expenditures of $4 billion, growth in inventory of $2 billion, net exports of $2 billion, business replacement expenditures of $8 billion and net business investment of $10 billion, a deficiency of $15 billion would remain. With net business investment of $15 billion, the deficiency would be $10 billion.

Assuming a multiplier of 2, the gross product would settle at $170 or at $180 billion, respectively. Consumers' expenditures might then be at about $127 or $137 billion, respectively, the remainder in both cases being $17 billion of public real expenditures and $26 billion of investment. This disregards a further fall in income due to reduced private investment.

If investment declines with the level of income, as it most likely will, the gap between realised and full-employment income might be much above the $30 or $20 billion here assumed, but similarly, when the level of overall income was raised through an appropriate fiscal policy, there would be a corresponding increase in private investment and income and, in choosing $30 and $20 billion as our gap illustrations, this '*income-induced*' effect on investment (as distinct from investment effects caused by specific revenue or expenditures measures), *has been omitted*. If it is assumed that the 'income-induced' drop in investment as income falls is the same as the 'income-induced' rise in investment as income increases, the autonomous increase in expenditures needed to close the gap may be estimated correctly while neglecting the 'income-induced' changes in investment in both directions.

10. While the investment effects of specific revenue or expenditure measures are thus not covered our definition of the initial income deficiency implicitly allows for 'income-induced' changes in investment. See note 9.

11. The community's marginal propensity to consume out of individual income after tax is assumed at 4/5. Allowing for such factors as changes in corporate savings and in transfer expenditures, this might make for a multiplier estimating very conservatively of 2. The α for public real expenditures is assumed at 2/3, that is, somewhat below the 4/5 applicable to *individual* income after tax, since allowance must be made for such factors as corporate savings and changes

in transfer payments. The α for transfer expenditures is assumed at .8. If r is assumed at .75 this gives a weighted average for the combined α of .7. As noted before, this simplified analysis does not allow for the fact that k varies with implicit changes in the tax rate.

12. With T equal to zero (and neglecting kI), expression (1) becomes $G = rE + k\alpha E$. Substituting $G = 30$, we obtain $E = 13.9$. Adding the initial expenditures of 10, we have total expenditures of 23.9. Deducting initial taxes of 10, we have $D = E = 13.9$. Similarly, for $G = 20$ we have $D = E = 9.3$.

13. Given any level of deficit, the limiting value for β is that for which the entire budget can be deficit financed. Thus with a deficit of \$16 billion for instance, the limiting value for β may be found by substituting $E + 10 = 16$ in expression (24-3). We then obtain

$$6 = \frac{30 - 32\beta}{.75 + 1.4 - 2\beta} \text{ or } \beta = .855.$$

For smaller values of β and a deficit of \$16 billion, hoarding of deficit-financed funds would be required to avoid inflation.

The relationship between E and β for $D = 16$ is determined by

$$E = \frac{30 - 32\beta}{2.15 - 2\beta}$$

for values of $\beta \geq .855$.

14 In both cases, expression (24-2) reduces to

$$E = \frac{G}{7 + k\alpha}.$$

15. Given any level of β the limiting value for D is again where $E + 10 = D$. Assuming $\beta = .6$ and substituting in expression (24-2), we have

$$D - 10 = \frac{30 - 1.2D}{2.15 - 1.2},$$

or $D = 18.37$. For larger values of D and a β of .6, hoarding of deficit-financed funds would again be required to prevent inflation.

The relationship between E and D for $\beta = .6$ is determined by

$$E = \frac{30 - 1.2D}{.75 + 2(.7 - .6)}$$

or $E = 31.58 - 1.26D$ for values of $D \leq 18.37$.

16. Note, however, that in choosing our gap illustrations we have excluded the more or less *automatic* changes in private investment which accompany general changes in overall income. See, however, notes 9 and 10 above.

17. In an unpublished study on the Impact of the Personal Income Tax on Savings, I have estimated the impact of alternative income tax rate structures upon savings and consumption at a high and low level of yield. While the results of this study are based on rather inadequate information as far as the consumption impact for *any one* rate schedule is concerned, they do give some idea of the differential impact obtained under various rate schedules.

For a yield of \$16 billion at a national income of \$140 billion, the impact upon consumption is estimated at 43 per cent, assuming rates in effect in 1944, at 30 per cent assuming a maximum degree of progression and at 50 per cent

assuming a flat rate (however, with 1944 exemptions). For a higher yield level
the impact on consumption would be substantially higher. Assuming such
proportionate increase in the 1944 rates as is necessary to raise the yield to, say
$30 billion (which might correspond to $40 billion at the higher income level
here assumed), the ratio would be well above 50 per cent. If excises were relied
upon, the average ratio would, of course, be substantially higher.

18. The explanation is similar to the preceding case, see note 14 above.
19. For the case of the $20-billion budget and the large gap assumption, expression
(24.5) reduces to

$$D = \frac{10\beta + 4.25}{\beta} .$$

The minimum value below which β must not fall is reached where D is equal to E
+ 10 or 20; at this point β is equal to .425. If β is smaller, the required deficit
exceeds the level of expenditures, i.e., the scheduled increase in expenditures is
insufficient to provide the necessary leverage even though the entire budget is
deficit financed.

For the case of the $28-billion budget and the large gap assumption,
expression (24-5) reduces to

$$D = \frac{18\beta - 4.35}{\beta} .$$

The minimum level below which β must not fall is now reached where D is
equal to zero and hence β is equal to .24. If β is smaller, the formula indicates a
'negative deficit', i.e., tax-financed hoarding is required to forestall inflation.

20. This principle, of course, does not indicate whether the budget should be large
or small. It merely requires that long-run expenditure planning should be
considered primarily a matter of resource allocation rather than of employ-
ment-creation.

REFERENCES

[1] Hansen, A. (1941) *Fiscal Policy and Business Cycles* (New York: Norton).
[2] Hansen, A. and H. Perloff (1944) *State and Local Finance* (New York:
Norton).
[3] Kaldor, N. (1944) 'Quantitative Aspects of the Full Employment Problem in
Britain', Appendix C, in Beveridge, Sir W., *Full Employment in a Free Society*
(London: Allen & Unwin).
[4] Lerner, A. (1943) 'Functional Finance', *Social Research*, 10, 1.
[5] Pigou, A. (1929) *A Study in Public Finance* (London: Macmillan).
[6] Rawl, B. (1941) *National Fiscal Policy and the Two Super Budgets* (Charlottes-
ville: University of Virginia Press).
[7] Samuelson, P. (1942) 'Fiscal Policy and Income Determination', *Quarterly
Journal of Economics*, LXI, 4.
[8] Wallich, H. C. (1944) 'Income-Generating Effects of a Balanced Budget',
Quarterly Journal of Economics, LIX.

25 Built-in Flexibility*
1948

I

The essence of compensatory fiscal policy lies in adjusting the level of
government receipts and expenditures so as to stabilise total income (and
employment) in the economy. This requires an increase in expenditures
and a reduction in tax revenue during periods of deflation and a decrease in
expenditures and increase in tax revenue during periods of inflation. Such
compensatory movements may be brought about by properly-timed
changes in expenditure programmes and in tax rates, but to some extent
they occur automatically. Certain public expenditures, such as unemployment benefits, are geared to move in a counter-cyclical fashion. Similarly,
tax yields under given statutory rates will fluctuate with changes in the
national income since the size of the tax base usually varies directly with
the level of income. Recently, the automatically compensatory movement
of tax revenues—generally referred to as 'built-in flexibility'—has received
increasing attention. The purpose of this paper is to appraise its importance as a stabilisation device.

II

The magnitude of the automatically compensatory adjustment will depend
of course upon the dollar change in tax revenue resulting from a given
dollar change in the national income, that is, upon the 'marginal tax rate'
and the problem might be formulated in terms of this marginal rate.[1] There
is, however, a more detailed and for our purposes more useful way of
stating the problem. The fiscal planner, from year to year, is confronted
with setting an 'average tax rate', that is, a rate which will raise the desired
amount of tax revenue at the expected level of income. This total revenue

---

* With Merton M. Miller (1948) *American Economic Review*, vol. XXXVIII, 1.

can be raised by various combinations of statutory rates and tax sources, and different combinations will result in tax systems which possess different degrees of sensitivity of yield in response to changes in income. It is the selection of one of these combinations and of the rates necessary to produce the desired yield from the expected level of income that determines the extent of 'built-in flexibility' or the marginal tax rate for the system as a whole. Consequently, the degree of flexibility will be analysed here in terms of the level of taxation (average tax rate at the expected level of income) and the sensitivity to changes in income of the selected combinations of tax sources.

To measure the effect of built-in flexibility, it is useful to start with a simplified model which assumes that public expenditures are fixed and wholly for goods and services, that all taxes are in the form of a personal income tax, that there are no corporate savings in the economy, and that the level of investment is independent of taxation. The expression for the *change* in income between two periods may then be written as

$$\Delta Y = \Delta I + c\Delta Y - c(r_1 Y_1 - r_2 Y_2) \qquad (25\text{-}1)$$

where ΔY equals $Y_1 - Y_2$ or the change in income from the first to the second period and ΔI equals $I_1 - I_2$ or the change in investment; (c) is the marginal propensity to consume out of disposable income which is assumed to remain constant; and (r_1) and (r_2) are the average rates of tax in the two periods.

The income elasticity (E) of the tax yield (T) is the ratio of the percentage change in tax yield to a given percentage change in income and may be expressed as

$$E = \frac{(\Delta T) Y_1}{(\Delta Y) T_1} \qquad (25\text{-}2)$$

Solving for ΔT and substituting the result for $(r_1 Y_1 - r_2 Y_2)$ in equation (25-1) gives

$$\Delta Y = \Delta I \ \frac{1}{1 - c + cE \dfrac{T_1}{Y_1}} \qquad (25\text{-}3)$$

and by substituting (r_1) for $\left(\dfrac{T_1}{Y_1}\right)$ we obtain[2]

$$\Delta Y = \Delta I \frac{1}{1 - c(1 - Er_1)} \qquad (25\text{-}4)$$

As a convenient measure for the compensatory effectiveness of built-in flexibility we may then write

$$\alpha = 1 - \frac{\Delta Y}{\Delta Y_\alpha} \qquad (25\text{-}5)$$

where ΔY refers to the change in income in the particular tax system under discussion (with its specific positive value for Er_1) and ΔY_α refers to a system where (E) is set equal to zero. That is

$$\frac{\Delta Y}{\Delta Y_\alpha}$$

is the ratio of the decline (or increase) in income in the particular tax system under analysis to the decline (or increase) in income if the system had no built-in flexibility; and (α), which is 1 minus this ratio, is the *fraction of the change in income which is prevented because of the existence of built-in flexibility*. If $\alpha = 0$, there is no built-in flexibility; if $\alpha = 1$, built-in flexibility is perfect, i.e. total income remains unchanged.

Substituting (25-4) in (25-5) we have

$$\alpha = 1 - \frac{1 - c}{1 - c(1 - Er_1)} = \frac{cEr_1}{1 - c + cEr_1} \qquad (25\text{-}6)$$

Given the community's propensity to consume, (α) will thus vary directly with (r_1) and (E), the level of taxation and the income elasticity of the selected combination of tax sources. But built-in flexibility can never be so effective as to eliminate all change in income. However high the values for (E) and (r_1), (α) will be less than 1 in any economy whose propensity to consume is less than unity. As a practical matter, of course, (Er_1) could not exceed 1, that is a marginal tax rate of 100 per cent. At this extreme (α) would be equal to (c) and the investment multiplier would be fully offset (eq. [25-4]). The change in income before tax would be limited to the change in investment and income after tax would be stabilised.

In interpreting the concept (α) as here developed, it should be noted that (c) is not a variable in the same sense as (E) or (r_1). While the numerical value of (α) will increase as (c) increases, the absolute amount of the remaining change in income will also be larger (eq. [25-4]). Consequently (α) has relevance only for comparing the effect of different tax systems in a single economy, all of whose other basic relations (including the value of [c]) are held constant.

III

Turning now to a consideration of the magnitude of (α) for various tax structures under ordinary conditions, the assumptions in the simplified model must be revised to take account of transfer payments, excise taxes and most important, corporate savings and taxes.

The introduction of transfer payments presents no particular difficulties. They may be handled either by introducing into equation (25-1) a new term which expresses consumption out of transfer payments or they may be treated as 'negative taxes' reducing (r_1).[3] By extending the analysis in this fashion a new equation (25-4) may be derived which allows for 'built-in flexibility' on both the revenue and expenditure sides of the budget.

The introduction of excise taxes raises no serious difficulty if they can be thought of as paid out of consumer expenditures, that is, as personal income taxes assessed on an expenditure basis. This procedure permits a measurement of their contribution to the flexibility of the tax structure but it does not account for the complications arising from the fact that excise taxes are reflected in the price level of output. These complications, however, do not bear significantly upon the major argument here developed and can be neglected for simplicity's sake.

Corporate profits and corporate income taxes may be introduced with a minimum of complication by treating corporations as unincorporated businesses. Total income is then defined as personal income plus corporate profits before tax (but after dividends which are already included in personal income) and (c) becomes the marginal propensity to consume out of disposable personal income plus retained corporate profits. The values for (E) and (r_1) would apply to the tax system as a whole, and (α) would measure the effect of built-in flexibility on the entire private sector of the economy.[4]

Figure 25.1 shows the value of (α) for the United States under normal conditions at various levels of tax yield (r_1) and for various degrees of yield elasticity (E), using what may be considered a 'normal' value for (c) of 0.65.[5] In reading the figure, (E) should be interpreted as a weighted average of the elasticities of the separate tax sources and a change in (E), as a change in the composition of the tax yield. An increase in (E), for example, would represent an increase in the proportion of tax revenue derived from taxes based on the more volatile income shares (such as corporate profits) or from taxes with progressive rates (such as the personal income tax). A decrease in (E) would represent increased reliance on taxes whose bases are relatively insensitive (such as excises and estate duty) or a reduction in the degree of progressivity of the sensitive taxes. As a reference point, it may be noted that for the present federal tax system (r_1) is about .20 and (E) about 1.5.[6] The yield is composed of corporation taxes at 24 per cent, income taxes at 50 per cent and other taxes at 26 per cent.

The figure shows that for an (r_1) of .20 and an (E) of 1.5, (α) will be .358, that is, somewhat more than a third of the change in income due to a

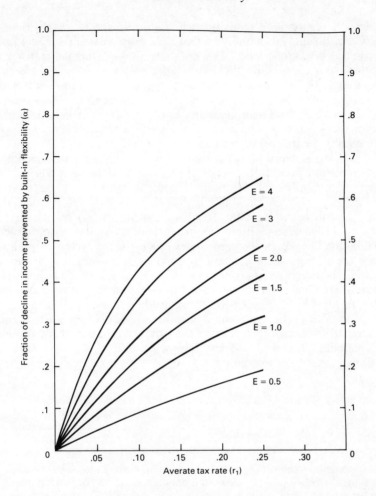

change in investment will be offset by built-in flexibility at that yield level. Should revenues be reduced uniformly by 50 per cent to an (r_1) of .10 without changing the composition of the yield, (α) will fall to .218. On the other hand, the effectiveness of built-in flexibility could be maintained at the lower level of yield by raising the average elasticity to 3.0.

IV

These preliminary considerations suggest that built-in flexibility may be an important factor in maintaining stability over the long run if taxes take a large proportion of income and if income-elastic taxes are relied upon. But the analysis here provided lends no justification to the view that built-in flexibility can do the job alone and that deliberate counter-cyclical fiscal policy can be dispensed with. The computations of the value for (α), despite their roughness, show that even under optimistic assumptions as to yield-flexibility, the automatic movement of tax yields can not offset the major portion of a decline in income and employment.[7] Moreover, it should be noted that built-in flexibility cuts two ways: If it is helpful in cushioning the downswing in a depression, it also serves to delay the return to a full employment level of income.

Actually there is every prospect that the value for (Er_1) will decline in the post-transition period. The level of (r_1) will be determined largely by average budget needs over the cycle. These will tend to decline as a per cent of income, although remaining higher than the pre-war average. It is unlikely that much can be done to offset the fall in (r_1) by raising (E) through qualitative changes in the tax structure or its composition. In fact it is probable that (E) will be lowered somewhat as the tax system is modified to reduce the impact on investment incentives.[8] The flexibility of the tax system might be increased if provision was made for automatic adjustments in tax *rates* with changes in income but this could hardly be called built-in flexibility in the usual sense of the term. Rather, it is a way of applying deliberate counter-cyclical adjustments in the rate of taxation and expenditures. Such adjustments must remain the primary reliance of fiscal policy when it appears (as it most certainly will) that the actual level of fluctuations passes tolerable limits.

NOTES

1. For a statement of the problem in terms of the marginal rate see note 2.
2. Expressing the relationship in terms of the marginal tax rate or (m) equation (1) is rewritten as

$$\Delta Y = \Delta I + c\Delta Y - cm\Delta Y \tag{25-1a}$$

and solving for Y,

$$\Delta Y = \Delta I \frac{1}{1 - c(1 - m)}$$

which of course is the same as (4) above because

$$(E) = \frac{m}{r_1}. \tag{25-1b}$$

3. For the simplest case where transfer expenditures are assumed constant, the decline in (r_1) would be offset by an increase in the value for (E) leaving (Er_1), the marginal tax rate, unaffected.

4. The redefinition of (c) as the propensity to consume out of disposable income plus retained corporate profits has the disadvantage of making (c) more subject to changes in (Y) and more dependent upon the particular tax structure in use. Thus (c) will be lower if the corporation tax is lower and changes in the corporation tax share in total receipts will affect the value of (c). To a lesser extent, the same problem arises with respect to differences in the consumption impact of, say, highly progressive income taxes and highly regressive spending taxes. For a fuller discussion of the implications of the differences in the consumption impact of various taxes see [1, p. 387].

5. This value of (c) was obtained by correlating total net private saving with disposable income plus corporate saving for the period 1929–41. This 13-year period was found to be divided into three distinct sub-periods 1930–32 ($[c]$ = .74); 1933–36 ($[c]$ = .63); and 1937–41 ($[c]$ = .54), giving .65 as an average. All data used were from the *Commerce* series.

   At the present time, the value for (c) is, of course, very much higher and for consumption out of disposable income is probably greater than 1. Under such abnormal conditions (α) becomes much higher than the numerical values shown in the figure even for relatively inelastic tax system. The same tendency would result if an acceleration factor is allowed for. However, as has been indicated above, (α) should not be compared for different values of (c). In view of the abnormality and instability of present (c) values, the discussion of built-in flexibility is confined to some more normal post-transition period.

   Attention is also called to the fact, not here allowed for, that (c) will differ with the rate and amplitude of income fluctuations. Instead of working with a fixed value of (c) a more elaborate analysis could be made in terms of consumption functions showing cyclical variations or time-lags in adjustments.

6. In 1946, personal income averaged $177.2 billion and corporate profits (before inventory adjustment.) $21.1 billion. For 1947, the corresponding figures based on data for the first half-year were $197.2 billion and $29.0 billion. Federal personal income tax *liabilities* for 1946 at current tax rates and size of labour force may be put at $17.8 billion (after adjustment for changes in the composition of income payments since 1946, mainly the decline in tax-exempt military pay and certain transfer payments). At the personal income level of $197.2 billion assumed for 1947, income tax liabilities would be very close to $21.5 billion. Federal corporation income taxes under the levels of profits assumed for the two years would be $7.3 billion and $10.4 billion, respectively. Other federal taxes (consisting of estate and gift taxes, excises and social security taxes) would increase from $10.7 billion to $11.2 billion. The total change in tax revenue is therefore estimated at $7.7 billion from $35.4 billion to $43.1 billion.

   For measuring (E), 'total income' should be defined as personal income plus corporate profits before tax (but after dividends which are already included in personal income) giving $220 billion for 1947 and $192.7 billion for 1946. On this basis, (E) for the present federal tax system works out to be 1.46. It may be noted that this estimate for (E) would not be too greatly affected by moderate errors in estimates of the level of tax yields under the assumed income conditions. An underestimate by as large an amount as $2 billion (which is rather unlikely) would raise (E) to about 1.8.

7. Changing levels of unemployment benefit are the major item of flexibility on the expenditure side of the budget. If these are taken into account and using present rates of benefit payments, the value for (d) might be raised by from 5 to 10 points. The results would thus not be changed greatly.
8. Much will depend upon what happens to the corporation tax rate and the share of the corporate tax in total receipts. Reduction of the corporate share in taxes will reduce (E) but reduction in the corporate rate applicable to dividends only would reduce (E) less than an equivalent reduction in the present uniform rate on profits because of the greater stability of dividends in comparison with total profits.

The value for (E) will also be decreased if weight is shifted from the personal income tax to estate duty and if present exemption levels are maintained while upper surtax bracket rates are reduced faster than lower bracket rates. In the other direction, decreased reliance on excises would tend to raise (E) somewhat. To the extent that the various adjustments described are successful in raising the average level of investment and hence income over the cycle, this will tend to compensate for decreased flexibility as well as lessen the need for deliberate countercyclical adjustment.

REFERENCES

[1] Musgrave, R. A. (1945) 'Alternative Budgets for Full Employment', *American Economic Review*, XXXV, 3.

26 Fiscal Policy in Prosperity and Depression* 1948

The objectives of public revenue and expenditure policies go beyond their traditional service and redistribution functions. Budget policy, also, is vitally important as a positive instrument of economic control. It is this latter function which is usually referred to as fiscal policy and with which this discussion is concerned.

After fifteen years of debate, the principles of fiscal policy are well established. The argument in its barest outline is: (1) that high employment and price level stability require aggregate expenditures just sufficient to take the high employment output, valued in current prices, off the market; (2) that this condition is not met automatically in our economy where private demand is subject to violent swings and where severe deflation or inflation may prevail for sustained periods; and (3) that compensatory budget policy offers one device, among others, for holding total expenditures fairly close to the proper level. By providing incentives for private outlays or adding more to the income stream on the expenditure side of the budget than is being withdrawn on the revenue side, deflation may be counteracted; by deterring private outlays or withdrawing more than is being added, inflation may be curbed. While born and reared in an environment of deflation and unemployment, the principles of fiscal policy apply no less to the boom and war economy.

These propositions may be qualified or stated in different terms, but most would accept their essential logic. Our time will be spent more profitably, therefore, if we proceed at once to certain issues of implementation which are more controversial.

I

Adjusting the size of deficit or surplus is the core of compensatory finance. If there is a need for checking inflation, the deficit should be reduced or the

---

* *American Economic Review* (1948) Proceedings, vol. XXXVIII, 2.

surplus be raised; if there is a need for checking deflation, the surplus should be reduced or the deficit be increased. While some tax revenues may be less deflationary than some loan receipts, this is not the usual case and we shall be safe to assume that changes in surplus and deficit will be reflected directly in a change of disposable income and private demand.

Whether the question is one of moving in the direction of greater surplus or deficit, the required compensatory effect may be accomplished by acting upon the level of public expenditures or the level of tax rates. During the depression of the 1930s when the early discussions of compensatory policy occurred, compensatory action was visualised largely in the form of deficit spending, implying the need for an absolute increase in the expenditure budget. By now it is recognised that anti-deflation measures may also take the form of tax reduction.[1] Similarly, inflation may be met either by lowering expenditures or raising tax rates.

This is not to say that the choice between the two approaches is a matter of indifference. The leverage effect per dollar of deficit (or the negative leverage per dollar of surplus) will differ with the technique used. If the deficit dollar reflects an increase in public expenditures on goods and services, the leverage will be greater than if it reflects transfer expenditures or tax reduction, unless the beneficiary's marginal propensity to consume is unity, which is unlikely. Under conditions of inflation, similarly, reduction in public expenditures will be more effective per dollar of surplus than increase in tax rates. Also, there may be substantial differences between the two approaches arising from political and other factors.[2] At times, these may be decisive. Under conditions of acute depression, for instance, relieving immediate distress is more important than providing for general income leverage, and until these immediate objectives are met, relief or public works outlays are preferable to tax reduction. Under conditions of wartime inflation, reduction in public expenditures, even though more helpful as an anti-inflation device, may not be feasible, so that reliance has to be placed upon tax adjustments. But granting these differences between the two approaches, it is more important for our purposes to note that the compensatory objective *can* be operated in either way.[3] The distance between Chicago and Cambridge is less than appears at first sight.

The two-dimensional character of the compensatory mechanism is important, because it permits us to dissolve a latent conflict between considerations of compensatory finance and considerations of optimum allocation of resources. Consider briefly a model of rational compensatory policy. Public expenditures in such a model would be planned on the basis of their usefulness relative to that of alternative (public or private) outlays. This allocation planning would be done on the assumption that resources are fully employed and tax rates would then be adjusted so as to provide such deficit or surplus as is needed to maintain high employment and prevent inflation. The distribution of the tax burden and of transfer expenditures would be eliminated by the community's preferences regarding the distribution of incomes. It is evident that there would be no make-work projects of any kind in such a system. Depending upon the availability of flexible projects, there would be, however, cyclical adaptation of expenditures within the basic blueprint of the longer run programme.

Actual policy, of course, will not fully comply with the rules of our model. Difficulties of prediction and delays of adjustment will render cyclical adaptations imperfect. Conditions may arise, for instance, where the planning of public expenditures cannot be conducted realistically on the basis of our full-employment assumption since the opportunity cost of public utilisation of resources may be merely unemployment.[4] But granting these imperfections, our model remains useful in demonstrating that there is no conflict as an inherent matter of economic principle between the objectives of compensatory finance and the objectives of optimum allocation of resources.

Given a fairly high level of tax rates, moreover, there is no necessary link between the idea of compensatory policy and a 'large' or 'small' budget philosophy. If we wish to check inflation without reducing public expenditures, we may usually do so by raising tax rates. If we wish to check deflation without raising public expenditures, we may do so by lowering tax rates. With a $30 or $40-billion budget, the scope for tax reduction is likely to be quite adequate. Our preferences regarding the desirable level of public expenditures, therefore, should not be permitted to dominate our attitudes towards the use of compensatory policy.

Compensatory policy requires changes in the level of public expenditures and tax yields which will meet the needs of the economic situation. In part such movements result automatically through the mechanism of built-in flexibility, but largely they require deliberate action.

The mechanism of built-in flexibility is this: If national income changes, the tax base and hence the yield derived from a given set of rates varies in the same direction. Moreover, there are certain public expenditure items, unemployment insurance in particular, which vary inversely with income. As a result, automatic and compensatory changes in surplus and deficit occur whenever income changes and thereby fluctuations in income are cushioned. To the extent that such reactions do occur and that the initial fluctuation is from a high employment level, they are to the good.[5] But what are the magnitudes involved?

The ratio of tax yield to national income, which is a first determinant of built-in flexibility, is considerably higher now than it was before the [second world] war. Yet it is still relatively small and will decline in future years. The income elasticity of the average tax dollar, which is a second determinant, now stands at about 1.5. It has been raised somewhat above the pre-war level by increased reliance on progressive taxation and the corporation tax, but it cannot be raised very much further; prospective tax reforms, on the contrary, are likely to work in the opposite direction. The income elasticity of the average expenditure dollar, finally, may now be lower than in the 1930s. On the whole, built-in flexibility is more important in the current setting [1948] than it was before the war, but its importance should not be overrated.

The automatic increase in budget surplus during current months is being helpful in meeting the inflation problem, especially with regard to credit control, and its shrinkage will be of help later when a depression sets in. Yet the automatic increase has been wholly insufficient to cope with the present problem of inflation, and it will also be insufficient to cope with a later problem of deflation. Using such assumptions as seem reasonable for a post-inflation year, we estimate that built-in flexibility may be expected to dampen the amplitude of fluctuations by perhaps one-third of what they would have been in its absence.[6] Unless potential fluctuations in income will be so small in the future that they may be permitted largely to run their course—and there is no reason whatsoever to assume that this will be the case—the major compensatory contribution will still have to come from deliberate budget adjustments. In view of this, the principle of all but exclusive reliance on built-in flexibility, such as advocated in the Committee for Economic Development Report [1] on fiscal policy, is quite unacceptable. If adopted it will lead to mentally and technically inadequate preparation for deliberate action.[7]

On the contrary, it is all-important that we provide for a mechanism by which changes in expenditure levels or tax rates may be put into effect promptly and with a minimum of friction. On the expenditure side we are confronted with the familiar problem of the public-work reserve and this is largely a matter of adequate appropriations and planning. On the tax side, the cumbersomeness of the legislative process looms as a more severe obstacle. One compromise approach might be through legislative provision for automatic changes in tax rates (and perhaps expenditure programmes), such changes to be geared to fluctuations in an official index of income or employment. While built-in rate flexibility retains the disadvantage of being too mechanical—the same initial fluctuation in income or employment may under different conditions require quite different degrees of compensatory action—built-in *rate* flexibility might be of great quantitative importance and permit prompt adjustments without requiring Congressional delegation of authority to vary tax rates.

We need not labour the point that our case for compensatory finance is no case against the use of other policies. Adjustments in budget surplus and deficit can impose effective checks to inflation or deflation where the excess or deficiency in aggregate demand extends broadly throughout the economic system, and the crucial importance of compensatory policy derives from the fact that the state of the economy is frequently one where such conditions exist. However, this is not the entire problem. The general deficiency or excess in demand may be caused (and is usually accentuated) by specific maladjustments which will continue to grow after the difficulty has become general and which will require specific remedies.[8]

While it is likely that expansionary fiscal policy, if sufficiently vigorous and sustained, can prevent a period of severe and prolonged unemployment, there is less reason to be optimistic about the efficacy of compensatory action to check inflation. The politics of fiscal policy undoubtedly are less favourable to proper action under conditions of inflation when the problem is one of curtailing money income than under conditions of deflation when the problem is one of supplementing incomes.

Limitations more specifically applicable to the fiscal approach arise from the dynamics of the inflation process which makes supplementary action along other lines (including credit and wage-profit controls) more urgent than in the deflation case. However, the lesser effectiveness in checking inflation also reflects more inherent difficulties in the fiscal approach to which our discussion will presently return.

II

But first let us turn to some issues of revenue and expenditure structure.

While the requirements of cycle policy are bound to be reflected in the expenditure pattern, expenditures should be based primarily upon considerations of need and usefulness of the projects as such.[9] Differences in the leverage effects of various expenditure projects exist, but they should not be overemphasised. Where relief expenditures are a more effective way to relieve distress in the depression, they should be preferred to public work outlays, even though a somewhat smaller leverage might result. Where public works are needed or are preferred as a matter of public morale, they should be given preference over relief even though they might involve a somewhat higher outlay per unemployed. At the same time, expenditure planning must account for the longer run as well as the more immediate merits of alternative expenditure projects. Thus developmental programmes will not only be useful in an immediate sense but have an important bearing upon the secular level of private investment and the growth of real income.

Passing over a more detailed analysis of expenditure policies, let us turn to some questions of tax structure. Again we refer back to our model of rational budget policy where the level of expenditure, the expenditure pattern, the level of tax yield (rates), and the kind of taxes used are all interdependent parts of the same planning process. Keeping this in mind, it will be permissible for purposes of the present argument to separate out the problem of tax structure. This involves considerations of equity in income distribution and of the economic effects of alternative taxes upon income and employment. While considerations of equity are an important datum for the economist, they are primarily a matter of social philosophy. But what can the economist say about the requirements of a tax structure which is 'good' in the sense of contributing most to the maintenance of high employment and price level stability?

Immediate needs to the contrary, it will be convenient to begin with the case of deflation. Under conditions of deflation, there is little difficulty in establishing the rule that the economy will be the better-off with any given level of tax yield, the less the average tax dollar depresses private expenditures on consumption and investment.

While the principle is simple, its application is difficult. With the use of the conventional-type tax instrument at least, the deflationary pressure of the average tax dollar cannot be reduced greatly below its present level. Partly this is due to the fact that revenue changes which relieve tax pressure on consumption also tend to increase tax pressure on investment, and partly it is the case because there are inherent limitations to possible reductions in the consumption pressure of the average tax dollar. These points will be taken up briefly.

First, with regard to consumption. We have attempted to calculate changes in the consumption impact of the tax system which would result if one were to switch between various revenue structures all of which provide the same yield [8]. These calculations—the validity of which hinges largely upon the evidence of available saving patterns by income groups—suggest that the gain in terms of released consumption which might be obtained by increasing progression is limited. The reason, of course, is to be found in the relative constancy of the *marginal* propensity to save over the income range and the fact that notwithstanding a highly unequal income distribution, the bulk of income is received in the lower and middle groups. Also, a considerable degree of progression does already exist in the federal tax structure. If comparison was made at a $30-billion yield level between the types of tax structure advocated on both extremes of the current range of tax proposals, I should doubt very much whether the level of consumption (at high employment income) under the most progressive proposals would exceed that under the least progressive plans by more than, say, $2 or $3 billion. Measured from the present in-between position, the change would be correspondingly less. Thus it does not seem likely that the consumption effects of increased progression could go very far in offsetting a serious decline in private investment or downward shift in the consumption schedule.[10] This is not to say that a more powerful effect might not be achieved through the taxation of saving or hoarding as such, but proposals of this kind which involve considerable technical difficulty cannot be considered here.

Increased progression, moreover, may result in a reduced level of private investment which would provide an offset to initial gains in consumption. Depressing effects upon investment may result (1) because the supply of available investment funds is reduced; and (2) because the willingness to invest available balances may fall off. With regard to the first possibility, a distinction must of course be drawn between the level of saving in general and the supply of particular kinds of savings. As long as the difficulty is one of an excess of intended saving, it does not make sense to talk about a shortage of savings in general. Yet a reduction in the level of savings may be reflected in the pattern of available savings, with the result that some type of investment is checked. Evaluation of this possibility is difficult, because relatively little is known about the qualitative composition of savings by income groups.

The extent to which increased progression may affect the willingness to risk the investment of available funds, depends greatly upon the way in which the tax base is defined. Provisions made for the offset of losses are of particular importance. Where losses can be offset against other taxable income the investor will save in taxes, if losses are incurred, what he must pay in taxes if gains are made. The return on risk-taking (defined as the ratio between the probable gain and loss net of taxes) will not be reduced by the tax [2,4]. But the complete assurance of perfect loss offset does not exist, except perhaps in the case of very large corporations or wealthy individuals, and could not be given short of a refund scheme which would provide for negative taxes (bounties) in the case of losses. Apart from improvements in the definition of net income, a shift in the emphasis from progression through income taxation to progression through estate taxation might help. Estate taxation not only provides an automatic loss offset (if a loss is made the estate is reduced) but it is also more removed from the immediate profit motivations of the investor. Beyond this the investment effects of the tax structure should be improved by eliminating bounties currently granted to certain relatively riskless investments; i.e. tax-exempt securities.

However, even though improvements of this kind are made, it is unlikely that they will wholly eliminate the effects of steep progression (and the inevitable result of high marginal rates) upon investment and, in a broader sense, upon entrepreneurial effort. The conclusion remains that there is an unhappy conflict between the least-pressure principle as applied to consumption and the least-pressure principle as applied to investment. The higher the level of tax yield the more painful does this conflict become.

But it must be asked, is this something to worry about? If conditions are deflationary and tax pressures on consumption and investment are too heavy, may we not simply reduce the level of tax yield until a proper balance is restored? Is it not the very purpose of tax finance to reduce disposable income to the extent to which this is necessary to avoid inflation, but not more? And if this is the case, why should a situation be permitted to arise in which the deflationary burden of taxation becomes excessive? There is a good deal of sense to Lerner's point.

A minor qualification arises because loan finance carries with it the by-product of public debt. Without suggesting that this is an alarming matter, we may assume that it is preferable when possible to accomplish compensatory action with a minimum of debt increase. It will be worth our while to lower the deflationary pressure of the average tax dollar, since this will raise the permissible level of tax yield and reduce the need for debt increase. The least pressure principle, therefore, remains valid even though the possibility of yield reduction is accepted. However, the possibility of yield reduction in the depression reduces the seriousness of our finding that there is only limited scope for lowering the deflationary pressure of the average tax dollar.

Let us now turn to the case of inflation. As a proposition in fiscal theory, it has been suggested that the tax pressure upon consumption and investment might be held to a minimum even under conditions of inflation. This will permit a higher level of tax yield and budget surplus, and hence debt retirement at a higher rate. This argument, though ingenious, is quite unrealistic. As the required level of tax rates cannot be counted upon, we shall be better off if we reverse our deflation rule and argue that, under conditions of inflation, the average tax dollar should depress private demand as heavily as possible.

If this condition is met, inflation can be checked with a lower level of tax rates. This is preferable politically and may also be preferable as a matter of economic policy. To develop this point, it will be helpful to distinguish between tax pressures on the level of private expenditures and pressures upon incentives to work and to produce, including managerial incentives. Whether pressure on investment incentives should be grouped with expenditure pressures or production pressures depends on the circumstances of the case and on the nature of the investment. The more short-lived the boom is expected to be and the more distant the output effect of the particular investment, the more clearly do pressures on investment incentives come under the heading of expenditure pressures.

Suppose now that we have a situation of heavy inflation, where the community's propensity to spend (on consumption plus investment) is well in excess of unity. In order to check inflation by taxation—and assuming the inflation pressure to be sufficiently severe—it might then be necessary to tax at an exorbitantly high rate, taking up, say, 50 or 75 per cent of total income. At some point the required rate of taxation will become so high as to interfere seriously with production incentives. As a result, real output will fall. This is undesirable, quite apart from the fact that it will tend to accentuate inflation. We are then confronted with a situation with which the fiscal mechanism cannot cope. The argument that tax rates might be lowered to reduce incentive pressures is not helpful, as this can only be done at the cost of raising the inflation pressure of money expenditures. A true impasse exists.

To some extent the impasse might be met by relying on taxes which will bear most heavily upon the level of expenditures while bearing least heavily upon work incentives. A tax imposed on pure economic rents or on a base unrelated to current earnings—such as a poll tax—might serve the purpose, but if a very high rate of taxation is required, such techniques are hardly feasible. Where excessive demand is a function of an excessive level of asset holdings, a capital levy may be better than a continued rate of very high income taxation. Moreover, the levy will be more equitable than an alternative impairment of the real value of money claims through price rise. In other instances, an expenditure tax or compulsory savings might help. But none of these devices will be so successful as to cancel the basic proposition that given a sufficiently high degree of inflation pressure, the tax check to inflation will break down.

All this, of course, is a matter of degree. While the problem of production pressure is potentially existent at even a low level of taxation, it does not become severe until a quite high level of rates is reached. Until then, increased rates will do more good in terms of reducing expenditure pressures than harm in terms of deterring work and production effort.

Conditions at the close of 1947 were of this kind. Current, or even somewhat higher tax rates, are hardly a deterrent to work, as far as the mass of workers is concerned. As far as pressures on investment go, the nature of the present [1947/8] boom appears to be such that a temporary abatement in the demand for investment goods is no less desirable than an abatement in the demand for consumer goods. Pressures on investment are thus largely to be classified as desirable expenditure pressures. On the whole we should have been better off if post-war tax reduction had been avoided and in particular if the excess profits tax (and with it the prerequisite for a more vigorous price wage policy) had been retained.

Before proceeding, another aspect of the possible conflict between production and expenditure pressures should be noted. In our previous illustration government expenditures were assumed not to figure as an active element in the inflation picture, but the same situation may arise as the result of a high level of public outlay. If these outlays, whether for goods and services or for transfer expenditures, are assumed to be sufficiently high (relative to productive capacity, the propensity to consume, and the level of private investment), the same dilemma will arise. Again the level of taxation required to check inflation becomes such as to check production incentives.

During the war, when we were confronted with just this problem, the solution was found in a moderate level of taxation, combined with direct price and rationing controls. The fiscal mechanism had to give way to other approaches.[11] The concern of traditional public finance writers—that public expenditures may become too high relative to national income to be sustained in an uncontrolled market economy—is thus not eliminated by the mechanism of compensatory finance. Adjustments of tax policy cannot offset the basic fact that an inordinately large fraction of total income may become unavailable as a market reward for production effort.

What do these considerations suggest regarding our plans for federal tax reform? Interestingly enough, most proposals advanced during recent years have aimed at a tax structure best suited to meet the requirements of deflation. But it now appears that we cannot be certain in assessing the future in these terms.

This leaves the tax planner somewhat in a dilemma, since the requirements for a good tax structure will be different under conditions of inflation and deflation. Both are similar in aiming at a minimum of pressure on work incentives, but are dissimilar with regard to consumption pressures and, in the short run, with regard to pressures on investment. It is hardly possible to look ahead and to predict which approach will be called for; yet the basic tax structure is rather rigid and cannot be changed frequently. It will thus be necessary to make the best of a difficult situation.

One requirement for the basic tax structure is that it should lay a foundation which will facilitate adjustment to more acute inflation or deflation situations without necessitating the introduction of new taxes or basic structural changes. The basic tax structure, accordingly, should retain a broad personal income tax base even though it may be desirable at times to hold rates in the bottom brackets to nominal levels. Also, it should continue to include a fully fledged corporation tax and an improved system of capital gains taxation. Given such a framework, changes in emphasis between different types of revenue sources may be accomplished by selective rate adjustments within the basic revenue structure.

The problems discussed in this paper have dealt with the current effectiveness of compensatory finance and tax policy in dealing with economic disturbances. Limitations of space have not permitted us to consider possible after-effects of such policies as may result in the form of increased public debt or money supply.

While it is evident that the vast increase in debt and credit during the war years has created serious problems, especially in curtailing the manœuvrability of monetary controls, this has been a wartime phenomenon. Indeed, it would have required some 75 years of deficit finance at the rate of the 1930s to match this increase. As far as the use of compensatory finance under future conditions of inflation is concerned, it will tend to remedy rather than aggravate the situation created in the course of war finance. As far as compensatory finance in a future depression goes, it is altogether unlikely that it would result in a drastic increase in the debt to national income ratio, and it is, of course, this ratio that counts. Examination of the problem of after-effects would not have greatly modified our previous conclusion that a vigorous use of fiscal policies is called for [7].

NOTES

1. As a matter of theoretical interest it should be noted that expansionary action may be obtained also by an equal increase in tax yields and expenditures, and contractive action by an equal reduction of both sides of the budget. A compensatory policy could thus be operated with a balanced budget. However, this proposition is of little practical interest. See my discussion of alternative approaches to budget policy [6].
2. Considerations pertaining to the politics of fiscal policy are emphasised in CED [1].
3. It is assumed that the initial level of taxation is sufficiently high enough in the depression case so that the problem can be met within the available scope of tax reduction to a zero level. While this was not the case in the 1930s, it is a realistic assumption for, say, the 1950s. This is one of the advantages of a large budget.
4. No precise definition of 'full' or 'high' employment need be given in this context. The argument is much the same, though the policy job is simpler, if the definition is in terms of 2.5 rather than 1 million unemployed.
5. If the economy is in a situation of unemployment, built-in flexibility will check recovery. Note that the built-in *rate* flexibility suggested below may be adjusted so as to escape this shortcoming.
6. For a discussion of this point see Musgrave and Miller [5].

7. The CED [1] principle, of course, is preferable to a rigid policy of 'balance the budget all the time' and in political terms might be a good compromise formula. However, this does not make it good economics.

A further difficulty with the automatic budget policy arises in determining the initial level of tax rates which is to be left alone thereafter. The proposed formula 'to set taxes so as to balance the budget at full employment' sounds attractive and may have some merit as a rule-of-thumb device, but it does not offer a satisfactory solution. The formula is satisfactory only if it can be assumed that in the average year a balanced budget is compatible with full employment. This assumption cannot be made and, accordingly, it is necessary to predict the economic outlook in order to determine the proper level of initial rate adjustment. Such prediction, of course, is most difficult if not impossible. Again, reliance will have to be placed upon periodic adjustment of rates.

8. Such specific controls may also involve fiscal action, as for example in the case of subsidy policies during depression or capital gains taxation in the boom.

9. Note that the scale of need for various projects will itself change with economic conditions.

10. As distinct from the optimistic view of earlier writers such as Hobson, this view now seems to be accepted by Keynesian theorists. See, for instance, Klein's [3, p. 59] extreme statement that 'a redistribution of income will leave total consumption approximately unaffected'.

More significant perhaps than the distribution of taxes paid by individuals is the extent to which the tax yield is derived from corporation savings, but even here there are obvious limitations if the yield total is large.

11. The vast changes in production structure required in the war economy further increased the need for direct controls.

REFERENCES

[1] Committee for Economic Development (1947) *Taxes and the Budget: A Program for Prosperity in a Free Society* (New York: CED).
[2] Domar, E. and Musgrave, R. A. (1944) 'Proportional Income Taxation and Risk-taking', *Quarterly Journal of Economics*, 58.
[3] Klein, L. (1947) *The Keynesian Revolution* (New York: Macmillan).
[4] Lerner, A. P. (1944) *Economics of Control* (New York: Macmillan).
[5] Musgrave, R. A. and Miller, M. (1948) 'Built-in Budget Flexibility', *American Economic Review*, XXXVIII, 1.
[6] Musgrave, R. A. (1945) 'Alternative Budgets for Full Employment', *American Economic Review*, 35.
[7] ___ (1948) 'Credit Control, Interest Rates, and Management of Public Debt', in *Income, Employment, and Public Policy, Essays in Honor of Alvin Hansen* (New York: Norton).
[8] Musgrave, R. A. and Painter, M. (1948) 'Importance of Alternative Tax Structures on Consumption and Saving', *Quarterly Journal of Economics, 62*.

27 Should We Have a Capital Budget?*
1963

Everyone is agreed that the economic effects of fiscal policy can be measured only by a *comprehensive* budget picture. This is not furnished by the administrative budget, but is provided by either the cash or national income base budget. As between these two, I find no clear preference, each being useful in its own way. A more potent issue is whether budget policy can be improved by the use of a capital budget. My comments will be limited to this aspect.

To begin with, one must distinguish between (a) proposals to separate current from capital items on the expenditure side of the budget, including expenditure budgeting for a longer period and appropriate accounting for capital items, but without assigning specific receipts to the current and capital parts, thus retaining the concept of a single, overall balance; and (b) proposals to assign specific types of receipts to specific types of expenditures, and to redefine the relevant concept of balance as that on current account.

The type of proposal involved under (a) is not controversial and deserves fullest support. There is an excellent case for budgeting capital expenditures over longer than a one-year basis and for improving allowance for capital costs (depreciation and interest) in evaluating the merit of particular programmes. Also, it is relevant to know, from the point of view of fiscal prudence, whether budget policy has increased or reduced the public capital stock. Our concern here will not be with these suggestions, but with the more controversial proposals of the (b) type.

Redefinition of budgetary balance as balance between tax receipts and current expenditures is highly tempting politically, since it would result in a more 'favourable' budget picture and, in a situation where fiscal policy is too tight, have a beneficial announcement effect. But would it make economic sense, and would it contribute to a more constructive budget discussion over the longer run?

Popular argument in favour of such proposals frequently draws a mistaken analogy between the corporation and government. As 'every

---

* *Review of Economics and Statistics* (1963) vol. 45, 21.

farmer in Maine' knows, no one can live on debt forever; but as 'every businessman' knows, business finance justifies borrowing, provided such debt is backed by acquisition of assets. If so, why not apply the same principle to government and offset debt by assets acquired, thus defining deficit as an increase in debt in excess of increase in assets, or putting it another way, a reduction in the government's 'net worth'? While possibly useful in making deficit finance politically palatable, this argument involves a complete misreading of the nature of fiscal economics. Government solvency is not a matter of assets held, but of taxable capacity; the reason for incurring debt is not to purchase assets, but to expand income relative to tax finance, and so on. While there is a case for separating out debt incurred in the finance of strictly self-liquidating public enterprises, that is, debt which does not require servicing from general tax receipts, this is where the analogy to business ends. Clearly, it cannot be extended to the larger problem of acquisition of non-fee-yielding assets in general.

There is, however, a more sophisticated and valid view of the capital budget approach. This is based on the idea of temporal or inter-generation equity: if the government incurs outlays, the benefits from which are spread over a future period, it is unfair to ask the initial generation to sustain the whole cost. Rather, 'prudence' requires that finance be based on a pay as you use basis, each generation contributing a cost share commensurate with its own share in the benefit stream. The proposition, then, is that tax finance of such outlays is unfair because it places the entire burden on the initial generation, while debt finance (with retirement as the asset is used and the benefits are received) results in an inter-generation distribution of cost which is in line with the corresponding benefit distribution.[1]

This argument bears a superficial resemblance to the net worth approach, but differs basically in that it deals with all outlays which provide for future benefits, and not only with those which involve acquisition of assets by government. Thus, teachers' salaries as well as school buildings are included, and the bias against investment in human resources and other forms of intangible capital formation is avoided.

We then come to the major question. Is it true that debt finance (with debt retirement synchronised with the benefit stream) actually serves to achieve the desired objective of pay as you use? This question cannot be answered in general, but depends on the kind of economy in which the budget operates.

Case 1

Suppose first that we have a system in which planned investment equals planned saving and full employment is maintained automatically. In this setting, no stabilisation policy is needed. When a government purchase is made, the economy must at once release from private employment the required resources, and private outlays must be cut accordingly. This can be done interchangably by either tax or loan finance since, in such a system, $1 of borrowing from the public will reduce private spending by $1, just as does a dollar of tax receipt. But if the outlay is loan-financed, the lenders are given a claim to being refunded later, when subsequent beneficiaries are taxed to retire the debt. In this fashion, the burden (in the sense of reduction in the private net worth of particular individuals) may be allocated properly over time for any one consumer, or between overlapping generations.

It may be noted also that substitution of loan for tax finance is likely to reduce private capital formation: depending on the elasticities involved, the increase in the demand for saving (due to increased public demand) under loan finance will drive up the rate of interest. This may raise the total supply of saving somewhat, but chances are that there will be a net increase in the rate of interest and reduction in the level of private investment. But though a reduction in private investment is likely to result, this is incidental to implementing the pay as you use rule among overlapping generations, and not its essence. The mechanism of cost allocation among overlapping generations also works in an economy where there is no private net capital formation. Only if the benefits are shared by non-overlapping generations, does the effect on private capital formation become crucial. In this case, a burden transfer to future generations may result if loan finance retards capital formation, thus reducing the to-be-inherited capital stock.

Case 2

Consider now a quite different system, where the supply of saving has no effect on the level of investment, be it because the rate of interest is stuck in the liquidity trap, because investment is wholly inelastic, or for a number of other reasons. Here fiscal policy has the function of providing for a full-employment level of demand. A tax dollar now reduces private spending, but a borrowing dollar does not. The level of deficit, required for any given level of public purchases (it being a matter of indifference in this connection whether they are for capital or current uses) is fixed by considerations of full employment policy. The same instrument (size of deficit), therefore, cannot be used for a second purpose, that is, the accommodation of inter-generation equity. If the latter is given priority, the level of employment (or price level stability) becomes a function of public capital outlays. Unemployment or inflation are likely to result, and neither the objective of stability nor of inter-generation equity is met.

It might be argued that the basic trouble (only one instrument for two objectives) may be met by introducing another instrument, for example, change in the level or composition of public expenditures, or greater reliance on monetary policy. Adjustment in expenditure policy (overall level as well as division between capital and current outlays) offers no solution since efficiency in expenditure planning would be sacrificed in the process. With regard to monetary policy, the basic question is how well the instrument works. In a system where monetary policy is always effective in securing a full-employment level of demand, we have essentially our first case. The deficit may be set on inter-generation equity grounds, and the residual stabilisation task be met by monetary policy. But in a system where monetary policy is not all-powerful, this solution is not available.

The case thus turns on the question of whether the burden for full-employment policy can be left with monetary policy, or whether fiscal policy is needed as well. The answer, to my mind, is clearly that fiscal policy is needed. Hence, I conclude that the dual budget is justified and desirable on the state and local level, where there is no responsibility for stabilisation policy and debt finance frequently involves capital import; but that it is undesirable at the federal level, where the use of fiscal policy for stabilisation is of crucial importance.[2] Given the popular folklore on what constitutes sound finance, it could be, of course, that a strategy of counter-confusion by appeal to the business analogy could improve the actual performance of fiscal policy (permit a larger deficit when needed) if a capital budget were used, but I would rather not bet on such an approach to public policy.

Notwithstanding these conclusions, the rate of public capital formation remains relevant for judging fiscal performance. If the concept of 'fiscal prudence' is reinterpreted from pay as you use to 'providing a net benefit to future generations', then such prudence is measured by the excess of public capital formation over capital use. As before, public capital-formation must be interpreted to include investment in human resources as well as acquisition of assets. The budgetary net contribution to capital stock, thus defined, should be assigned a significant place in the budget picture, but the nature of [US] economy is not such that it should be linked to the question of tax versus loan finance.

NOTES

1. The requirement of 'comprehensiveness' would hold for the combined dual budget system, but an excess of OASI receipts over expenditures would not be recorded as a surplus and be treated as now done in the administrative rather than the cash budget. Since an obligation for the future is incurred (the opposite of providing for future benefits), coverage through tax finance is required. In other words, if one *had* to defend a principle of balance in the present budget system, then the administrative balance is the more meaningful one.

2. Reference is to a capital budget system where capital expenditures are excluded in striking the balance in the current budget. There is no objection, of course, to supplementing a single budget, including all expenditures and receipts by a financial statement showing uses and sources of funds in debt transactions.

28 Public Debt and Future Generations*
1965

[In the early 1960s] there has developed a new debate over an old question: Can debt finance lead to a burden transfer from the present to future generations; and if so, by what mechanism?. . .

While the hunt has been great fun, the snark (if it exists) remains an elusive quarry.

To begin with, it cannot be overemphasised that this discussion relates to debt burden in an economy of the classical type, where full employment in the private sector is maintained automatically and no stabilisation policy is required. In such a setting, a dollar of loan finance is as deflationary as a dollar of tax finance, both reducing private expenditure by the full amount. The choice between the two means of finance is not made as a matter of controlling aggregate demand. Rather, the question is whether the choice between loan and tax finance may be used to distribute the burden of public expenditures between present and future generations.

The contributors to the debate are agreed that the resource withdrawal from private use must occur at the time when the public outlay is made. This must be the case whether tax or loan finance is used. If burden is defined as release of resources from the private sector, it is evident that no burden transfer can occur. Some contributors to the debate accept this definition, but most do not. Quite properly, they wish to define the burden on any one generation as the effect on that generation's lifetime consumption or (as I prefer) its potential lifetime consumption.

One way in which this burden may differ under tax and loan finance is through what Shoup has referred to as the Ricardo–Pigou mechanism. Suppose that taxation results largely (or, to simplify, entirely) in reduced private consumption, while borrowing results largely (or, to simplify, entirely) in reduced private capital formation. If generation 1 taxes itself when a given public purchase is made, its consumption is reduced, and the burden is shouldered by generation 1. If loan finance is used instead, consumption remains initially unimpaired, but private capital formation is reduced. As a result, generation 2 will inherit a lesser capital endowment,

---

* Review of Ferguson, J. M. (ed.) (1964) *Public Debt and Future Generations* (Chapel Hill: The University of North Carolina Press), in *The American Economic Review*, (1965).

thus reducing its potential (or actual) consumption. The burden is transferred to generation 2. To be sure, generation 2 also inherits the government bonds, but with them it assumes the tax liabilities needed to finance interest thereon. Unless there is a 'debt illusion', this constitutes no net gain and cannot offset the lower level of real wealth that is passed on.

This mechanism of burden transfer depends on the condition that loan finance falls more heavily on saving, while taxes fall more heavily on consumption. It does not require overlapping generations. It remains the most clear-cut and perhaps the most important type of burden transfer in the full-employment setting, but it is not the only one. The focus of the debate is precisely on demonstrating that there may be other mechanisms as well. A common characteristic of these mechanisms is that the comparison is not between tax and loan finance proper, but between initial tax finance and initial loan finance with subsequent debt retirement. This mechanism will therefore be referred to as the postponed taxation effect.

One of the earliest contributions to this approach was offered in Buchanan's *Public Principles of Public Debt*. While it must be credited with stimulating much of the discussion, Buchanan's position remains difficult to follow, as evidenced by the rather diverse interpretations given it by the various authors. The essential point seems to be that lending is a voluntary exchange and hence cannot involve a burden. A burden results only when taxes are paid, which requires a compulsory surrender of wealth. Hence burden is incurred only when taxes are paid to retire the debt. As long as the debt is not retired, burden is postponed. This is the case whether the released private resources incidental to the initial lending were from consumption or from capital formation. Effects on the future level of GNP, as indeed the entire Ricardo–Pigou effect, are not considered relevant to the point.

A subsequent thesis by Bowen–Davis–Kopf sets out to demonstrate that burden transfer can occur even in an all-consumption economy without inheritance, where each generation consumes its entire income over its lifespan. Suppose generation 1 finances a public outlay by bond issue. As it purchases the bonds, its consumption is reduced. Later on, generation 2 arrives on the scene, overlapping generation 1. At this later period, generation 2 is taxed, and the bonds held by generation 1 are redeemed. As a result, generation 1 increases its consumption, while 2 reduces its. The burden is thus transferred from 1 to 2. Generation 1's lifetime consumption is kept intact, if partly postponed, while generation 2 suffers the full reduction in consumption. A burden transfer through the postponed taxation effect has occurred, even though the Ricardo–Pigou effect has not been operative.

The present writer has presented a somewhat similar model of generation overlap, but again the argument is stated in unnecessarily restrictive terms, thereby diverting attention from the basic issues involved. This is the proposition that loan finance postpones the final settlement of an expenditure burden, simply because it postpones the final reduction in net worth which is implicit in taxation. This indeed was precisely the point advanced by Keynes in his *How to Pay for the War*.

The fact of the matter is that burden transfer through the postponed taxation effect can occur in an all-consumption or a capital-formation economy; whether lifetime consumption is assumed equal to lifetime income or not; with or without inheritance; and whether or not the saving consumption impact of tax and loan finance differs. The only condition which must be met for the mechanism to work is that there should be generation overlap.

While the Ricardo–Pigou effect and the postponed taxation effect involve distinct mechanisms of burden transfer, they are not mutually exclusive, but may coincide. The conditions required for the Ricardo–Pigou effect (inheritance and differential savings impact of tax and loan finance) are compatible with that needed for the delayed taxation effect (overlap of generations). Thus if both sets of conditions are met and only part of the initial lóan is retired, generation 2 will be burdened partly via the postponed taxation effect (which is independent of the initial saving consumption response) and partly by the Ricardo–Pigou effect (which depends on this response).

Having learned that burden transfer may occur by either of these mechanisms, what are we to conclude about the politician's dictum that debt finance is bad because it mortgages future generations?

First, he must be told that this entire debate, as previously noted, refers to a hypothetical economy where full employment is maintained automatically by the private sector. The Ricardo–Pigou mechanism breaks down in an economy where the tax loan (or tax loan monetary) mix is determined by considerations of stabilisation policy; and the postponed taxation effect, in this more realistic setting, can be invoked only at the cost of unemployment or inflation. As far as central government is concerned, the debate therefore seems of little importance for a country such as the United States even though it is significant for low-income countries or for local finance.

Secondly, even in a classical setting, it cannot be concluded that burden transfer is necessarily bad. Indeed, the principle of intergeneration equity demands that public expenditures on durables which involve the transfer of intergeneration benefits should be matched by a corresponding burden transfer. This, of course, is the element of validity behind dual budget systems involving a current and a capital budget.

Nevertheless, the fact remains that burden transfer is possible, and the contribution of the discussion has been to show that the Ricardo–Pigou effect is not the only mechanism by which it can be accomplished.

29 The Changing Image of Fiscal Policy*
1985

In the preceding papers of this section, the role of fiscal policy was viewed first in a Keynesian setting and then in the context of the broader macro model which emerged in the 1950s. In that model, both fiscal and monetary policy were taken to provide effective control over aggregate demand; and with inflation in a minor role, this meant effective control over the level of employment. Bridging a purely fiscal and monetary perspective, the model left the choice of policy mix the main issue. Various policy mixes would generate the same effect on aggregate demand and employment, but they would differ in other aspects. In particular, an easy money-tight fiscal mix would be more favourable to growth than an easy fiscal-tight money mix. This consensus peaked by the mid-1960s but did not withstand the onslaught of subsequent events. A changing scene shifted attention from unemployment to inflation and new views of macro theory emerged. A detailed discussion of these matters has been undertaken elsewhere [Musgrave and Musgrave, 1984, Part Six], but a brief review of some key points may be added here.

FISCAL POLICY AND INFLATION

The inflationary record of the United States economy since the late 1960s is frequently blamed on budgetary growth and on loose fiscal policy. Overly expansionary finance of the Vietnam War did indeed set an inflationary spark at the outset, but such a pattern did not prevail unbroken throughout the 1970s. The ratio of Federal expenditure to GNP showed little change from 1970 to 1979, nor did that for the entire public sector (including the state and local levels). The ratio of Federal deficit to GNP rose in the mid-1970s, but by 1979 returned to its 1970 level. Over the same period, state and local budgets gained a surplus. Inflation peaked in 1979–81, that is well before the deficit exploded in 1982; and while the deficit was largest, inflation abated and the economy went into a recession.

* 1985. Adapted from 'The Changing Image of Fiscal Policy', in *Öffentliche Finanzen und Monetäre Ökonomie Festschrift für Karl Häuser*, Frankfurt, Knapp Verlag.

A similar picture emerges from the monetary perspective. The increase in money supply, accounted for by monetisation of the debt (as measured by commercial bank absorption) accounted for only 3 per cent of the increase in M2 during the years from 1969 to 1979 and 5 per cent from 1979 to 1982.[1] While the contributions of monetary and of fiscal policy cannot be separated easily, as one is set in response to the other, overly expansionary fiscal policy hardly provided the major source of inflation; nor, for that matter, did monetary policy. Rather, aggregate demand policy sustained an inflationary process largely caused by outside shocks, beginning with the oil crisis and extended by cost-price escalation.

It became painfully evident, however, that instruments of demand control—be they fiscal or monetary—cannot deal with the dynamics of cost-price push. Or, more precisely, they cannot deal therewith without inducing severe recession with its cost of output loss and unemployment. The experience of 1980–81 provides an unhappy illustration. But though aggregate demand controls of the traditional type failed, selective fiscal instruments might have done better. Such tools have been suggested [Perry, 1976; Lerner, 1980]. They would place tax penalties on taking part in wage-price escalation, or grant rewards to reduce the risk of abstaining. While untried so far, such selective devices might restore the effectiveness of fiscal policy under recurring conditions of stagflation.

EFFECTS OF INFLATION ON THE FISCAL SYSTEM

We now turn to the reverse picture, that is, the impact of inflation on the fiscal system. Here resulting distortions of the income tax have been the major concern. With exemptions and bracket limits set in nominal terms, inflation raises the effective rate of tax for given levels of real income. This may be welcomed as increasing the built-in flexibility of the tax system in checking inflation, but it also distorts the distribution of the tax burden. As the increase in bracket rates flattens off when moving up the income scale, the progressivity of the tax is reduced, especially so over the middle income range. Since tax-free amounts and bracket limits of the U.S. income tax are to be indexed beginning in 1985, this distortion will be avoided henceforth, but its past impact has been a major factor in the declining popularity of this tax.

There remains, however, the more difficult problem of dealing with the inflation-induced wedge between nominal and real changes in the value of assets. For appreciation of capital values to be taxed fairly, the gains should be measured in real terms, that is, the base should be indexed. For interest to be treated neutrally, interest received and paid should be adjusted to deduct the inflation rate from the nominal rate of interest. Such adjustments for realised gains and interest have been recently proposed [U.S. Treasury, 1984], but it remains to be seen whether they will be enacted.

On the expenditure side of the budget, the impact of inflation depends on whether adjustments in appropriations lead or lag behind the inflation rate. With lags more likely, the fiscal system once more exerts a built-in brake. A special concern arises, however, with regard to interest on the public debt and the tax rate required to service it. This is no serious problem if the debt is long term, but may become one if the debt is short. Assuming the debt to be of infinite maturity (i.e., in the form of consols), the dollar amount of interest for a given level of debt is fixed. As income rises with inflation, the tax rate needed to finance the debt falls and declines toward zero. The fall in rate begins at once and proceeds rapidly. Suppose the level of income is $1,000, the debt is $400, and the real rate of interest is .03. In the absence of inflation, the interest bill is $12 and the required tax rate is $1.20. Now let inflation set in and continue at a steady rate of 10 per cent per annum. After one year, the required tax rate falls to $1.09. After five years it has fallen to 74 cents and after 20 years to 17 cents, approaching zero. The debt is gradually repudiated and the bond holder cannot help it. But suppose now that the debt is quite short and has to be refunded each year. In that case, the tax rate t will rise from 1.2 to 3.6 in the first year of inflation and thereafter it will once more decline towards zero. Thus, it will fall to 3.3 in year two of the inflation, to 2.5 in year five, and to 0.6 in year twenty.[2] Initially the required t, as the U.S. now experiences, rises sharply and the increase remains substantial for a considerable period. This will come about even if the nominal debt remains constant, although the problem will of course be more severe if the nominal debt rises, and less so if real income increases as well.

POLICY MIX

The traditional reasoning on policy mix, as noted before, was that a tight money-easy fiscal mix favours consumption at the cost of capital formation and thus retards growth. Tighter money forces up interest rates, as does the placing of additional debt needed to finance the deficit. Lower taxes in turn permit a higher level of consumption. While the U.S. Treasury asserted in the early eighties that 'crowding out' does not occur, this can be sustained only on the extreme and unreasonable assumption that changes in money supply only matter. The continuing high level of U.S. interest rates, not withstanding declining inflation, sustains the crowding out interpretation.

These consequences were to be expected, given the chosen mix of U.S. policy since 1981, but its global repercussions were not foreseen. When exchange rates were fixed, the rising level of income (independent of mix) would give rise to increased imports and a balance of payment deficit. To close the latter, a shift towards tighter monetary and easier fiscal policy would be called for, thereby attracting capital inflow. The domestic level of interest rates needed to accomplish this, however, might not be that required to secure the desired rate of growth. To meet all three policy objectives—high employment, desired rate of growth, and balance-of-payments equilibrium—an additional policy instrument (e.g., tax incentives for investment) would be needed.

However this may be, the issue of imbalance in the balance of payments disappeared with the turn towards flexible exchange rates. But with it the policy mix now came to have a more powerful impact on the balance of trade. A tight money-easy fiscal mix again raises interest rates and attracts capital inflow, but this now raises the value of the currency on the international exchange. As the value of the dollar rises, imports increase and exports fall off. The export sector, as well as sectors sensitive to foreign competition, suffer while the opposite change occurs abroad. Thus structural changes are forced upon economies which do not reflect basic changes in competitive advantage and which may be temporary only. Moreover, the inflow of capital reduces the growth deterrent otherwise exerted by tight money, while forcing higher rates of interest and reduced growth upon foreign countries. Given the increased ease of capital flows, the international repercussions of policy mix have become of major importance and point to the need for policy coordination in the choice of mix among trading partners.

SUPPLY SIDE EFFECTS OF TAX REDUCTION

In the traditional model of fiscal policy, tax reduction was viewed as a way to increase aggregate demand, just as a tax increase was viewed as a way to reduce it. This indeed was the essence of Lerner's model of functional finance [Lerner, 1943]. While it was countered that adjustments should involve both the expenditure and tax side of the budget [Samuelson, 1951], primary emphasis was placed correctly on the tax side.[3] An inflationary situation would thus call for a tax increase. It was thus startling to find that the supply-side argument of the early 1980s called for precisely the opposite adjustment. Stated in its extreme (Laffer curve) form, the contention was that tax reduction by raising net rates of return would increase hours of work and investment at given before-tax returns. As a result, there would be such an increase in output as to recoup the loss of tax revenue. No deficit would result and an increase in supply would serve to check inflation.

This argument overlooks the fact that such increase in output as might result would also be matched by additional income, so that there would be no offset to inflation. Moreover, an increase in output sufficient to recoup the revenue loss assumes that tax rates already exceeded the level at which maximum revenue is obtained. This theoretical possibility has long been recognised in fiscal theory, but it is most unlikely that tax rates had reached this level. The reasonable proposition that high marginal tax rates tend to reduce work effort must not be confused with the extreme contention that a further increase therein would reduce revenue, or that a reduction would raise it. Moreover, and most important, such supply-side effects as may result will take time to come about. This holds especially for effects upon capital formation. While high rates of taxation may have significant long-run effects on continued investment, the primary short-run effects of tax rate reduction will be to raise income and add to demand, thereby raising output via its leverage effects. As the tax reduction of 1981 occurred under conditions of recession, this leverage served to stimulate the economy, but it did so primarily via a demand rather than supply-side response.

RATIONAL EXPECTATIONS

A more fundamental reinterpretation of the role of stabilisation policy has been generated by renewed concern with the role of expectations. While expectations had played a unique part in macro theory prior to the great depression [Keynes, 1926], they were lost sight of in a subsequent turn to comparative statics, lag-driven dynamics and equilibrium rates of growth. Thus reemergence of expectations is all to the good, especially in explaining fluctuations in the rates of interest and exchange. Expectations regarding future rates of inflation in particular influence the nominal level of interest rates and have been responsible for the persistent gap between real and nominal rates.

A distinction need be drawn, however, between the role of expectations in economic change, and the hypothesis of economic behaviour based on 'rational' expectations and, most important, perfect foresight. Assuming the latter, stabilisation policy (other than random changes therein) may be shown to be ineffective. This applies in particular to the role of fiscal policy and the implications of debt finance [Barro, 1974]. Confronted with tax reduction (and assuming expenditures constant), a rational person with perfect foresight will be aware that higher taxes will be needed in the future to finance interest charges on the additional debt. The taxpayer will discount this tax stream and find its present value to equal that of the tax payment needed under tax finance. The taxpayer's net worth will be reduced equally in both cases, and his/her response will be the same.

This argument was first advanced by David Ricardo who also hastened to reject it as unrealistic [Ricardo, 1817]. In this he was correct. Consumers can hardly be expected to anticipate the future consequences of loan finance. Lenders and taxpayers will not be the same people, future tax laws and their burden distribution are uncertain, and future debt (especially if long term) may be devalued by inflation. It thus seems most unlikely that individuals will respond equally to tax and loan finance. Nevertheless, it is a useful and interesting exercise to explore the role of policy instruments in a model based on rational expectations and on perfect foresight—especially so since such a model incarnates the image of a perfectly functioning market system, a system in which no such policies are needed. But this does not render the model a realistic guide to actual policy choices. The Ricardian equivalence, similarly, offers an intriguing proposition, but it can hardly be accepted as a policy rule.

FISCAL POLICY AND FISCAL POLITICS

Matters of fiscal politics are discussed in detail in later chapters [Vol. 2, Part IV], but they have become too important a factor in the choice of policy mix to be bypassed here. To be sure, the role of politics in the choice of stabilisation instruments is nothing new. In its early stages, fiscal policy was viewed in terms of expansionary measures, and these were taken to call for an increase in expenditures. This associated fiscal policy with growing budgets, appealing to the liberal side of the spectrum and greeted with suspicion on the conservative side of the scale. Reliance on expenditure adjustment subsequently reversed the political stripes of fiscal policy, especially for restrictive measures to check inflation. Cutting across, reliance on tax reduction and increase, rather than expenditure adjustment would neutralise this impact in both directions, but such counsel has remained academic. There continues a presumption that monetary policy will be more neutral, less likely to involve interference with the market or the state of distribution, than does fiscal policy.

In recent years, a new set of considerations entered. A first line of reasoning opposes deficits because they are taken to hide the true cost of public services. They thus lead to excessive expenditures growth, that is, a rate of growth above that which voters would accept if the opportunity cost of public services was realised at once through taxes. This has provided the rationale for a balanced budget amendment to the constitution. This argument is not without merit, although it overlooks that debt finance may be appropriate for the case of capital expenditures. Also, such an amendment would sacrifice the active use of fiscal policy as a stabilisation device, which seems to me too high a cost.

A second line of reasoning is based on the opposite behavioural premise. It is now assumed that voters sooner or later will insist on a balanced budget. This means that expenditures will follow tax revenue so that tax reduction will lead to an expenditure cut. Those who consider the budget too large will now force tax reduction as a remedy. If expenditures follow at once, the resulting 'balanced budget shrinkage' will not be expansionary and indeed may become slightly restrictive. But if expenditures lag, fiscal policy is eased and a shift in policy mix towards tighter money will be needed. This, it appears, is what happened in Washington in recent years. The big tax reduction of 1981, though not matched by an absolute expenditure cut, has indeed retarded expenditure growth. Given the Administration's overriding desire to reduce the size of the public sector, the tax cut thus accomplished its objective. But the expenditure response was insufficient to avoid a sharp increase in deficit, thus calling for a shift towards tighter money. This line of reasoning, more than faith in the rapid working of supply-side responses, may well explain how the lopsided monetary-fiscal mix came about: setting reduction in the budget size as the primary objective, the choice of policy mix became the dependent variable in the system.

The hypothesis that expenditures follow revenue, and do so fairly promptly, also bears on the desirability of a revenue system which is responsive to income change. Traditionally, this feature of built-in flexibility was hailed as an automatic mechanism through which the fiscal system would serve to stabilise the economy. Indeed, it was thought to provide the main form of adjustment, calling for a system in which tax rates would be set so as to balance the budget at full employment [Friedman, 1948]. But built-in flexibility becomes perverse if expenditures follow revenue. A recession-induced decline in revenue now reduces expenditures equally and (with a balanced budget multiplier of one) becomes deflationary on balance, just as an inflation-induced revenue gain when matched by expenditure growth becomes expansionary. Built-in elasticity becomes ineffective or even counterproductive.

These changed perspectives nicely reflect a major shift in approach to the issues of fiscal economics. An earlier generation of fiscal economists had thought it their task to prescribe efficient policy action, based on the assumption that government would follow this prescription. A newer generation now proceeds from the premise that government cannot be trusted to act wisely, and that policies and institutions should be designed so as to prevent foolish action. While this latter perspective has its point, it hardly follows that the former should be discarded.

In concluding, we may note that the two lines of reasoning traced above rest on opposite behavioural assumptions. The case for a balanced budget amendment is based on the assumption (1) that voters, if permitted to indulge in deficit finance, will over-expand the budget. The case for tax reductions, as applied in 1981, is based on the assumption (2) that voters will not tolerate an increase in the deficit. Which then is the correct assumption? Perhaps (2) may be expected to apply if the deficit is already large, while (1) may be taken to hold with regard to lesser departures from a balanced budget position. This might permit the two policy prescriptions to be reconciled, but I wonder. The safer path for a democratic society, it seems to me, is to make the case for efficient policy, rather than to adjust institutions to presumptions of devious policy behaviour.

NOTES

1. To be sure, there was an additional absorption of Federal debt by the Federal Reserve Banks. While accounting for only a small share of the increase in Federal debt, this did account for most of the expansion of federal reserve

credit. But this does not mean that the resulting expansion in M2 is to be debited to the financing of public debt. The purchase of US debt by the Federal Reserve merely reflects its role in open market operations, with the resulting expansion of the reserve base reflected largely in the extension of private credit by the commercial banks.

2. Assuming the debt to be in consols, the tax rate t equals $iD/(1+\alpha)^n Y$ where D is the nominal amount of debt, i is the real rate of interest, α is the inflation rate, and Y is the level of money income. Suppose, now, the bonds have a one-year maturity. The government each year withdraws and issues an amount D. To be able to keep placing the debt in the face of inflation, it must keep the bond holder whole. That is, it must pay the holder an amount of αD to compensate for the loss of real value of D (the level of real consumption which the lender could enjoy upon liquidation) plus an amount of $(1+\alpha)rD$ which is needed to maintain an interest payment of constant real value. The debt service bill thus equals $[\alpha+(1+\alpha)r]D$, and the tax rate equals

$$\frac{[\alpha+(1+\alpha)r]D}{(1+\alpha)^n}$$

which may be approximated by the simpler term $(\alpha+r)D/(1+\alpha)^n$. As inflation sets in, the debt service bill rises from D to $(\alpha+r)D$ and t rises from rD/Y to $(\alpha+r)D/(1+\alpha)$. Thereafter the debt service bill remains constant while t declines toward zero.

3. The case for use of both tax and expenditure adjustments begins from a position of unemployment. It then argues that consumers will wish to spend part of their additional income (received when moving to full employment) in the form of public services. When taking action to restore full employment, public expenditures should thus be raised accordingly, with the remainder of the leverage provided by tax reduction. But suppose instead that we begin at a position of full employment with compensatory measures to be undertaken to prevent a decline in income. In that case, the level of public services, corresponding to the full employment level of income, already prevails so that preventive compensatory action is to be in the form of tax reduction only. The conclusion thus depends on how the problem is formulated, that is, whether the compensatory action is seen to restore full employment or to prevent a decline. Applied to corrective measures aimed at preventing inflation (and beginning from full employment), similar reasoning calls for tax increase, not expenditure reduction.

REFERENCES

Barro, R. J. (1974) 'Are Government Bonds Net Worth?' *Journal of Political Economy*, 82.

Friedman, M. (1948) 'A Monetary and Fiscal Framework for Economic Stability', *American Economic Review*, XXXVIII.

Keynes, J. M. (1930) *Treatise on Money* (London: Macmillan).

Lerner, A., and Colander, C. (1980) *MAP: A market anti-inflation plan* (New York: Harcourt Brace).

Lerner, A. (1943) 'Functional Finance and the Federal Budget', *Social Research*, 10.

Musgrave, R., and Musgrave, P. (1984) *Public Finance in Theory and Practice*, 4th ed. (New York: McGraw Hill).
Perry, G. (1976) 'Stabilization Policy and Inflation', in H. Owen and C. Schultze (eds.), *Setting Priorities, The Next Ten Years* (Washington, D.C.: Brookings Institution).
Ricardo, D. (1817) *Principles of Political Economy and Taxation*, ch. XVII.
Samuelson, P. (1951) 'Principles and Rules in Modern Fiscal Policy: A Neo-Classical Reformulation', in *Money, Trade and Economic Growth, Essays in Honour of John Williams* (New York: Macmillan).

Acknowledgements

I am grateful to the editors and publishers of the following journals and books for permission to reproduce the articles which appear in this volume: *The Quarterly Journal of Economics*; McGraw-Hill Book Company for material from *The Theory of Public Finance*; St. Martin's Press for material from *Public Economics*; *Finanzarchiv*; the American Economic Association for material from issues of *American Economic Review* and *Journal of Economic Literature*; *Journal of Political Economy*; Wayne State University Press for material from *Effects of Corporation Income Tax*; *Harvard Law Review*; *Public Finance Quarterly*; *Journal of Public Economics*; the Australian Tax Research Foundation for material from *Taxation Issues of the 1980s*; *Review of Economics and Statistics*; Fritz Knapp Verlag.

Name Index

Topical Index